NATURAL RESOURCES AND
INTERNATIONAL DEVELOPMENT

Essays by D. GALE JOHNSON

M. A. ADELMAN

ANTHONY D. SCOTT

DEMITRI B. SHIMKIN

P. LAMARTINE YATES

ARTHUR GAITSKELL

JOSEPH GRUNWALD

CHARLES P. KINDLEBERGER

CHANDLER MORSE

EGBERT DE VRIES

NATURAL
RESOURCES
AND
INTERNATIONAL
DEVELOPMENT

EDITED BY MARION CLAWSON

PUBLISHED FOR *Resources for the Future, Inc.*

BY *The Johns Hopkins Press*

© *1964 by The Johns Hopkins Press, Baltimore, Maryland 21218*
Printed in the U.S.A.
Library of Congress Catalog Card Number 64-12731

Second Printing, 1965

CONTENTS

FOOD AND THE WORLD

RESOURCES IN EUROPE, AFRICA, AND LATIN AMERICA

RESOURCE DEVELOPMENT AND UTILIZATION

PROBLEMS, SITUATIONS, PROCESSES

EDITOR'S INTRODUCTION

Almost the whole world seems preoccupied with economic growth and development these days. There is rivalry among the advanced countries, most marked between the leading nations of the two great world power blocs, as to the rate of economic growth achieved this year and anticipated for the years ahead. The poorer countries seek economic improvement to obtain the full advantages of political independence, and to escape the brutal poverty which has so long been their lot. Rich and poor alike have learned from experience that economic adjustments of all kinds are far easier to accomplish during periods of growth than of stagnation, and that — within wide limits — the faster the growth rate, the easier are the adjustments and changes necessarily required by economic evolution.

It has not always been thus. Traditional societies deny both the possibility and the desirability of growth; change is not valued, but shunned. The old and the familiar are preferred above the new and the strange. These attitudes are fast disappearing, at least among the leaders of even these countries. Economic growth is widely, if not universally, sought today.

This emphasis upon economic growth is reflected in a concern over natural resources and their use, especially in the lower-income countries. In such countries, capital is scarce, manpower is unskilled, and entrepreneurship is weak. Lacking these other assets, the low-income countries are specially concerned to appraise their resources, to ascertain the ways in which fuller use of the natural endowment may lead them to prosperity. The richer countries can make substitutes for many natural resource products — the magic of modern chemistry and industry has opened vast new avenues in this direction; and they can buy what they need in the world's markets, from other advanced countries or from the poorer ones. They can trade skill and capital for Nature.

Economic growth is a complex process. The United States has experienced a discouragingly low growth rate in the past several years. Why? There is no lack of diagnoses, but there is far from full agreement among economists, to say nothing of divergence among politicians and the general public. During these same years, Western Europe has grown amazingly, confounding earlier dire prophecies made by many. Why? Again, there is no lack of diagnoses. Some of the lower-income countries seem to have made greater economic progress than others. Why? Some factors seem evident, but others are less apparent.

There are many theories on economic growth and development, of varying complexity and generality. Some give a modest role to natural resource endowment such as soils, climate, forests, mineral deposits, and the like; others scarcely mention these factors. Can we totally ignore the natural resource base? Is not the economic growth problem easier of solution if a nation is generously endowed with the conventional natural resources, than if it is barren of them? We doubt if anyone will assert that natural resources alone, no matter how high their quality or how large their quantity, are sufficient for rapid economic growth. Even in the simplest cases too many other factors are involved.

The central concern of Resources for the Future is with the conservation, development, and use of natural resources, especially as these relate to economic growth. The main focus of our research to date has been upon the United States scene, but we have carried out or financed a few modest inquiries in other countries. It is our hope and expectation that this extension to other lands will grow in the next few years.

During most of the past several years, RFF has conducted an annual Forum. Each has resulted in a book. The first symposium, in 1958, was concerned with conservation in its broadest aspects; its papers were published as *Perspectives on Conservation: Essays on America's Natural Resources*. The second, held in 1959, dealt broadly with the relationship of science and technology to resources, and the results were published as *Science and Resources: Prospects and Implications of Technological Advance*. The third, held in 1961, brought to an American audience a discussion of selected resource programs in other countries, aspects of which might be useful in certain U.S. situations. The papers were published as *Comparisons in Resource Management*. The fourth Forum was held in 1962, on the general subject of urban and suburban space as a natural resource. Its results have recently been published under the title *Cities and Space: The Future Use of Urban Land*.

The theme of the 1963 RFF Forum was The Role of Natural Resources in International Development. This book, which presents the results of that Forum, consists of ten essays: three are on commodities or groups of commodities — agriculture, oil, and fisheries; four focus on resource problems in regions of the world — Western Europe, the Soviet Union, Africa, and Latin America; and three deal with problems and sit-

uations — the potentialities and hazards of foreign investment for resource development, the terms of trade between raw material exporting
and importing countries, and the transfer of knowledge and capital across
national boundaries.

A brief word as to the organization of the Forum may aid in understanding the structure of this book. The general pattern of the Forum was
planned by the staff of Resources for the Future. Several internationally
noted scholars were asked to prepare papers on the general subjects.
Each was given the option of developing the broad topic as he chose.
Drafts of papers were circulated among the authors. The Forum itself was
held in Washington on January 28 and 29, 1963. Each author briefly
summarized his paper, then the authors as a group formed a panel for discussion of each paper, and finally an invited audience was given a chance
to ask questions and make comments.* Two or three papers were thus
taken up at each of four half-day sessions. The discussion was lively. After
the Forum, each author was encouraged to revise his paper to the degree
he thought appropriate in light of the discussion at the Forum.

The essays in this book do not purport to cover completely the complex subject of natural resources and economic growth on a world scale.
They are rich samplings of some of the best thought on the subject, but
they are samplings only. The papers are loosely, not closely, integrated.
They are related to each other, but not as intimately as would normally be
the case in a book by a single author. If the result lacks the central core
and close integration that single authors strive for, and sometimes achieve,
we hope it more than compensates in the variety and freshness of the individual contributions.

Resources for the Future is pleased to present this book of essays, and
commends it to readers of our books. We believe that the diverse personalities of these men, apparent at the Forum, will emerge through the
printed page, and we hope you will enjoy a visit with each.

The editor wishes to add his personal word of thanks to his colleagues
at Resources for the Future who helped plan and conduct the 1963 Forum; to the Brookings Institution for the pleasant surroundings in which
the Forum was held; to the public officials, scholars, and others who attended and participated; and lastly, most important of all, to the ten able
and interesting men whose papers made this Forum a notable experience.

Marion Clawson
August 1, 1963   Resources for the Future, Inc.

* Due to circumstances beyond their control, P. Lamartine Yates and Arthur
Gaitskell were unable to be present at the Forum itself.

Commodities with International Significance

The Role of Agriculture in Economic Development
D. GALE JOHNSON

The World Oil Outlook
M. A. ADELMAN

Food and the World Fisheries Situation
ANTHONY D. SCOTT

THE ROLE OF AGRICULTURE
IN ECONOMIC DEVELOPMENT

D. GALE JOHNSON

Viewed in terms of international relations, political and economic, the problems of agriculture are now probably as universally important as they have ever been. First, agriculture is, or should be, a point of major concern in all efforts to increase the rate of growth in underdeveloped areas; all programs of economic aid and assistance must sooner or later come to grips with the problems agriculture presents. Second, some of the most intractable problems of the European Economic Community (the Common Market) revolve around trade in agricultural products. Third, the Soviet bloc area has been unable to achieve a satisfactory solution of its farm problem, a fact that probably has had some impact on its international policies. Fourth, as a result of its domestic farm policies, the United States has severely limited its role as a world leader in efforts to achieve a more liberal trade policy for agricultural products. As an example, some of the features of trade policy for agricultural products adopted by the European Common Market are of the same restrictive nature as U.S. quotas and import duties; furthermore, our extensive use of export subsidies

---

D. GALE JOHNSON is professor of economics and dean of the Division of the Social Sciences at the University of Chicago. Prior to 1944, when he went to Chicago as research associate, he was assistant professor of agricultural economics at Iowa State College. Mr. Johnson is consultant to several U.S. government agencies and to numerous private organizations. He is author of *Agriculture and Trade: A Study of Inconsistent Policies* (1950), *Forward Prices for Agriculture* (1947), and many journal articles and chapters of books on agricultural economics and policy. Mr. Johnson was born in Iowa in 1916. He received his B.S. degree from Iowa State College, did graduate study at the University of Wisconsin and University of Chicago, and received his Ph.D. from Iowa State College.

makes it extremely difficult for the United States to oppose high import duties imposed by others. Fifth, many other industrial countries have policies designed to increase agricultural output.

The last two problems are clearly significant to the problems of the development of low-income areas and to the role that agriculture can play in that development. The policies that most industrial nations are following clearly limit demand for the agricultural products of the underdeveloped areas of the world. It is sometimes argued that the agricultural and related import and export policies of the industrial nations have little effect on exports of the tropical products that are typical of underdeveloped areas; and it is true that some of the most restrictive measures undertaken by industrial countries affect cereals, which are grown mainly in temperate zones and in developed nations. But sugar is heavily protected in most industrial countries, and cane sugar is a tropical product; and rice is a tropical or semi-tropical cereal. Underdeveloped areas are a major source of vegetable fats and oils, which are subject to import duties in several industrial countries. Sugar, rice, fats and oils are major sources of foreign exchange earnings for many underdeveloped areas; the ability of these countries to import capital equipment and other requirements for economic growth is affected quite directly by the agricultural and trade policies of the industrial nations. We only mislead ourselves when we think otherwise.

A few general comments about the state of our knowledge and of our ignorance, concerning interrelationships between agriculture and the rest of the economy during the process of economic development, may facilitate discussion. A fundamental characteristic of economic development is that as it proceeds the relative importance of agriculture as a source of national income and of employment declines. This phenomenon, apparently universally applicable, occurs as a result of forces affecting both the demand for and the supply of agricultural products.

After per capita income reaches a certain level, the income elasticity of demand for farm products is less than unity and thus lower than that for all other goods and services. Moreover, as real income increases the income elasticity of demand for farm products declines gradually and persistently and eventually approximates zero. This means that as real income grows a smaller and smaller fraction of any addition to income is spent upon farm products and a larger and larger fraction is spent upon non-farm products and services. Thus the demand for farm products grows more slowly than does demand for other things.

With advancing scientific knowledge and increasing specialization, many functions formerly performed on farms are performed elsewhere at lower cost. More advanced technology and the availability of substitutes for land (such as fertilizer), as well as for labor and animal power, make it possible to almost entirely overcome the limitations on expanding output that may at one time have been imposed by the principle of diminishing returns and a limited land supply.

It is generally recognized that in most developing or growing economies agriculture has made one or more highly significant contributions to the growth of the economy as a whole: (1) the release of labor for non-farm employment; (2) the provision of an increased supply of food and fiber at moderate cost; (3) the availability of agricultural exports as a major source of foreign exchange to pay for capital goods and technical services not available domestically; and (4) savings from agriculture to be invested in industrial activities.

Each of the contributions requires a more or less continuous increase in output per worker. Without this, it is virtually impossible to expand output in the non-agricultural sector of an economy. And the real cost of industrialization will be substantially reduced if the output of agricultural products is sufficiently elastic to provide for the increased per capita availability of food and fiber that is required by higher per capita incomes. Sometimes, of course, the very elastic supply of agricultural products is outside the borders of the country that is industrializing, but the existence of such a supply still remains an important element in economic growth.

It is clear from these brief comments that we know a great deal about the impact of economic development upon agriculture and the kinds of contributions that agriculture makes to economic development. However, there is much that we do not know about the forces that initiate or lead to economic development and the role of agriculture as an initiating force. We do not yet understand whether in most cases the reduction in factor costs of agricultural products, which makes possible transferring labor out of agriculture and an elastic supply of agricultural products, has occurred mainly because of actual or incipient developments in the non-agricultural sectors of economies or has been due to circumstances that were largely unique to agriculture. Perhaps this is something we shall never know — it may be nothing more than the old query as to which came first, the hen or the egg. We do not know why technically advanced agriculture may emerge in small sectors of some nations — tea plantations in India and sugar plantations in the Philippines, for example — with seemingly little impact upon peasant farming. Nor can we say why in areas faced with what appear to be similar circumstances, some seem to have achieved remarkable economic growth while others have stagnated, or nearly so.

ECONOMIC DEVELOPMENT AND THE
DEMAND FOR AGRICULTURAL PRODUCTS

For a given period of time, the change in total use of a product is the multiple of the change in population and the change in per capita use. This is an obvious truism, but some further exploration of it will help us to understand some of the differences in the agricultural problems of high- and low-income countries. The change in per capita demand (not necessarily consumption) is due to the change in per capita income and the income elasticity of demand, assuming constant relative prices. Based on developments during the 1950's, the following tabulation indicates very roughly the differences among high- and low-income countries, with the latter divided into slowly and rapidly growing:

| | Annual per cent change in | | |
	Population	*Income per capita*	*Income elasticity of demand*
High-income countries	Moderate or low	Low, moderate or high	Low
Low-income countries			
Slow growth	High	Moderate or low	High
Rapid growth	High	High	High

With respect to population growth, *moderate* means between 1 and 2 per cent per annum, while *low* means less than 1 per cent and *high* means 2 per cent or more. With respect to income growth per capita, *high* means 3 per cent or more, *moderate* from 2 to 3 per cent, and *low* less than 2 per cent per annum. A low-income elasticity is one of 0.5 or less, with some approaching 0.1, while high-income elasticities are those exceeding 0.5 with some approaching 0.9.

Let us consider some examples of anticipated growth rates for demand for food for the period 1957–59 to 1969–71, based on the Food and Agriculture Organization (FAO) study, *Agricultural Commodities — Projections for 1970*. Table 1 includes certain relevant data for four areas that illustrate some of the conditions noted above.

Table 1. Projected Annual Growth of the Potential Demand for Food,
Selected Areas, 1957–59 through 1969–71[1]

Item	Asia and Far East[2]	Latin America[3]	EEC[4]	North America[5]
Basic assumptions[6]				
Population	2.3	2.7	0.7	1.8
GNP/capita	1.3	2.0	3.9	1.3
Income elasticity	0.9	0.6	0.5	0.16
Potential increase[6] in				
Total demand	3.4	3.7	2.1	1.9
Per capita demand	1.0	1.0	1.4	0.16
GNP/capita[7] (1957–59)	$165	$491	$1,285	$2,190

[1] Food and Agriculture Organization, *Agricultural Commodities — Projections for 1970* (Rome, 1962), p. A–2.
[2] Excludes Japan and Mainland China.
[3] Excludes Argentina and Uruguay; includes Mexico and Central America.
[4] European Economic Community.
[5] Canada and the United States.
[6] Per cent increase per year; compound rate.
[7] Converted into U.S. dollars at 1955 prices.

The projections for Latin America indicate the highest annual rate of increase in the total demand for food. A high rate of population growth, a moderate to high rate of increase of per capita income, and a high income elasticity of demand generate a projected growth of demand for food of 3.7 per cent per annum. Crudely speaking, approximately a quarter of the increase in total demand is attributed to the effects of rising per capita income and the remainder to population growth. North America illustrates a high-income area with a moderate rate of growth of population, a slow rate of growth of per capita income, and a very low income elasticity of demand. The projected annual increase in the demand for food is 1.9 per cent. Almost all of the increase in demand is attributed to population growth; if the rate of growth of income doubled, the annual rate of growth of total demand for food would be no more than 2.1 per cent.

The European Economic Community is illustrative of an area with a slow rate of population growth, but a high rate of increase of income per capita and a moderate- to high-income elasticity of demand. In this region, the only one of the four illustrated, income change is the major source of increase in the demand for food. Even so, the expected increase in the total demand for food is at a rate of only two-thirds the expected increase for Asia and Latin America.

The difference in annual growth rates of demand of, say, 2 and 3.5 per cent do not appear at first glance to be very large. However, because of the mysterious and alarming characteristics of compound interest, the difference in the percentage increase over a decade is quite large. In a decade, a 2 per cent growth amounts to an increase of about 22 per cent; 3.5 per cent growth accumulates to an increase of 41 per cent.

The above simplified analysis indicates why a relatively high growth rate for agricultural output is important in the underdeveloped areas of the world. Economic development results in a sharp increase in the demand for food products compared to a situation of stagnation. The many forces associated with economic development bring with them the conditions for declining mortality and thus a significant increase, at least for a period of several decades, in the rate of population growth. Furthermore, the rising per capita income that flows from economic development leads to a substantial increase in the per capita demand for food. If food output does not increase as rapidly as the demand conditions change, either the pace of economic development will be slowed or farmers and workers will be forced to pay a relatively high price for the economic growth that is achieved. This price will be a decline in per capita consumption, if the previous level of living makes this possible without increased mortality, or a maintenance of per capita consumption with increased mortality and slower population growth.

CHANGING THE SUPPLY FUNCTION FOR AGRICULTURAL PRODUCTS

We still do not know as much as we should about the factors or conditions that make possible increases in agricultural output. But from the experiences of a variety of countries and areas — the United States, Canada, the Soviet Union, Japan, for example — we know a substantial amount. We know that increased output is a result of one or more things occurring: (1) increased use of inputs; (2) improving the quality of inputs; (3) increased knowledge or a change in the production function; and (4) a change in incentives for farm operators and their families.

If all of the increase in output must come as a result of increased inputs — more labor and/or land — it is unlikely that agriculture will be able to make any significant contribution to economic development. If this is the case, the growth of the agricultural population in a low-income or underdeveloped economy will have to occur at the same rate as the growth of total population unless per capita food consumption is to decline. Labor cannot be released to other sectors of the economy for their development and the real factor costs of food cannot decline. In fact, unless additional land can be brought into cultivation or land developed through irrigation or reclamation at about the same rate as the population grows, average output per worker in agriculture may decline and real factor costs of food increase.

We should not assume that long periods of unchanged production functions or static productivity conditions have not or cannot prevail. As indicated in Table 2, there was virtually no change in the ratio of output

Table 2. Indexes of Output, Inputs, and Productivity,
United States Agriculture, 1880–1930

(1947–49 = 100)

Indexes	1880	1890	1900	1910	1920	1930
Farm output	37	43	56	61	70	72
Production inputs	53	63	73	82	93	97
Farm labor	100	116	127	135	143	137
Farm real estate	56	66	79	93	97	96
All other	18	24	31	39	53	62
Productivity	70	68	77	74	75	74
Output/labor	37	37	44	45	48	52
Output/real estate	66	65	71	66	72	75

Source: Ralph A. Loomis and Glen T. Barton, *Productivity of Agriculture, United States, 1870–1958*, U.S. Department of Agriculture, Tech. Bul. No. 1238 (April, 1961), pp. 57, 58, 60–61.

to input in the United States for a period of fifty years, from 1880 through 1930. There was a slow increase in output per unit of labor, but this was due to capital investments and increased purchases from the non-farm sector. For a period of three decades, 1880 through 1910, output per unit of land remained unchanged. The expansion of agriculture into the Great Plains area was in part responsible for the stable output-to-land ratio because lower-yielding land was brought under cultivation, but the effect was not very large.[1]

It is not implied that under some circumstances economic growth cannot or does not occur when there is little or no change in production techniques in agriculture. The experience in the United States seems to clearly contradict this for the period from 1880 through 1930. If the particular techniques of production are such as to permit a relatively high level of income for the farm population and moderately low prices of food, and if the income elasticity of demand for food and other agricultural products

[1] D. Gale Johnson and Robert L. Gustafson, *Grain Yields and the American Food Supply* (Chicago: University of Chicago Press, 1962), pp. 19–26.

is significantly below unity, the farm labor force and agriculture's contribution to the national income can both decline relative to the non-farm sector. During this period, significant amounts of new land were brought under cultivation and modest substitution of purchased inputs for labor were possible and occurred. It should be remembered, however, that in the United States of 1910 national income per capita was of the order of $1,000 in 1955 U.S. dollars — several times the per capita income in Asia or Africa or many parts of South America today.

But when per capita incomes are low and the income elasticity of demand for food is almost unity, agricultural employment must increase absolutely and remain a relatively stable proportion of total employment unless technological change occurs.

It is quite likely that improved quality of inputs and a change in the production function (change in technology) usually occur together. In an underdeveloped economy the most important input — as measured by the share of total product paid to it — is labor. Fortunately, labor is also an input whose quality can be changed by well-understood procedures. Unfortunately, these procedures involve the expenditure of significant amounts of scarce resources. But the history of Japan from 1870 through 1910 indicates that a poor country can organize its resources to provide for nearly universal education for the farm population, for agricultural research, and for education of the adult farm population in new and improved methods of production.

The increase in the ratio of output to input, which is a measure of the effect of the change in quality of inputs as well as of technological change, makes it possible to transfer labor from the farm to the non-farm sector. Rapid economic growth requires such a transfer. However, rapid economic growth does not require an absolute decline in farm population or farm employment. If the farm employment is to be stable in an absolute sense, the annual change in the ratio of output to input in agriculture in low-income countries must be very large if population and income growth per capita are of the order of 2 per cent per annum. In this situation the increase in demand for farm products (assuming little international trade) will be about 3.5 per cent per annum. Even if half of the increased output is due to increased quantities of non-labor inputs, the ratio of output to input must increase by about 1.5 per cent each year. This implies a doubling of the output-input ratio in about forty-five years; in the last fifty years the output-input ratio has increased by about 75 per cent in the United States.

I should hasten to add that it is not essential for the absolute level of farm employment to remain stable during the early period of industrialization. The usual pattern has been for the farm labor force to increase absolutely for several decades after per capita incomes have started to increase. In fact, if an economy starts from a position of, say, 80 per cent of its labor force engaged in agriculture and if total population is increasing by 2 per cent per annum, it would be nearly impossible for non-farm employment to absorb all of the increase in labor force. Under these assumptions, the non-farm labor force would have to grow at a 10 per cent annual rate or double about every seven years. Such a growth cannot be said to be impossible; between 1926 and 1934 the annual increase in non-farm employment was about 9 per cent in the Soviet Union.

In a growing economy, starting from a low income level, savings in or from agriculture are an important source of investment funds for the entire economy. The degree to which savings are extracted from agriculture — through taxes, rents, low prices or forced deliveries at nominal prices — has an important effect upon agricultural output. In my opinion, the relatively poor performance of agriculture in the Soviet Union from 1928 through 1953 was due to lack of incentives provided by the price structure, forced deliveries, and institutional arrangements. On the other hand, Japan apparently transferred significant amounts of savings from agriculture into non-agricultural investment and still achieved rapid modernization of its agriculture.

A part of the support for land reform in underdeveloped areas is the expectation that reform will lead to an improvement in the incentive structure and thus to increased investment in agriculture and greater interest by the farm operator in increasing output. Some land reforms seem to have achieved this result (the short-lived reform in the Soviet Union after World War I and the post World War II reform in Japan and Taiwan), but many others seem to have failed.

To sum up: In this section I have tried to indicate briefly some of the interrelationships between the supply of agricultural products and the process of economic development. It has been indicated that an improvement in the output-input ratio is required before rising per capita incomes can be achieved in a low-income area; and that if population growth is moderate or high and the income elasticity of demand is high, the increase in the output-input ratio must be a significant one if agriculture is not to act as a restraint on economic growth. It has also been indicated that while farm employment must decline as a share of total employment, it may increase absolutely during the early period of industrialization.

Recent Trends in Total and
Per Capita Agricultural Production

As a rough approximation, agricultural production in the industrial countries of the world has increased at a faster rate than consumption of agricultural products during the past quarter-century. Again as a rough approximation, consumption of agricultural products in the underdeveloped areas of the world has increased at the same rate as output over the same period. But this difference in pattern is apparently not due to any significant difference in output trends, but to differences in the underlying factors affecting demand.

Table 3 summarizes the available data on changes in total and per capita production of agricultural products for the past quarter-century. In general, the Southern Area includes most of the underdeveloped areas of the world, while the Northern Area includes the high-income countries. With respect to total production, the increases are of the same general order of magnitude. In fact, if adjustment were made for the unsatisfactory weather conditions in North America during 1935–39 and the good weather conditions there from 1958 through 1960, total output probably increased more in the underdeveloped areas.

The discussion in the first few pages of this essay indicated that the tasks of increasing agricultural output in the underdeveloped areas of the world are relatively much greater than in the high-income areas. The high-income countries will create surplus problems if output increases at about 2 per cent per annum, while the underdeveloped areas will face food stringencies if output increases at a rate of 3 per cent annually. For the high-income countries, an annual growth of food production of 2 per cent is not a difficult task; if anything, the problem is to restrict growth to that level. But for the underdeveloped countries, a growth rate of 3 per cent or more requires substantial investments in fertilizer, research, adult education, tools, seeds, and chemicals.

Agriculture in the Sixties

Agriculture presents a very different problem to various groups of countries in the world. In North America and Western Europe the primary concerns are with the level of income of the farm population, actual or potential excess of supply relative to demand at "acceptable" levels of prices and/or incomes, and the means to dispose of surpluses or to re-

Table 5. Indices of World Agricultural Production: Total and Per Capita, by Region, Average 1935–39 and Annual 1958–59 to 1960–61[1]

(Average 1952–53 to 1954–55 = 100)

Region or country	Total production						Per capita production					
	Average				Average annual per cent change		Average				Average annual per cent change	
	1935–39	1958–59	1959–60[2]	1960–61[3]	1935–39 to 1960–61	1952–54 to 1960–61	1935–39	1958–59	1959–60[2]	1960–61[3]	1935–39 to 1960–61	1952–54 to 1960–61
					Per cent						Per cent	
Southern Area												
Latin America	72	121	123	124	3.1	3.4	103	107	106	104	.04	0.6
Africa and West Asia	77	117	118	121	2.5	3.0	100	106	105	105	0.2	0.7
Far East less Japan[4]	89	114	119	119	1.5	2.7	111	104	106	105	-0.3	0.7
Communist Asia	96	120	115	117	1.0	2.4	112	109	102	102	-0.4	0.3
Total	85	118	118	120	1.7	2.9	106	106	105	104	-0.09	0.6
Northern Area												
Western Europe	81	110	112	115	1.8	2.1	92	106	107	109	0.8	1.3
Eastern Europe[5]	108	132	130	131	.9	4.4	106	123	120	119	0.5	2.7
United States and Canada	69	113	114	117	3.0	2.4	87	104	103	104	0.9	0.6
Japan	83	132	140	145	3.3	6.4	102	125	131	134	1.3	4.9
Australia and New Zealand	76	120	121	124	2.7	3.4	100	107	106	107	0.3	1.0
Total	84	118	119	122	1.9	3.1	93	111	110	111	0.8	1.6
World total	85	118	119	121	1.8	3.0	101	108	107	107	0.3	1.0

[1] Value of production at constant prices. Revised. Crops included in the index are harvested mainly between July 1 of the first year shown and June of the following year. For a few crops and most livestock production, estimates are for the calendar year of the first year shown.
[2] Preliminary.
[3] Estimated.
[4] Includes Pacific Islands.
[5] Includes Soviet Union.
Source: U.S. Department of Agriculture, Foreign Agricultural Service, *The World Food Budget, 1962 and 1966* (Washington), p. 76.

strict competition from more efficient regions. In the low-income areas of the world the major agricultural problem is to achieve a rapid advance in output with a minimum expenditure of resources to provide a more adequate and cheaper food supply for a rapidly growing population, to obtain desired levels of foreign exchange, and to release labor for non-agricultural development. In the Soviet Union and other Communist-bloc countries the basic problem is to achieve a rapid increase in agricultural output, especially marketed output, to provide a growing urban population with a diet that compares more favorably with that available in the Western countries and to do this without requiring a significant diversion of investment from the industrial and military sectors.

If the data used by the U.S. Department of Agriculture to prepare Table 3 are of reasonable reliability, the differences in the agricultural problems of the three broad regions are not the result of striking differences in the rate of output growth over the past quarter-century. It is true that the growth of agricultural production in the Communist areas (Communist Asia and Eastern Europe) was the lowest of any of the areas for the period 1935–39 through 1960–61. However, during the 1950's output increases were of reasonable size. Admittedly, these increases followed long periods of output stagnation. As noted, the output increases in the low-income areas (excluding Communist areas) have been as large as in the high-income countries.

It can be argued that the regional averages of changes in agricultural production conceal substantial variations by country or smaller area. This is true, just as it is true that the average change in farm output in the United States conceals the considerable differences in output changes by regions or states. If one compares the variation in output changes among the high-income countries with the variation among the low-income countries, after some rough adjustment for the size of the areas, one finds that there has been about the same variability in output changes in one as in the other.[2] The fact that all low-income areas have not increased output at the same rate as the average for the low-income areas does not contradict the point that has been made, namely that the level of per capita income and the rate of increase of farm output have not been related.

The remarkable similarity in the growth of output in the various areas of the world means that the underlying causes of their quite different problems must lie somewhere else. In the case of the low-income coun-

---

[2] *The World Agricultural Situation, 1962* (Washington: U.S. Department of Agriculture, Foreign Agricultural Service), pp. 18–50.

tries, the source of the problem is not difficult to detect. If there is rapid economic growth, the demand for farm products will increase at an annual rate of 3.5 to 4 per cent. This increase may be compared to an estimated annual growth rate of about 1.5 to 3.0 per cent for the past quarter-century or 2.7 to 3.4 per cent for the past decade.

Eastern Europe

The nature of the problem in Eastern Europe is similar to areas with rapidly growing demand for food, though there is an important distinguishing element that will be noted below. In Eastern Europe the growth in the demand for food will be substantially greater than in Western Europe or the United States. While the growth of population may be expected to be somewhat less than in the United States, it will probably be much more rapid than in Western Europe.[3] The income elasticity of demand for food in Eastern Europe — based on scanty information from the Soviet Union — is relatively high; it is probably about 0.75 and almost certainly greater than 0.5. Thus rising consumer incomes, perhaps at an annual per capita rate of about 3 per cent, combined with an annual population growth rate of 1.4 per cent, would result in a growth of demand for food of 3 to 3.5 per cent annually.

But the growth in demand is here estimated on the assumption that there now exists an equilibrium between the demand and supply for food. In the Soviet Union there is excess demand for most food products at the fixed prices in the state store. Generally the prices in the free market are substantially higher than those in the state stores — for several important products, 50 to 100 per cent more. An increase in the retail price of meat by 30 per cent and of butter by 25 per cent on June 1, 1962, without eliminating all of the excess demand (reports of queues and bare shelves persist) indicates that some of the food markets are substantially out of equilibrium. While it is true that state food store prices are generally substantially below prices in the free market, they are not low by comparison with prices in Western Europe and the United States, nor are they low compared to the income of the population in the Soviet Union. Approximately 50 per cent of consumer income is expended for food, of which about 90 per cent is purchased in state stores at controlled prices.

· · · · · ·

[3] *The World Food Budget, 1962 and 1966* (Washington: U.S. Department of Agriculture), p. 72.

Some comment and discussion of development in Soviet agriculture since 1950 seems appropriate. Following Stalin's death in 1953 changes were made in the treatment of the agricultural sector, and agricultural output increased substantially (perhaps by 40 per cent) until 1958. However, since 1958 agricultural output has apparently stagnated; 1962 output probably exceeded the 1958 output by no more than 5 per cent. During 1962 there were two reorganizations of the control and administrative structure for agriculture, resulting in the raised retail prices of meat and butter mentioned above.

The increased output between 1953 and 1958 was in part due to the favorable climatic conditions in the latter year, but after this factor is appropriately discounted a substantial increase is still evident. This increase was the consequence of a number of important changes, one of which was a significant increase in incentives for the members of collective farms. The added incentives resulted from sizable increases in the fixed prices paid by the state for products sold to procurement agencies, reduced taxes charged against the collective farms and the members of the farms, and reductions in the obligatory deliveries imposed upon the private agriculture of collective farm members and workers and employees. By 1958, the average prices paid by the procurement agencies to collective farms had risen sevenfold for grains, tenfold for potatoes, elevenfold for meat animals, almost fourfold for milk, and more than double compared with 1950 prices for sugar beets. Only cotton prices remained unchanged. After crude adjustment is made for the absorption of collective farms into the state farm system during 1957 and 1958, it appears that money payments to collective farms for products delivered to the procurement agencies were about five times as great in 1958 as in 1950.

As a result of the new lands program, the total sown area increased by 40 million hectares (about 99 million acres) or by a quarter between 1953 and 1958. The corn silage program added to the quality of the feed supply and improved its seasonal distribution, though the effect upon the total quantity of feed was fairly modest. Substantial increases were achieved in the inventory of machinery and in fertilizer availability.

Between 1953 and 1958 it probably appeared to Soviet officials that their agricultural problems were on the way to being solved. It might even have been assumed that the Seven Year Plan goals (1958–65), aggregating to a 70 per cent increase in agricultural output, could be achieved — the first time ever for an aggregate goal for agriculture. But with the plan period four-sevenths gone, only one-fourteenth of the goal has been achieved. Why has stagnation again appeared after five years of progress?

A partial answer to this question is that the extent of stagnation is exaggerated by the comparison of 1962 output with 1958 output. The output in 1958 was probably at least 5 per cent above "normal" because of the favorable climatic factors. If this is taken into account, agricultural output has grown at a rate of about 2.5 per cent per annum since 1958. On this basis, the increase in output probably has failed to keep up with the increase in demand, but the short fall has not been very great and would not be particularly troublesome except for the existence of a substantial degree of excess demand in 1958.

It is not possible to give a definitive answer to the question posed above. I believe that three factors are important in explaining the failure to achieve rapid output growth since 1958. First, there has been no significant improvement in the incentive structure since 1958. The rapid progress made following 1953 was certainly related to the substantial increase in incomes obtained for work done on the collective farms. Second, a large fraction of the increase in output achieved between 1955 and 1958 was the result of bringing 40 million hectares of previously idle or fallow land under cultivation, and in the process resources of all kinds were brought into play in the new-lands area. Third, I believe that certain structural changes in agriculture have had a negative influence since 1958 — possibly, in fact, since 1950. I refer especially to the amalgamation of the collective farms which resulted in a reduction in the number of such farms from about 250,000 at the beginning of 1950 to 121,000 at the end of that year and to 44,000 by the end of 1960. And one must also note that the climate for private agriculture has deteriorated significantly since the mid-fifties.

The organizational structure of Soviet agriculture has in it features that increase costs of production and seriously affect its adaptability. At the one extreme are the very large collective and state farms. In 1960 there were 44,000 collective farms with an average sown area of 2,745 hectares (6,783 acres) and an average total area of 6,300 hectares (15,-367 acres). There were 7,375 *sovkhozy* (state farms) with an average sown area of 7,000 hectares (17,297 acres) and a total area of 26,200 hectares (64,740 acres) per farm.[4]

Alongside these giant farms are approximately 35 million of the tiniest "farms" that exist anywhere in the world. The members of collective farms have about 17 million plots that average perhaps 0.3 of a hectare (0.74

---

[4] There were also 107,000 auxiliary state farms of various economic institutions with an average sown area of 55 hectares (137 acres). These farms controlled approximately 3 per cent of the total sown area.

acre) and there are approximately 18 million plots of state employees living both in rural and urban areas. Altogether, the 35 million plots involve about 3 per cent of the total sown area of the Soviet Union, while the 51,-000 giant farms control 94 per cent.

One of the basic problems of the collective farm system has been (and is) to induce the members to work for the collective farm. Until 1953–54 a major explanation for the low reward for work on the collective farm was the very low level of prices paid by the state for most of the deliveries to the state procurement agencies. But in recent years the low reward must be blamed largely upon the many inefficiencies that have become imbedded into the collective farms. The prices now paid by the state for products delivered by the collective farm cannot be said to be exploitive, at least not by comparison with prices in other parts of the world. While international price comparisons are beset with many difficulties, one can get some idea of the level of prices paid to collective farms by assuming that a new ruble is equivalent to one U.S. dollar. On this basis, the following comparisons with prices received by farmers in the United States emerge (per metric ton):

	U.S.S.R.	*U.S.*
Wheat	70	72
Milk	125	85
Beef (live weight)	900	485
Hogs (live weight)	1,050	375
Chickens (live weight)	1,400	350
Sugar beets	24	15
Cotton (unginned)	340	260

But the productivity of and the return to labor on the collective farms are so low that the return to members of collective farms is much higher per unit of time for work performed on their tiny plots. Members of collective farms, including all working family members, distribute their time worked in agriculture in about the following proportions: 75 per cent on the collective farms and 25 per cent on their individual plots. I have estimated that in 1957 only 37 per cent of the income of collective farm members came from payments for work performed on the collective farms. The remainder came from the private plots, except for a small amount received as wages. Thus the return to labor performed on the tiny plots, where the hoe and the spade are the capital equipment, is much higher than on the large collective farms with their tractors and combines.

The agricultural output from all of the tiny plots represents a significant fraction of the gross output of Soviet agriculture. If the outputs of eleven commodity groups are weighted by the 1958 prices paid to collective farms, we find that in 1959, 16 per cent of all crop output and 49 per cent of all livestock output was produced in the private sector. A third of all agricultural output came from the plots yet, it may be remembered, the private plots control only 3 per cent of the total sown area. It may also be noted that about 35 per cent of all labor used in agriculture is devoted to private plots.[5] Thus the average gross labor productivity on the private plots is nearly the same as on the giant farms; the average net productivity is probably much higher on the plots.

It seems fairly obvious to me that a different mix between socialized and collectivized agriculture in the Soviet Union — and most other countries in Eastern Europe — would result in a larger output and more effective utilization of labor and other resources. But any significant change in the relative role of private agriculture is fraught with many political problems in the Soviet Union.

But we should perhaps not be too smug; we cannot claim very great success in solving our own farm problems, and one of the reasons for our limited success is that we have ruled out certain approaches largely on political grounds, and have maintained numerous programs that complicate and exacerbate our difficulties because of expected political benefits.

.   .   .   .   .   .

The governments in the Soviet Union and other Eastern European countries are faced with two alternatives other than significantly increasing the role of private agriculture. One is to wipe out the excess demand by a significant increase in state store food prices. The other is to eliminate the excess demand by achieving a very short-run increase in the quantity of food available. The second alternative would involve substantial investments and inputs from the non-farm sector and might entail certain institutional changes that would be difficult politically. The first alternative would not be a popular one; there is some evidence that there was resistance and unrest as a result of the recent butter and meat price increases in the Soviet Union. In my opinion, neither of these alternatives is likely to be chosen. The costs of meeting the annual increase in

[5] The distribution of labor referred to in the previous paragraph was for the members of collective farms; the estimate that 35 per cent of all labor in agriculture was devoted to private plots includes the time spent by workers and employees and the members of their families in addition to the collective farm members and their families.

demand will in themselves place a strain upon the available resources, given the priority granted to military power and industrial growth. Thus it is unlikely that the necessary additional resources that would make possible a substantial output increase will be made available. While under Stalin it might have been possible to wipe out the excess demand by higher retail prices — though even he never did it — I do not think that the present governments can do so.

Consequently, the governments in Eastern Europe will continue to be plagued by agricultural problems. Food output will continue to be too small and numerous programs and measures to increase output will be undertaken; generally the success achieved, if any, will be slight.

In early 1961, Arcadius Kahan and I completed a study of the possible increases in output that might be achieved in the Soviet Union between 1958 and 1965. Our study, which was based upon an examination of resources likely to be available and possible improvements in farming methods for eleven major groups of farm commodities, indicated that farm output might increase by 24 per cent or a little over 3 per cent per annum. Such an increase, if achieved, would have been about equal to the change in demand over the period. Thus, the increase would have made no contribution to eliminating the excess demand, though there would have been a small improvement in per capita consumption. It now appears that our projected increase in output was definitely on the high side. With four of the seven years now history, farm output has increased by about 5 per cent. Actual performance during the seven years may be that of maintaining per capita consumption of food, but even to accomplish this would require a more rapid growth of output in the last three years of the plan period than were realized in the first four.

Western Europe

The underlying demand and supply situation in Western Europe (all of Non-Communist Europe) is a happy one, if one takes the point of view of benevolent governments that wish to provide their farmers with "fair and reasonable" prices. The quantity demanded exceeds the quantity produced by farmers of Western Europe; for the area as a whole, imports provide about a quarter of the food consumed. Output of domestic farmers can be increased through various forms of protection and only local consumers and taxpayers are the worse for it. In other words, in these circumstances governments face a manageable task — a task that is far less intractable than that faced by an exporting nation that wishes to increase the incomes of its farmers through the price mechanism.

All countries, of course, are not in this enviable position. Denmark, which has had least interference with its agriculture and the highest farm income in Western Europe, may well have difficult days ahead if EEC adopts a protectionist policy with respect to agriculture. Generally, the markets for meat and milk may reach a point of equilibrium between demand and local supply from the area as a whole.

In terms of output, the agriculture of Western Europe is approximately the same size as U.S. agriculture. Agricultural production in Western Europe for 1958 has been estimated as $26.3 billion compared with $26.5 billion in the United States.[6] Furthermore, the rate of increase in agricultural output in Western Europe during the past quarter-century has not been much smaller than in the United States. If U.S. output during 1935–39 is adjusted upward by 7 per cent to reflect the adverse effect of climatic factors, output in 1960–61 was 60 per cent greater than "normalized" output in 1935–39; in Western Europe the increase was 42 per cent. The increase in agricultural output per capita since 1935–39 has been slightly larger in Western Europe than in the United States, if the adjustment referred to above is made for the United States.[7]

An FAO study,[8] projecting changes in demand and supply for agricultural products for the period 1956–65, indicates that in the nine-year period farm output will increase by more than 20 per cent while demand (measured at the farm level) is expected to increase by 16 to 18 per cent. The FAO projections indicate a continuation of a trend in the relationship between food output and food consumption that has been under way for at least a quarter-century. The trend referred to is the relative decline in the importance of imports in the food supply of the area. Before World War II, Western Europe imported 31 per cent of its food supply; in the latter part of the fifties, about 25 per cent. The FAO projections imply that by 1965 imports may supply approximately 22 per cent of the total food supply.

More recent projections made by FAO for the period from 1957–59 through 1970[9] do not indicate any change in expectations. Production is expected to increase more rapidly than consumption for most food prod-

[6] *The World Agricultural Situation, 1961* (Washington: U.S. Department of Agriculture, Foreign Agricultural Service), p. 5.

[7] *Ibid.*, p. 2.

[8] "Trends in European Agriculture and Their Implications for Other Regions," *Monthly Bulletin of Agricultural Economics and Statistics*, IX, 11 (November, 1960), 1–8.

[9] Food and Agriculture Organization, *Agricultural Commodities — Projections for 1970* (Rome, 1962), pp. 1–30, 32, 33, and Part II.

ucts and thus the share of imports would decline below the 22 per cent projected for 1965.

United States

There is little point in reviewing in detail the potential increases in demand and production of agricultural products for the United States. Numerous such efforts are available. In general, the conclusion is that total demand or consumption will increase only slightly more rapidly than population. Certainly for the next decade there is no question that production can increase as rapidly as demand. In fact, the basic problem seems to be that of restraining production so that it does not increase more rapidly than domestic demand and our willingness to supply our farm products to low-income countries under foreign disposal operations.

In the United States there are various governmental policies that have an effect upon the agricultural output of the country and upon the markets for the exports of most other producers of agricultural products. The programs that affect output are frequently inconsistent — some are designed to reduce output while others have the effect of increasing it. Among the latter programs are support prices, reclamation and irrigation projects, watershed projects, agricultural conservation programs and the Soil Conservation Service, and the imported farm-labor program. Output is restricted by rationing the use of land or withdrawing land from agricultural production. Whether the net effect of the programs upon output is positive or negative has not, so far as I know, been determined.

The United States clearly illustrates the conflicts between politics and economics that affect agricultural policy in all Western industrial nations. In most industrial countries there is a clear economic base for reducing the quantities of resources engaged in agriculture. Except for a few isolated cases (Sweden and West Germany), the governments of these countries are unwilling to adopt positive measures to bring this about. And West Germany, even though it has recognized the need for a smaller labor force in agriculture, supports farm product prices at extremely high levels and induces an expansion in farm output.

Low-Income Countries

It is not possible for me to indicate the prospects for agricultural production in the low-income countries. The variations from country to country are great and the amount and quality of information available leaves much to be desired. As has been indicated earlier, the evidence on output indicates that the low-income countries have, on the average, been increasing output at about the same rate as the rest of the world. The rapid increases in population during the past two decades in most of the low-income areas of the world are certainly consistent with the estimates of agricultural output.

There is now rather general agreement that the technological possibilities for increasing food output in the low-income areas are good. Many of the low-income areas — Africa, Latin America, and Southeast Asia — have room for substantial expansion of the cultivated area. But the experience of Japan over the past century clearly indicates what can be done in an area where only moderate increases in the sown area are possible. In the half-century from 1881–90 to 1931–40, the cultivated area of six major crops in Japan increased by only 18 per cent. However, yields increased by 66 per cent and production by 95 per cent. The excellent *Report on India's Food Crisis and Steps to Meet It,* prepared by The Ford Foundation team under its chairman, Sherman Johnson, clearly indicates that it is technically possible to substantially increase food production in India.[10]

That it is technologically possible to increase food output is, of course, only a necessary pre-condition for a solution of the agricultural problems of the low-income areas. A great deal must be done before the technological possibilities can be translated into food available for an increasing population with a rising per capita level of consumption. But the changes that are required are not impossible of achievement, even in very poor countries. It will be necessary, however, for substantial quantities of resources to be invested in agriculture or industries supplying agriculture.

I have noted earlier that agriculture can make four important contributions to economic development: provide an increasing supply of food at constant or declining real prices, release labor for non-farm employment, release savings for investment in non-farm activities, and provide foreign exchange earnings to pay for imported capital goods and equipment. I wish to comment briefly upon the prospects for the latter of the contributions during the decade of the sixties.

It should be remembered that trade among low-income countries is quite modest in volume or value. Most of it is with the high-income or industrialized areas. Consequently the changes in export earnings from ag-

---

[10] The Agricultural Production Team (Sherman Johnson, chairman), *Report on India's Food Crisis and Steps to Meet It,* sponsored by The Ford Foundation (issued by the Government of India, Ministry of Food and Agriculture and Ministry of Community Development and Cooperation, 1959).

ricultural products in low-income countries depend mainly upon import demands of the high-income areas, and these in turn result from change in the balance between consumption and production in the high-income areas. As has been noted, growth of demand in North America will be quite moderate, while growth of demand in Western Europe will be greater than in North America but much slower than in the low-income countries. Demand will grow rapidly in Eastern Europe, but it is impossible to predict how much of the growth will be translated into effective demand for imports from the low-income areas.

In both Western Europe and North America it is likely that output will grow at a faster rate than internal consumption. Thus the relative importance of imports in total consumption is likely to decline. This does not mean that the absolute quantity of imports will decline, but it probably does mean that there is little chance for the export earnings of the low-income countries from agricultural products to increase during the decade. Consequently, unless there is a radical change in the agricultural policies of Western Europe and the United States and a substantial change in the willingness of Eastern Europe to meet its domestic food demand through importing, it is unlikely that agriculture in the low-income countries will make any additional contribution to the financing of economic growth through expansion of foreign exchange earnings.

The U.S. Sugar Act of 1962 is indicative of our failure to effectively consider the effects of our agricultural legislation upon the prospects for economic growth of nations whom we attempt to assist through our foreign aid programs. Sugar is an agricultural product with a very considerable potential in several low-income countries; it is quite possible that in Brazil sugar could provide a substantial source of foreign exchange earnings and more than offset the potential loss of earnings from coffee. If the almost 800,000 tons of the increased quota allocated to domestic producers had been made available for the much lower cost of imports, the impact on foreign exchange earnings through increased quantity and higher prices would have been substantial.

SUMMARY AND CONCLUSIONS

I have attempted to substantiate the following main points:

1. There are sharp differences in the rate of growth of demand for food between the industrialized countries and the low-income coun-

tries; this difference is due to generally more rapid rates of population growth in the low-income countries and to higher income elasticities of demand. In the United States, for example, the growth of demand for food is predominantly a function of population growth, while in South America both population growth and per capita income growth are important.

2. The available data indicate that growth of output over the past quarter-century has not differed substantially among the major areas of the world, except perhaps for a somewhat slower rate in Eastern Europe.

3. The agricultural problems of the low-income countries result from the fact that if a reasonable rate of economic development occurs, the increase in demand for food may be at a compound annual rate of 3 to 4 per cent; even under the best of circumstances this is a rapid rate of sustained growth for agricultural output.

4. The efforts of the Western industrial countries to maintain or increase the incomes of their farmers by measures that result in larger domestic output of agricultural products have serious consequences to the markets for the agricultural products of the low-income areas. This is true whether the farm programs result in a reduction of imports, as in Western Europe, or an expansion of exports, as in the United States. One of the major contributions that agriculture can make to the development of an economy is to supply foreign exchange for the purchase of capital goods. The policies of the industrial countries may seriously impede the efforts of the low-income countries to obtain the necessary capital items.

5. The East European countries are faced with a food demand that is growing at a more rapid rate than is true of other industrial countries. In addition, because of past failures of their agricultural output to grow at a satisfactory rate, a substantial excess demand exists for food. Consequently, even if food output grows more rapidly than population and some increase in per capita income is achieved, the continued existence of excess demand will imply the continuation of an agricultural output problem.

6. Both the Communist countries and the Western industrial nations are inhibited from finding solutions to their agricultural problems by political considerations. Except for Poland, the Soviet bloc has not been willing to provide an accepted role for private activity in agriculture. In the Western industrial countries, with only one or two exceptions, there has been an unwillingness to treat the agricultural problem as an aspect of the long-run adjustment required in any growing economy. Programs are

maintained that impede the transfer of resources out of agriculture and induce additional resources to be employed in agriculture. Such programs are adopted and continued primarily for political reasons.

FURTHER READING

Iowa State University Center for Agricultural and Economic Adjustment. *Food — One Tool in International Economic Development.* Ames: Iowa State University Press, 1962. 409 pp.

Johnston, Bruce. "Agricultural Productivity and Economic Development of Japan," *Journal of Political Economy,* LIX, 5 (October, 1951), 498–513.

Lindholm, Richard A. "The Farm: The Misused Income Expansion Base of Emerging Nations," *Journal of Farm Economics,* XLIII, 2 (May, 1961), 236–46.

Mellor, John W. "The Process of Agricultural Development in Low-Income Countries," *Journal of Farm Economics,* XLIV, 3 (August, 1962), 700–16.

Nicholls, William H. "An 'Agricultural Surplus' as a Factor in Economic Development," *Journal of Political Economy,* LXXI, 1 (1963), 1–29.

THE WORLD OIL OUTLOOK

M. A. ADELMAN

SUMMARY AND CONCLUSIONS

The world oil market has and will continue to have great excess capacity. Greater output can be had nearly everywhere at lower costs, and hence the price will be under pressure. Yet petroleum is not an industry of inherent surplus (or "natural monopoly"), where greater output is usually and necessarily to be had at lower cost. This influential but rarely explicit thesis must be rejected, even when it is today advanced no longer as universally true but true everywhere outside the United States. The start of any understanding is in the opposite direction. Fields and areas are of widely unequal cost, and under either competition or rational monopoly the cheaper sources are preferred to the dearer. This suffices to make petroleum an industry of increasing costs like almost every other and, as with almost every other, there is mild paradox but no contradiction in the fact that, over time, costs are expected to be gradually lowered by greater knowledge. (The supply curve slopes upward, and shifts gradually to the right; irregular shifting does not change "up" into "down.")

Hence the excess capacity is not to be explained in the manner of Molière's doctoral candidate, as "inherent," like the "dormative power" in

M. A. ADELMAN is professor in the Department of Economics at the Massachusetts Institute of Technology, having been with that Department since 1948. During the academic year 1962–63 he was on leave in Paris, where he conducted a study of the world petroleum market. He is the author of *The Supply and Price of Natural Gas* (1962) and of articles on industrial organization and public policy in economic and law journals. Since 1958 he has been U.S. editor of the *Journal of Industrial Economics*. Mr. Adelman was born in New York City in 1917. He received his Ph.D. degree from Harvard University.

opium which puts people to sleep, but by the facts of recent history. The reason is in the market, not in nature. The market has been neither simply competitive nor simply monopolistic and, therefore, the cheaper sources have not gradually displaced the dearer.

The first basic reason for oversupply was the appearance of incredibly rich fields in the Middle East. The intrusion of these fields was essentially a chance event, but the type of random shock is intrinsic to the industry. It does not modify the basic fact of higher costs with greater output, but it does explain why a long-term tendency to lower prices can be disorderly, can manifest itself in an irregular, unforeseen way, awarding to some the shock of pleasure and to others the shock of dismay. These new low-cost sources entered the market at prices set by higher-cost output, and hence afforded large scarcity rents — as, indeed, they always will. But, secondly, prices have not been allowed to fall far enough to eliminate enough of the higher-cost sources to remove excess capacity over time. In particular, and rising to the dignity of a third basic reason, the new areas were largely shut off from the largest consuming market in the world, the United States. None of these three causes is likely to be changed much in the near future.

Under any kind of economic system, there must be some method or mechanism to determine output in total and as among the various producing centers. In petroleum, if it were left to the usual disorderly play of competitive forces, the mechanism would be marginal cost equating to price, in accordance with a complex and shifting set of demand and supply conditions. (Price equal to marginal cost does not mean lack of profits; quite the contrary.) Since this mechanism is suppressed, with nothing clear and predictable to replace it, all parties concerned are troubled. Every producing interest feels entitled to about as much as it can profitably produce at today's prices, and in the aggregate this adds up to considerably more than 100 per cent of the market, in any given place and in total.

The present condition will not cure itself by demand catching up with supply, because incentive to explore and develop still more oil will remain. The probabilities of development are good enough to take care of any foreseeable demand at costs no greater and perhaps even lower than today's. Indeed, if we take account of the reserves of natural gas, which were never even estimated before 1962 because they had too little economic importance, world petroleum reserves since 1957 have not only held steady in proportion to world production, but have even increased.

Competition in world oil has been on the increase because economies of scale are large absolutely, but are diminishing and already small in relation to the size of the market. In the long run, this is perhaps the most important factor of all. The current Middle East entrance fee — money needed for exploration up to the time a profitable discovery is found — may be guessed at from the fact that in 1958 a Japanese company, lacking experience in oil finding or production, succeeded with an investment of less than $10 million. Venezuela is less expensive. We must therefore assume that new companies, mostly private, some public, will be more numerous in the future than in the past.

Control of the market has passed from the small group of international oil companies, who had it in only a very special and passive sense, but it has not yet found any firm possessor. The governments of the producing countries are supported for a variety of reasons by the governments of those consuming countries who want a high price for crude oil. The Soviet Union, both as an exporter and for political reasons, wants a high price but may set unacceptably high terms for its membership in some kind of controlling group. Whether the other producing countries, who are largely gathered in OPEC (Organization of the Petroleum Exporting Countries), can control the market and keep prices from declining further remains to be seen. No predictions can be made, but OPEC has given no sign of recognizing that either they control total output and its division among areas or they fail to control the market. It is not decisive, but it is relevant that these governments are acting to increase the growth of new capacity. They have retrieved much acreage in the original concessions in the Middle East and North Africa, and have reserved much in Venezuela. Some of these areas have been offered for private exploitation, some will be held for the respective national oil companies.

The private oil companies and their host governments are naturally in agreement on wishing to maximize total profits, but not on how to share them. The governments are getting perhaps 60 per cent today, and it is generally expected that they will get rather more than this. But if this is so, the really vexing question is: how much more?

The situation is fraught with difficulty because rents (including both scarcity rents and monopoly gains) are so large a part of total revenues and constitute so much room for disagreement. There is dangerous uncertainty on each side of the bargaining table as to just how far the other side can be pushed before an undesirable (and undesired) showdown is brought about. The suggestion made here is that in any case royalty payments should not specify any per-barrel payment because so rigid a requirement would break down in practice; a percentage sharing has a basic flexibility which, in the present and continuing state of ignorance, the parties cannot afford to do without. Indeed, there may be too much rigidity even in a uniform percentage.

At the other end of the spectrum, the consuming nations are embarrassed by prices too high in one sense, too low in another. A key question seems to be that of heavy-fuel-oil prices in Europe, which, it is urged, are not abnormally low and are unlikely to rise unless the price of crude is raised. No guess is made on this point, but the revision of royalties, without further reforms, will not put up prices; it may even lower them if the governments cannot control the market more effectively than they have in the past.

This essay nowhere mentions "administered prices" or "countervailing power." The first, when not purely formal, is a too-clever way to insinuate market control while evading the awkward necessity of proof. The second confuses two different phenomena: buyers able to promote and to benefit from sellers' competition, and buyers able to impose their monopoly. The latter is unimportant and not expected in world oil; the former has been important and may become more so.

SOME BASIC NOTIONS

The petroleum industry is fortunate in having some independent experts whose great experience is matched by their integrity, and from whom we should be prepared to take more than a little on faith; people steeped in some art, as distinct from science, know much more than they can prove.

I am not of that fortunate company; the object of this essay is to expose a way of thinking, or an economic theory, about the world crude oil problem, with few substantive conclusions and fewer recommendations. But the problem will be with us for some time to come. The facts are going to change; our impressions of them will change even more; "solutions" will seem for a while to work and then fail. If we have some body of general ideas of how the markets operate, we can better adjust to change.

The world oil market today is said to be in a state of chronic imbalance. If so, we need to ask the nature of balance. The answer cannot be precise. But then a doctor would have some trouble in defining precisely an individual's bodily equilibrium. He could, however, state confidently that a lack of nourishment or some mechanical strain or shock would yield abnormal symptoms or effects. When, therefore, we ask under what conditions a system like the world oil producing industry would be at rest, it is not implied that so dull a state could ever be reached; still less, that it should be! But to understand disequilibrium, we must have some concept of equilibrium: a condition where nobody in the market can increase his profits (or decrease his losses) by doing something to change output and prices. That is plainly not the case today; we wish to know why and how much.

Three general cautions are in order at this point. First, a system may be in disequilibrium for a long time or forever, if strong enough blocks are built into it. The seas off Holland are in disequilibrium with the level of farmlands on the other side of the dikes; but so long as those dikes are strong and well maintained, they will stay that way. If strong enough barriers can be interposed into the world oil market, then the seemingly irresistible force of the market, or of competition, has met a truly immovable object, and the market stays at rest. There will be strain but no rupture, and current prices and supply patterns will continue.

Second, given the many gaps in our knowledge, there may be more than one way to explain a set of facts. In choosing one hypothesis over the other, we are best off saying no more than is absolutely necessary; the simpler theory is almost always the better. Common sense, indeed, cautions that if to explain something you need a special story, it had better be a good one. If, therefore, we reject such notions as Russian "dumping," or an international petroleum cartel (even hedged and qualified), it is because we do not need them — though there happen also to be facts to disprove them.

Finally, the notion of balance or equilibrium in a market has absolutely nothing to do with what is good, bad, desirable, or undesirable. Not that any economic policy can exist without some notion of what is good or bad, and for whom. Discussion of this kind is far from trivial or secondary, and I wish there were more of it. It is not the confrontation but the admixture of what *is* with what *ought to be* that endlessly confuses and exhausts so much industry economics, including that of oil, and if we cannot keep the two viewpoints distinct we had better adjourn. Let me risk offense where none is meant by giving a simple example. I could not count the number of times the price of oil or gas, crude or products has been called "fair and reasonable" (or unfair and unreasonable). Now, when businessmen describe their prices as "fair and reasonable," they are saying to a university or government economist (and not only to them) that "they do not compete strongly with one another, sheltering behind price agreements or tacit understandings to live and let live."[1] Yet perhaps they

[1] Sir Robert Hall, *Planning,* Rede Lecture 1962 (Cambridge: Cambridge University Press), p. 25.

are not trying to say this and do not mean it; they have merely confused their audience and done themselves an injustice. All too often does someone in industry, when told that prices diverge from the competitive level, answer like the proper Bostonian rebutting the notion that his ancestors hanged witches: they didn't do it; besides, it was a good thing; and anyway, the Quakers were even worse.

The principal theses of a general theory of oil production economics may be baldly stated as follows, for later elaboration.

1. The crude oil industry, contrary to common belief, is inherently self-adjusting; more precisely, it has a strong adjustment mechanism for determining the level of output and its division among various sources of supply, by the *price* acting upon the cost which must be incurred to bring up more output. This incremental or marginal cost, for every individual unit and *a fortiori* for the system as a whole, increases rather than decreases with greater output. It therefore serves as the governor of the producing mechanism in general and in any particular place: so long as marginal cost is less than anticipated price (or net revenue), there is a profit incentive to produce more; when the marginal cost rises above the price it chokes off further expansion of output. The current spasms of the world oil market express both a strong adjustment mechanism trying to make itself felt and also strong barriers to it.

2. The adjustment mechanism is always under strain — or always has work to do: (*a*) Changes in cost conditions may be quite large and unforeseen, particularly because the cost of finding oil is subject to some large random disturbances. (*b*) The "prices" and "marginal costs" which count are always those existing in the future: expected or planned. Hence changes in expectations and changes in the rate of discounting must affect, and may powerfully affect, the relative marginal costs of different supply areas and for the industry as a whole.

3. To speak of the average cost of oil, or of total or average profit, or even of marginal cost, without specifying the level of output, is to say very little. Given (1) above, strongly rising incremental costs, it follows that there must be large rents in the system: a price which barely pays the expense of bringing up the highest-cost barrel yields large profits on the extraction of the lower-cost. And given (2), an industry of several time horizons, some very long, the rents must be even greater, for a payment needed to evoke greater output in the long run may be superfluous to keep current output going in the short run. Rents by their nature are upsetting because they form a large area for appropriation and for disagreement. And finally, given a world price level which is far above marginal cost

under present or almost any conceivable conditions, the rents are that much greater and more disturbing. (Perhaps wrongly, we include in "rent" both scarcity rents and any other above-minimum profit — not because the distinction is trifling but because it seems not to be necessary for our purpose.)

An Industry of "Inherent" Surplus?

Petroleum production costs, conventionally divided into the three stages of exploration, development, and extraction, are generally considered to be rather unusual. This opinion is justified, but the usual reasons offered are so wrong and so deeply held that we must begin by disposing of them; for it is impossible to face up to the real problems before getting rid of the false ones. But our object is constructive; the facts disproving the false theory are the elements of the correct one.

The common opinion, though it is assumed everywhere and breathes from the pores, so to speak, of almost every general discussion of the petroleum industry, is almost never explicitly stated. We only catch hints, e.g., that oil production has "an inherent surplus," because at all times more is available, at the current price, than is wanted at that price; hence "it has been found necessary" — in the United States by law, elsewhere by industrial statesmanship — to restrict output, not because people are greedy, but because there is no other way to keep the industry going. It is, however, impossible to come to grips with any theory so briefly mentioned, or urbanely assumed. The nearest we come to a statement is in a United Nations publication.[2] Petroleum production is stated to be an industry of decreasing costs, or increasing returns.[3] A "decreasing cost" industry will often be called a "natural monopoly," because the facts of nature compel a monopoly. Not only would there otherwise be waste and extreme, senseless price fluctuation, but anything except a monopoly must in time break down. The market if left to itself must evolve toward monopoly even regardless of the desires of any of the firms in it; so we ought to recognize that fact from the beginning and base our policy upon it.

One's opinions, even on basic economics, tend to be formed by interests and prejudices. But this vision of oil as an industry of decreasing costs

---

[2] *The Price of Oil in Western Europe* (E/ECE/205; Geneva, 1955).
[3] Much of the following is from M. A. Adelman, *The Supply and Price of Natural Gas* (Oxford: Blackwell, 1962), hereafter cited as SPNG; but the treatment here is wider in some respects, narrower in others.

and natural monopoly is held clear across the political-economic spectrum. Perhaps it is just as well — or perhaps very bad — that we must reject the one opinion that seems common to all.

Decreasing Costs and Natural Monopoly

We will need to show explicitly why an industry of decreasing costs is also one of natural monopoly. The basic problem is one of *unlimited economies of scale*. For example, within very wide limits the larger an electrical generating plant, the lower its unit costs. Therefore additional capacity can always be had at a lower unit cost. Hence there must be a monopoly in any local area where electricity is generated and sold. For, if there were two or more independent concerns, each of them could always make a little more money, for the moment, by producing more and selling it for anything even a little in excess of the cost of the increment. But the cost of previous capacity, as we just saw, is higher than that of the increment. Hence (barring price discrimination) each concern, though making a profit on the increment, would be losing money on the rest of the output.

In almost all industries being very small is uneconomic and it pays to be bigger, but only within limits. After a while, being bigger becomes a neutral factor, swamped by the usual run of management problems. In an industry of decreasing costs this brake on size is absent, and the management is under constant compulsion to be bigger and produce more at all times, no matter how much is already being produced. But the more the industry produces, the more it pushes down prices, and the greater are the losses suffered by the group as a whole. This is the process summarized in the UN document (pp. 16–18) as "the well known economic theorem" that in an industry of increasing returns, individual producers acting individually must operate at a loss. If they get together on prices and output, of course they are no longer acting individually. Since a large number of producers cannot (usually) get together, the idea of independence is often expressed indirectly, i.e., as large numbers; but the key concept is independence.

Under these circumstances, monopoly is inevitable. Perhaps there is a written agreement not to produce past a certain point, or else all are wise enough to live and let live and not try to produce and sell past the amount expected of them. But this is an uneasy kind of existence, for the pressure is still there all the time and must always be resisted. The most economic solution is simply one company.

A single company is of course still confronted with the fact of nature that it could lower its costs by being larger, but the fact is no longer an inducement or pressure. A monopolist can compare the cost of the additional output not with the current price nor with the expected lower price, but rather with the net impact on revenues, or marginal revenue. Thus, if current costs are 100 and revenues 110, and if at doubled capacity costs would be 175 but revenues only 185 because prices would drop, the marginal revenue would be barely equal to the marginal cost of 75, and there would be no inducement to build. Whereas if the company had been one of a number of independent ones, the management would have known that all the other companies would be trying to produce more, thus bringing down the price, and it would have no choice but to increase capacity and hence, by increasing output, help to bring about just the result it did not want!

Obviously the model of natural monopoly describes many persons' thinking about the oil producing industry, except that they do not trouble to set it out. Indeed for many people this is a model of all or most industries: everywhere the bigger the better, or more efficient. But our business is only with crude oil.

Increasing and Decreasing Cost in Petroleum Production[4]

"Production" is sometimes used to refer only to extraction; sometimes, as in "the producing industry," to the whole spectrum of activities: exploration, development, and extraction. This double usage is not precise, but because it has become customary we will follow it, trusting to the context to make the meaning clear.

We must at the outset pay our disrespects to some of the more usual clichés. The greatest one of all, "Remember East Texas in '30; we'll have 10 cents a barrel if we don't watch out!" will be discussed later (p. 72). Another time-worn cliché, "Once an oil field is found, all you can do is produce it to get your money out," says only that before there can be production there must be exploration and development, which cost money. But before there can be production of widgets, there must first be investment in a widget factory, which can do nothing profitable except turn out widgets. A third cliché is: "Most oil producing costs are overhead, and the fixed : variable ratio is very high." So it is in agriculture, and in retail trade, which are most typically atomistic industries.

The fixed : variable ratio is being confused with economies of scale, and while the two may loosely correlate, they are certainly not the same, as our two examples show. Furthermore, the fixed : variable ratio is often strik-

---

[4] "Petroleum" is used to denote both oil and natural gas.

ingly low in oil when found but not yet developed: in the Middle East, sunk costs per unit are in fractions of a cent per barrel; in a stripper well, operating costs are much higher than investment costs. As a matter of fact, there is really *no* ratio of fixed : variable costs which can be called broadly representative of the industry, even in the loosest sense. And this extraordinary variability, as will be seen, is the key to the whole problem.

A Warning and Example. Even experienced readers may need the warning that an industry of "increasing costs" does not mean costs rising over time. (See Figure 1.) A functional relation at any given time is not a

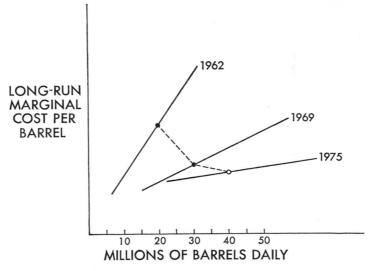

Figure 1. Expected Costs, 1962–75

trend over time. The petroleum industry has increasing costs, but not because most or all of the large low-cost fields have already been found. We venture no prediction on that score. Nor does our analysis assume or imply that Middle East or Venezuelan costs will rise by 1975; in fact, the contrary is asserted. Above all, it is not denied that right now every unit and the industry as a whole could lower its cost by increasing its output. We start from this fact, and ask whether it follows from the physical determinants of finding-development-production costs. We demonstrate that it does not. The way is then open to analyze the real, not fancied, peculiarities of the industry. It is then possible to try finding the true reasons for the present condition and to predict what may happen to costs and prices over time. Opinions will differ on how well the two latter tasks are done, but this does not affect the first housecleaning job.

The supply function of an industry, which is essentially the cumulation of all the costs of all conceivable producing units, traces out the lowest cost at which any given amount of output could be produced. If the optimum is violated — either by chance, ignorance, unforeseen change, or by deliberate market control — it may or may not be considered unfortunate; one can argue about that indefinitely. The objective fact is that pressures are set up for business enterprises to take advantage of others' non-optimum conditions through underselling their rivals; and these pressures may cumulate to violent strength. If, therefore, the present functioning of the oil industry does not much resemble the industry of increasing costs which the facts of nature would make it, that discrepancy does not discredit the theory, but it does express the present tension.

A useful exercise in the theory of increasing and decreasing costs is had by looking at two closely allied activities, pipelines and tankers. A single pipeline, or tanker, is a classic example of decreasing costs or economies of scale, because for basic physical reasons the larger one builds, the lower are the unit costs at optimum volume. Now, a pipeline *may* be an example of a decreasing-cost industry, or natural monopoly, *if* the market is so small as only to permit one or two to exist. Hence, in studying the natural gas industry in the United States it was necessary to analyze in some detail the special case of a pipeline as first having a buying monopoly in a producing area, then gradually losing it as more reserves were found and new pipelines were built into the region.[5] Thus even a clear case of decreasing costs in the single producing unit does not necessarily mean an industry or market of decreasing costs — one must also consider the size of the market. Consider now the world tanker fleet, which serves a single market (with the partial exception of U.S. coastal traffic). Taken as a whole, that fleet is one of the clearest examples of increasing cost, because tankers form an array from lowest to highest cost. When, as during the winter of 1962–63, demand is especially high, more and more inefficient tankers are pulled out of layup, or out of the grain trade, and the marginal cost and the market price of the transport service are higher.

In longer perspective, the increasing cost is moderated because many more ships can be built. The pressure is transmitted to the shipbuilding yards, and therefore greater output still means higher cost, though to a milder degree. In the very long run, however, given time enough to adapt

[5] SPNG, *op. cit.* (Note 3), pp. 44–50.

shipyards also, the tanker industry is one of approximately constant marginal and average cost. But there can be striking technical progress and cost reduction over time. At any given time, therefore, taking the tanker fleet as it exists and will exist, it is an increasing-cost activity. In 1970, it will still be one, but the whole range of cost, or most of it, will be lower than it is today. Let us note, first, that in order to answer the question we had to specify the time period we had in mind and, second, that to speak of the laws governing the cost of the single tanker was no answer at all to the question of industry costs. In fact, it is a good example of the logical fallacy of composition.

The petroleum industry, to which we now turn, is like tankers in that the variability among producing units makes it an increasing-cost industry. But here the case is much stronger, because within each producing unit costs also rise with increasing output, and because we cannot build petroleum deposits to most efficient sizes — we must take them as we find them.

Exploration is a process of spending money to find oil deposits, and the more barrels found per dollar the lower is the unit finding cost. At any given time there are a number of places to look, and the better places are preferred. The business of an exploration department, or of an independent wildcatter, is to decide which prospects are expected to be lower-cost oil. Shallower deposits are preferred to deeper because the incremental per-foot drilling cost increases very rapidly with greater depth; only a higher price makes it worth drilling deeper.[6] A concessionaire deciding which area to turn back and which to keep is doing another exercise in increasing costs; so are the Russian oilmen who concentrate on shallow, permeable, porous reservoirs of low-viscosity oil, who know about the more difficult (hence more costly) stratigraphic traps, but prefer to explore only structural indications as long as there are plenty of them, and who ascribe their exploration success to their concentration on the most favorable prospects.[7] The same has been true in the Middle East, which is, indeed,

---

[6] Joint Association Survey (American Petroleum Institute, Independent Petroleum Association of America, and Mid-Continent Oil & Gas Association), *Report on Petroleum Industry Income and Expenditures in the United States* (New York, 1944, 1948, 1953, 1956, 1959).

[7] Robert Ebel, *The Petroleum Industry of the Soviet Union* (New York: American Petroleum Institute, 1962), pp. 41, 44, 53, 58. See also SPNG, *op. cit.* (Note 3), p. 104 citation. For the greater desirability of structural traps, see A. I. Levorsen, "Exploration for Stratigraphic Traps," in *Economics of Petroleum Exploration, Development and Property Evaluation* (New York: Prentice-Hall, 1961), hereafter cited as EPEDPE, pp. 17, 31, 36.

mostly unexplored.[8] The higher the output of oil aimed at, the more must the costlier prospects be explored; conversely, the higher the price, the poorer the prospects it pays to evaluate and explore. This is what we mean by an increasing-cost activity.

This does not mean that over time the better prospects get used up, so that exploration costs per unit must necessarily increase. They may or may not. So far, increasing knowledge of the geology of more of the earth's surface and progress in technology have outrun exploration and production, thus bringing costs down. But where knowledge does not sufficiently grow, costs must go up and Hodges and Steele[9] were therefore rightly concerned with the possibility that in the United States new technology in exploration had not been important enough, after around 1940, to overbear the otherwise inevitable tendency to rising costs over time. Their opinion was that the statistics did show this exhaustion, and I believe that later data on oil and gas for the United States provide further proof. Averages mean little when the dispersion is so great, but there has been a persistent and large fall in the percentages of larger size new oil reservoirs found, and an irregular decline even in the absolute numbers.[10]

Period	Total New Fields	Per Cent of New Fields with Reserves Over: (in millions of barrels)		
		50	25	10
1945–48	1,018	1.0	1.1	2.4
1949–52	1,801	0.8	0.9	3.7
1953–56	2,290	0.2	0.7	1.2

[8] Norval E. Baker, in *The Science of Petroleum*, VI (Oxford: Oxford University Press, 1953), 83.

[9] John E. Hodges and Henry B. Steele, *An Investigation of the Problems of Cost Determination for the Discovery, Development and Production of Liquid Hydrocarbons and Natural Gas Reserves* (Rice Institute Pamphlet, Vol. 46, October 1959). The approach of Bruce C. Netschert, *The Future Supply of Oil and Gas* (Baltimore: Johns Hopkins Press for Resources for the Future, Inc., 1958) is partly opposing, partly complementary. Noting what nobody would dispute, that existing statistics of "proved reserves" are far less than ultimate recoverable reserves from any given deposit, and also that there are a number of promising new techniques of exploration and development, he concludes that the supply of oil and gas in the United States can in the future be greatly expanded at no increase in real cost. This conclusion is not absurd or implausible, but neither does it follow from the evidence adduced, which could at best prove that some cost-reducing factors will operate. On an important error in analyzing natural gas cost, see SPNG, *op. cit.* (Note 3), p. 54.

[10] J. Ben Carsey and Marion S. Roberts, in *Bulletin of the American Association of Petroleum Geologists*, Vol. 43 (1962), p. 920, tables XIX, XX. The estimates are for after six years' development history. The distributions on log-probability paper show a shift for both oil and gas, though gas is much less pronounced.

This may be incorrect. The important point is that, at any given time, with exploration plans and commitments to be made according to what is then known of available choices, the more exploration, the more must it go into the less promising places. Over time new and better places may be found, but if so the whole range of choices, from best to worst, is displaced — it is not inverted.

Development is the next stage. It consists of finding the horizontal and vertical limits of the reservoirs in any given field, largely by drilling wells and equipping them for production. Obviously there is no clear-cut division between exploration and development, and many activities could as reasonably be put into one box as another. Basically, as one moves along a very extended scale, uncertainty is less and knowledge greater. And the greater the certainty the more strongly do increasing-cost elements enter. First, as with exploration, all discoveries must be evaluated. Most are discarded right off as non-commercial; others look better but finally are abandoned; others are developed. "Only about 2.7 per cent of all new-field wildcats discover a profitable field, although 11 to 12 per cent produced some oil or gas."[11] The higher the price of oil, the more it pays to drill the poorer discoveries; and the more oil to be produced, the more must be drawn from the poorer discoveries.

Second, as a reservoir or a whole field is developed, the chances increase of getting to and past the edge. Hence, there is increasing risk in any single instance, increasing cost for any group of operations, as one gets closer to the edges and begins to get either thin and skimpy productive strata, or gets nothing.[12]

Third, fields are not uniform and the more productive areas or strata are normally developed first. The operator of the world's greatest field, now that salt water is encroaching and being produced with the oil, solves the problem temporarily and very cheaply by plugging back the lower perforations, but anticipates the time when the production so lost

---

[11] *Ibid.*, p. 752. See also Frederic H. Lahee, *Statistics of Exploratory Drilling in the United States* (Tulsa: AAPG, 1962); and J. J. Arps, in EPEDPE, *op. cit.* (Note 7), p. 163.

[12] On the difficulty of distinguishing local from general structural dips, and mistaking the boundary, see Edgar N. Owen, "Petroleum Exploration — Gambling Game or Business Venture," in EPEDPE, *op. cit.* (Note 7), p. 12. Again, in a given field, with past development costs at 92 cents per barrel, increments could be had at respectively $1.48, $1.71, $2.01, and $2.40. With a price at $1.50, the last three projects would not be worth doing; at higher prices, they would. (Arps and Roberts, in AAPG *Bulletin*, Vol. 42 [1958], pp. 2549–56.)

will be too great to accept and special separators will be needed to handle wet crude.[13]

Fourth, the productivity of a field is less than proportional to the number of wells because past a certain point there is well "interference." The area over which oil migrates through permeable sands is very wide, so that one well could ultimately drain a very large reservoir.[14] If time — meaning the value of money — were no object, that would indeed be the best because it would be the cheapest way.[15] If the demand for oil ever fell to a small fraction of what it is today, most or all of it might be produced this way. But if the price is high enough, it pays to drill more wells into the reservoir and drain it faster, accepting the higher costs.[16] And at some point, the cost of the additional oil which would thus be produced goes up to the point where one must consider the alternatives of either such further expenditures as fluid injection, or development of another field. Instead of just continuing to drill more wells, therefore, some Middle East operators combine it with fluid injection;[17] but elsewhere, as in the Khursaniya field, engineers advise against further developing for fear of excessive — which means expensive — pressure drop, so the company turns to developing Manifa.[18]

We turn now to *producing* strictly considered, the extraction from an existing and known and fully developed field. This is the usual stereotype. Exploration and development costs are already sunk. The relatively small outlays for labor, some fuel and power, etc., are practically independent of the volume of output per month (or any given convenient period). Therefore, up to well capacity, the more barrels produced, the lower the cost per unit. As in our electric power example, the cost of additional barrels is less than the cost of the barrels already produced. The price can fall to absurdly low levels without the operator cutting back production — and then he will not cut back, he will shut down. For the ultra-short run — say about a month — this is a fairly accurate picture of petroleum produc-

---

[13] A. F. Fox, "The Development of the South Kuwait Oilfields," *Institute of Petroleum Review* (London), Vol. 15 (1961), pp. 373, 378.

[14] Morris Muskat, *Physical Principles of Oil Production* (New York: McGraw-Hill, 1949) pp. 591, 858–62, 899; and Rupert C. Craze, "Development Plan for Oil Reservoirs," in T. C. Frick and R. W. Taylor (eds.), *Petroleum Production Handbook* (New York: McGraw-Hill, 1962), pp. 33–5 to 33–20.

[15] Muskat, *op. cit.* (Note 14), pp. 897–99.

[16] *Ibid.,* and C. C. Miller and A. B. Dyes, "Maximum Reservoir Worth — Proper Well Spacing," *Journal of Petroleum Technology,* Vol. 216 (1959), p. 334.

[17] *Oil and Gas International,* March, 1961, pp. 29–33; April 1961, pp. 22–25.

[18] *Ibid.,* September, 1962, pp. 82–83.

tion. After that, as will soon be evident, it is wrong. But in any case, petroleum production cannot be and is not geared to the ultra-short run; it is too expensive. Costs are considered over the remaining life of the field, which at the beginning is the whole life, and decisions on investment and production are made on that basis. Over the remaining lifetime of a field or well, marginal cost is a rising function of output: the greater is the output the higher is the cost of additional output. Even neglecting the cost of well workovers, fracturing, waterflooding, etc., the basic fact about oil and gas production is *the production decline curve*. Every annual reserves bulletin of the American Petroleum Institute–American Gas Association[19] draws attention to it. In his well-known book,[20] Ball states that ". . . no one can understand the oil business who has not grasped the universality of the decline curve. . . ." This is quoted approvingly in a recent work by the U.S. Geological Survey.[21] The forces determining the curve are too complex for summary in a simple formula, as Muskat's treatise is at pains to show, but many empirical approximations are used. There is a very large literature on the subject and the thinking of engineers shows increasing economic sophistication.[22] Its importance from the operator's point of view is to let him know just *how much* more profitable production he can get out of a lease, and *at what point* the unit cost of producing more is going to go above the price. During 1961–62, for example, the *Oil and Gas Journal* carried a series of over forty articles, by E. T. Guerrero and F. M. Stewart, on the many kinds of production decline curves and practical ways of forecasting them at any given time. Other writers remark that many different formulas give results that in practice are not far apart, and hence that a simple exponential curve is often appropriate. Their example shows a fixed outlay per month and diminishing production per month; the operator forecasts the time to abandonment, which will come about

[19] E.g., API-AGA bulletin for 1961, p. 8.

[20] Max W. Ball, *This Fascinating Oil Business* (New York: Bobbs-Merrill, 1940), p. 143.

[21] A. D. Zapp, *Future Petroleum Producing Capacity of the U.S.*, Geological Survey Bulletin 1142-H (1962).

[22] J. J. Arps, "Estimation of Primary Oil and Gas Reserves," Chapter 37, in Frick, *op. cit.* (Note 14), pp. 37–41 to 37–52. "The economic limit rate is the production rate which will just meet the operating expenses of a well [i.e.] . . . how much would actually be saved if the well were abandoned." *Cf.* J. L. Hopkinson, "Modern Method of Reservoir Assessment and Control," in *Planning for Productivity in the Oil Industry* (London: Institute of Petroleum, 1960), pp. 53–61, and references cited there.

when the value of the monthly production no longer exceeds the monthly cost.[23]

The calculation of production-decline curves and forecasting of output belong both to the development and production stages. Every development plan forecasts production over the life of the field or well. A convenient example of earlier-stage calculation is to be seen in a paper presented by an Aramco representative at the Second (1960) Arab Petroleum Congress.[24] This shows the cash flow and expenses anticipated "over a 15-year period at a declining production rate due to a normal decrease in reservoir pressure." As a variant of great practical importance, the writer shows how a waterflooding project would put production on a much more steady basis and would increase total recovery; but the waterflooding would cost additional money and the incremental cost per barrel would be some 19 per cent above the non-waterflood design. Moreover, recasting the computation to take account of discounting, he shows that the additional output is not worth this higher marginal cost, because it ties up money in an unduly low-profit activity.

Of course, these calculations lend an appearance of far more precision than is normally the case. But this merely means that the operator must refigure and refigure as he proceeds, gaining more and more knowledge of the deposit as he drills more wells and produces more from them. For porosity and permeability are not like "a nice uniform sponge down below," holding the oil in place.[25] In so tremendously rich a deposit as the Burgan field of Kuwait, the increasing knowledge might seem trivial, and yet is discussed in a report on its development.[26]

To sum up: looking at development-production program *ex ante,* we must take account of the fact that both total output and total cost are functions of time. In general, if the expenses per unit of time are fixed (and *a fortiori* if they are increasing, as in fact they are), and if the production per unit of time decreases, *then the production cost per additional unit increases the greater is the total production.* Or, as a variant, if total output can be both increased and stabilized at greater expense, then it again follows that unit variable costs rise with greater output.

[23] William F. Stevens and George Thodos, "New Method for Estimating Primary Oil Reserves," *World Oil,* Vol. 153 (December 1961), p. 163.

[24] Lawrence Ison, "Financial Analysis of Oil Projects."

[25] See the discussion following Hopkinson, *op. cit.* (Note 22), pp. 61–67, for some fascinating examples.

[26] A. F. Fox, "The Development of the South Kuwait Oilfields," *Institute of Petroleum Review,* Vol. 15 (1961), p. 373.

There is one minor but not negligible qualification. In a very large field, much additional capacity is had at approximately constant cost before the operator starts approaching the thinner strata, or the end, or the possible need for denser drilling. Furthermore, this process must take some considerable time. Therefore, if it will take some years before we can go from x barrels to $x + a$, we must assume that when the time comes to produce the increment a, we will know more than we now do about the field, and perhaps have some better methods available. Hence the increment a is produced at a lower cost than the previous output x. To be sure, this conclusion does not necessarily follow, because the rate of discount may be such that the cost of waiting until we can produce the increment may exceed the gains in knowledge. At this point, the cost becomes too entangled with expectations, too much of an inventory phenomenon, and its analysis must be deferred. But we can at least take note that the best approximation to the cost function of a very large field is a long flat stretch where new capacity can be brought in at about the same cost as the old. This is an economy (or the postponement of diseconomy) of high-level output, not an economy of scale. The distinction is important, because economies of scale imply a freedom to choose or build that size of productive unit which is most efficient at its optimum volume. In petroleum this freedom does not exist; one must take fields as he finds them.

The Industry as the Sum of All Reservoirs. In dealing with production, we have met the decreasing-cost hypothesis on its strongest and most familiar ground, that of the single field, already developed, considered in isolation from all other fields. Even here it fails, because it conflicts with the basic physical laws governing petroleum production. But even if it had been true that the individual field (like the individual tanker) operated under decreasing costs, it would still have been untrue of the industry as a whole, because production costs, even in the very short run, vary widely, and therefore the higher the price, the higher-cost fields it pays to operate; the lower the price, the more the industry is restricted to the very low-cost fields.[27]

---

[27] For commercial wells in the United States, direct operating costs vary from $200 to $1,000 monthly, with much clustering around $300. (Arps, in Frick, *op. cit.* [Note 14], pp. 37–22 ff.) Of the 231 oil leases from which Champlin Oil & Refining Co. made sales in 1955, about a fourth had development-plus-production costs of 75 cents per barrel or less; the other quartiles varied as follows: 75 cents to $1.65; $1.65 to $3.60; over $3.60. (Federal Power Commission, Dockets Nos. G-9277 and G-9280, Exhibit No. 52.) "In the same field, even with wells producing in the same manner from a single zone, individual well costs will vary widely." Eight wells

We have already considered exploration and development costs, and seen that they are much more clearly (but less precisely!) examples of increasing cost. Hence we must conclude that at every single one of the three grand stages the producing industry is dominated by increasing costs. It would be hard to find a stronger example, or one better documented, in the whole literature of economics; at any rate, I know of none.

It is therefore worth asking: why is the error of petroleum as a decreasing-cost industry so firmly imbedded in the thinking of the industry and of friendly, unfriendly, and neutral critics outside? Perhaps because the industry has for years existed both in the United States and abroad under a set of restrictions strong enough to keep the price up, but not strong enough to prevent the resulting over-capacity. In order to keep over-capacity from becoming over-production and breaking the price, the United States has a system of law, and the industry outside the United States has the complex mixture of forces public and private.

Given the system, it is literally true that every single producing unit, field, and province is working under excess capacity: if it were free to produce more, it would lower its cost. Hence the economic theory of a decreasing-cost industry seems to be such a perfect description. One must be sincerely grateful to those stating the idea in terms of an economic theory, which can then be compared to the facts to show how wrong it is — that is what theories are for. And those with experience in applying economics to public policy, who know how agonizingly difficult or impossible it is to get any accepted idea or cliché clearly enough stated so that one can test and prove or disprove it, will understand that here gratitude is not mixed with irony.

There is, however, a more sophisticated version of the decreasing-cost argument; it has never, I believe, been put in print, but discussions with some thoughtful observers in and out of the industry permit one to state it as follows. True, so far as physical laws govern the industry, it is one of increasing costs. But how can we ignore the laws of man, in conjunction with those of nature? For reasons with which all are familiar, the industry never has and never will be left to its own devices. Why not, therefore, take into account both nature and man-made laws? If one does so, the net

---

forming a single lease cost in dollars per month: 97, 112, 153, 170, 209, 235, 239, 244; so that the high was 2½ times the low. (Marion H. Stekoll, "Cutting Costs of Well Completion and Operations," in EPEDPE, *op. cit.* [Note 7], p. 26.) A rising-cost supply curve at various times is in the *Report to the Joint Committee on Atomic Energy*, 86th Cong., 2nd Sess., Vol. 4 (Washington, 1960), pp. 1520 (coal), 1533 (oil).

result is clearly, as we have just seen, built-in excess capacity and decreasing costs.

This argument must be treated with respect: indeed, this paper is perhaps less a disagreement than an exposition. The essential point of difference is simply that excess capacity caused by certain man-made arrangements is not the same animal as excess capacity due to nature. Under natural monopoly, any kind of competition is under a strain it cannot ultimately bear. But man-made excess capacity registers a force in exactly the contrary direction — a competitive strain which a system may or may not be able to resist. Since the one does not yield the same results as the other, or give the same response to a given stimulus, any public policy founded upon an assumption of the one will sooner or later go wrong and be ineffective or perverse. And this is independent of whether we like the policy or not.

There is always a basic qualification in any kind of scientific disagreement. Within certain limits, two theories may be equally good in explaining some fact of nature or of society; past those limits, one may break down and the other remain. But if we have no desire to go past those limits, we do not need to choose. The Copernican theory of earthly revolution and the Ptolemaic theory of solar revolution are, for many purposes, mathematically equivalent. Similarly, for some kinds of public policy it might not make much difference why the industry suffers from universal excess capacity today. But a theory which makes the oil producing industry peculiar for the wrong reasons blocks our appreciation of why it really *is* peculiar. This is what we must soon explore.

MARGINAL COSTS, MARKET SHARES, AND "PEACEFUL COEXISTENCE"

The Industry Cost Function

To sum up the preceding discussion: under any given conditions of knowledge, the more exploration is done, the higher, probably, will be the finding cost per unit of what is found. The more a given deposit is developed, the higher will, almost certainly, be the cost of additional development. Finally, from the time a well begins to operate, the greater the output the higher the cost of additional output. When the additional cost of another increment of output goes up above the current price, production ceases; when incremental development cost rises above the anticipated near-term price, development ceases; and much more hazily, when finding cost in any place goes above a longer-term price anticipation, exploration stops.

This is commonplace but sounds unnatural to many in the industry because of the popularity of the term "marginal cost" or of that famous "incremental barrel" which is often so heartily damned in the trade press. It is a reflex reaction among oilmen to think of marginal or incremental cost as exclusively the short-run cost of producing somewhat more from a unit that is not fully utilized and is being held back to less than its most efficient rate of output. But government or other regulation aside — we do not yet consider it — marginal cost in production always rises with greater output, even in the individual producing unit. More important, the promise of lower-cost oil is preferred to the promise of higher-cost oil. Most important, when discoveries are made, in general, it is the *farthest, deepest, smallest,* and *least permeable* discoveries which are highest cost and least worth drilling up; it is the *nearest, shallowest, largest,* and *most permeable* which are lowest cost and most worthwhile; and the others are distributed in rising order between. Henceforth I will relate higher output and prices to the reaching after the higher-cost sources, leaving unstated but understood the effort of rising costs within each unit. Our industry cost function or supply function consists of all the reservoirs lined up from lowest to highest cost, with the current or expected price as the line marking off the worthwhile from the non-worthwhile. Then, if the price goes to x dollars per barrel, it will pay to exploit sources A through F; if the price is lower, they will not be developed, and we will be confined to A, B, C; and so on.

Marginal Cost-Revenue Gap as the Engine of Supply and Price Change

If this is the true shape of the industry cost function, then the crucial relation is between the current or anticipated revenue from additional output (which under simple competitive conditions is simply the price) and the marginal cost. An economist would usually say that the equality of marginal revenue (or price) with marginal cost was the stability condition of the oil market. But one might with more truth call it the instability condition. For what it means is that if price is above marginal cost, there is an incentive to produce and offer more, i.e., supply exceeds demand and there is pressure on the price. The market is then unstable until and unless something is done to get rid of the excess supply. In seeking, therefore, to understand the petroleum market, it is always marginal cost we want to know about, and better a few rough indications of its magnitude than the most exact figures on average cost: better to be approximately right than precisely wrong. The average cost, whether of a given reservoir or area or the whole industry, is only an after-the-fact summary of what has been spent. It cannot be compared with price, and it has no implications for output. Reservoir A may be very cheap to find and exploit, but if it is of limited size, then to get more output out of it would send marginal cost far above what would pay, so a modest rise in price will give us nothing more from it. On the other hand, Reservoir B may be more expensive oil, whether now or in final retrospect; but because it is a much bigger deposit than A, current marginal cost will increase only modestly even with a great deal of development, so a small price rise will give us a great deal more oil.

Hence it is of little help to talk about "the cost" of oil or "the profits" of "the industry." At any time, the profits of the lowest-cost units are very large, others are mediocre; others just breaking even; other such units are losing money if they take account of sunk and unrecoverable costs, but breaking even or better on current account. It is the cost of the marginal or highest-cost facilities which makes the price in a competitive industry and puts pressure on it in a non-competitive market. For if the price is too low to keep the highest-cost facilities operating, these operations will shut down, supply will be less than demand, and price will rise. Hence the price must be high enough to remunerate them. If demand surges and sends up the price, that is a signal that higher-cost facilities are needed and can be profitably operated; and at the higher prices, the profits of the best pools will be all the better. Conversely, if productive capacity exceeds demand, price will fall and squeeze out the highest-cost units no longer needed. This is what has not been permitted to happen over the last decade; hence the high- and low-cost facilities all stay in operation, and supply exceeds demand. Anyone who questions the world price of oil because Middle East costs are so low as to allow high profits is telling us only that the best fields earn a big producers' rent, which we already know. But if he means that there is so much available oil that can be cheaply developed and that incremental costs will continue to be low over a long stretch, so that Middle East oil could displace costlier oil and bring down the price, then he is at least talking sense, even though he may be wrong on the facts. (I happen to think he is right, but that is secondary.)

The Market-Sharing Mechanism of Relative Marginal Costs

To what extent, given free competition, would the lower-cost units displace the higher-cost? We might as aptly ask to what extent, given free competition, would the higher-cost units displace the lower? Both questions are equally meaningful. For if our basic theory of petroleum costs is sound, it becomes perfectly easy to understand "peaceful" — or even non-peaceful — coexistence among centers of production of vastly different average costs. If development in each area is carried to the point (or is cut back to the point) where its incremental costs equate with that of every other area, account being taken of transport, then there is no further pressure to cut back in one place to make room for any other. Incremental cost then serves as a mechanism to divide markets; the division may not be "equitable," but it is stable in the sense that it is not within anybody's ability and to his interest to increase or cut back his offerings on the market. Again, the principal significance of this market-sharing mechanism is negative; if markets are divided any other way — on the basis of what is considered "equitable" or more suitable by governments or producers' groups — then the incentive remains for some people to expand their output, supply exceeds demand, and the price is under pressure.

We must of course beware of the logical fallacy that because peaceful coexistence is to be expected under even the most rigorous competition, the particular pattern of coexistence we see at any given time is thus explained. It may or may not be. But the mere fact that oil keeps on being produced in various parts of the world at widely differing average costs and profits needs little explanation. Neither government regulation nor industrial statesmanship nor any other special reason is needed to explain why the United States and Venezuela continue as big producers; they always will. But if relative marginal cost were the governing factor, the United States would produce less, the Middle East more, and there is no telling about Venezuela. The important matter is *more or less*, not *yes or no;* and the fact that we never hear this question asked in the United States, that it is always "the domestic industry" which is to be preserved for national security, is itself an important fact, not of economics but of public policy, which could stand some prolonged meditation by policy-makers.

In Europe, it has been estimated that about 90 million tons of coal can be produced annually at the lower prices which would rule if oil could be freely brought in, as compared with current output of around 250 million.[28] With smaller amounts, that is, long-run marginal coal cost will drop to about the same level as oil prices. The saving to the European economy would consist in the elimination of the real costs of the excessive and most expensive 64 per cent. This means, of course, much more than a 64 per cent saving. Or, what comes to exactly the same thing, it means the elim-

---

[28] Council of Europe, *European Energy Problems* (Strasbourg, 1962), p. 90, incorporating the estimates of the European Coal and Steel Community (ECSC).

ination of much more than 64 per cent of the coal mining jobs and the coal mining enterprises — which is of course why Western Europe will not opt for the policy. Hence the capacity to produce both the excessive 64 per cent of the coal, *and* the equivalent in oil, are both in the market and exerting pressure on price.

Thus the market-sharing mechanism or coexistence mechanism, the equating of marginal costs, holds as well among various fuels as it does for the same fuel from two different sources, and has about the same predictive significance.

Transport Cost

We must now speak explicitly of transport cost, which is a very large factor in comparative incremental cost, and usually offsets it very much. Relatively high-cost oil (or gas or coal) near to consuming centers is able to compete with very much lower-cost fuels from farther away. And our earlier discussion of costs and prices was too simple in one crucial respect: there can be no such thing as *the* world price of oil, but only a world price *structure*. The structure cannot be stable unless certain conditions are satisfied. First, in any exporting area f.o.b. prices are uniform to all destinations; otherwise, there is an incentive to elbow your rivals aside (with their customers' help) in attempting to get to the markets with higher realizations, until all are equalized. Second, in any importing area price should be the same for any given quality of fuel regardless of point of origin; otherwise it is buyers (with sellers' help) who have the incentive to change. (So there is no cause to wonder, for example, why cheaper Venezuelan or other oil has always gone at the same price as dearer U.S. oil.) Third, if the price in the export countries and the price in the import countries are in the neighborhood of the respective marginal costs, which differ approximately by the amount of transport cost, then the system is under no strain.

This last condition is the most difficult to set forth, but it is the unifying principle of the whole world market. There needs to be such a balance among marginal costs in the various production centers and transport costs to the various consuming centers, that there is no incentive to change the pattern of trade. Or, what comes to the same thing, to expand production anywhere would cost more than it was worth; to contract production would be to sacrifice profit.

If this sounds too vague, some examples may help. Residual fuel on the U.S. East Coast has long been described, and correctly, as selling at coal parity. Yet there is also truth in adding that coal sells at residual-oil (and natural-gas) parity.[29] A shortage of residual oil, and rise in price, would mean a greater coal demand and a rise in coal price. That is, after all, the purpose of the current import restrictions. The "parity" concept is useful, but only over small intervals, or only for small increments to the supply of one fuel, all else being equal. But if there is a sizable increment to supply (or demand) we are again reminded that the price of all fuels taken together is made by the total supply of all. To say that the price of heavy fuel in Northern Europe, today or over the next decade, depends on the f.o.b. price in Venezuela (plus transport) is a half-truth, or much less than half. For the price f.o.b. Venezuela depends on the marginal cost, which in turn depends on the level of output. The price in Europe determines the price in Venezuela as well as vice versa; the dependence is mutual; but if most European fuel oil is from European refineries, the European influence is much greater and the dependence less. Marginal higher-cost fuel oil from Venezuela sets the price only if there is available additional Venezuelan capacity at a lower cost than additional European capacity. Over the next decade, Europe will produce much more heavy fuel oil. If output over a certain level can only be had at greater additional cost than an increment to Venezuelan output, then the marginal output would be from Venezuela.

Yet, if after carefully examining prospective supply one concluded that cheaper Middle East crude will be available up to the limit of any more expected output, then the increment would be more cheaply produced in European refineries, Venezuelan output would be backed out of Europe and output cut back, starting with the highest cost, until the two refining centers were producing at about equal marginal cost, allowing for transport cost: which means Venezuelan output f.o.b. the refinery at some 30-odd cents less than European. Observe that if we assume transport service as available in any desired amount (given enough time to build additional ships, if needed), the structure of price is such that Europe is always about 30 cents over the Caribbean; but this says nothing about what the price level is going to be, only about its structure. Depending on the amounts available at given cost levels, it *may* make sense to say that with long-run Caribbean supply price around x cents, the price in Europe must be $x + 30$; but we may today be nearer the truth to say that with the long-run European supply price at y cents, the price in the Caribbean must be $y - 30$.[30]

[29] *Cf.* SPNG, *op. cit.* (Note 3), table 9.

[30] For an example of this error in an otherwise excellent article, see "What's Happening to Fuel-Oil Prices in the European Common Market," *Oil and Gas International*, I (December, 1961), 24.

Figure 2 shows these relations in a simplified manner. It is assumed that it costs 80 cents per barrel to haul crude oil from Export Area to Import Area, and that, given time enough to build more ships if need be, there is no practical limit to the amount of transport service available at that price. We assume that in Import Area production costs are such that for every additional 10 cents added to the per-barrel price, one can have another million barrels over the appropriate time period for which output is calculated. Export Area is assumed to have much cheaper oil: every additional 10 cents in the supply price will give us not 1 million but 4 million barrels capacity. These conditions are shown in the two light lines labeled "domestic availability" and "foreign availability," respectively. If demand is as shown by D_1, then production will be 3 million, all supplied by Import Area, despite its much higher production costs. Only when the price in Import Area goes above 80 cents is there any point in starting production in Export Area.

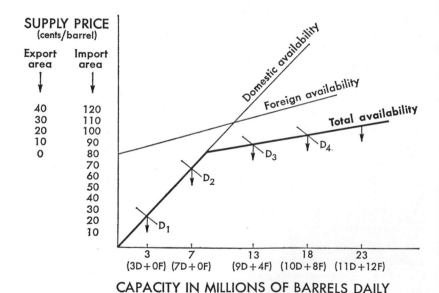

Figure 2. Relation of Supply to Price Level and Structure

If demand is as shown by D_3, or greater, the effective supply curve will no longer be the domestic one alone; to get it, we must add horizontally the domestic and foreign, which gives us "total availability." At an Import

Area price of 90 cents, 13 million barrels are supplied, of which 9 million are domestic and 4 million foreign. Foreign output is then "supplementing but not supplanting" domestic, and the rate of supplementation is governed by relative marginal cost, or relative supply price: four to one.

Now suppose that with demand at D_4, price is fixed at \$1.10; then total capacity is 23 million barrels, of which 11 million are domestic and 12 million foreign. But total demand is only 17 million (we have assumed it rather inelastic, so that a 10 per cent higher price lowers demand by less than 6 per cent). Hence there are 6 million barrels of excess capacity. Import Area producers will now argue that with the price at \$1.10, they can and should produce 11 million barrels, letting Export Area make up the difference; while Export Area producers might argue that they could, and should, produce 12 million, letting Import Area producers make up the difference. If each side insists on its "rights," and they together produce 23 million barrels, the price would for at least a time drop far below \$1.10, and the repercussions would take some time to die away.

But setting this aside, the diagram shows that we can only explain a structure of prices by means of transport costs, not its level. How tempting it would be to say, for example, that the price in Export Area must be 90 cents because the price in Import Area is 10 cents. For small amounts, this is true; for higher demand, price will be higher in both areas. Assuming equilibrium of supply-demand everywhere, and questioning only the one price, it is fully determined by subtracting a freight disadvantage or adding a freight advantage; but only under these circumstances. In the short run, for small factors, it makes good sense to assume these factors away; over the longer term, it does not.

One important qualification: changes in transport cost do have an effect on total availability, as one can see if one assumes the transport cost from Export to Import Area to be not 80 but 60 cents, and redraws the figure accordingly; at a price of one dollar, total availability would be not 18 million but 26 million barrels.

It is necessary to warn at all times that when one sets forth briefly a theory of what makes prices, one cannot help but give an impression that the process works neatly and precisely. It does not. The establishment of price parities among various sources of supply is done by sellers and buyers always looking for a better deal, guessing ahead and often guessing wrong. Moreover, when the market mechanism works best it conceals itself. If, for example, it is known that for a substantial time there must be imports from some farther-off place, at a higher price because of higher transport cost, importers do not necessarily bid against each other for a limited supply from nearer areas, gradually raising price to the point where product begins flowing in from farther areas. It is more likely that, since all know what the final outcome will be, prices are raised immediately. Thus the process is short-circuited and the final result appears quickly and seems "natural" to all concerned.

This theory is useful because it is not a realistic *description* of the world industry at any given time. By showing how rigorous are the conditions for stable markets, it lets us understand how numerous and important and ever-present are the destabilizers. First and foremost, whenever there is a saving anywhere in cost of either production or transport, it lowers marginal delivered cost somewhere and there is an incentive for someone to produce more, changing the structure. As the U.S. railroads lower coal hauling costs with integral trains, the ripples will reach the oil market in Western Europe, to say nothing of markets nearer home. The swift growth of the giant tanker (ten years ago anything over 35,000 tons was a supertanker; today most new ships are half again that size) has meant a substantial reduction in the long-run marginal cost at which Middle Eastern oil could be laid down at the European or U.S. dockside. Thus even a price structure in balance around 1950, i.e., which gave no incentive to import more, would in any case have become obsolete. The incessant changes in production and transport costs are a set of incessant shocks which the system is always in process of adjusting to. So, strain in the markets and price structures diverging from competitive stability may indicate either the adjustment process or a block to it.

Finally, not only may uniform f.o.b. price and a uniform c.i.f. price be hard to establish — because of variations in quality, spot quantities versus long-term supply contracts, and fringe benefits varying from one sale to another — but in addition the tendency to uniformity might be perpetually disrupted by unforeseen supply-demand changes. The student of markets must often admit that he cannot tell what is going on, but that he can at least tell one or two things that are not happening — e.g., that there are substantial and persistent variations in f.o.b. or c.i.f. prices at any given time, which are not explained by cost, quality, contract, or other aspects.

Changes in Total Output and Demand May Transform Relative Marginal Costs

Both the world price structure and price level, and both the total of production and its share among various sources, are affected by the total level of demand. At high levels of output relative marginal costs may be completely different from what they would be at lower levels, and hence world channels of supply may drastically change. It was known for decades that there was probably a lot of cheap oil to be found in the hills of the Middle East — the flat plains being long unjustly denigrated — if anyone wanted to spend the money to try to find it.[31] But we need no special theory to explain why there was relatively little exploratory effort. Given the low levels of U.S. Gulf and Venezuelan output, and therefore very low marginal cost; given also the very high cost of hauling Middle East oil as refined products in small tankers (for refineries were mostly crude-oriented and world trade largely in products), the marginal delivered cost of Middle East oil in the large markets of the world was too high to compete.

Things are very different today, but the important question is again: how different? The student, government official, and the responsible officer of either a private or public oil enterprise are vitally concerned with the question, for if ever an industry was oriented to the future and was in constant need of making intelligent forecasts and decisions, this is it. Yet the information is painfully sparse. Worse yet, it is hidden by irrelevancies. How many times have we been told that average daily production per well is 11 barrels in the United States, 300 in Venezuela, and about 5,500 in the Middle East? Yet this says almost nothing about comparative marginal cost. For the United States, it says nothing even about average cost. If one eliminates the stripper wells, the U.S. average goes to 45 barrels daily. In addition, high U.S. costs are in very large measure determined by two factors. First is the high price of crude, which makes it profitable to find small deposits and produce under expensive conditions: price determines cost as well as vice versa. Second, most U.S. crude output is subject to a unique regulatory system.[32] When we read of eight producing days in Texas, it is the wells capable of producing much more that are being held to this limit. The "marginal" or high-cost wells pre-empt the market and the productive wells are only permitted to make up the difference.

In the East Texas field, a marginal well is permitted up to 600 barrels monthly; non-marginal wells, some of which could produce thousands daily, are restricted to 184 monthly. Small wonder that people have found it worth while to deviate wells illegally in order to get the few more barrels daily that they were allowed (since this resulted in a considerable per-

[31] G. M. Lees, "The Oil Fields of the Middle East," *The Science of Petroleum*, I (London, 1938), 140, and VI (1953), 67.

[32] The best brief account is in Wallace F. Lovejoy and I. James Pikl, Jr. (eds.), *Essays on Petroleum Conservation Regulation* (Papers delivered at a Seminar in Industrial Organization and Public Regulation, Department of Economics, Southern Methodist University, Dallas, Spring, 1960).

centage increase in daily output and hence a considerable reduction in unit cost), or to treat dry wells as "grandfathers" and divert production into them so that the allowable could be retained.[33]

But these are surface phenomena, however regrettable. The important point is elsewhere. Given either a competitive market or a rational monopoly, the low-cost sources are exploited to the maximum and high-cost sources the least. But in the United States an elaborate and stringent regulatory system is needed to institute the exact contrary: the high-cost wells produce before the low-cost. We maximize costs and minimize efficiency. Of course, the more output is cut back, the more unit costs go up, and the better the "justification" for raising prices further.

Since allowables are given per well, there is in any case a strong incentive for each operator to drill unnecessary wells to get higher allowables; if all do this, output per well must again be cut, and so on around the circle. With the higher crude price, the incentive is all the stronger. Today, when crude prices can no longer be raised to subsidize deliberate inefficiency, there is a searching of hearts and a questioning of current regulatory practice. When Mr. Halbouty, the well-known operator, states that: ". . . we have drilled a minimum of 100,000 wells in this state that are not needed, at a cost of several billion dollars," one suspects him of exaggeration, because after all the whole state has only 204,000 wells.[34] Yet it may be that Mr. Halbouty should, if anything, be criticized for understatement. During the first quarter of 1962, production in the southwest producing states of Texas, Louisiana, Alabama, Mississippi, and New Mexico was 4,485 thousand barrels daily (MBD).[35] Assuming that 15 per cent spare capacity was needed,[36] total capacity should be no more than 5,382 MBD. Assuming a light per cent attrition rate and hence 1,590 MBD lost during 1954–61 inclusive, total gross incremental capacity needed was 2,047 MBD. But actually 3,538 (1,590 + 1,948) MBD was provided. The 43 per cent superfluous development (1,491/3,538) would account for more than 43 per cent of all expenditures, since under any rational system the higher cost capacity is avoided in favor of the lower; furthermore, many wells added little or nothing to

[33] *Oil and Gas Journal*, May 2, 1962, p. 80; and June 18, 1962, p. 16. This is not meant to imply that directional deviation of wells is a qualification for marginal status.

[34] *Platt's Oilgram News Service*, August 17, 1962, p. 2.

[35] U.S. Bureau of Mines, *Monthly Petroleum Statement* No. 481, July 6, 1962.

[36] See National Petroleum Council, *Petroleum Productive Capacity* (Washington, 1952), p. 25; and Zeb Mayhew, in *International Oil and Gas Development* (Dallas: American Institute of Mining, Metallurgical, and Petroleum Engineers, jointly with International Oil Scouts Association, 1961), Part II, p. 614.

capacity. Actual capacity, however, was 6,873,000 barrels daily. On January 1, 1954, it had been 4,925,000.[37]

Waiving any claim to precision, it is difficult to escape the conclusion that the bulk of development work in those eight years was waste, and done largely to get additional allowables. Spare capacity is said to be needed for national security (and I think it is), but no concern over its lack was voiced ten years ago by the National Petroleum Council, and it is difficult to take seriously a preparedness which appeared as the undesired side-effect of regulation. There is no reason to think we have the right producing and pipeline spare capacity at the right places.

Regulatory practice in the United States, and especially in Texas, is at least moving in the direction of more economy, but the process will be slow and painful.[38] In 1960, two operators in the East Texas field proposed to shut down seven-eighths of the non-marginal wells, without cutting field output. That savings would have been considerable is proved by the protests of the local residents who would have lost jobs and markets. That is what it means to economize scarce resources. The decision went in favor of making work and against economy.[39] It lit up the landscape for a moment. Nobody doubts that a good nine-tenths of the non-marginal wells could be shut in with no loss, to say nothing of the 20 per cent of wells that are marginal — some 92 per cent all told.[40] Of course, East Texas is an extreme example, but one would like to know how extreme. At any rate, we can draw two useful lessons from it.

First, the 11-barrel-per-day figure for the United States means literally nothing and perhaps, given a drastic change in regulation, will be multiplied many times. Second, to be quite literal-minded, the state regulatory bodies are not "obedient tools of the industry"; they are elected officials, trying to do what is good for their constituents, enforcing a law which forbids unitizing or co-operation where it would save money. Prorationing is generally recognized as price-fixing, but even more basically it is featherbedding. Regulation has sacrificed the more efficient to the less ef-

[37] Independent Petroleum Association of America, *Report of Productive Capacity Committee* (Tulsa, respective years).

[38] The Canadians are more flexible; when Alberta went from 40- and 80- to 160-acre spacing last year, development costs were expected to drop 40 per cent. (*Oil and Gas Journal,* April 23, 1962, p. 59.)

[39] For a good account of the proceedings, see *Oil and Gas Journal,* August 22, September 26, and December 5, 1962; and the documents filed by Tidewater and Atlantic.

[40] One would need at most 1,500 wells to drain East Texas. Thomas C. Frick, in *Journal of Petroleum Technology,* 10 (1958), 12. In round numbers, there are 15,000 non-marginal and 4,000 marginal wells.

ficient output, and has sacrificed the industry as a whole to the local supplying population to promote jobs and incomes within the state. Nothing
could be more commonplace. How much more exciting to talk about the
"vast political power" of "the oil industry" or, better yet, of the huge corporations in it!

This lengthy detour into the United States was worth while because we
have so long heard the per-well figures quoted as though they showed
some physical difference between domestic and foreign conditions. Freed
of the regulatory incubus it now supports and also of the illusion that imports are the source of its woes, and with a huge natural gas market, the
domestic industry might, if given a chance, surprise itself as to how tough
a competitor it can be. We might even have a revival of exploration, of
which little will be worth while so long as an oil operator must risk his
money with nothing better to look forward to than eight days' monthly
production of a shrunken allowable. Stiff import controls have failed to
increase exploration[41] and stiffer ones will fail. All they bring us are more
weeds in the garden — more stripper wells.

Let us look a bit afield. What does it mean to say, for example, as is
often said, that average or representative Venezuelan development costs
are five times Middle Eastern, and that Middle East development-operat-
ing costs are 5 to 10 cents? (I cannot vouch for the figures but that is in-
essential to the argument.) To approach the problem in these terms leaves
us helpless before so simple a fact as Sun Oil Company's 1960 discovery
of a deposit with 1,800 feet of productive oil sand[42] which Sun calls as
good as the best Middle East.[43] This is surely exaggerated, if only because the best Middle East is practically on tidewater, but the field is
surely better than much Middle East, and the relevant economic question
is at what point the two areas equate. But even this aside, if Venezuelan
costs are 25–50 cents, Middle East crude cannot compete with Venezuelan oil on the East Coast of the United States even today, for the Venezuelan freight advantage there can hardly be lower than 60 cents,[44] and even

[41] *Cf.* D. M. E. McLarty, "Reducing Hidden Exploration Costs," in EPEDPE,
op. cit. (Note 7), pp. 76, 96.

[42] *Oil and Gas Journal,* December 26, 1960, p. 148; the well tested 7,500 b/d.

[43] Sun Oil Co., *Annual Meeting of Stockholders: Proceedings* (1962), p. 3–3.

[44] Tanker rates are usually expressed in terms of percentages of Scale (or more
recently Intascale), a world-wide matrix of payments per ton of cargo between
many origins and destinations, published by the London Tanker Brokers Panel.
(Other matrices are less widely used, but mention should be made of the American
Tanker Rate Schedule, or ATRS.) Statement in this form, of Scale plus or minus a
per cent, permits the immediate comparison of any number of actual transactions
covering many different voyages, since they have all been reduced to a single sys-

in Europe it is about half that. So what looks like a huge cost disadvantage — costs five times as high — turns out to be a substantial advantage.

But let us now change just one variable: much higher production rates. If Venezuelan capacity was approached, marginal cost would tend to rise pretty sharply, while Middle Eastern would not. Soon the two marginal delivered costs would equate and then any further increase in consumption would be supplied from the Middle East. Venezuelan producers would, of course, earn a considerable rent, and the less efficient would complain that they were not getting their "fair share" of the market growth.

I would not claim that this explains what has actually happened; on the contrary. Nor does it prove that Venezuelans are wrong in fearing Middle East competition. What it does suggest is that the fear is not based on cost disadvantage, but rather on a break in a price structure. Because of excess capacity, the relative competitive strength of Middle East and Venezuelan crude oil does not have much relation to relative marginal cost, and nobody can use the two cases as guides or reference points. And so long as this is true, there will be more supply than is demanded.

The final corollary that must be drawn from petroleum as an increasing-cost industry is that the operators incurring lower-than-marginal costs earn higher profits, or rents. But the subject of rents must be postponed for a while, since our analysis of petroleum production costs, although sufficient for some preliminary conclusions, is still incomplete. We have shown its basic tendency to stability and self-adjustment; we have now to show the powerful destabilizers to which it is subject because of *random effects* and because of *inventory effects*.

DESTABILIZERS: I. THE RANDOM ELEMENT IN FINDING COSTS

One basic peculiarity of the petroleum industry is in the response of productive capacity to investment. At any given time, in nearly all industries, investment will be governed by expected prices and costs, and capacity for new production will be pretty well calculable from the investment. Hence there is a fairly good (sometimes, to be sure, not so good) line of inference from current prices and prospects to the new capacity which businessmen will be moved to supply.

In oil production, on the contrary, the relation between investment and

---

tem. At Scale less 45 per cent, which is roughly today's term charter rate, the cost of shipment to the U.S. East Coast from the Middle East is 66 cents per barrel plus 12 cents Suez tolls; while from Venezuela it is about 16 cents.

basic new capacity, i.e., between expenditures to find oil and the new oil found, is unpredictable in any one place and poorly predictable even in the aggregate. The reason lies in the causal mechanism governing the incidence of oil and gas deposits. This mechanism is little understood in the large, though much is known in detail. But we can at least roughly organize the confusion by some statistical analysis. On some very general logical grounds the distribution of the sizes of fields, which is the resultant of the cubic volume of the trap and its porosity (or oil per cubic foot of sands), might be expected to follow the so-called logarithmic-normal law of distribution. Whether it is really governed by this law is, for me, an unsettled question, though Allais, Arps, and Kaufman[45] think so, and their opinions must command respect in view of their work. The log-normal distribution is basically a refinement of the law of proportional effect, that for certain kinds of phenomena the probability of any unit being by chance greater or less than an estimated size is independent of that size, so that a deposit of n barrels may turn out to be $2n$ whether n is 1 million or 50 million. And Allais does argue that the kinds of chemical reactions producing mineral deposits are subject to the law of proportional effect and should generate log-normal distributions.

But first, conceding this to be true even of the population of deposits in a large area, and owing their existence to a common geological force,[46] can the reasoning be extended to a larger area containing a number of independent basins? Second, this reasoning omits the second and more important part of the reserve creating process, which is oil and gas migration from the original source rocks:

> Hydrocarbons are by nature fluid and mobile, generally found scattered in the places where they first appeared, and only become exploitable after undergoing displacement, or migration, more or less long, right through various places of accumulation, and sometimes very far from those where they were formed. . . . Petroleum geologists [have] relatively little interest in looking for source-rocks [because] many important deposits of oil and/ or gas can exist in sedimentary layers which have no source-rocks in the

[45] Maurice Allais, *Evaluation des Perspectives Economiques de la Recherche Minière sur de Grands Espaces* (Alger: Bureau de Recherches Minières de l'Algérie, 1957); J. J. Arps, "The Profitability of Exploratory Ventures," in EPEDPE, *op. cit.* (Note 7), pp. 154–59; Gordon Kaufman, *Statistical Decision and Related Techniques in Oil and Gas Exploration* (New York: Prentice-Hall, 1963). According to an unpublished analysis of the four principal U.S. areas by Irwin Silberman, the largest and most important area does seem to conform closely, but not the others. G. Mathuron, "Application des Méthodes Statistiques à l'Evolution des Gisements," *Annales des Mines*, Vol. 144 (1955), pp. xii–52.

[46] Arps and Roberts, *op. cit.* (Note 12).

locality or even the region, these deposits having resulted from a lateral migration which can be as much as several dozen or even several hundred kilometers. [Furthermore] it is still difficult, in the present state of knowledge, to designate with certainty, in a series of sedimentary stopping places, the horizons which gave rise to the hydrocarbons.[47]

The deposits of the Middle East usually are not assigned any source rocks at all, there being an embarrassment of possibilities.[48] At any rate, there seems no general or a priori reason why the migration and entrapment of oil and gas should follow the law of proportional effect, though it is certainly worth the attention of some geologist-statisticians.

Third, the basic unit — the field — is not an altogether clear-cut idea, especially for the largest fields, and the curve is much affected by the size of the largest. For the engineer, if a number of pools are connected and oil can move from one to the other under suitable pressures, or if the pools are, as it were, scattered over a single structure, they are regarded as one field. Yet in terms of economics, this may not be the case. If discovery effort brings in a field, but it takes further discovery effort to find what eventually turns out to be an extension of the same field, and if, furthermore, movement between the two or more components of the field is improbable or very difficult, is it correct economics to call this a single field and count it as a single unit in the statistical table? This is the case with the Burgan field of Kuwait,[49] where the Magwa and Ahmadi extensions were found as the result of exploration begun in 1948, ten years after the original discovery well at Burgan. The Khafji field off Saudi Arabia, discovered by the Japanese, has turned out to be an extension of Aramco's Safaniya. Again, the "Bolivar coastal fields" of the eastern shore of Lake Maracaibo are considered as essentially a single field;[50] yet this comprises five distinct pools, each discovered at widely varying times and each, as may be seen in Table 1, showing very different production characteristics.

Hence if we are to treat fields as units representing economic inputs, we should almost certainly treat the "Bolivar coastal fields" as four or five, Safaniya-Khafji as two, Kuwait as two or three. Obviously, reasonable men can differ here, and hence the logarithmic-normal distributions that one or the other might compute will also differ. It is still harder to classify distinct fields with a common water drive (see page 67).

[47] Jacques Flandrin and Jean Chappelle, Le Pétrole (Paris: Editions Techniques 1961), pp. 17–18, writer's translation.
[48] Lees, op. cit. (Note 31).
[49] A. F. Fox "The Development of the South Kuwait Oilfields," Institute of Petroleum Review, Vol. 15 (1961), p. 373.
[50] Flandrin and Chappelle, op. cit. (Note 47), pp. 200, 202, 206, 280.

Table 1. The Bolivar Coastal Fields

Pool	Year of discovery	Gravity °API	Depth (000 ft.)	Daily average production per well, 1961
Bachaquero	1930	14–35	3.4–11.5	423
Cabimas	1917	20–26	2.2	n.a.
Lagunillas	1926	16–32	3.0–8.6	461
Pueblo Viejo	1940	14–19	2.0	n.a.
Tia Juana	1928	14–27	3.0	153

n.a. = not available.
Source: Oil and Gas Journal, December 26, 1955 and December 25, 1961. In the latter issue, Pueblo Viejo has been merged with Bachaquero.

Finally, our reserve estimates are for the remunerative portions of a deposit, so that there is yet another mechanism at work; although there is some reason to think it might itself be subject to a law of proportionate effect.

For these reasons and also because of some doubts as to the significance tests, I am unwilling to treat the log-normal distribution, so far, as anything more than a plausible approximate description. Even so, we can get some interesting results out of it, with some definite implications from the world oil outlook. It is, above all, a radically unequal distribution. In the United States, for example, there are something like 10,000 oil fields but a mere 200-odd fields account for more than half of their total reserves.[51] In Kuwait, the Burgan field, the greatest ever found, accounts for about one-third of current Middle East reserves. It is rather startling to learn that "if Upper Cretaceous erosion had cut 100 feet deeper, the whole content of the Burgan field would have had free channels of escape to the surface"; indeed, bigger ones may have got away.[52]

Where fields are so subject to chance and vary this much in size, and where discovery is so much a process of looking into the unknown, we must expect that the results of any given amount of effort will vary radically according to chance. It is not only that in one place a large money outlay is almost completely wasted (though never completely, as is explained on pages 67–68), while in another place a small expenditure brings in a big field. If the distribution of fields were not so radically and asymmetrically unequal, the law of large numbers would govern very nicely and for a big enough sample of companies or operators one could predict with

[51] *Oil and Gas Journal,* January 28, 1962.
[52] Lees, *op. cit.* (Note 31), p. 71.

fair enough accuracy the relation between outlay and results. Given anything like the log-normal distribution, we must expect to see a lot of variation even among big samples.

The Middle East as a Huge Random Disturbance

If we treat the exploration effort of any given year as a sample, we must
be prepared for huge variation year to year, and even decade to decade.
It cannot yet be rigorously proved with existing data,[53] yet it is not, perhaps, hard to believe that if one takes the largest fields in the United
States as a sample to be used as a predictive device for South America
(adding perhaps Africa and the Far East — it makes little difference),
the distribution of fields by size is not too far from what might have been
expected. But if one then turns to the Middle East, the results ride clear
off the chart — one could not possibly have forecast such a succession
of gigantic fields. It seems impossible for so many huge oil-bearing structures to be grouped in one relatively small area, and yet there they are.[54]
It is also peculiar that the processes shaping the great fields in the moun-
tainous areas of Iran and Iraq seem to have been quite different from
those shaping the even greater fields in the flat country of Kuwait and
Saudi Arabia; but the end result, for economic purposes, has been much
the same.

To be sure, we must not be too bedazzled by size. If, for example, an
investment of $10 million brings in a field of 10 million barrels, the dis-
covery cost is a discouragingly high dollar per barrel. If the field is 100
million barrels, the cost is 10 cents; if it is a billion-barrel giant, the cost
is 1 cent. The relative difference between 1 and 10 is the same as between
10 and 100, but the absolute difference is 90 cents per barrel in the first
case and only 9 cents in the second. A cost difference of 90 cents may be
overwhelming; that of 9 cents may not even be substantial because there
are so many other costs to be considered in evaluating the competitive advantages and disadvantages of the two fields. And indeed, ten 100-million-
barrel fields in the Western Hemisphere, costing ten times as much to find,
would be much more valuable — regulation aside — than a billion-barrel
field in the Eastern Hemisphere, for the freight advantage is several times

[53] Cf. George M. Knebel and Guillermo Rodriguez-Eraso, "The Habitat of Some
Oil," AAPG Bulletin, Vol. 40 (April 1956).

[54] Vincent C. Illing in "Factors which Control the Assessment of World Resources of Oil and Natural Gas" (Sixth World Power Conference, Melbourne,
Paper 185 I. 1/2, p. 21), surmises that the three crucial optima — source rocks,
reservoir rocks, and cap rocks — are independent or even inversely correlated. The
Middle East is the statistically unlikely spot where they coincide.

the production cost disadvantage. Yet this is true only because the demand pattern is such that the United States is an import area.

The Middle East fields have not only had remarkably low discovery costs, but also remarkably low developing-producing costs, largely because of their unusual permeability. The more permeable the sands of an oil trap, and the greater the pressure to which the deposit is subject by gas or water drive, the more will flow out of the trap daily wherever a well is drilled. The distribution of permeability and of other relevant characteristics does not seem so radically unequal as that of the size of fields, yet it is obviously very unequal and often quite capricious. It is instructive to compare the Agha Jhari field of Iran, the Hassi Messaoud field of Algeria, and the Spraberry field of West Texas. All three fields have a rather non-pourous sand, so that the oil per cubic foot is not high. But all three structures are so huge that the total amount of oil in place runs into the billions of barrels. Hassi Messaoud is broken up into many pockets of permeable sands surrounded by almost impermeable sands, so that unless one wants to wait until doomsday a fairly large number of wells must be drilled. In Spraberry the pockets are smaller and the barriers are greater; it seems today that only a small proportion of the oil in place (estimated by some at over 7 billion barrels) will ever be produced, and it may never pay out. Agha Jhari is in even worse shape than Spraberry, but one additional element makes all the difference. The field is extensively fractured horizontally and vertically. The result is that migration and pressure are unprecedentedly high, and a successful well, which takes some difficult and costly drilling, comes in as though somebody had accidentally struck a high-pressure pipeline. Hence, Hassi Messaoud is a great oil field, Agha Jhari is amazing, and Spraberry is a fiasco.[55]

The Middle East fields are by no means uniformly good — some are rather mediocre even by Western Hemisphere standards — but the best have the highest producing rates in the world; and as to their marginal costs, we at least know that even for a very large increment to output they cannot be appreciably higher than average costs today because there are such large undeveloped reserves.

Thus we can consider the Middle East as a huge random disturbance

---

[55] On Hassi Messaoud, see J. J. Rousseau, in *World Oil*, Vol. 152 (February 1961), p. 23; C. de Lapparent, in *Oil and Gas International*, January, 1961, p. 43. On Agha Jhari, *Oil and Gas International*, April 1962, pp. 38–45. Spraberry is a sad oft-told tale.

which only began to be foreseen in 1944, with the publication of the De Golyer report,[56] and has been making itself increasingly felt ever since.

We can see why the oil trade is subject to some uncomfortable shocks which are difficult or impossible to foresee. Investment which, according to the best information available at the time, ought to have been profitable, may turn out to be unprofitable as new low-cost output comes into the market from somewhere else, at much lower marginal cost, and pushes down the price. A rightward-shifting supply curve looks harmless on paper (Figure 1) but can be devastating in practice. Yet even here we should not exaggerate. The novelty of the Middle East lasted roughly from 1944 to 1953; the ten years since have seen less adjustment than strenuous avoidance. The industry's built-in stabilizers (see pages 69–70) are now exhausted.

If the producers can shield themselves directly or through government, and keep the price from dropping, this encourages the even faster growth of new supply. The effort to bring in this new supply may just happen to coincide with a period of dearth. But if the exploratory effort stimulated by the price is highly rewarding, then supply can go very far above demand.

This kind of situation deprives people in and out of the industry of the price-cost data they need. It is practically impossible to say today just how great is the gap between marginal cost and price in any particular place, how persistent will be the pressure of excess supply over the years ahead, and how much we might expect to see it relieved by a price decline or strengthened by a price increase.

DESTABILIZERS: II. THE INVENTORY ASPECT OF PETROLEUM PRODUCTION COSTS

Reserves as Types of Inventories

So far we have considered petroleum production costs at any one time, and as changing over time. But we have still to consider how the lengthy production process both simplifies and complicates the picture.

[56] *Oil and Gas Journal,* March 23, 1944, p. 56, estimating, respectively, proved reserves and proved plus probable reserves in fields discovered but not developed, in billions of barrels: Iran 5–6 and 6–7; Iraq 4 and 5, Kuwait 4 (only); Saudi Arabia 2 and 4–5; Qatar ½ and 1. Iran, Iraq, and Saudi Arabia were all close together, with "Qatar a somewhat distant fourth and Kuwait a definitely distant fifth."

The basic point may be stated as follows: Exploration and development are production *for* inventory, while "production" in the usual narrow industry sense is delivery *out of* inventory. Newly discovered but undefined fields are raw material; reservoirs under development are work in process; while fully developed or "proved reserves" are the shelf inventory, ready to flow out to the pipeline or tanker. "Proved reserves" are those known with near-certainty to exist, to be worth recovering, and to be within reach of existing wells. Only a small part of the proved reserves are undrilled.[57]

The inventories are very large relative to current production. Over the past quarter-century in the United States, the ratio of the shelf inventory only (proved reserves) to annual production has held quite steadily at around 13 : 1. This does not contradict what was said earlier about the radical fluctuations of new discoveries from year to year, but it does greatly moderate its force. Nobody knows in any given year what have been the new reserves discovered that year, or even a few years before, as the DeGolyer Report shows dramatically. The practice of the AAPG (American Association of Petroleum Geologists)[58] has therefore been to make estimates only after three and again after six years of development, and then only within broad size classes. At any given time, an oil operator has certain reserves proved and others in process. Obviously it does not pay to move goods onto the shelves at a faster rate than justified by expected sales, so that the rate of proving up reserves out of discoveries resembles to a considerable degree the rate at which a merchant orders his goods, or the rate at which manufacturers take up raw material partly to fill orders already received, partly to anticipate new orders. There is, therefore, a rough kind of technical optimum in this neighborhood, and it is interesting, though not at all conclusive, that the Soviet producing managers figure on a fairly steady annual production rate (due to heavy emphasis on water flooding) of 25 years' supply.[59] This would correspond to a ratio of 12½ times annual output, almost precisely the same as in the United States.

Types of "Proved," "Published," and "Probable" Reserves

Beyond the current inventory of proved reserves, statistics thin out very quickly. For the world outside the United States, the *Oil and Gas Journal* and *World Oil* provide estimates, generally considered of good quality, of

[57] See API-AGA Bulletin, *op. cit.* (Note 19).

[58] See J. Ben Carsey, "Exploratory Drilling in 1960," AAPG *Bulletin,* Vol. 45 (June 1961) pp. 701–27.

[59] Ebel, *op. cit.* (Note 7), p. 41.

"proved reserves" in a somewhat more elastic sense than is used for domestic supplies. In the Middle East particularly, it is often impossible to figure proved reserves because wells are so far apart that one cannot be sure of the underground strata in between. Adherence to API practice would lead to crediting no reserves to the area between two wells a mile apart, though any geologist would take oath that there was a continuous oil sand between them and be willing to estimate the reserves it contained. These estimates are "conservative" not in the sense of deliberate underestimation, but rather in the sense of saying, "That's what we are sure we would have there if we drilled; there must be more, but we don't know how much."

Beyond this less rigorous kind of "proved reserves," which we might call "published reserves," lies a mass of data and knowledge not so easily reduced to numbers, and of course with much greater margin for error. An excellent example of how knowledge grows can be seen in Saudi Arabia. The behavior of an oil reservoir can be represented by an electronic model, with the parameters of the oil pool and its water drive supplied by a trial-and-error process: calculated from past behavior, compared for a time with actual behavior and then corrected. The trial-and-error may go on for a varying time, depending on how important are the unknowns. In the Abqaiq field of Saudi Arabia certain persistent anomalies *could* have been interpreted as an undiscovered hydrocarbon accumulation in the neighboring Ghawar field (or fields); and there were some other less attractive possibilities. During 1960–61, four wells were therefore drilled on the east flank of the Ghawar field; because they were productive, the boundary had to be redrawn three kilometers farther east, thereby adding a billion barrels to published reserves; but the anomaly is not yet altogether explained, and perhaps the flank delineation is still not complete.[60]

This is the kind of investment which transforms less precise into more precise indications of the inventory; for reasons indicated elsewhere,[61] I think the Soviet system of calculating reserves by six pre-defined stages of precision is at the very least a commendable (and so far unique) attempt to face the problem and adapt the statistics to it.

Finding Costs Reconsidered

The peculiarity of *past* finding costs is that they are often unknowable, usually unknown, and always uninteresting. No dry hole is ever a com-

---

[60] W. R. Bartlett, "Saudi Arabian Oil Fields Performance with an Electronic Model" (Third Arab Petroleum Congress, 1961), pp. 1, 3, 5, 15, 16, 19.
[61] SPNG, *op. cit.* (Note 3), Appendix p. 113; *cf.* Arps, in Frick, *op. cit.* (Note 22), p. 37–7.

plete waste, and many a duster is well worth its cost in more information. "Most exploration and some development are literally wasted effort, a chasing after false leads. . . . The cost of a successful effort cannot be ascribed to that effort alone, but rather to the combination of all efforts, and the cost of all efforts, with which it was associated. The cost of the individual project does not exist."[62] Furthermore, even if the finding cost *were* precisely known, it would be of no interest because it would be a sunk cost, and whether vastly above or below price would not matter.

This is, of course, what gives the decreasing-cost theory its appearance of realism, but once we think of petroleum as an industry producing for inventory, the false problem is replaced by the real one: What does exist in looking ahead, and does control the price, is the reproduction cost. How much must one expect to spend, taking in the good discoveries with the bad, to reproduce a given reserve? The answer may be wildly imprecise, or never even formulated — though actions may speak louder than words — but the question should not therefore be avoided.

Replacement Cost and Price

Let us consider, as a first approximation, that supply and demand are in balance, and that the cost of finding, developing, and producing crude is not expected to change in the future. For convenience and to make the maximum concession to the decreasing-cost theory, we further assume that extraction cost is zero. Then the price stays in the neighborhood of the marginal finding-plus-development cost, i.e., the amount needed, including a barely sufficient return on investment, to pay for the highest-cost crude producing capacity just barely needed to meet demand. The price will be stable at this profitable level, even if it costs absolutely nothing to bring up the oil. Discounting does not change the case. For, to have that barrel ready years from now, we must keep spending money right along. When the present value of the reserve, at today's prices, is equal to both the present value of its expected price and the present value of the cumulated expected reproduction cost, there is no incentive to produce more and thereby push downward on the price, or to produce less and push upward. Conversely — and usually — the discrepancies among these three values put the oil market under upward or downward pressure. In management terms, then: it makes no sense to sell the barrel today for less than one dollar if one will have to spend so much money, year after year, to replace the barrel, that the present value of the sum total of all these expected expenditures is at least one dollar. If one sells for

[62] SPNG, *op. cit.* (Note 3), p. 6 (condensed).

less, one is giving or throwing away some of the assets of the business. For example, let the current price be one dollar, and the discount rate 10 per cent. Suppose we expect to spend 1.8 cents a year for twenty years in order to find and develop enough reserves so that, on the average, their date of sale is twenty years off. The present value of those expenditures is 15.2 cents, and the present value of receiving a dollar twenty years hence is also 15.2 cents, so that we are in balance, with no incentive to speed up or slow down development.

The oil producer is like the retailer; he does not sell off his shelf inventory at any price merely because it is already there and paid for and his operating expenses are fixed anyway. For then he must restock and he will merely have exchanged old inventory for new, at a loss. Only if the retailer finds he has more inventory than he needs to run the business, will he stop ordering and perhaps consider cutting prices to move the stuff.

Inventory as Stabilizer: Development as Strategic

Inventory production works two ways. It stabilizes and smooths greatly the shock of new discoveries; in fact, the market would otherwise be far more unstable. Nobody knows how big a new reserve may be until developed, and the pace of development is governed by current and near-term expected prices. Hence development is the most strategic of the three stages. Upon discovery, a big reserve can only be guessed at, and if prices and prospects generally are not auspicious, it will be developed slowly and its effect on the market will be gradual, since the new producible capacity will build up only gradually, along with the knowledge of how much is yet to come. With a 12½-year inventory, equating roughly to an 8 per cent annual loss, and an annual demand increase of 4 per cent, current producing capacity must always be increased by about 12 per cent just to stay in place and prevent any shortage. Hence an unanticipated surge of new development of lower-cost oil means only that retirements of declining wells take place somewhat sooner than usual.

Adjustments by which one producing center gains at the expense of another are by nature gradual and continuous because of the fact that direct producing costs are in most cases considerably less than total finding-plus-development-plus-producing costs, and may indeed be only a small fraction of them. This means that in the short run many fields can continue to operate without any sudden shutdown until the depletion of their reserves and consequent rise in their unit producing cost makes them shut down. Furthermore, over the near term, many development projects are still worth carrying to completion even if they never pay out their exploration costs. Thus the fact that operating costs are often a small part of total costs turns out upon analysis to be a stabilizing factor and a help in adjustment.

Inventory as Destabilizer

First, there is the rate of discount. Whether one wants to hold an asset or sell it off depends on how heavily one discounts future as against current receipts. This is in part determined by the cost or the value of money, or the alternative uses to which a sum might be put during the waiting period. In general, the higher the alternative rate of return, the more it costs to wait.

But the future is discounted for a host of reasons other than the rate of interest available on alternative uses of the money. Political instability or fear of unfavorable government policies certainly makes operators discount the future more heavily. A government, such as the Soviet Union, or an enterprise, National Iranian Oil Company (NIOC), which feels keenly pressed by development needs, may also heavily weigh the present against the future. We can conceive of a schedule of discounts, from lowest to highest, which is analogous to a schedule of marginal cost, but with a contrary effect.

Discounting factors are of necessity mingled with price expectations, so that the two must be considered together. Anyone who expects the future price of oil to be lower than it is today will try to sell the oil today. In so doing, if he forecasts correctly, he pushes the excess supply onto the market today and lets the price decline be spread over a long period, moderating the pace. But right or wrong, he brings his pessimistic expectations to the attention of others in the trade and lets them judge whether or not they agree. Differences of opinion are what make horse races and the petroleum industry. It is surely desirable that people should put their opinion on the line and back it with money for all to see and reflect upon, for the forces determining the price of oil are complex.

The future demand for energy in general, and in the form where oil has a near monopoly (the internal combustion engine); future incomes; the relation between income levels and energy: these are all factors that compound uncertainties about future energy use. Substitute fuels compound them still further.[63] The greater the demand for energy, especially in the form of liquid fuel, and the more expensive the substitutes, the

[63] See papers by Walter J. Levy and Milton Lipton, Nathaniel B. Guyol, Paul R. de Ryckere, *Proceedings, Fifth World Petroleum Congress* (New York, 1959), Section IX, and discussion afterward, pp. 45–51.

greater will be the demand for oil, and — for reasons indicated above — the higher will be the marginal cost which must be covered if the additional supply is to be forthcoming.

All these possibilities can and perhaps should be expressed in terms of expected prices of oil in the future. But it is more useful, I think, to conceive of them as factors causing expected future receipts to be discounted rather heavily as compared with the present, and hence giving an incentive either to sell in the present and bring prices down, or to hold for the future and push prices up.

The second possible destabilizing aspect of inventory production is the size of the inventory. An inventory costs money to hold, whether in operating expenses or in money tied up in the business, or in both. We suggested above that in the United States and the Soviet Union a 12½-year supply of proved reserves — which implies a higher stock of semi-proved — was considered adequate, and anything above it an unnecessary burden. Arps, who has done a great deal to put risk and cost ideas into quantitative terms, points out that with plausible discount factors profitability is very sensitive to the net realized price and the rate of production.[64] Under U.S. conditions, writes a banker, "it is doubtful that a barrel of oil which is not going to be produced for, say, twenty-five or thirty years from now . . . is worth a penny for loan purposes."[65] It is not of course worthless for all purposes; the point is merely that the present value does go down sharply with time and the far-off dollar becomes smaller compared with the present. Anything in excess of some maximum is really deadweight inventory and ought to be drilled up and its production sold off. Where a concession is due to end at some time, oil expected to be left in the ground then is worthless to the operator today, as is of course true in much of the Middle East and Venezuela. Even denser drilling at higher unit costs (since it would be cheapest to drain the deposit with as few wells as possible) is worth while if those higher costs are yet below prices obtainable over the period of development and production. Hence an increase in inventory beyond the term necessary for efficient production has the same effect as an expected fall in future prices, or an increase in the rate of discount. It makes present production much more attractive compared to future production, and therefore supplies an incentive for people to develop, drill, produce, and sell more than they would otherwise do.

[64] Arps, in EPEDPE, *op. cit.* (Note 7), pp. 169–70.
[65] Eugene McElvaney, "Financing Property Acquisitions," EPEDPE, *op. cit.* (Note 7), p. 182.

The Rule of Capture and the Bogey of East Texas

We have finally the analytical tools to understand an interesting bit of history and the folklore it left behind. Nothing, said Joseph Schumpeter, is so durable as a folk memory. And the influence on oil industry thinking of the catchwords "Remember East Texas in '30; we'll have 10 cents a barrel if we don't watch out!" is extraordinary. Europeans who reproach Americans for thinking too much in terms of U.S. experience will in almost the same breath expound on East Texas. The UN memorandum treats it as a convincing affirmative test of its decreasing-cost theory; others point out that oil is by nature an industry of inherent surplus, as witness East Texas in 1930, and hence "it has been found necessary" to take such steps as seemed necessary. Surely we should hesitate to generalize from a pattern so wildly unrepresentative: the Great Depression, the only time in history when oil consumption actually declined; a new field with reserves (of 2 billion barrels as they were then known) which were seven times the annual output of 330 million barrels a year; and perhaps most important, the law of capture, which holds nowhere but in the United States and which, having once made clear the inventory nature of oil production, we are now able to analyze.[66]

Imagine a group of retailers, each of whom carries a considerable stock. At any given moment, the inventory is already there and paid for, and operating costs are mostly fixed anyway, so that additional sales would be almost clear additional profit in the ultra-short run. But if one intends to stay in business he must reorder; the cost of the inventory thus prodigally sold off is the cost of restocking. Hence there is no tendency to throw goods into the market for next to nothing, and the trade can function and earn profits quite normally.

Suppose now that every retailer suddenly gains possession of the keys to the stockrooms of a dozen or so of his nearest competitors, and is told that he may legally and in good conscience help himself to as much of their wares as he and his employees can move away. Furthermore, he knows that every one of the other dozen retailers has a similar key to his own stockroom. Obviously his cost of replenishing inventory is no longer the manufacturers' price; it is the much lower one of renting a truck and paying some overtime. To remain in business now, he must not be left holding the goods; he must sell off as fast as possible, at any price above zero, both his own and his competitors' stocks. It is fatal for him to do

[66] For a classic description and legal analysis, see Northcutt Ely, "The Conservation of Oil," *Harvard Law Review,* Vol. 51 (1938), pp. 1209–44.

otherwise. Of course the goods will be flung into the market or into the streets; nobody will want to reorder, so that manufacturing will slow down or cease. Finally, after the debauch is over, the goods are gone, and prices have shot far up, manufacturing must be started up again and some plans must be made to prevent the madness from recurring. But, had it been illegal or physically impossible for competitors to help themselves to each other's stocks — hardly an unusual state of affairs in capitalist society — the market could have been stable all along. To complete the analogy, one must suppose that the retailers' trade paper is full of complaints about how strange and murderously competitive is the retailing business *in general;* and the editor, in collaboration with a professor at the local university, publishes a study showing with technical citations and terminology that retailing *in general* (and not merely because of the strange ground rules in this town) is an industry of decreasing costs which must break down into wild extremes of chaos, waste, and scarcity unless the merchants are allowed to get together to fix prices and regulate sales — or have the government do it for them.

Given the rule of capture, therefore, and nothing more sweeping or pretentious in the way of economic assumptions, the discovery of every new field will mean a sudden and wasteful rush to overproduce. But this results from a legal system peculiar to the United States. It is even more narrow than that. For, as was recognized by 1916, the waste is not only a burden on society but even on the producers themselves, and it is therefore in their interest to "unitize" operations in order to minimize the number of wells drilled and to insure that there is no longer any "neighborly" appropriation of oil from beneath their land.

The technical problems of reconciling unitization with private property in subsoil rights are admittedly great. Even in the Soviet Union there has been slant drilling from one side of a republic's boundary into a pool on the other side; Texas cannot claim to be first here. Unitization is best done soon after the pool is discovered, when there is still no adequate basis for determining the field's vertical and horizontal limits, variations in thickness and permeability, and water drives and the effect of differing rates of encroachment. This lack of knowledge means that one cannot determine precisely the relative values of surface rights. Estimates made on the basis of what is known are bound to be unfair to some owners without some kind of retrospective adjustment. But nobody has thought these problems insuperable,[67] and our federal system would have provided

[67] Herman H. Kaveler, "Unitization," in American Petroleum Institute, *History of Petroleum Engineering* (New York, 1961), especially pp. 1170, 1173.

room for three or four separate trials with an eventual pooling of experience in a model statute. Even today, it would be a worthwhile experiment in any state to set allowables by fields instead of wells, and watch how quickly the operators react! Had the United States not settled in the 30's for prorationing — which seemed then like a satisfactory halfway house between unrestrained drilling and compulsory unitization — the private interests of oil operators and of the states would have driven them to unitize, and the industry and the country would be much better off today. (We are all wise in retrospect.) We would also have been spared much misunderstanding. For outside the United States the special situation of the rule of capture does not exist, and therefore any theory based on that rule, however rich in corroborative detail, must be put in the same category with the Loch Ness Monster and the Abominable Snowman. People may have seen "it" all right, but they did not see what they thought they were seeing.

Two Kinds of Rents in Petroleum Production[68]

The final peculiarity in petroleum cost is in connection with rents. When prices everywhere are in the general neighborhood of incremental costs, the system is not under tension because there is no incentive for anyone, acting independently, to change output and thereby affect price. A price equal to incremental cost does not result in low or zero profits, as is too often assumed; on the contrary, it may mean very high profits for the more efficient and better located producing units, which can benefit from their lower transport or production costs. These amounts above bare production cost (including a minimum necessary return on investment) are known in economic jargon as *rents,* or surpluses, and they exist, even under the most stringent competition, in all industries. But in the three-stage petroleum industry, there is another species of rent. In the very short run, anything above bare production (extraction) costs is a rent. But unless the price is high enough to cover also the costs of development, we will soon find ourselves with a dwindling output. If, therefore, new production is needed a year to six years ahead, a payment sufficient to evoke it is not a rent at all. Now consider whether or not we need new exploration: if not, anything above development cost is surplus; if we do need to find new oil, a sufficient inducement is not rent but a cost. In petroleum, therefore, we see two kinds of rents: differential

---

[68] This section deals only with scarcity rents, existing even under the most rigorous competition. See pp. 32–33.

rents, and also what might be called horizon rents which are surplus only in the short run.

In general, costs are outlays which cannot be reduced without losing some supply, for some at least of the suppliers can go elsewhere. But rent is a return or income which can be decreased without any supply response. It does not matter how much of the profits of the low-cost oil go to the landowner, the wildcatter, the producer, the men who put up the money at the right moment, or the government.

Differential rent is obvious enough, especially in the Middle East: the best oil fields in the world will make money under any circumstances — they will never be forced down to bare cost. But the horizon rent is more nearly peculiar to the oil industry and it is more complex.

Consider first a piece of completely unexplored or "rank wildcat" acreage. An oil company is not willing to pay much for the right to explore and produce because it is the few good discoveries that pay for the many failures. It will therefore offer only a sort of composite value, averaging in all tracts of this type. That is the most it will pay, and it will go elsewhere if the landowner wants more. If the company succeeds in paying less than its maximum, it is getting some rent and the owner has lost some in the bargaining. Of course, opinions may vary on how good the tract really is. This is clearly seen under competitive bidding, when the high bidder may offer far more than the next highest.

In general, if it turns out that there were others who would have paid more, the landowner is sorry he let the tract go so cheaply; contrariwise, if the nearest price was much lower than the price accepted, the landowner is glad and the producer sad. But the fact that the rent of a particular tract — the margin between its price and the cheapest tract — went either to the landowner or to the company bidding, has no effect on whether that tract is drilled up or not.

Once the tract is drilled, uncertainty gives way to real knowledge. This is the great divide of the petroleum industry. If there is no oil, or none worth developing, the producer's money has been wasted. If, on the other hand, the deposit is large, shallow, permeable, with a powerful water drive, so that developing-producing profits will be large, the landowner is going to wish he had held out for much more and with foreknowledge the producer would willingly have paid much more.

Because of the nature of petroleum costs, a rich discovery means a dissatisfied landlord who knows that his tenant's profit is far greater than is necessary to keep him producing. Here, there can be a curious reverse echo from the rule of capture when the individual cost of an oil inventory is nearly zero but the social cost is substantial. It is evident that the rent for some individual projects is always going to be very large, even if the price is so far below industry marginal cost that the industry is failing to replenish reserves. As has been pointed out earlier, the cost of searching in one place is not completely independent of the cost of searching in many, and it may even be inseparable. In the larger view, it is the return over the cost of all together which counts. Therefore, if oil explorers are deprived of the hope of making big profits occasionally by finding a lot of low-cost oil — the so-called "lure of the big strike" — then the expected profit of good and bad discoveries taken together will fall and less capital and enterprise will be available, ultimately reducing supply. If for some reason no additional oil finding was desired, the surplus could certainly be confiscated with no ill effects. This is the basic economic distinction between "pure rent" and "quasi rent," which is a surplus in the short run but not the long run. But what is true for the industry as a whole may safely be neglected in any one instance. A given landlord, accounting for only a small part of all leases, could confiscate all the rent being gained on his acreage without any perceptible effect on the industry.

Whenever as a result of a bargain the alternatives open to the parties are transformed, the new situation puts a strain on the bargain itself. The classic example is the Pied Piper of Hamlin. In prospect (as with no oil found), the burghers were willing to pay a thousand guilders to get rid of the rats. But after the rats were gone (oil found) they wanted to renegotiate at 95 per cent discount: "A thousand guilders? Come, take fifty!" With no higher authority around to enforce his contract, fifty guilders was all the Pied Piper could get. He retaliated so brutally that the burghers in turn would have paid much more than a thousand guilders to have gotten their children back. Both parties were too hasty, too ignorant of the harm the other could inflict, and too passionately sure they were right to come to any agreement, and in the end both were much the worse off. This is the kind of showdown one would not like to see.

BACKGROUND TO THE CURRENT PROBLEM

It is time to put the theory to work. As we saw, the petroleum industry is, in general, one of increasing costs with greater output. It has no general tendency, always operative and only occasionally overcome, to drive prices below costs. If a large unmanageable surplus begins to appear, it must be explained by some combination of: (1) a strong random factor in the discovery (but only to a lesser extent in the development) of new fields; (2) changes in the rate of discounting of the future by oil operators, including governments, who must compare present with future receipts; (3) changes in the ratio of inventories to current sales and expected sales; and (4) changes in expected prices of substitutes for oil, and therefore, in the expected prices of oil. I do not believe (4) has been operative; (2) and (3) have been. Effect (3), inventories, could conceivably in any given case be explained by chance alone. But it does not necessarily result from it, since the time needed for development is an inherent slower-down and damper of the random reserve effect, and development is governed by near-term price expectations and costs which can be estimated approximately. Hence to explain a *persistent and growing* surplus of supply a fifth factor needs to be invoked, namely (5) a persistent holding of prices above the cost of reproducing inventory.

For the situation outside the United States, the five reasons suggested above could bear more elaboration than can be given here, but one must be mentioned. An oil company can scarcely avoid investing in some surplus capacity as insurance against a variety of embarassments: severe winters like 1962–63 and (much aggravated by wartime shortages not yet made up) 1947–48; natural disasters or political disagreements in one place or another; and so forth.

Investment in spare capacity is therefore cheap insurance and good business, and there always will be some spillover into the market. But its importance is at best interstitial; it cannot exert much pressure on price. For if an operator uses the spare capacity to make a sale, it ceases to exist as insurance and must be replaced — which is to say, this sales contract under consideration requires more drilling for its fulfillment, or else the surplus capacity was not needed for insurance at all. Particularly in the Eastern Hemisphere, with demand growing at around 10 per cent annually, and therefore something more than that needed as additional capacity merely to stay in the same place, it is hard to see the "insurance surplus" as much of a market factor. Nevertheless, there may be more to it; I profess no great confidence in this judgment so long as the development plans and procedures of individual companies are so little known.

Finally, the fact that many individual companies are still short of "adequate" reserves in spite of an industry-wide surplus is merely another way of saying that the current price does not reflect that surplus. If it did, few companies would seek their own reserves; they would be content to sign long-term contracts or buy participations.

The price of oil has not been left free to move down, and it will probably not be left much freer in the foreseeable future. In the United States, for reasons indicated earlier, the ratio of reserves to production has if anything decreased, but the immediate producing capacity — wells actually drilled and functioning — has increased greatly, and is in burdensome excess. Abroad, on the other hand, the immediate producibility problem is not so great, but what presses on the market are huge published reserves which can be developed on fairly short notice into proved reserves.

To be in any kind of equilibrium between present and future sales, the oil industry needs to be in a perpetual state of looking for new reserves, below whose expected cost the price cannot fall. Allowing roughly for the difference between proved and published reserves, we need something higher than 12½ years' supply abroad — perhaps of the order of 15. In fact, Venezuelan reserves are only 14½ times annual output, which is hardly excessive.[69] Were Venezuela alone in its markets, replacement cost for both finding and developing crude oil capacity would serve as a firm underpinning for the price, though not necessarily the present price. But Venezuela must live in the same world with the Middle East, where published reserves are about 111 times current output. For the large Middle East producers (and some in Venezuela), finding cost is not merely low, it is zero, because the inventory they use up by developing new capacity today is without value to them — the future revenues they sacrifice are too heavily discounted, both by time and by uncertainty of receipt, to be worth anything today. To be sure, if the world formed one single market, estimated reserves would be a much less crushing though still excessive 35 years' supply, but that is not the case. Outside the United States, replacement cost has disappeared as a floor for price; in the United States, development cost has also disappeared.

The current world oil crisis is the combined result of higher demand triggering the huge low-cost reserves of the Middle East, and a price persistently far above long-run marginal cost — i.e., the cost of finding, developing, and producing new oil. Price maintenance may be good policy for many reasons, but even the best reasons do not change economic consequences. Price maintenance means both a general surplus and, of equal importance, it suppresses the market-sharing mechanism of carrying output everywhere to the point where marginal cost is in the neighborhood of prices. The current price level is an incentive for every operator to produce and sell more than he now does; hence he must curtail his offerings

---

[69] This and other years' supply estimates from *Oil and Gas Journal,* December 31, 1962, p. 87, or earlier issues.

to suit more nearly the interests of all the sellers. But the incentive remains, and the unceasing urge for additional sales and profits has put the market under a severe continuing strain. In order to reconcile the two objectives of more sales volume and no price cutting, producers give away some of the excess of price over producing cost by making special deals for some customers, trying to gain business by non-price competition at the final customer level, operating refining-market facilities which bring little or no profit, and trying to tie up long-term outlets by loans or other inducements that cost money. On the other side of the table, independent refiners and large consumers and governments try also to get special deals, and sometimes prefer even to engage in the search for oil, which they regard as an El Dorado.

What can we expect by way of further evolution? We must first ask what has been the mechanism by which price has been maintained.

Petroleum Cartel or Commodity Agreement?

What is the current market structure in the world oil trade; what is the degree of control of price and output, and how is it maintained? This is a practical question. If, as we shall try to demonstrate, the cartel is a myth no matter how the meaning of "cartel" is diluted, then anyone who desires the current price level to continue is wrong to sit back in the comfortable expectation that the great companies, with perhaps a bit of help, will make everything all right. On the other hand, if one is opposed to the current price level, he is wasting his time trying to discover ways of preventing the companies from running the market.

One thing seems well settled; this is that the international oil companies do not get together to fix prices. In the United States there has now been a study by the Federal Trade Commission[70] and three suits by the Department of Justice;[71] whatever else they came up with, consultation on prices and output was something they did not find.

Because everybody knows this, it is elaborately discounted and dis-

---

[70] *The International Petroleum Cartel, Staff Report to the Federal Trade Commission submitted to the Subcommittee on Monopoly of the Select Committee on Small Business,* U.S. Senate, 82nd Cong., 2nd Sess., Washington, 1952; hereafter referred to as FTC Report.

[71] *U.S.* v. *Standard Oil Company (New Jersey), et al.,* D.C. D.C. Civil Action No. 1779–53, hereafter referred to as World Oil Complaint; and D.C.S.D.N.Y., *Final Judgment,* November 14, 1960; hereafter referred to as World Oil Consent Decree. *U.S.* v. *Standard Oil Co. of Calif., et al.,* 155 F. Supp. 121 and 210 F. 2nd 50 (2nd Circ. 1959); hereafter referred to as MSA Case. *U.S.* v. *Arkansas Fuel Corp., et al.,* CCH Par. 69.619 (N.D. Okla., 1960); hereafter referred to as Arkansas Fuel case.

missed. Even a hardened sceptic, insistent on facts and logic, will often collapse altogether in the face of: "Now, my dear fellow, let's not be naive! They don't actually need to get together. I mean — oligopoly and all that." But the mystery lies precisely in the "all that," much as in the "etc." in the title of Queen Elizabeth I, when all Europe wanted to know if she did or did not proclaim herself the head of the Church of England, and that great and prudent lady "et-ceterated herself."

As it happens, there was a cartel between the wars, and the companies did have to get together, repeatedly. They started with an agreement on principles and a sound distaste for detailed regulation. In many industries, to settle strategy and let tactics take care of themselves makes good sense, but with a product mixture as odd as petroleum, and with so many new channels for competition to find when it was dammed up in others, the companies found themselves writing more and more detailed specifications.[72] And therefore, in a postwar period even longer (from the Achnacarry oil agreement to war was only eleven years; World War II has been over for seventeen) and more turbulent, the impossibility of getting together has meant at the very least a substantial limit on their power to act. "Oligopoly" is a fact in world oil, but it does no more than open the discussion.

But perhaps the companies were able after the war, without any explicit agreement, by means of a wink and a nod, at least to keep prices much higher than they would otherwise have been? There is no doubt about the price level, but to attribute it to the companies' winks and nods is to beg the question. We find ourselves looking around for evidence which will confirm or refute the hypothesis of tacit understandings. The postwar evolution of crude oil prices, particularly up to the end of 1949, has been described in the last chapter of the FTC Report, which can be used as an example of the most that could be said by the most unfriendly source. This may be a mistake, since the chapter was not meant for economists, but for the judge in a great antitrust suit that never came off. The repetitive rhythmic beat of "identical delivered price, regardless of point of origin" was meant to lull the critical sense of a judge who might otherwise see that if delivered prices are *not* the same, regardless of point of origin, there are few more definite signs of a block to competition. Putting aside the subliminal persuader and looking only at the facts, it is instructive to read them in the light of a complaint made, some eight years later by

[72] FTC Report, *op. cit.* (Note 70) Chapters VIII and IX, pp. 275–79, 282–86, 288–304, 311–48.

Sheikh Abdullah Tariki.[73] His reproach was that the oil companies should have set the price to equal the natural ceiling, at London, or perhaps just barely undercutting Venezuelan oil, instead of equating with it at New York. The cumulative difference between the one and the other was around five billion dollars. Now whatever may be said of Mr. Tariki's policy advice, an economist must admire how he got to the heart of the problem and put it in at least rough quantitative terms. If the Middle East producers had been able to act as a group, they would have equated at London because it would have increased profit. Like all good things, this would have taken some self-denial. For it meant that since the net return on shipments to London was much higher than on shipments to New York, the normal competitive response would have been for each individual seller to channel as much output as possible toward London, and to keep doing so as long as any such differential remained, driving it toward zero. For each company to resist this pressure, and equate the price to a London sale in the confident expectation that everybody else would, was what a small group *could* have done without any actual correspondence.

Thus, in trying to think out the price structure, we are brought to realize that monopoly price and output are what is best for an industry or group as a whole, i.e., what would be charged and supplied by a single seller, who *is* the industry as a whole. I do not find control of a market as always or necessarily offensive. To paraphrase: "A little monopoly now and then / Is relished by the wisest men." But it is important to know the phenomenon for what it is. A price well above incremental cost is a source of tension in the system, which, good or bad, is not to be talked away by calling it fair, reasonable, natural — or even "competitive," in view of the nearest substitute. It can be maintained only by a united front and refusal to supply at any lower price. The kind of price structure that Mr. Tariki wanted was that of an effective Middle Eastern monopoly, and the fact of his complaint is sufficient evidence that it was far from being fully effective. So if one turns back to the FTC study with a fresh view, what is actually chronicled there is a swift and drastic revolution in the price structure — just the change we should expect under the hypothesis of a competitive market. From Gulf-plus we ended up with a single f.o.b. price that just equated with the price, net of transport cost, in the most

---

[73] Sheikh Abdullah Tariki, "The Pricing of Crude Oil and Refined Products," *Proceedings, Second Arab Petroleum Congress* (Beirut, 1960), pp. 13, 15, 20. The "hidden profits" thesis, which in any case I may not understand, appears unrelated to the main argument. It is instructive to compare it with the FTC Report, *op. cit.* (Note 70), pp. 366–67.

distant market — the U.S. East Coast. Hence the FTC Report's own data do not bear out its hypothesis of a cartel acting through "trade custom" or other means. But do they establish the contradictory hypothesis — are they only compatible with competitive behavior? For this purpose the evidence is ambiguous. The price revolution was made in the anxious presence of the U.S. government, guided by a particularly competent group of advisers. I for one cannot say if it would have happened had the government been less interested or less ably advised.

Let us try another test, over the time period following 1949: failure to import into the United States on an increasingly large scale. It has been in the interest of each Middle East and Venezuelan producer to bring a great deal more oil into the United States. For the domestic price covers the costs of much more expensive wells, even with costs raised yet further by the regulatory system.

With such an inducement, why did the oil companies not import much more? One logical explanation would be, again, group interest. All the Middle East producers except Compagnie Française des Pétroles (CFP) and British Petroleum (BP) were big U.S. producers, and some were also very big in Venezuela. Hence, to help bring down Western Hemisphere prices would on balance lose rather than gain for them. This is the kind of agreement that can be reached simply by everybody waiting for somebody else to start something, and hoping he won't. Yet this explanation, although logically sound, is not satisfactory. First, it does not explain the self-restraint of BP and CFP. Second, it assumes that the losses in the Western Hemisphere would have outweighed the gains in the Eastern, which is at best unproved. (In my opinion, which is also unproved, a rational Middle East monopoly, with large U.S. and Venezuelan interests, would have been money ahead even at much lower U.S. prices and output.) Third, it is hard to believe that companies having crude deficits in the United States and therefore benefiting most by imports, would not have insisted on some kind of compensation for their forbearance, and of this there is no evidence.

Unlike the FTC theory, the hypothesis that by business statesmanship the large American companies refrained from spoiling the American market is logically tenable but has some weaknesses. Even if it were stronger, however, we would have to reject it in favor of a simpler one. The American companies were in fact never free to import, and therefore their statesmanship or lack thereof was never put to the test. Between late 1949 and late 1954, the United States (because of Korea and then Iran) had no more than two to three years of easy supply. One can review the Congressional hearings in 1949–50 and later years,[74] or read the FTC Report, noting that its Senate sponsor considered the most important problem to be not whether oil prices were too high and imports too low, but whether the big companies were importing too much and ruining the domestic producers.[75] One can examine the Justice Department Complaint in the 1953 world oil antitrust case, where the large companies are accused both of restricting imports into the United States *and* of excessive dumping into the United States.[76] Or one can examine the reporting system set up in early 1953 by the Texas Railroad Commission (which could shut down any well), whereby importers reported detailed programs in advance and filed a compliance report afterward.[77] In the light of this continual vigilance and pressure, nobody can possibly suppose that the oil companies were free to import large amounts even before overt regulation. When the situation became more difficult, the national administration intervened: in July 1954 President Eisenhower named an Advisory Committee on Energy Supplies and Resources Policy, which issued a report the following February, recommending an imports ceiling. In 1957 imports again seemed to be getting out of hand because of the activities of many smaller importers who were less vulnerable politically and administratively than the big oil companies, which did not themselves, I would say, keep ranks any too well at that time. But the "voluntary" and then mandatory programs came immediately, in July 1957 and March 1959, and the breakdown of the former indicates that the big importers would not or could not control the situation. We must conclude that the failure substantially to import, like the price revolution of 1948–49, is inconclusive evidence; the companies never had the chance to show what they would do if left to themselves because in fact they were not left to themselves.

Let us shift our attention somewhat to Western Europe. It could plausibly be contended that the demand for oil was rather inelastic, i.e., unre-

[74] *Effects of Foreign Oil Imports on Independent Domestic Producers, Report of the Subcommittee on Oil Imports to the Select Committee on Small Business,* House of Representatives, 81st Cong., 2nd Sess., Washington 1950; hereafter referred to as 1950 House Report. *Causes of Unemployment in the Coal and Other Specified Industries, Report of the Committee on Labor and Public Welfare,* U.S. Senate, 81st Cong., 2nd Sess., Washington 1950; hereafter referred to as 1950 Senate Report. *Petroleum Study: Petroleum Imports, Progress Report of the Committee on Interstate and Foreign Commerce,* House of Representatives, 81st Cong., 2nd Sess., Washington 1950; hereafter referred to as 1950 Wilson Report.

[75] FTC Report, *op. cit.* (Note 70), Preface by Senator John Sparkman, Chairman, Select Committee on Small Business, p.v.

[76] World Oil Complaint, *op. cit.* (Note 71), IV–8–b and V–11–(2), (3), (4).

[77] It may be found adequately reported in the *Oil and Gas Journal* and the *Journal of Commerce* (New York).

sponsive to price, and that this inhibited price cutting. If true, this would be a group rationale; demand may be inelastic for the product as a whole, therefore price not worth reducing for the group as a whole, but it is certainly elastic for each seller. To say, therefore, that the group refrained from price reduction because of inelastic demand is to say that they practiced statesmanship. But was even aggregate demand that inelastic? Econometric studies of demand elasticity must be used with care because elasticity is essentially a condition in the immediate neighborhood of some price, and changes as the price is higher or lower. If, in the neighborhood of the current price, elasticity is, say, 2.0, then a 1 per cent decrease in price implies a sales increase of 2 per cent. It does not follow at all that a decrease of 10 per cent should increase sales only about 20 per cent. For a large price cut may completely change the relative attractiveness of two different fuels, or two different ways of spending one's money. Elasticity is a function of standards and habits of living, and of knowledge of the advantages of substitutes. The demand for gasoline is generally considered as quite inelastic, and in the short run it is (though recent Italian experience makes one wonder). But over the long run it is not; for if it were, how could we explain the difference in car design, and in average consumption per mile, between Europe and the United States? Moreover, some of the middle distillates, and all heavy fuel oil are extremely competitive with coal, and when the price of oil is only a little higher, the elasticity becomes very high indeed. As of 1956, a 10 per cent drop in fuel oil prices implied more than a doubling of sales, i.e., an 80 per cent increase in total receipts.[78] In later years it went much higher than that; indeed, one might say that it is today infinitely high in that even with no change in price many more people would buy fuel oil if they were free to choose. Once fuel oil occupies a major part of what might be called the boiler fuel market, further decreases in price bring a smaller sales response, until at some point the demand becomes quite inelastic again. This is the price a reasonable monopolist would aim at, to maximize his profit, but of course it has not come about in Europe and probably even less would have happened if the increase in coal prices had not happened to coincide with some new elements of independence in the fuel market.

For crude oil as a whole, which is a composite of the moderate gasoline elasticity, the very great fuel oil elasticity, and the intermediate one for middle distillate, elasticity is at least high enough so that the action of European and Japanese governments to restrict imports either directly or by means of heavy taxation does act as a substantial depressant.

[78] R. Regul, "Energy Studies," *Institute of Petroleum Review,* Vol. 12 (1958) pp. 299, 303.

Now, the greater the price elasticity for oil as a whole, the greater the sales response to price reductions, and the greater the likelihood that a price cut would be worth making even for the group as a whole. If it were worth making, then we cannot explain the failure to cut prices as being group interest; we can only explain it by some inhibition preventing the group from acting as it would like to. We are not justified simply in *assuming* that the oil companies were free to cut prices and import all the oil they wished, but restrained imports to maximize their profits. Coal protectionism in Europe is and always has been a basic fact. A reasonable and well-informed oil producer with European refineries would refrain from cutting price even if he thought if would benefit the whole group, himself included, if he also thought it would lead to governmental restriction on imports and a loss of investment in new output.

Let us now try to appraise the role of the international oil companies. They were a small group, seven in all, with several joint ventures and long-term supply contracts. We know little enough of these agreements, but they did provide a vehicle (not merely a forum, which is trivial) by which every company knew and had to know the development plans of every other: even before the Iranian concession, BP's plans had to be known to Gulf in Kuwait, and to Jersey, Socony, Shell, and CFP in Iraq; and Jersey's and Socony's Iraq plans could not but affect their Aramco offtake and development plans, known to Texaco and California Standard. And Jersey and Shell accounted for most Venezuelan output. As for the supply-requirements contracts, notably Gulf to Jersey, Socony, and Shell out of Kuwait, in themselves they did nothing but bring together companies with a crude surplus and crude deficit in some given part of the world. Such contracts will always exist under any degree of competition. But given a small group of suppliers, they supplied additional reassurance that the rock on which the whole structure rested was still there: nobody was contemplating a price cut. Add to this an inhibition on price cutting to get more business either in Europe or the United States, because of protection for coal and domestic oil; add further what was then highly probable and is now certain, that the governments of the producing countries would not stand for price cutting, and I submit we have enough in hand for a reasonable explanation.

Because of the growth of lost-cost capacity, the competitive pressure after World War II was toward lower prices. The oil companies were reluctant to yield, as sellers always are. The one thing they could do about price was to leave it alone. "The House of Lords, throughout the war, did nothing in particular, and did it very well." Each of the companies was resolved not to cut the price until somebody else forced them to. Had there been a large group — say of the order of twenty or more — prices would have started to fold earlier, and then the governments would have intervened earlier. But a small interrelated group was able, without any consultation, to stand fast, try to gain business by all possible non-price methods, and leave the price alone.

To do nothing was, indeed, to do much, and of course it was the Middle East-Caribbean oligopoly that permitted this to happen. But by refusing to take "oligopoly" as a general explanation of prices, and by focusing on what actually happened and the need to explain it, we rid ourselves of the notion that the companies did or can do any more. True, they are now, by special leave of the U.S. Department of Justice, permitted to get together to fix prices, divide markets, and limit output.[79] Some may find it odd that antitrust proceedings should have this result; but the guiding genius of the law has always been Mr. Facing-Both-Ways. In any case, the situation has gone too far to permit the companies simply to get together to work things out on their own, as they might have done ten years ago.

Summing up: during most of the 1950's, in effect if not in form or intent, we had a world commodity agreement in crude oil, sponsored by nobody in particular but maintained by the co-operation of the governments in the consuming countries and the international oil companies; the governments each restrained competition at home, the companies did practically nothing, but all refrained from doing what might have brought the agreement to an end. My opinion, for what it may be worth, is that the commodity agreement worked very well. Large amounts of oil were forthcoming at a price well below that of other sources of energy. The high price provided an incentive to establish reserves for an unprecedentedly long period ahead. But that is a receding bit of history, and I make no prediction about a similar solution for the current crisis, to which we now turn.

The Deterioration of the Market, 1957–62

How long the commodity agreement would have lasted under quiet conditions we cannot say. The disappearance of Iranian crude from the

---

[79] World Oil Consent Decree, *op. cit.* (Note 71), Selection V, subsections (A) and (C). The companies did well to get this provision into the decree; they will do even better to treat it as a shield, not a tool for setting up a cartel.

world oil markets in 1951 offset the tendency to over-capacity, and so did the Suez crisis. The turn came some time either in 1957, when Iranian output again exceeded its pre-crisis level, or in 1958, the first year of large Soviet exports, and also of a significant buildup of non-Soviet producing capacity, from 17 to 22 per cent of output.[80] Perhaps there was also the beginning of serious price cutting by two of the old major companies as they pushed their refined products into new areas,[81] notably CFP and BP, who was held particularly to blame.[82] And of course the robot-like following of the U.S. price increase at the beginning of 1957 strained the system all the more, for the increase was related to nothing at all in world supply and demand. By late 1958, it seemed that Middle East crudes were being discounted by roughly 11 to 13 cents per barrel.[83] We cannot begin to give an adequate account of changes in prices since then, but a hurried condensation may be adequate, using as a yardstick Arabian crude of $34.0°–34.9°$, and bearing in mind that using any other yardstick would give us a different set of discounts even with the same observed prices. From $1.93 before the Suez crisis, it was raised to $2.08 in May of 1957, and the reduction led by BP to $1.90 in February 1959 did perhaps no more than take formal note of discounts.[84] Early in August 1960 came a further reduction to $1.76, then a partial restoration to $1.80 after the strong disapproval of the producing nations and the formation of the Organization of the Petroleum Exporting Countries (OPEC).

As of 1962–63, it is impossible to speak of any single price because of the many types of explicit and implicit discounting. However, it is possible to discern, dimly, several layers. Some sales may still be at posted prices.[85] Then there is a sort of official discount at approximately 8 per cent, or about 14 cents off;[86] below that may be discerned a sort of semi-

[80] Cf. editorial in *Oil and Gas Journal*, December 30, 1957, suggesting worldwide prorationing. On capacity, see Mayhew, "A Review of Foreign Oil Production in 1960," *International Oil and Gas Development, op. cit.* (Note 36).

[81] *Petroleum Press Service*, Vol. 26 (1959), p. 87.

[82] *Oil and Gas Journal*, August 15, 1960, p. 83.

[83] *Oil and Gas Journal*, August 25, 1958, p. 66, announcing that the posting of Getty crude prices at 13 cents below the equivalent Aramco crude caused no flurry since that was about in line anyway.

[84] *Petroleum Press Service*, Vol. 26 (1959), p. 87; *The Economist*, February 28, 1959.

[85] In early 1962, Zelten crude was selling at posted prices to affiliates, but this had (apparently) ceased later in the year, when sales were sought to non-affiliates. (*Petroleum Intelligence Weekly*, January 28, 1963.)

[86] Cf. the statements of Burmah Shell, BP, Standard Vacuum, and Caltex, sum-

official discount of about 35 cents.[87] Perhaps the greater part of arm's-length transactions are in the neighborhood of this latter figure. (The transfers within integrated companies are not meaningful unless some account is taken of refining realizations and losses — which will be discussed later.)

But it is also clear from published data that some sales are being made at considerably lower prices. For example, to land a barrel of crude on the U.S. East Coast costs about $2.13 over and above the price paid for the crude oil itself. That is, a producer or refiner can get transport by a time charter at around 66 cents per barrel (or some 10 cents cheaper if he is content to keep relying on spot charters), plus 12 cents Suez Canal dues, plus 10.5 cents import duty, plus approximately $1.25 for a "ticket." ("Ticket" is the trade name for the import permits given to domestic refiners in proportion to refinery runs; inland refiners, having no use for the permits, in effect sell them, by making favorable exchanges of domestic crudes, to refiners having tidewater capacity.) Obviously there can be no nice regular series of current quotations on the market value of a "ticket"; my impression is that its value has risen from about 80 cents per barrel in early 1959 to the current figure, which is said by the president of the Independent Refiners Association of America to be from $1.00 to $2.00 per barrel, but is usually perhaps in the neighborhood of $1.25.[88] Anyone who wants crude oil can have all he needs landed on the East Coast for

---

marized in *Report of the Oil Price Enquiry Committee* (Government of India, Ministry of Steel, Mines and Fuel, Department of Mines and Fuel, July 1961), pp. 16–24. Unfortunately, the discounts do not clearly distinguish between f.o.b. and c.i.f.

[87] *Oil and Gas International*, September 1961, p. 57; Edward Symonds, *Oil Prospects and Profits in the Eastern Hemisphere* (New York: First National City Bank, September 1961). *Cf.* the quoting of Khafji 27° crude at $1.30 (including 12 cent discount off the nominal $1.42), which is 36 cents below the $1.66 it would take to bring 27° crude into line on the basis of 2 cents per 1°. See also *Petroleum Intelligence Weekly*, July 16, 1962, giving an EEC estimate of 27–36 cents. Since the heavy fuels are in especially good demand, the traditional 2 cent allowance is really too large. One can as well say that the true discount on heavy crudes is greater than indicated, as that the lighter crudes are overpriced in relation to the heavy. Unfortunately, many reports of discount prices cannot be used because it is not made clear what crude is being discounted.

[88] M. H. Robineau, in *Small Business Problems Created by Petroleum Imports; Hearings before Subcommittee No. 4 of the Select Committee on Small Business,* 87th Cong., 1st Sess., Washington, 1962, Part II, p. 745. At the same hearings, a Sinclair official estimated the price of a ticket as "a dollar plus" (p. 690). The Independent Petroleum Association of America has estimated the value at $1.15 (*Oil and Gas Journal*, August 7, 1961, p. 96). A later report, in *Platt's Oilgram Price Service*, July 5, 1962, puts it at $1.25, and implies that it had not changed much in the past year.

about $3.35.[89] Therefore, if a purchaser buys Arabian 34° crude at the Persian Gulf for $3.35 less $2.13, or $1.22, he is no better off than if he bought U.S. domestic crude at prevailing prices. He must be paying somewhat less, or he would have no incentive to buy. Hence substantial amounts must be moving at, say, a trifle under $1.20, or at most just under $1.30 if spot charters are used — which would have been a painful experience last winter. Venezuelan discounts are probably greater; on a comparable basis, parity would be not at about 58 cents ($1.80 less $1.22), but around a dollar off; Oficina 34° crude, posted at $2.78, probably sells as low as $1.65 — though I should stress that that is the low end of the range (based on published sources), and not *necessarily* an average or representative price. For all I know, oil is moving at even larger discounts, but that cannot be proved.

The current state of the market is glimpsed by some recent offers and bids, as shown in Table 2.

We reckon freight throughout at available term rates of around Scale less 45 per cent. To some extent, it is a fiction to quote term charter rates

Table 2. Offers and Bids for Crude Oil, 1962, 1963

| | Crude | | Price (U.S. $) | | | Yardstick (U.S. $) | |
Time	Origin	Gravity	C.I.F.	Freight	F.O.B.	Equiva-lent	Dis-count
(1) July	Kirkuk	36°	1.94	(.52)	(1.42)	1.38	.42
(2) September	Kuwait	31°	2.00	(.69)	(1.31)	1.39	.41
(3) October	Libya	39°	1.80	(.10)	(1.70)	1.24	.56
(4) October	Khafji	26°	offered-not accepted		1.00	1.16	.62
(5) December	Algeria	41°	—	—	1.85	1.31	.49
(6) January	Khafji	26°	—	—	1.20	1.36	.44
(7) February	Safaniya	27°	—	—	1.32	1.46	.34
(8) March	Algeria	41°	—	—	1.83	1.27	.51
(9) March	Lybia	39°	2.27	(.53)	(1.74)	1.28	.52

( ) = computed.
Sources: (1) *Platt's Oilgram Price Service* (New York: McGraw-Hill), August, 1962; (2) *Petroleum Intelligence Weekly,* September 10, 1962; (3) P.I.W., October 22, 1962; (4) P.I.W., October 29, 1962; (5) Platt's P.S., P.I.W., December 3, 1962; (6) Platt's P.S. and P.I.W., January 28, 1963; (7) P.I.W., February 4, 1963; (8) P.I.W., March 18, 1963; (9) Platt's P.S., March 13, 1963.

[89] West Texas sour crude, which is in particularly strong demand, lays down at a Gulf Coast refinery at about $2.95 per barrel for 32° gravity. Since the prevailing differential is 3 cents per degree, and is adhered to, 34° material must sell for $3.01. (*Oil and Gas Journal,* December 18, 1961, p. 45.) To this is added 34 cents per barrel tanker rate (flat Scale, and 7.5 barrels/long ton).

at this time, when there is very little term chartering going on. Nearly all new charters are at spot, which until the distressing winter 1962–63 was some 10 points lower. But since we must think in terms of a sales contract for a year or more, the buyer or seller must have an assurance of shipping for that period, either by his own ships — in which case the market value of their services is what can be got for them under current conditions — or by hiring others. The margin of term over spot rates also represents an insurance premium or risk allowance for the possibility of spot rates rising before the contract runs out.

It should not be supposed that the above table represents "the" market. Some sales are made with terms not announced, some have fringe benefits which greatly modify the price, some are simply unintelligible. But the one criticism which can *not* be legitimately made is that they represent only the open market and hence do not apply to the great bulk of crude oil, which moves through integrated channels. A short answer might be that a "price" set without arm's-length bargaining is not a price at all — it is noise in the circuit, not information, and should be disregarded. Equally important, refined-product prices now reflect crude prices at about these levels everywhere in Western Continental Europe except France, and they are heading that way in Britain. These two reasons, as will now be seen, are partly related.

Reasons for the Post-Suez Change

Why did the oversupply translate itself into market instability after the Suez crisis? The usual explanation is the entry of newcomers, including the Soviet Union. Others stress that these newcomers have little of the total world productive capacity and markets and that the old internationals were already cutting prices before the impact of the newcomers was felt. We may never know which of these explanations is the better, partly because some facts will never become public and partly because the two factors are interdependent. Had the old internationals been able to form some sort of cartel, or at least an understanding, they could have followed the most profitable road, which would have been to disregard the price cutters, who had little crude and still less access to markets. Thereby they would have sacrificed little in the way of sales volume and nothing at all in prices. But this they were not free to do because where a newcomer took business away from an old international the latter would try to recoup from somebody else. The resolution of each member of a small group to do nothing about price can last only as long as he feels certain that others will do the same. Because the older concerns could not, in fact, be sure of this, each feared to reject one sale lest it lead to loss of sales all along the line, like a row of dominoes. It is a fact of common notoriety in the United States that Texas has served as the balance wheel of the oil producing states, absorbing most of the restriction in output because there is no mechanism of agreement or efficient collusion among the states. (The Compact Commission has sometimes been accused of acting this role, but with no justification; still less, the Bureau of Mines, or the American Petroleum Institute.) And therefore the companies, under the necessity of following their particular rather than the general interest, have been in the position of competitors rather than statesmen, and have met price cuts at least part way at crude and product levels.

Therefore, even if the newcomers really dealt in much smaller quantities of oil than did the older concerns, their influence was out of all proportion to their sales. Furthermore, it was to be expected that in the longer run the newcomers would account for more oil. It is a basic axiom in the study of industry economics that the larger the market, the more room there is for competition and the smaller, relative to the market, is the minimum size of a firm which has all necessary economies of scale; also, the larger the market, the greater and more available is the complex of service and supply companies. Since in Venezuela and the Middle East it was clear by the fifties that relatively small companies could successfully find oil, governments made a point of getting as many independent firms as possible to explore. Today, a single lease covering the whole country is unthinkable. Reasonable men may disagree on whether oil was ever a "natural oligopoly," but it clearly is not one today.

In this sphere the Japanese, rather than the Russians, have been the true revolutionaries. Their Arabian Oil Company was formed by a group of businessmen, including refiners, electric power companies, and other large consumers. It was not "access" or "assured supply" they were after. They could have signed up all the oil they wanted, undoubtedly at less than posted prices. Plainly, they considered even the discounted price to be far above the cost of finding-plus-development-plus-production, even for newcomers who cannot do it as cheaply as the old concerns. Furthermore, they had no producing experience and conducted a pure checkbook operation. They raised $10 million, a rather small sum in the Middle East, and hired the talent.[90] Once oil was found, sums for development came in with little difficulty.[91] Those who think oil can only be found and developed out of past oil profits ought to reflect on the Japanese example.

[90] See *Petroleum Press Service,* Vol. 28 (1961), p. 224; *Oil and Gas International,* Vol. 2 (January, 1962), p. 29.

[91] As of April 1961, they had spent $55 million and planned another $108 million.

Let us now consider the biggest of the newcomers, the Soviet oil trust, which is far more traditionalist than the Japanese, being a large, old-established company which talks in statesmanlike fashion of regaining the traditional share (19 per cent) of world trade it had in 1930–33.[92] The Russian incursion into world markets has been well and extensively covered in the trade press; there are also a volume issued by the American Petroleum Institute and two issued by the National Petroleum Council, not to mention some technical papers at various congresses.[93] When one reads these sources, the notion that the Russians do not sell at prices unrelated to costs, or are dumping in order to disrupt world markets for political ends, appears to be unfounded and downright frivolous. Nothing is so easy and cheap as to accuse the price cutter of selling below cost in order to drive all others out of business, leaving him in a position to exploit without mercy.[94]

Of course the Soviet Union is trying to get all possible political advantages from its oil exports. But if political ends are so important that they are worth buying at a price, there is a quicker, cheaper, and easier way to fulfill them: buy for storage large quantities of crude oil and products, and then dump them adroitly at just the time and places to do the most political damage. This has obviously not happened. The Russians have mounted an impressive oil and gas finding effort, which has taken, and is still taking, a lot of their scarcest resource — trained manpower — to run. We should rather ask why they were so late in putting their economy on a petroleum basis; they paid heavily for their neglect. Perhaps it was bureaucratic conservatism, or fear of the whims of a ferocious dictator, or, most basically, the lack of any mechanism to take account of comparative advantage and relative prices. Soviet insulation from Western economic thought was not the only disadvantage; Polish fuel policy, too, was a drag on the economy.[95]

The Soviet attempt at oil and gas finding in the mid-1950's was primarily to satisfy their energy requirements more cheaply. Their success was

[92] *Oil and Gas Journal,* October 31, 1960; and *Petroleum Press Service,* Vol. 27 (1960), p. 406.

[93] Ebel, *op. cit.* (Note 7); National Petroleum Council, *Impact of Oil Exports from the Soviet Bloc* (Washington, 1962). See also sources cited in SPNG, *op. cit.* (Note 3).

[94] This is not to deny that if the Soviet bloc furnished a large part of the supplies of the non-Soviet world, they might cut it off for political reasons. *Cf.* Harold Lubell, *The Soviet Oil Offensive and Inter-bloc Economic Competition,* RM 2812-PR (RAND Corp., December, 1961).

[95] On the Polish fuel economy, I rely on an unpublished paper by T. Paul Schultz, graduate student in economics, Massachusetts Institute of Technology.

considerable, but they found much more gas than they had expected. This had a double effect: to the extent that gas satisfied fuel needs, it pushed corresponding amounts of oil out of the region, a process no different from that experienced in the American Southwest after World War II. But gas transmission is a voracious consumer of steel line pipe, which the Russians did not have in sufficient amounts. To get the pipe they had to have foreign exchange, and so oil was exported, perhaps a little more abruptly than would otherwise have happened, but much later than if they had operated on old-fashioned private-enterprise principles in the first place.

Any respectable discussion of the Soviet oil export drive starts with the basic fact that, at present prices, oil finding, development, production, and export are a rational, profitable activity for the Russians to undertake. True, we know very little about the costs of the oil. In particular, such scanty facts as we have on permeability of four big oil fields (in millidarcies, respectively 150–500; 30–40; 1,000; 280), suggest that development-production costs are not unusually low,[96] but this is hardly weighty evidence.

But if we hold fast to marginal rather than average costs, we can see that the old high-cost oil fields in the south have become a valuable asset. There is no question of further development, or of building new pipelines. But the lifting cost in the different Azerbaijan fields plus the current operating cost of shipment through old small-diameter pipelines is well under a dollar a barrel, and it is being sold for more than that. On any principle of bourgeois economics, this makes sense. It did not make sense when the oil was needed inland, and its true cost to the Soviet economy was not that of extraction but of the losses imposed by not having it. But that condition has ceased to exist because of the discovery of newer fields, at much lower costs, and closer to consuming areas. Hence the old higher value has vanished, and today the constraint is only the current resources used to bring up the oil and put it aboard the tanker. These old oil fields are obviously a wasting asset; the prospects of future Soviet exports are governed by the costs of developing (and probably even of exploring) in the new areas, plus the cost of shipment through new pipelines. Here is

[96] Ebel, *op. cit.* (Note 7), pp. 77–98. *Cf.* J. Flandrin and J. Chappelle, *op. cit.* (Note 47), p. 22; 1,000 millidarcies is considered very good, 100–1000, good, below 100, poor. *Cf.* Charles E. Webber, "Estimation of Primary Reserves Discovered," in Graham B. Moody, *Petroleum Exploration Handbook* (New York: McGraw-Hill, 1961), Chapter 25, table 25-v, presenting a random sample of thirty-two reservoirs, of which seven were over 1,000, eighteen from 100–1000, and seven below 100.

where we know least. But finding costs, which do enter into long-run marginal costs, tend to be low because they are incurred jointly by oil and gas. This basic advantage over Middle Eastern oil will not soon disappear; nor will the better location for shipment to Northern Europe. If Middle East long-run marginal costs are in the neighborhood of 17 cents per barrel, which Sheikh Abdullah Tariki thought to be the average cost of all crude there,[97] and Soviet costs, even with the gas finds, are as much as four times as high, or 68 cents,[98] the net disadvantage is only 35 cents because of an approximate 33-cent freight advantage. (Freight costs are reckoned at current discounted term charter rates of about Scale less 45 per cent; if we used higher rates, such as those of the Average Freight Rate Assessment [AFRA], the advantage would be much larger.)

As for Soviet prices, it ought to be easier today to find acceptance for the proposition that they are set low enough to make the sale, and no lower.[99] It should have occasioned no surprise that the Soviets were repeatedly underbid in 1962, and in 1963 were complaining that the international companies were practicing "artificial competition" and meanly underselling; that when an offer was made to take ships for oil, the deal was not to be sweetened by "cut prices" for the oil; that a "cutthroat" price war by U.S. oil companies was said to be damaging all sellers.[100] How familiar it all sounds to anyone who studies markets in capitalist economies!

Much is made, and rightly, of the wide discrepancy between prices to members of the Soviet bloc and prices to buyers outside. That prices to bloc members are always part of a bilateral trade deal may mean that the apparently very high prices are really lower — or really higher. So far, at least, we cannot tell. Such evidence as exists indicates very great discrimination in Soviet export prices. But surely this is the only conduct to be expected of a rational monopolist who meets competitive offers when he must and otherwise exacts a high price. The notion that these high prices "subsidize" and hence make possible the low prices to non-Soviet buyers is unfounded. The sales to non-bloc buyers are well worth making because they are well above costs, and the sales to Soviet-bloc buyers even

[97] *World Oil*, Vol. 153 (October 1961), p. 12.

[98] Average Soviet costs, including finding and developing, are estimated at 64–68 cents in 1960. (National Petroleum Council, *op. cit.* [Note 36], I, p. 63.) Natural gas costs are estimated around 2½ cents per mcf. The figures must be treated with great caution, if indeed used at all, since they are not explained.

[99] SPNG, *op. cit.* (Note 3), pp. 107–11.

[100] *Platt's Oilgram News Service,* February 15, 28, March 7, 11, 1963; *Platt's Oilgram Price Service,* February 12, 1963.

more worth making because they are even further above costs. This is the simplest theory and it fits the facts. There is of course plenty of price discrimination in the non-Soviet industry, but here it expresses not a single state monopoly but a mixture of competition and control.

As for prices to the non-Soviet world, we have perhaps heard a bit too much of the $1.00 per barrel f.o.b. the Black Sea on sales to Italy. First, I have never seen official or other authority for that figure and wonder if it has not achieved recognition by repetition.[101] Second, assuming authenticity, it was a single transaction, made in 1960, and it is simply incorrect to say that the U.S.S.R. is "today" selling at that price. It is the same error, though not nearly as bad, as saying that natural gas is sold "today" in the United States at 5 or 10 cents per mcf, under contracts made years ago. Third, since we do not know the value of the pipe and other Italian products delivered in return, we cannot be too sure of the true price. And finally, as of 1960, average prices to Italy were far above that figure, so that if prices to other buyers were at substantial discounts, the alleged dollar price seems impossible. Soviet prices to non-Soviet nations for that year are worth a brief glance:[102]

Overseas destination	F.O.B. price ($/bbl.)	Equivalent Persian Gulf (or Caribbean) price ($/bbl.)
Brazil	1.73	[1]1.86
Cuba	1.54	[1]2.01
Egypt	1.63	[2]1.37
Finland	1.72	1.49
France	1.60	1.27
W. Germany	1.38	1.05
Greece	1.79	1.46
Italy	1.42	1.10
Japan	1.34	1.70
Morocco	1.83	1.50
Yugoslavia	2.27	[2]1.95

[1] Caribbean equivalent.
[2] Bilateral deals involved.

[101] *Petroleum Press Service,* Vol. 27 (1960), p. 418, says only that the price was believed "advantageous." Nor is it mentioned in *Petroleum Press Service,* Vol. 28 (1961), pp. 8, 124.

[102] Prices, from Trade Statistics of the U.S.S.R. (*Vneshniya Torgovlia SSSR*), quoted in *Oil and Gas Journal,* December 11, 1961, p. 87. See also *Petroleum Press Service,* Vol. 29 (1962), p. 27. Freight disadvantage calculated at Scale less 45 per cent and 12-cent Suez toll where applicable.

Assuming a 34° crude, Brazilian and Cuban refineries paid 80 cents to $1.00 under Venezuelan posted prices; assuming a 27° crude, it was about 66 to 86 cents discount, which is above but not far above current discounted prices. As for the three biggest buyers — Germany, Italy, and Japan — the price is nearly uniform for the three, which would be expected under keen bargaining when the sales are large and regular rather than spot or filler-in, as with France. The equivalent Persian Gulf prices for Germany and Italy were probably below most discounted prices to arm's-length buyers; if so, one would expect further non-Soviet discounting in 1961 and 1962, and also some stiffening of Russian offers as the two price levels approached one another, as seems to have happened.

All this makes no sense if political ends are really paramount, and presents few problems if we treat it as a profit-seeking venture by the Russians. Surely their attempts, starting late in 1961, to raise prices — and their occasional losses of contracts — are only consistent with a seller trying to make the most of his every bargain and now and then overreaching himself. Since the Russian market in Europe is a politically limited share of the governments and independents, they cannot, for the time being, increase their sales by further price-cutting. Hence they would indeed not cut further, they might even raise a bit if profit were their aim; which is what they have done.

Summing up: exports are profitable business for the Russians, even at lower than present price levels. They flattened out in 1962, but I doubt that this lack of trend will long continue. But I would also suggest that the Soviet Union *for both political and economic reasons* desires a new and more stable commodity agreement to maintain prices. They want to be charter members of the new club, on their terms.

We come now to the third element in the change since Suez, and it is not altogether independent of the other two. The independent refiners are again an important part of the landscape. Some of them are private, like Petrofina, which from 1954 to 1960 tripled its sales and its crude deficit alike, preferring to supply largely through term contracts.[103] Some were government enterprises, and some were quasi-government, notably the late Enrico Mattei's Ente Nazionale Idrocarburi (ENI).[104] Or a government might bargain on behalf of its refining industry, as did India. But

[103] *Oil and Gas International*, March, 1961, pp. 18–21.
[104] In 1961, 62 per cent of Soviet crude and 20 per cent of product exports went to governments; non-integrated refiners took 34 and 51 per cent; "others," 4 and 29 per cent. (National Petroleum Council, *op. cit.* [Note 36.])

what all these enterprises had in common was independence from the producing companies, and the ability to do arm's-length bargaining. By selling finished products at prices not too far below those of integrated companies, which reflected the high posted price of crude, and yet buying at discount prices, these refiners were able to expand sales and market share; eventually they brought product prices down.

Take the most quickly expanding product, fuel oil, in the three most quickly expanding markets: Germany, Italy, and Japan. In such markets one expects prices to be most buoyant, yet reflection enables us to see that here the price comes under the greatest downward strain. Because none of the established concerns can be sure of what the others are doing, and because rewards for success in getting and keeping the market share — and penalties for losing it — are the greatest, it is hardest to maintain a given price. Furthermore, since fuel oil distribution, unlike gasoline, is relatively easy to enter, independents were soon playing a significant if minor part. And their uncontrolled capacity was soon playing its traditional role. Thus the resounding paradox that *the rise in the price of coal in the mid-50's, increasing the competitive advantage of oil, caused the price of oil not to firm up but to collapse.* By the end of 1957, the price of heavy fuel oil in Germany, Italy, Belgium, the Netherlands, and France had settled back to a little above the pre-Suez level. Nor did quoted prices fall precipitately; but discounting started early in 1958, in Germany, and by late 1959 effective prices had fallen roughly by 40 per cent, to a level where they have remained more or less stable.[105] (France is an exception, since the industry is so tightly controlled there; and indeed the discrepancy is a constant source of tension within the European Economic Community.)[106] Gasoline was for a long time a safer product, but the rising demand for fuel oil brought a great deal of gasoline into the market (which we might well remember the next time we hear fuel oil called "a mere by-product"), at the same time that independent refiner-marketers were also coming in.[107]

Had the U.S. crude oil market been open to substantial imports around 1950, the presence of large refiners independent of Middle East and Venezuelan production would have brought the price down then, some eight

[105] *Oil and Gas International,* December, 1961, pp. 24–27; Walter J. Levy, *Current and Prospective Developments in World Oil* (Zug, Switzerland: Bundesverband Deutscher Industrie, 1961), pp. 1–35–40.

[106] *Cf.* Alain Murcier, "La Politique Energétique Française à l'Epreuve du Marché Commun," *Le Monde,* September 13, 14, 1962.

[107] *Petroleum Press Service,* Vol. 28 (1961), p. 163; and *Oil and Gas International,* November, 1961, p. 38, and July, 1962, p. 59.

or nine years earlier. For it would have meant that a group of large buyers were able to shop around and to offer large and profitable outlets. To the extent that such outlets open up here and there in the world, it becomes more difficult to support the current price level.

Thus the post-Suez history may be summed up by saying that the growth of oil volume outside the vertically integrated companies, not restricted by product sales, reacted back upon those companies: some independence in buying and selling mobilized, though it did not cause, the huge and growing excess capacity in the international oil trade and made it bear down upon the price. It is not easy and perhaps it is not correct to reduce all the colorful parade of events to the gray theory of some slippages in the market structure. But to blame the Russians or the late Signor Mattei for sagging prices comes perilously close to — I will not say amounts to the same thing as — blaming the messenger for the bad news he brings. Nor does one belittle any bold actor on the business scene by recalling what Justice Holmes said: "Effort is the means by which the inevitable comes to pass."

The Current World Oil Outlook

Having dwelt at great length on the general economics and recent history of the industry, we can now analyze the outlook for world oil. The preparation, however lengthy, has been necessary, I believe, to understand the problems as they exist today.

The short- and long-run prospect for the price of oil may serve to bring various parts of the problem into focus and show the relations among them. I propose first to look at basic supply-demand factors, then at the market structure, since they may conceivably push in two opposite directions. As we have seen, the swift growth of demand in Europe and Japan acted to push the price up, but it also acted to draw in more competition and thereby push the price down; and the second influence was stronger than the first.

The Supply-Demand Factors

The general consensus can be summarily stated: by 1975, according to Levy and Lipton,[108] world non-Soviet demand will be around 15 billion barrels annually, twice the current level. For this rather stupendous con-

---

[108] Levy and Lipton, *op. cit.* (Note 63).

sumption, present world reserves of 284 billion will be hardly more than comfortable. As inventories become much smaller relative to production, replacement cost will rise from its present zero level. Furthermore, it would be imprudent to expect any more complexes of fields like those in the Middle East. Hence in little longer time than that which separates us from the installation of the Trans-Arabian pipeline, the present oversupply will be history. Moreover, not only will finding cost reappear, but it will be a higher finding cost than it is today, and there will also be higher development-production cost. Therefore long-run marginal costs must presently start picking up, and prices with them. The pressure of increasing demand, it is thus concluded, will eventually absorb the present excess capacity and cause a hardening of prices.

Such is the consensus. But I think this expectation is basically wrong. Unless demand turns out to be much greater than is foreseen, the outlook is for continuing surplus. In short, the supply function for the period 1962–75 looks now to be lower than that for 1962, so much lower that on balance the marginal cost and the shadow competitive price may be if anything lower than they are today. (See Figure 1, page 36.) If annual non-Soviet consumption increases linearly from 7.3 billion barrels in 1962 to 15 billion in 1975, total consumption in that period will be approximately 142 billion barrels. Today, published reserves in the non-Soviet world are about 284 billion barrels.[109] But we must recognize how expansible a figure this is. In the United States reserves have continued to grow by horizontal and vertical boundary extension and by new methods to increase per cent of recovery; the growth has been "achieved with negligible reliance on major new discoveries."[110] The National Petroleum Council points out that proved reserves discovered in new fields and pools in 1937–44 were currently given at 3.9 billion barrels, but by 1944, original reserves in those same fields were already figured at 10.6 billion, and in 1959, at 17.6 billion or two-thirds higher. If we take the 1945 estimates of U.S. reserves, which on the average were in fields aged 12–14 years, and compare them with 1960 estimates of original reserves in those same fields, the latter are 50 per cent higher than the former. Even eliminating the 1940–44 period, the increase is 45 per cent.

I see no reason to suppose that the basic physical and technological factors are any different in or out of the United States. The corresponding growth abroad will, just as in the United States, "not take place automatically with the passage of time, but [will be] . . . the direct result of fur-

---

[109] *Oil and Gas Journal,* December 31, 1962, p. 89.
[110] E. V. Corps, *Institute of Petroleum Review,* Vol. 15 (1961), pp. 269, 271.

ther drilling, the development of additional information, and the application of improved recovery procedures."[111] That is to say, the supplies are available at something a little higher or lower than current development costs, which are so low as to be almost lost in freight rates. If, therefore, we apply an increase factor of one-third to the United States and one-half to the rest of the non-Soviet world, we may guess that reserves in deposits *already discovered* at the end of 1962 are around 421 billion barrels. Subtracting the 142 billion consumed through 1975, we are left with 279 billion, or nineteen years' supply of the estimated 1975 annual consumption. It would appear, then, that there is really enough oil on hand to take care of all demand in the interim, at development costs little different from today's, with enough left over for at least an adequate start in whatever direction may be indicated after 1975. Perhaps after 1975 the prospect will be for greater scarcity; it seems futile to guess.[112] (In particular, we need and make no assumption about ultimate reserves or the "resource base.")

For the interim, these estimates of 421 billions-plus are rough indeed, and the only excuse for presenting them is that for forecasting they are nearer to the truth than the published reserves — far less precise, far more accurate. In point of fact, supply should be even greater than the estimates indicate. First, they take no account of new discoveries. Middle East discovery effort has neglected all but the most obvious structures, and perhaps the use of new methods will offset the higher cost of looking for others. We may therefore find at least one new Middle East right in the old one. Then there are other areas. It is the total laid-down cost of crude oil at a given market which determines the cheapest source. Judging from a little information just released by a big Libyan operator, and by the daily producing rates of the wells operating there, I would guess that

---

[111] National Petroleum Council, *Proved Reserves and Productive Capacity of Crude Oil, Natural Gas and Natural Gas Liquids* (Washington, 1961), pp. 14–20. Anibal R. Martinez, "Prediction Technique Applicable to the Venezuelan Oil Industry" (Second Arab Petroleum Congress, 1960), p. 14, applies a 50 per cent factor to Venezuela. See also Vincent C. Illing, "Factors which Control the Assessment of World Resources of Oil and Natural Gas" (Sixth World Power Conference, Paper 185, I. 1/2), p. 19: "No doubt this process [assessment of reserves] is continuing in many of these Middle East fields at the present time." My guess, for what it may be worth, is that a 150 per cent factor is much too low. See *Report to the Joint Committee on Atomic Energy, op. cit.* (Note 27), p. 1544, where the Bureau of Mines uses a factor of 300 per cent, for a concept perhaps a little wider than this.

[112] Illing (*op. cit.* [Note 111] p. 22) is confident of plenty "for at least a half century ahead, in spite of increasing consumption. Further than that we cannot see, for the future will involve fields not yet discovered. . . ."

the production-development cost of Libyan oil is only about 15 cents higher per barrel than Middle East. But the oil runs, on the average, about eight degrees higher, which even today ought to be worth at least 10 cents, and the freight advantage is around 38 cents. Hence for the European market, Libyan oil is cheaper, on balance, by about 33 cents.[113] Hence it makes good sense to explore and develop Libya even in the face of Middle East competition entirely aside from the perhaps temporary advantage of paying royalties on the basis of actual, not posted, prices. The opinion often heard in the trade that operators in Libya have found their investment unprofitable and hence must sell at unprofitable prices, seems ill-founded, at least on the basis of the information that is publicly available.

There are other Libyas, but even if there were not a great deal of exploration would take place for purely economic reasons. Large amounts will be found, but we cannot predict how large they will be relative to existing deposits.

The second reason for thinking petroleum resources are greater than the estimated 421 billion barrels is the existence of natural gas, particularly non-associated gas. It has been intensively sought only in Canada, the United States and the U.S.S.R.; in the first two countries certainly, and in the last possibly, its reserves exceed oil in heat content. It is not altogether reckless, I think, to expect it at least to come near equality in other areas where it has not yet been looked for.[114] Because of high transport cost, gas is less important economically than physically, but there are plenty of pipelines to be built, and commercial transport of liquid methane is not even in its infancy — it is still *in utero*. Moreover, some rethinking will have to be done about gas reserve location, even in highly faulted old Europe. The reserves of Lacq and Slochteren are already well over twice European oil reserves (at roughly 24 trillion cubic feet, they equate to about 4 billion barrels, as against only 1.8 billion in oil reserves). Slochteren reserves are probably more valuable, because of location and availability in high-end uses, than a 6-billion-barrel field in the Middle East. And its indirect effect may possibly exceed the direct, for it appears to lie on a structure extending under the shallow North Sea to England, where a small gas discovery, itself of no importance, was

[113] See *Petroleum Intelligence Weekly*, February 18, 1963, p. 1; *Oil and Gas Journal*, December 31, 1962. The average daily production rates are understated there because the region is rapidly developing. Average Middle East oil is assumed to be 31°, Libyan 39°. Freight is assumed as Scale less 45 per cent.
[114] *Cf.* SPNG, *op. cit.* (Note 3) and the estimates of Lewis G. Weeks in *Oil and Gas Journal*, March 12, 1962, p. 74.

made some years ago. If gas was formed and accumulated at the ends of a structure so large, it is hard to believe that the rest of the structure is barren. A group will test that hopeful possibility before long.[115]

Natural gas is of course of peculiar importance because it is a joint product with crude oil; therefore the more gas that is found, the more oil is available at low marginal cost. But even if it were an altogether unrelated product, cheap gas available in greater and greater supplies will displace higher-cost oil and push us down upon the lower-cost supply. This holds true of any substitute.

Nuclear power, which has for so long been a thing of promise but not performance, may be starting its commercial life soon in such disfavored areas as New England, where nuclear power is expected to be as cheap as conventional by 1967.[116]

The Luxembourg-Brussels working party expects nuclear energy to be competitive with heavy fuel oil at $2.07 to $2.47 per barrel, and it projects a price of $2.50 to $2.80 delivered at Rotterdam.[117] I disagree with the forecast (see below, p. 118 ff.), but if it is believed, it will be acted upon, and nuclear power will absorb some of the demand which otherwise would be met by coal and oil. Under U.S. conditions, which probably are little different from elsewhere, costs have been calculated on the basis of 7 and of 14 per cent fixed charge rates for a very wide range of plant sizes. If we take the 7 per cent rate as more likely to be used in practice, and the 80 per cent capacity factor because a nuclear plant will inevitably take the base load, the result is truly striking. With heavy fuel oil at $2.20 per barrel or more, practically any size of nuclear plant will produce electricity more cheaply; with fuel oil below $1.60, not even the largest plant will.[118] Thus the whole range between upper and lower limits of economic feasibility about coincides with the spread of f.o.b. fuel oil

[115] On Slochteren, see *Petroleum Intelligence Weekly,* July 23, 1962, p. 5, and February 25, 1963, p. 1; but see also *Oil and Gas Journal,* July 2, p. 82, and July 23, 1962, p. 66. On the North Sea search, see *Petroleum Intelligence Weekly,* February 25, 1963, p. 1, and *Platt's Oilgram News Service,* same date, p. 4. What will one eventually say about "the cost" of either the English gas, or Slochteren gas, or North Sea gas?

[116] *New York Times,* November 27, 1962, reporting the proceedings of the Atomic Industrial Forum.

[117] *Etude sur les Perspectives Energétiques à Long Terme de la Communauté Européenne* (Document No. 6600/3/62f), p. 95.

[118] Frank K. Pittman and U. M. Staebler, "Nuclear Power Technology and Costs," in Vol. I, *Natural Resources — Energy, Water and River Basin Development,* U.S. papers prepared for the United Nations Conference on the Application of Science and Technology for the Benefit of the Less Developed Areas (Washington: Government Printing Office, 1963) pp. 163–72.

prices today, from about \$1.50 in the Middle East to about \$2.06 on the U.S. East Coast.[119] In view of general expectations, whether right or wrong, that prices of crude oil and products are going to rise, there is little doubt that nuclear plants are on the way in unless there is an unexpected fall in heavy fuel oil prices. Thus the market for oil will be further narrowed, particularly for the heavy grades which are now in strong demand.

In fine, some optimistic but not foolish assumptions about natural gas and nuclear energy would mean no need for any but the cheapest oil, so that long-run marginal cost might fall quite appreciably between now and 1975. It is safe to conclude that it will not rise. The competitive pressure on prices will not be any less.

Market Structure: General Considerations

The previous discussion might be summed up by saying that if the price of oil today were set simply by competition, we would probably, though far from certainly, need to look for a mild long-term decrease. But the price as it is will most likely continue to generate further increases in reserves and further excess capacity. This is, of course, subject to the basic indeterminacy discussed earlier. Large amounts of money may be spent to no purpose, but they will be spent. Outside the United States and Venezuela, despite the erosion of prices since 1957, the finding effort has continued with little letup. "Oil reserves continue to grow because the boards of directors of oil companies decide that they should grow."[120] Refiners with crude deficits, like Shell and Indiana Standard, have recently gambled in the Persian Gulf (Indiana apparently with great success) because they expect to get crude more cheaply that way than they can buy it even at discounted prices — and governments favor them because they have sales outlets. Companies with crude surpluses also continue to search. Sometimes they hope to get lower-cost crude for some particular market, such as Australasia. Sometimes they seek greater diversification as insurance against losing their present holdings.

Moreover, if a new field is found, it may for political reasons obtain a kind of pre-emptive right over some portion of the world market, because

---

[119] The low of \$1.50 represents a 15-cent discount off the Ras Tanura posted price, while the high represents the undiscounted Boston price. The delivered Northern Europe price is higher as of March 15, 1963, but will come down by the summer of 1963 to more normal levels.

[120] A. A. Fitch, in *Institute of Petroleum Review*, Vol. 15 (1961), p. 305. Wells drilling, mid-1961, were higher than in mid-1957 for the Middle East, Asia, and Africa.

the older regions will acquiesce in making room for some at least of the new source, whereas they would not do so for each other. Hence established producers may find it worth spending more money to find new crude, because there is a chance of selling it at a profit, whereas they cannot sell more of the old. And finally, governments are increasingly searching or subsidizing the search either because they hope for oil cheaper than at present-day prices, or hope to save foreign exchange, or for other reasons. Chance alone guarantees that there will at least be a substantial increment to reserves.

The continued search outside the old concessions also reminds us that this matter of division of the markets among producing countries is one of the most delicate of all. Where production is near capacity, a petroleum operator is governed by the comparison between expected price and expected cost. If any given project is not expected to pay, it is not undertaken, and that ends the matter. The division of markets among production centers takes no special planning; it comes about by the operator's going as far as he can in each country, to the point where price cuts off further expansion, in accordance with incremental (not average) costs. Hence a low-cost area with only some small remaining pools available would be passed over in favor of a higher-cost area, which has better remaining prospects. In any case, the decisions stay within the sphere of ordinary profit-making business management.

But consider a company operating in two countries. In both places, because of excess capacity, plenty of new oil could be developed at unit cost less than current price. Then the decision to produce this much in *A* and so much in *B* may not turn at all on relative costs, but rather on political considerations and pressures. The petroleum operator finds himself willy-nilly making, in effect even though not in intent, decisions about *A*'s balance-of-payments difficulties versus *B*'s development needs; while *C* insists that its oil is also profitable, and that it deserves a better share by reason of past production or exports, or present reserves, or some other reason. Under excess capacity, reasons are as plentiful as blackberries.

Will Concession Revisions Put Up Prices?

It is widely expected that as concessions are revised to give governments more royalties (including also taxes and other payments), this increased "cost" will also push up the price of crude oil. Revisions are generally expected, though I am not competent to say that they have or have not any basis in law. As was pointed out earlier (pages 75–76), it is axiomatic in the finding of petroleum that a good discovery means a concessionaire who is earning a big differential and horizon rent, and a dissatisfied landlord who wishes he had held out for more. From the moment oil was found, the bargaining position of the concessionaire was less and that of the host government was greater. More recently, the concessionaire's power of disposal has decreased because of independent refiner-marketers, excess capacity, and the possibility of other concerns doing exploration and development; and so the basic economics of petroleum production explains the paradox that new sources of suppy, such as those of North Africa and the Soviet Union, far from weakening the bargaining power of the old host governments, actually strengthen it. The entry of new concessionaires strengthens it also.

Certainly it is over the last few years of oversupply that the tendency toward higher government take has been most visible. The upper limit is the whole producers' rent, leaving the companies enough of a good management fee to keep them from leaving. The lower limit is zero, since the landlord with no alternative use for the land will not withdraw it from oil extraction. But it is a safe guess that neither party will suffer himself to be pushed to his maximum limit.

A year ago, the UN General Assembly urged member nations:

> To pursue policies designed to ensure to the developing countries an equitable share of earnings from the extraction and marketing of their natural resources by foreign capital in accordance with the generally accepted reasonable earnings on invested capital; . . .[121]

Presumably there would be some disagreement over what was meant by the "generally accepted reasonable earnings on invested capital" to which profits were to be limited. Undoubtedly some countries would consider it as a bare management fee for development and production, and some only for production; others, for some allowance for reproduction cost, etc. But it seems safe to say that the resolution goes further toward removing the operator's rent than the government's. The trouble is that each side's bargaining power is so ill-defined that it is hard for either side to see the other's; rent is that kind of object. Hence the anxiety one cannot help but feel when reading of the progress of current company-gov-

---

[121] UN General Assembly, Report of the Economic and Social Council, *Economic Development of Under-Developed Countries. Questions Relating to International Trade and Commodities, etc.* (Report of the Second Committee) A/5056, December 18, 1961, pp. 20, 43, 56. The resolution was adopted December 19, 1961. See A/RES/1710 (XVI), January 5, 1962, p. 2.

ernment discussions.[122] However doubtful the economic content of distinctions drawn by the Organization of Petroleum Exporting Countries (OPEC) between royalties and income taxes, etc.,[123] it is better to have two points on the agenda than one, and better four than two. For it gives the parties a chance to understand each other and get some notion of how far any revision can go; it gives each side a chance to withdraw gracefully from one position in return for some real or fancied concession on some other point.

Yet granting that government take is on the increase and that the current split is 60–40, not 50–50, one may ask why this should tend to raise prices. Since Suez the government's take has increased, yet prices have quite substantially decreased. Perhaps the idea that every expense is a cost which gets automatically passed on as a price could only seem so self-evident after two decades of inflation and the mythology of "administered prices" which could forever be pushed up if you only wished hard enough. Unfortunately, when people believe a myth they act on it, and their subsequent education can be painful to them and others.[124]

At first sight there would seem to be no effect on price in any arrangement for sharing profits; we would seem to be confusing cause with effect. If prices and costs are such that the profit per barrel is, say, $1.00, then 50–50 will give each party 50 cents, 70–30 will give one 70 cents and the other 30 etc. If profit sank from $1.00 to 10 cents per barrel, the profit shares would all shed one zero, and that would be all. Now, anyone who urged this today would probably be viewed as rather naive and ill-informed. The only possible explanation is that profit-sharing does not in fact exist any more, having been replaced by some kind of minimum per-barrel guarantee, which a producing company must regard as a cost. There are two important difficulties here. First, nobody outside a company knows just what is the minimum. (Presumably the oil companies

---

[122] If I understand the companies' position, it is that there are no negotiations in progress, in any normal sense. Governments have suggested modification in the agreements, but the companies are free to reject them because the existing concessions have the force of law, and therefore the companies will consider modification of agreements only when unforeseen events bring about inequities or distortions related to the original intent of the parties. Whether this position is compatible with the recent changes in the Aramco concession, and accounting methods, is an interesting question.

[123] See OPEC Resolutions IV. 33 and IV. 34; and the Explanatory Memoranda reprinted in *Petroleum Intelligence Weekly,* July 30, 1962; and *Platt's Oilgram News Service,* August 7, 1962. No opinion is expressed on the legal validity of such distinction.

[124] *Cf.* M. A. Adelman, "Steel, Administered Prices, and Inflation," *Quarterly Journal of Economics,* Vol. 15 (1961), pp. 16–40.

have reckoned their minima, and yet I wonder what force these will have if a real crisis arrives — much as one thinks of the war plans of a general staff.) Secondly, a government's rent or royalty is not a cost, and past the short run it is not going to behave like one, even if we call it a cost and dress it to look like one. If people make commitments based on this misconception, just as if they build houses upon the sand, they are headed for trouble.

In theory, the landlord's share of profit is not a cost, and has no effect on the price because it has no effect on supply. A development is undertaken if it promises at least some profit over and above the costs, including the necessary minimum return on investment. The landlord may get some or all of the excess, but he cannot take any more or there will be no project. Therefore, to the extent that the landlord is well informed and follows his own interest, his rent has no effect on what is produced and offered on the market, and no revision of terms to give him a bigger percentage will have an effect on supply and price. However, this may be obscured when the rent is a per-barrel royalty, and hence we take this more difficult case.

Let us suppose the following: that a host government decides, in substance or even in form, that it will accept no less than 75-cents-per-barrel royalties (including associated payments); that development-extraction cost of a given deposit is not less than 15 cents per barrel; that the operator can get a long-term contract at a price no higher than $1.00 because the buyer can do as well elsewhere; and that a profit of 10 cents per barrel would not be a sufficient return to the operator development investment, but that at 20 cents it would pay. If the facts are as stated here, it is in the government's interest to accept a lower royalty, because either they get 55 cents on a large number of barrels, with no investment or risk, or else they get nothing.

The situation is quite different from what it would be if, say, a distorted and broken formation made expected development costs, exclusive of royalty, 90 cents per barrel. The project could not pay, and there would be nothing to negotiate. But on the conditions stated here, there would be an inducement, and if one company or government passed it up, others might pick it up. To call both kinds of payments "costs" is to misunderstand or hide the problem. For it is in the interest of the host government to approve, though it might want to disguise the fact in order not to call other royalties into question.

But if the government suspects that the facts are not as stated, then it may ask for proof, or simply refuse. A company proposal for more offtake at a lower price and royalty may look like — and, for all I know, may be — a deceptive way of stopping the company's profit erosion. Or, the government may believe the facts to be as stated, but hope that other governments will co-operate in refusing to approve any contract at so low a price, so that the buyer will have no outside alternative and be willing to pay a higher price. A government will not permit its per-barrel royalties to drop if it can be avoided, and it only becomes necessary if buyers have an alternative source of supply, i.e., only if the sellers cannot hold the line. The governments are obviously watchful that this should not happen. The problem is not costs but communication, or control of the offers of rivals, or both. Once we are rid of the illusion that payments to a landlord or sovereign are "costs" we can see a complicated situation for what it is.

Some reflection on the non-cost nature of payments to the landlord shows that the competitive advantage, which may be substantial, of not paying any royalty really reduces to the lack of any communications problem. For, so long as any profit expected after rent or royalty is less than enough to induce a private company to make the investment, it is to the landlord's benefit to take a lower royalty. For his alternative is no operation, and no royalty. The landlord, as residual claimant, simply gets what is left, much or little.

To complicate the matter further, the return to the operator, while it cannot be a pure rent, may yet contain large amounts of rent. In the above example, if the project was worth undertaking at 20 cents, the operator was better off taking that return than not. Hence, if the old royalty had been less than 55 cents, the government could, on the same reasoning, get its share *up* to that figure.

One is struck by the difficulty of getting the considerations involved, the supply-demand factors which determine both sides' bargaining power, into quantitative terms. The greater the gap between cost and price, the greater the total rent, and the more there is for the parties to negotiate, and possibly disagree on. But what makes the situation delicate is that the information is very imprecise, so that neither party knows how far the other is willing to go if he must. Anyone attempting to guess how far profit sharing will diverge from 50–50 needs to guess at both economics and communications; I would rather state the question than try to answer it. But the warnings we hear nowadays to both parties to proceed carefully are no mere pious cant; they reflect the difficulties inherent in the subject.

Summing up: in order to raise or maintain the price of oil, it is necessary to insure unity among the sellers, such that none will offer any at less than the agreed-on price. If this cannot be done, then it is impossible to raise the price by raising royalties and rents. But if it can be done, then all that now matters is how high the price can profitably be raised. *The whole problem of rents and royalties is superfluous to the determination of price.*

In my opinion, the governments associated in OPEC recognize this principle. For they have insisted from the beginning on the need for high posted and actual prices as providing a bigger fund out of which rents may be paid, and they do not seem to be under the illusion that bigger payments to them are merely a cost to be passed on.

Two suggestions may be in order for the discussions which began in the fall of 1962. The first is that the royalty agreements should not specify any per-barrel amount. It is one thing to start with that as an objective, and then translate it into some set of percentage or other terms to which the parties must adhere; but it would be a dangerous mistake to make it an explicit agreement, because this would require the companies to do something they cannot do, and which perhaps even the governments in concert cannot do.[125] The French word for disappointment is *déception,* and indeed the two ideas are close. A feeling by the governments that they have been fooled will not make future relations any easier. In the current state of ignorance, a percentage has an inherent flexibility which the parties, in my opinion, simply cannot do without. In fact, even a uniform per cent is probably too rigid.

The second point is that the more the governments get and the closer the companies are pushed to the incompressible management fee, the more have the governments taken over the price decisions. The more of the profits they take, the more of the problems they have. Governments only stepped front and center in late 1960, like the U.S. government imposing mandatory import controls: exercising openly a power that had always backstopped the price but which proved insufficient as the pressure increased.

When OPEC had just been organized, I wrote that it "obviously . . . will stand or fall by its ability to control total output, and also to establish some effective prearranged sharing of markets."[126] Clearly I must retract that first word; it is not obvious at all, judging by the way that prorationing and market sharing have died out of the discussion since then. But I think the rest of the sentence still holds good. If the allocation of markets

---

[125] This would seem to be in opposition to the suggestion in *The Economist* (October 6, 1962, p. 69) that the producing countries be guaranteed a minimum per-barrel royalty, while prices should be left to the play of market forces.

[126] SPNG, *op. cit.* (Note 3), p. 83; the original draft was written in 1960.

is not to be done by price acting on relative marginal costs, it must now be done consciously and explicitly. Account must be taken of the diversity of costs among producing areas, such that a given price is much more favorable to one than to another, and some means of compensation must be found. If there is nothing but a high price, or a high per-barrel guarantee to every producing government, every one would be constantly confronted with the knowledge that there was considerable additional profit to be made by shading the price — preferably, of course, hiding the reduction in some of the many other terms of the bargain, such as freight. Most of the governments most of the time would doubtless resist the temptation to make a mutually profitable deal with a concessionaire. But that is not enough under great excess capacity. It takes only one, either fearing that it is being left out, or resentful of an unduly low share, or badly pressured by a treasury deficit or a balance-of-payments problem, to start the stampede to the exit. Unless there is a market sharing agreement, which will be adhered to, the price cannot be held no matter how many people sign.

The Consuming Countries, in General

From the foregoing, one might expect a forecast of a decline in the price of oil, but this is uncertain. I do, indeed, believe that the pressure on price will increase, but so will the resistance, and I have no way of telling which force will be greater. As in the United States, where it seemed a foregone conclusion that imports would greatly increase sometime after 1950, but where every threatened break called forth stronger resistance, the same kind of challenge and response is to be seen in world oil. The emergence of the producing governments is the most important challenge thus far. But although the consuming countries could, if they wished, bring the price down, they will not try to do so, at least over the near term. The United States is by far the most important factor. It is clear after the Kennedy-Kerr agreement[127] that no large flow to the United States will occur, bringing with it disruptive effect experienced in Western Europe and Japan. Furthermore, the maintenance of a high level of U.S. domestic prices is the more difficult the higher it is above world price levels. Hence the influence of this country will be exerted in favor of keeping up the world price.

[127] *Wall Street Journal,* October 30, 1962, p. 2. *The Economist,* in its "American Survey" (September 22, 1962, p. 1099), states that the agreement runs through 1968, but the correspondent's cliché-spangled prejudice against the oil industry does not make the report more credible.

The underdeveloped countries are extremely concerned with price maintenance for primary commodities: it was incorporated in the UN resolution noted earlier, and has been repeatedly and forcibly demanded since then, at all official and non-official levels. The former Council chairman of the Food and Agriculture Organization has called for it as part of the world-wide struggle against hunger: "We must de-mystify the problem. . . . We must have done with neo-colonialism and must re-establish trade equilibrium, constantly degraded by the fall in the prices of primary materials."[128] The 1964 United Nations conference on trade problems will demand greater economic equality, to be achieved by price supports. The United States and Britain agree with this aim: President Kennedy has called for support of primary product prices as a basic part of this country's foreign economic policy, and the world coffee agreement fits the action to the word. Sir Eric Roll, Edward Heath's assistant in the recently lapsed Common Market negotiations, has called for more such agreements. The Council of Ministers of the Organization for Economic Cooperation and Development (OECD) has urged "concerted policies" to "increase the receipts [of] the less developed nations [from] their exports, as much from basic raw products as manufactured goods."[129] The Soviet Union had for some time been in favor of a world economic conference for this purpose. As a petroleum exporter, obviously hoping to export much more, and trying for the allegiance of the underdeveloped nations, the Soviet political and economic interest is in supporting the price. At their August 1962 conference of Marxist economists, accordingly, the principal paper estimated that the developed nations were getting $14 to $16 billions annually from the underdeveloped by means of "unequal exchanges."[130] Since the total exports of the developed countries to the underdeveloped amounted to around $20 billion in 1961,[131] this implies either that their "equitable" value was only $4–$6 billions, a 400 per cent overcharge, or else that the "equitable" value of the underdeveloped nations' exports was really around $34–$36 billions, a markdown of 40 per cent. It is a round sum either way: *"Si vous faites cela, vous ne ferez pas peu."*

[128] *Le Monde*, March 20, 1963, p. 17, interview with Josué de Castro.
[129] See *Le Monde*, September 28, 1962, p. 17; October 11, p. 18; November 30, p. 22.
[130] *Current Digest of the Soviet Press*, September 19, 1962, pp. 13–14.
[131] OECD, *Foreign Trade, Series A*, August 1962. The "developed" nations are taken as the United States, Canada, Japan, OECD Europe, Australasia, South Africa, and Israel; the Soviet and the Chinese blocs are excluded; the rest of the world is taken as "underdeveloped."

If price support for primary commodities is sought, oil will not be last on the list. As *The Economist* put it:

> The Six cannot afford to consider the incomes of the oil-producing countries in quite the way that they affect to consider the incomes of other primary producers; these are not poor countries to be fobbed off with the assurance that commodity agreements will be considered some time.[132]

The underdeveloped countries are mostly oil consumers. But solidarity, whether this means principle or log-rolling will make them favor price maintenance for oil, at least in the short run. Furthermore, some of them have or hope for their own oil industries, and the higher the price, the better these look.

We turn now to the industrialized nations, chiefly Western Europe and Japan, which outside the United States are much the most important consuming countries. Western Europe in particular has been in a torment of indecision about energy policy. They officially desire the cheapest energy consistent with security, which would in any case be difficult to determine. Diversification of non-European sources is no answer at all. For if it means anything, it means that the various non-European sources are independent of each other; that an interruption in one will not mean an interruption in any other. This seems unlikely; in union there is strength, and if the producing countries, whether acting through OPEC or not, are really so disunited that they will not act together to support the claims of any one, then the problem is really much simpler than *The Economist*,[133] or I, or any other student of it thinks.

It is, however, the desire to protect coal that makes the problem not difficult but insoluble. An informed guess is that perhaps a third to a half of the existing coal industry is competitive with imported coal and oil.[134] European recognition of the problem as a problem is much greater than in the United States; considerable progress has already been made in reducing the size of the coal industry, and more is planned.[135] But the limits to further or faster action are well seen in the history of Common Market at-

---

[132] *The Economist*, October 6, 1962, p. 69.

[133] *Ibid.*, ". . . over the years, the oil suppliers' bargaining power will not fail to be exercised."

[134] Council of Europe, *European Energy Problems* (Strasbourg, 1962) pp. 90, 140.

[135] *Ibid.*, pp. 88, 92 ff. For an excellent statement of the problem, see: Assemblée Nationale, Première Session Ordinaire de 1961–1962, *Projet de Loi portant Approbation du Plan*, Tome III, pp. 390 ff., and its underlying document, Commissariat Général du Plan d'Equipement et de la Productivité, *Rapport Général de la Commission de l'Energie* (Paris, 1961), esp. pp. 71–73, 253–57.

tempts to formulate a policy. In October 1959, an inter-executive work-ing party was formed of representatives of the Common Market, the Coal and Steel Community, and Euratom. They reported in 1960, 1961, and June 1962; action on this third and apparently final report was postponed to the meeting of the Council of Ministers in October 1962. The reports had obviously been made with a fairly close attention to what was practi-cally possible; and each report had been discussed by the Ministers, so that the working party must have been fairly sure they knew what could and could not be considered. Yet in October the report was abruptly re-jected, and action now seems years away, all of which bespeaks men who know what they want to do, and cannot do it.

It is perhaps not too surprising that when the moment of decision ar-rived the Ministers found it impossible to act. To let uneconomic coal mines disappear, and to promote an orderly and rapid transfer of labor force (of which Europe is chronically short) is politically impossible.

Oil is further complicated because Britain and perhaps France and Holland think of themselves as primarily sellers not buyers. More sales would be desirable because their nationals would profit and because the balance of payments would improve; but for that same reason, they do not wish the price to be allowed to fall. And finally, Europe wants to have good relations with the oil producing nations, and the special French in-terest in Algeria is the strongest example. Hence the French position in the Common Market is most clearly in favor of high prices, while the Ital-ian position is mostly clearly in favor of low. British adherence to the Community would tilt the balance in favor of maintaining high prices, since the British are sellers, have much coal, and have large political in-terests in the Middle East.

Perspectives

The present uneasy balance may not last, though it is hard to say which way it will tilt. If ENI makes large discoveries of high-cost oil (the one off Iran does not qualify in either way), the Italian position will be more fa-vorable to higher prices. If co-operation between France and Algeria does not work out, the French position will change in the opposite direc-tion. The coal mining labor force will diminish as unremunerative mines are closed, and its political power will therefore be less. The lower the profits earned by the British, Dutch, and French companies, and the smaller the contribution to the balances of payments, the less interest will their governments have in protecting the price. The desire for good Mid-dle East relations will presumably stay.

Finally, and perhaps most important, the very fact that there is no common energy policy leaves each country free to go its own way for the time being, and makes it all the more likely that some of them will do something to undermine the inherently fragile structure of prices.

First — and I now widen the scope beyond Western Europe — an independent refiner, private or government, cannot but keep probing its sources of supply to try to find cheaper ones. A number of underdeveloped nations, for example, are setting up their own refineries. This may or may not always be an economic choice — in some cases it seems obviously uneconomic — but it will exist as a fact.[136] These nations may be all in favor of the current UN resolution, and may in principle favor supporting the price of oil, but when it comes to making supply contracts, the official responsible for the refinery profit will do his best to get the price down to the lowest possible level; and a harassed finance minister will not be loathe to co-operate. Not that I expect an active open market to come into existence; producing companies would in any case try to get long-term contracts by offering loans of money, as they have to the Japanese independents, or some other means of getting the outlet assured. But the very existence of independent refiners, and their continued growth, means more shopping around than has hitherto existed.

The second kind of action which consuming-nation governments will find themselves taking is in taxation, especially profits taxation. In most countries, most local refining and marketing is done by subsidiaries of the international oil companies. These subsidiaries are subject to local income taxation, and it is impossible to compute income tax without putting down a price for the imports. The higher the price at which crude (or product) is transferred to the local subsidiary, the less its profits, and vice versa. Now, the transfer price set by the company itself has no public validity in itself. Two decades ago, a similar problem arose in the United States; under the revenue codes in force during 1934–41 inclusive, corporations were not permitted to consolidate the tax return of all subsidiaries, and had to compute and pay income tax on the earnings of each one. Transfer price needed to be that which would be set by arm's-length bargaining between independent buyer and independent seller. The principle remains in effect though its importance is now much less.[137] I hope it is not being merely provincial to say that I do not see what other principle

[136] *Petroleum Press Service,* Vol. 29 (1962), pp. 143, 248.

[137] See U.S. Treasury Department, Internal Revenue Code of 1954, Section 482; Technical Information Release 441 (1963); Revenue Ruling 57–542.

a government could consistently follow. In view of the developments in world oil over the last few years, certain serious problems are presented.

It has for some time been common knowledge that the refining-marketing subsidiaries of the integrated companies in Western Europe have declared little or no profit; in some countries there have been losses. Edward Symonds, of the First National City Bank, has estimated that the "down-stream profits" of the seven large companies, never very large, turned into losses in 1958, and during 1958–60 were around $300 million annually.[138] In 1960, he calculates, roughly $70 million was due to the seven companies' direct discounting of crude oil, which leaves $230 million as the net refining-marketing deficit calculated at posted prices. Since refinery through-put in Western Europe in 1961 was about 1.3 billion barrels, a difference of 46 cents per barrel (see Table 3) would mean nearly $600 million, and if the integrated companies have about four-fifths of the market, the disputed revenue would be around $400 million per year. These figures are too rough except for one purpose: to establish that the amount of money involved in any recomputation of income tax would be too large for a government to ignore if it was thought that the basis of computing tax was in error. And as Mr. Symonds was not slow to point out:

> . . . The tax gatherer . . . is . . . struck by the fact that the value added in processing and distributing oil within the national boundaries gives rise to little or no income on which he can levy tax . . . [And even in the United Kingdom, France, and the Netherlands, the only countries where] dividends and other advantages [are] gained from the participation of national companies in the international oil business . . . the tax credits allowed to the companies on their payments to foreign governments remove much of the tax revenue that would otherwise result.[139]

It is doubtful that a democratic government, committed to non-discrimination among taxpayers, will fail to consider that a large oil company, and perhaps a foreign company at that, may be underpaying its income tax. Certainly the parliamentary opposition can be expected to remind them. Furthermore, some of the refining-marketing companies are partly

---

[138] Edward Symonds, *Oil Prospects and Profits in the Eastern Hemisphere* (1961); *Oil Advances in the Eastern Hemisphere* (1962); both New York: First National City Bank.

[139] Symonds, *Oil Prospects . . .*, op. cit. (Note 138), p. 7. Apparently tax payments to the British and other home governments on crude oil production income are based on posted prices, which are no longer real market prices, however valid they may be in law.

owned in their local countries. If, therefore, the integrated companies reckon the cost of their crude oil at anything higher than what would be paid by an independent importer, large enough to command all economies of scale, it is a good bet that in some of the developed countries, at least, they are going to face demands for higher income taxation; and this might well include a large bill for back taxes.

Table 3 shows the difference in cents per barrel of landed cost computed on the basis of posted prices and Average Freight Rate Assessment which is an average of all rates in force at any given time (much like the average price per mcf of gas sold in the United States under all contracts, whenever negotiated); and roughly estimated discounted prices and current term tanker rates. These figures are only approximate and raise some theoretical and statistical problems. First, the use of a term charter rate implies that an independent importer (or seller) would find it necessary and prudent to sign up tonnage two to five years ahead, rather than use spot freights as anything but a supplement. This may be untrue, or exaggerated. The discounted price estimate is very rough: some oil was moving at less, and some at more. Now, were the oil market a freely competitive one, we would expect prices to fluctuate irregularly in response to random supply-demand changes, just as spot tanker rates fluctuate. Hence it would be as unreasonable to make the lowest or the highest price granted anywhere within any time period *the* arm's-length price for anyone, as to say that the lowest or highest spot rate granted during the year should be considered as *the* arm's-length spot tanker rate. But since the oil market is not a freely competitive one, it is incorrect to try to strike a balance between irregular ups and downs by taking the average. If others can get a persistently low price, why should the taxpayer be credited with paying a higher one? But then, what is the "persistently low" reference price?

Every country has its own methods of tax administration, rules of legal procedure, and standards of proof. The tax collector will have wide fact-finding powers in one country, few in another. Hence the table must by no means be considered as an approximation to the discrepancy between declared and actual f.o.b. and landed cost that a treasury would calculate. But it may show orders of magnitude. It would be a great mistake to take lack of precision as a reason to disregard the facts thus roughly sketched.

Perhaps future negotiations will throw further light on the subject and provide better figures than these. Doubtless some companies whose tax accounts are questioned will present facts and argument to prove that by

Table 3. Approximate Nominal and Discounted Landed Crude Cost, 1958–1962

(dollars per barrel)

Year	Posted price 34° Arabian Crude	AFRA		Total nominal landed cost	Discounted price	Term charter		Total discounted landed cost	Difference, nominal less discounted
		Per cent over (+) or under (−) Scale	Per barrel, Ras Tanura — Northern Europe[1]			Per cent under scale	Per barrel[1]		
1958	1.90	+24.4	1.31	3.21	1.85	−40	.69	2.54	.67
1959	1.90	+ 8.5	1.17	3.06	1.80	−45	.64	2.42	.64
1960	[2]1.87	[3]−10.6	.98	2.85	[4]1.72	−45	.64	2.39	.46
1961	1.80	−14.7	.83	2.64	1.45	−45	.64	2.09	.55
1962	1.80	−18.0	[5].77	2.59	1.35	−45	[5].63	1.98	.61

[1] To Germany west of the Baltic and including 12 cents Suez Canal dues. Flat Scale 50/9, or about 95.6 cents at 14 cents per shilling and 7.4 barrels per long ton.
[2] Includes $1.90 first eight months, $1.80 last four.
[3] Large vessels only, 1960 and after.
[4] Includes 20 cents discount first eight months; 10 cents thereafter.
[5] Ras Tanura Hamburg flat 49/9.

the standard of arm's-length bargaining their f.o.b. and landed costs and their losses were genuine. Is it too much to hope that none will wave the flag, tear a passion to tatters, protest their "fair and reasonable" prices, great benefits conferred upon the country and its balance of payments, etc.? Such companies may never have their day in court, having conceded the case against them, and more, from the outset.

Before turning to the final way in which non-Soviet governments will keep coming back to the oil price problem, we should note the light which these calculations throw on the problem of heavy fuel oil competition with coal in Europe. It is widely considered that heavy fuel oil prices just now are "abnormally" low, in some sense or other. Dumping by the international oil companies is unproved and unlikely. The processing margin between the price of heavy fuel oil and the price of crude, it is widely said, must in the long run be more favorable than it is in Europe today. Fuel oil is a very small part of the total output; even a drastic fall in price is not much of a check to greater output. Hence in the United States residual fuel oil sells for a dollar or so under the price of crude. But where the desired output of fuel oil is higher, and gasoline is lower, the price of fuel oil is much more important in choking off output at some maximum point. Hence it need not fall anywhere as low as minus $1.00 in order to be in equilibrium with crude and processing costs; indeed, there is no necessary reason why it should even be negative.

In the special but not unreal case of a very simple refinery, with no cracking, and running a fairly heavy crude (deficit of higher-octane gasoline made up by imports), all products might be selling at a (small) margin above the price of crude. In any case, with heavy fuel oil selling in recent years under $2.00 a barrel, if the landed cost of crude were in the neighborhood of $2.77, the refinery margin of minus 77 cents would seem much too low to be permanently maintained. But with the actual landed cost figures around $2.00, a margin of about 9 cents under 34° crude or of one cent under 31° (Kuwait) seems quite within the range of reasonableness, and the expectation that it must begin to rise is unfounded. Refiners have been buying at $2.00 or less; we cannot assume that they are losing money selling heavy fuel for around $2.00. The growth of independent refining is hard to reconcile with such a hypothesis. Fuel oil is sold profitably at under the price of crude oil when the other joint products are sold sufficiently over it to insure that the total output is sold profitably. If the other products could no longer be sold high enough above crude value, the problem would simply vanish — as has already begun to happen in Japan — by the crude being burned entire without any refining at all.

In general: the greater the share of heavy fuel oil in the total product output, the higher its price. But the upper limit is not much over the price of crude itself. For if fuel oil went appreciably higher, it would pay to install crude-burning apparatus.[140]

There is also the idea that products are being sold in Europe today at "marginal cost," which by (somebody's) definition does not include investment costs, only current costs. This holds only under excess capacity in refining — it is our unhappy old friend, known in the United States as "the incremental barrel," renamed "la tonne supplémentaire" or "die übrige Tonne," but neither sounding nor working very well in Europe today. More important is the fact that this kind of marginal cost, that of idle capacity, can scarcely have been of much importance when refinery output was increasing at 10 to 20 per cent annually. The growth of independent refining in particular, and at an even faster pace than the majors,[141] is incompatible with such a hypothesis. But whatever truth there is in it, it applies to the whole range of refined products, and it is sleight-of-hand to load it on to heavy fuel.

Marginal cost is as essential a concept as it is misunderstood. It is the cost of producing a product, everything else being equal, versus not producing it; or, what sometimes is not quite the same, the saving on nonproducing versus producing. In the case of heavy fuel oil, the cost of turning out another barrel is the cost of the additional crude *plus* processing *plus* or *minus* what the additional other products bring. If the additional other products cost so much or so spoil the market that their total net revenue is less than zero, then the marginal cost of the incremental fuel oil is prohibitively high. A rather more important type of marginal cost of fuel oil exists as a choice between different forms of refining and different types of crude charged. The marginal cost of turning out more heavy fuel oil with the same refinery is the sacrifice of gasoline revenue, offset to some degree by the expenses saved of less catalytic cracking. This may well be less than the revenue from additional fuel oil if the ratios of the various prices become more favorable to fuel oil and less favorable to gasoline. If the price ratio is expected to persist, the marginal cost of heavy fuel becomes submerged in the problem of choosing the simpler type of refinery over the more complex. And in both the short term (using the refinery on hand) and the longer term (designing the new refinery) one can

---

[140] *Petroleum Intelligence Weekly,* February 25 and March 4, 1963, for the Japanese plans.
[141] *Ibid.,* March 11, 1963.

calculate the marginal costs of running a heavier crude in order to get more heavy fuel.

If one squeezes water out of a sponge, it is obvious that the more water he squeezes the more effort it costs him. Now "costs" in economics are nothing but the registration, in money terms, of effort needed and resources used up to accomplish any end. In this perspective it is easy to see that the rapid displacement of coal by heavy fuel oil has put producing facilities under a strain and *raised* marginal costs, directly or by turning out excess gasoline. The demand has been good enough to support the greater real cost of getting more fuel oil and, most obviously of all, the strain of getting more heavy fuel oil has in part been transmitted back to the crude producing branch of the industry, resulting in the great and increasing popularity of the heavy crudes. In time, a better adjustment may be expected, and hence easier heavy fuel supply. It may also be that excess supplies of all crudes may be transmitted into attempts to sell it off at the product stage. On either ground, and still more on both, the current margin of fuel oil over crude is not abnormally low, it is if anything abnormally high, and should drop in the future.[142]

True, relative prices, product marginal costs, and refinery margins are today in a most unsettled state, because refinery patterns are unsettled. The European gasoline surplus is pushing refiners to try to use naphtha as a boiler fuel, or crack residual into middle distillates, now in strong demand,[143] or discover an economic way of making bigger molecules out of smaller ones and so getting middle distillates out of light ends. To the extent that such efforts are successful, heavy fuel oil prices will also tend to fall somewhat lower than the present near-equality with crude.

Only a strangely insensitive man would think that the problem of heavy fuel oil versus coal was nothing but relative costs. As this paper is being finished there is evidence to the contrary. The French coal miners are on strike, and job insecurity is surely an underlying cause of their discontent. The German government has gone so far to discourage refinery expansion as to ask the U.S. and British governments to pressure their respective internationals into refusing to let their German subsidiaries build, and it is contemplating more stringent fuel taxes and regulations. In northern Scot-

---

[142] Nor is there merit in the cost categories of "miscellaneous costs and storage," which are either part of refinery cost and hence already considered, or else part of distribution cost and do not belong in an ex-refinery price. See *Petroleum Intelligence Weekly*, March 4, 1963, summarizing an ECSC study not yet available to me.

[143] *Cf.* the interesting possibility, which would solve or mitigate the growing sulfur problem, in E. S. Sellers and L. C. Strang, "The Refining Pattern," in M. J. Wells (ed.), *The Oil Industry Tomorrow* (London: Institute of Petroleum, 1962), pp. 65–67.

land a large electric generating plant has received a favorable offer of heavy fuel oil despite a sizable tax to protect coal, thus precipitating a warning from the nationalized electricity industry to the nationalized coal industry that it refuses to pay "fancy prices" for coal, and a retort from the coal chief that the savings are chicken feed compared with loss of thousands of miners' jobs.

The Soviet Union has offered heavy fuel at $11.20 the ton ($1.65 per barrel), which is slightly below prevailing prices, and the Russians do not intend to pay over the market price for the ships they will take in exchange. The Mineworkers are of course opposed, but the Scottish miners, whose area would benefit, are in favor — provided non-Soviet imports are cut by an equal amount.[144] All an economist can say is that $1.65 per barrel is a profitable price, so that suppliers will keep offering it in Northern Europe, and it is far below the $2.50 to $2.80 which is officially projected.

The great recovery of the Western European economy could not have happened without heavy fuel oil. Universally, this is realized, along with a feeling exactly like that of the ex-Dauphin in Bernard Shaw's *Saint Joan:* Yes, Joan had done a lot of good and he was grateful, but now if she would only clear out, go home! Sainthood, in Shaw's view, was like a force of nature which once unleashed could not be recalled. I do not know if we can go quite that far in analyzing heavy fuel, but the notion that its price will now of itself settle far enough above the present level to leave most or much coal in existence, just to suit our convenience, is as unfounded as it is natural. And if the price of crude continues to fall, the problem will grow.

The last way in which Western European and other large consuming nations cannot help but run into the price of oil is in working out a storage program. Ever since Suez, the OECD has urged its members to store larger amounts, but the degree of compliance, if any, is not publicly available. The suspension of the Common Market program on oil forces each nation to face the problem on its own. The problem lies in insuring availability of crude oil, since refinery capacity is sufficient. Refinery crude storage costs today are probably around $1.50 per barrel.[145] To store very large amounts would permit certain economies, such as the use of underground caverns, but also some diseconomies, such as avoiding large

[144] *Platt's Oilgram News Service,* February 15 and March 9, 1963.

[145] *Cf.* W. L. Nelson, in *Oil and Gas Journal,* December 25, 1961, pp. 168–70, where cost in an "average" tank of 8,000 barrels is put at about $1.43 in 1948. Since then, the general price index (GNP deflator) has increased by about 25 per cent, but technical progress has kept the cost increase much lower, and perhaps $1.50 is as good an approximation as we can get.

population centers for the sake of such factors as safety and appearance. Hence we might be better off allowing a higher storage cost figure, or $1.75.[146]

If we think in terms of amortizing the $1.75 over a period of fifteen years on the assumption that by that time the need for storage will be past, we must recognize that the steadily increasing demand will mean a steadily increasing need; hence the average amortization period will be less than fifteen years, perhaps only ten, or 17.5 cents per barrel per year. Maintenance of the facilities is around 10 cents per barrel,[147] though this too may be a bit high because it is based on refinery storage facilities. We must also consider the interest charges on both the facilities and the fill. If the cost of tankage and fill is around $3.75 per barrel, at 5 per cent interest, this would come to 19 cents per barrel. Hence the cost of storage would be, rounding fraction, somewhere in the neighborhood of 18 + 10 + 19 = 47 cents per barrel.[148] Then if a full year's consumption of crude oil had to be stored, that would be the cost of storage per barrel consumed. If a government thought that by severe rationing, more U.S. and European coal, a little from domestic petroleum, and the normal commercial fill, it could cut petroleum consumption in half for a year, then six months' supply would guarantee a year's safety. Again, I have no inkling of what is actually being prepared, but the public discussion seems to point more toward the neighborhood of ninety days; therefore twice that

---

[146] The cost of storage of an assortment of refinery products, finished and intermediate, is of course considerably higher. Thus M. E. Hubbard estimates it at around £10 per ton, or $4.00 per barrel. (*Petroleum Press Service*, 29 [1962], 462.) But this is to provide for seasonal and irregular swings, and tends to be high. For the U.S. product storage has been estimated at only $2.00 per barrel. In Sweden, it has been estimated at 1.7 to 1.8 million kroner for 100,000 cubic meters. Taking the middle figure of 1.75 million kroner and converting at 19.5 cents the kroner and 6.29 barrels the cubic meter, we have an estimate of $3.10 per barrel. That storage of an assortment is contemplated is clear from the mention of widely different costs of types of fill. See *Petroleum Press Service*, Vol. 29 (1962), p. 67. The *Rapport Général de la Commission de l'Energie, op. cit.* (Note 135), p. 58, speaks of a range of 80 to 100 F per ton, or about $2.28 to $2.86 per barrel for an assortment near refineries, and 15–35 F per ton, or 43 cents to $1.00 in salt caverns. An over-all figure of 70 F per ton, or $2.00 per barrel, is used for crude, for further calculation (conversion at 7.3 barrels per ton and 4.9 F per dollar).

[147] Nelson, *op. cit.* (Note 145).

[148] The Swedish calculation came to 54.4 cents per barrel. Since this was based on a capital cost roughly half again as large as ours (cost of fill ranging from $2.17 to $3.73, of which $2.95 is the mid-point, added to $3.10 for facilities), it indicates that our other factors were perhaps high. The *Rapport Général, op. cit.* (Note 135), estimated a year's storage cost at about 13 F per ton, or about 37 cents (same conversion factors as earlier). The method used is much more refined than mine, and deserves to be read carefully.

or half a year may perhaps be taken as an extreme upper limit. The cost of storage would then be half of 47, or 24 cents per barrel.

This is indeed a heavy charge which it would be a mistake to impose on private companies and which a prudent government would cover from general or special revenues. But of course it is truly a cost to the economy, just as much as if the market price of oil were 24 cents per barrel higher. Certainly it ought to be reckoned in when searching for the point where coal starts to be competitive with oil: there are bound to be a certain number of mines which can pay the expected price plus that figure, and it makes as much sense to subsidize coal output as oil storage. But leaving this problem aside, it is clear that the government which provides and pays for the storage (even though it would doubtless be easiest to have the oil companies operate the facilities) will have a direct interest in keeping its cost to the minimum.

Therefore, both in planning and in operating storage facilities, some governments will need to raise the question of the landed cost of crude in very much the same way as for purposes of income taxation. A government, in buying or underwriting the purchase of large amounts, may, like the U.S. government in 1948–49, consider itself committed to bring about the lowest possible competitive price. If, today, sizable amounts are moving at low prices, a government could successfully insist on paying no higher. We would in effect have an official policy of not recognizing higher price for purposes of taxation or regulation. There is much any government can do to enforce its conviction that some price is needlessly high, and it would be tempting if oil storage for security would not only be costless, but would return a good profit.

Thus, quite without any concerted action by Western Europe, but merely because some governments might seek individually some modest additional revenues and some protection against shortage, the present fragile price structure could lurch pretty far down. I am not speaking of a Western European attempt to exercise its predominance as a Middle East outlet to bring the price down below competitive levels, much as pipelines were once able to do in some U.S. gas fields. That prospect is, fortunately, as unreal as the attempt would be unwise. I am, rather, speaking of the disruptive effects upon the present price structure when special prices, well below the prevailing level but far above marginal cost, tend to become generalized to more and more buyers.

I do not argue that such a policy or result would in some general sense be wrong; each government must judge its own interests. (My desire not to see too drastic a price decline rests on what I consider the political interests of my own country, and I have no political expertise; I make the remark only for the sake of disclosure.) But there is one purely economic objection to letting the price fall to where it would be under immediate free competition, and it goes back to the three-stage nature of production analyzed in some detail earlier. A price equal to short-run marginal cost under excess capacity may be very far below long-run marginal cost after the excess capacity has disappeared. Worse yet, a drastic fall in price would so derange expectations that the anticipated price, with which operators would compare development cost, would surely be lower than what the price turned out to be, because trends are projected into the future and a decline is extrapolated like an increase. Forces long pent up and then let loose act with violence, and they tend to over-correct by far. Hence a collapse of the present system could give such a blow to development (and exploration) as to result in shortages and in higher future prices than would otherwise exist. A collapse is not likely, but if I did not consider it more than just possible, I would not mention it.

Such, in early 1963, is the general shape of the world crude oil outlook. It is fascinating as a problem in economics and in the lag of ideas behind events. Nobody will make the mistake of thinking it only an economic problem; many will fall into the opposite error of thinking they can neglect the economic aspects. The basic thesis stated here, that the world industry has changed its cost structure in ways to which the market has not yet adapted, will be wrong in detail and perhaps in general. But to reject economic analysis because the theory does not seem to describe the market is to head for the school of experience — an expensive one. The evolution of prices must be "discreetly handled: does it not call into question the conduct of business firms, labor unions, and even nations? There is no disputing this, but it is also well to note the errors to which we have often been led by fear of seeking the truth," in part by not wanting to take a "wide enough view . . . of the costs of world oil."[149]

---

[149] Lucien Gouni, "L'Economie Energétique Française et ses Problèmes," *Bulletin de L'Association Française des Techniciens du Pétrole,* 151 (January 1962), 5. And M. Gouni points out how most studies thought to find the key to the European fuel oil problem in the price of American coal delivered in Europe, and were sadly wrong.

Note: This paper is based on research done in the course of preparing a study supported by Resources for the Future, a study of the post-World War II world petroleum market. The essay was written on a leave under a Ford Foundation fellowship. I am indebted to both these organizations. For hospitably providing an office and library facilities, my hearty thanks go to the Institut Français du Pétrole, particularly Jean Chappelle, Secrétaire-Adjoint. Valuable comments were received from Georges Brondel, Leslie Cookenboo, Jr., Nicholas G. Dumbros, Richard B. Heflebower, J. E. Hartshorn, Joseph Lerner, Walter J. Levy, S. Morris Livingston, William J. Newby, Francisco R. Parra, Anthony D. Scott. None of them is responsible for any errors, but they are responsible for there not being many more. This paper is still regarded as a peliminary essay, and the author will much appreciate further criticisms and suggestions.

SUGGESTED READING

Flandrin, Jacques and Jean Chappelle. *Le Pétrole*. Paris: Editions Techniques, 1961.

Frankel, Paul H. *Essentials of Petroleum*. London: Chapman & Hall, 1946.

——*Oil: The Facts of Life*. London: Weidenfeld & Nicholson, 1962.

Hartshorn, Jack E. *Oil Companies and Governments*. London: Macmillan, 1962.

Levy, Walter J. "The . . . Price Structure for the International Oil Trade," in *Proceedings of the Third World Petroleum Congress* (1951), Vol. 10.

——*Current and Prospective Developments in World Oil* (in English, report for the Bundesverband Deutscher Industrie), Zug, Switzerland, 1961.

Owens, David. "Crude Oil Prices: the Next Five Years," in *Competitive Aspects of Oil Operations*. London: Institute of Petroleum, 1958.

FOOD AND THE
WORLD FISHERIES SITUATION

ANTHONY D. SCOTT

The contribution that fisheries development can make to international economic development is probably small compared with that to be expected from agriculture and mining. But the word "probably" is important, for the rational exploitation of the seas is still in its infancy.

In at least one scheme of the "stages of history," agriculture passed through its great revolution more than three thousand years ago, when hunting was converted to husbandry.[1] Although it has adopted from other industries their innovations in the application of power and new materials, fishing has yet to take this step. Consequently, appraising our oceans on their ability to produce food is akin to valuing the great plains merely as a habitat for buffalo. We are just beginning to assess the seas' full potential productivity.

ANTHONY D. SCOTT has been acting head of the Department of Economics and Political Science at the University of British Columbia in 1962 and 1963. He has taught there since 1953. During 1959–60 he was Visitor, Department of Applied Economics at Cambridge University, and in 1955–56 served on the staff of the Royal Commission on Canada's Economic Prospects. During 1950–53 he was Lecturer at the London School of Economics. He is the author of "Economics of Regulating Fisheries" in *Economic Effects of Fishery Regulation* (1962), *Canadian Economic Policy* (1961), *Output, Labour and Capital in the Canadian Economy* (1957), and *Natural Resources: The Economics of Conservation* (1955). Mr. Scott was born in Canada in 1923. He received his B.A. and B. Comm. from the University of British Columbia, his M.A. from Harvard University, and his Ph.D. from the University of London.

[1] Carlo Cipolla, *The Economic History of World Population* (London: Penguin Books, 1962), pp. 17–32.

When better developed, the seas will certainly be an important source of food. It is with this aspect of international economic development that this essay is concerned; for many millions of people already rely on fish for protein and vitamins, and this resource can be relied upon to expand and continue.

But the problems that have, presumably, slowed the arrival of the "fisheries' revolution" are still present. Fish are hard to find and catch. Man has almost no control over their location or numbers and little knowledge of their individual or population biology or psychology. To this lack of control must be added his lack of legal control over the seas. The phrase "the open seas" is apposite, for all nations can hunt, deplete, and destroy ocean fish populations. Thus the problem of ocean cultivation, like that of land cultivation, requires a revolution in legal approach as well as in biological and physical knowledge.

It is difficult to predict the impact of fisheries development on economic development, apart from the greater yield of food and materials. We do not know what nations will take part in the cultivation and the harvest; we do not know whether it will be located in the depths or in the shallows, whether it will be labor-intensive or automatic, whether it will be in the tropics or the Arctic.

Recent increases in demand and in the pace of ocean exploration have led to some progress. On the legal side, nations have made claims to waters previously open or unused. Fish populations have been discovered and opened to exploitation. New hunting and catching methods have been vigorously adopted. International agreements for research, exploration, and conservation have been made. Indeed, we are well beyond the expectations of the scientific writers of the last century.

But none of these changes is really revolutionary. Increased exploitation is leading to conflict, congestion, and compromise, but not to proposals for new approaches. The most elementary proposals for enclosing and genetically controlling fish are still well beyond today's techniques or ambitions. Consequently, it is difficult to distinguish the impact of world fisheries development on the major developed nations from that on underdeveloped countries. All that can be said is that the newest techniques of high-seas fishing are being pioneered by developed countries, using their own resources of mechanical technology, capital, and management. But tomorrow we may see other countries come to the fore. Just as domestic fisheries are overcrowded with vessels today, the high seas may be overfished tomorrow. As Peru has shown, a country does not have to be rich and powerful to make use of a newly discovered fishery.

In thus deciding to concentrate on fish supplies, I have nevertheless had to narrow my field even further. The new promise of fish meal and flour from low-value species is barely mentioned, though it is certainly important to undernourished nations today. And the yield of inland fisheries is merely touched upon. I must concede that both these developments are instances of bringing the fishery "under control" and making its products widely and cheaply available. But I have chosen to concern myself with the ocean fishery and its potentiality as a food source.

THE GROWTH OF DEMAND

To an increasing extent, it is becoming correct to speak of a *world* demand for fish. It is true that there has always been some international trade in fish, particularly in Europe. But for the most part, each country has depended upon its own coastal and inland waters for its supplies. Even when its fleets ventured onto the high seas, as the Western European fishermen crossed to Newfoundland, there was a tendency for each country to consume only the catch of its own efforts. This self-sufficiency was still to be seen in the Japanese entry into Antarctic whaling in the first three decades of this century, and in the current Russian policy of intense exploitation of high-seas fisheries.

But self-sufficiency, which has also been encouraged by tariff protection of national fleets, has been countered by a broadening world trade in fish, which has been traced by the Food and Agriculture Organization (FAO) biennial yearbook of fishing statistics.[2] At the present time (1960–61) the world catch amounts to about 40 million metric tons. Of this, about one-quarter (by weight) enters into international trade. Five years ago the fraction was only one-fifth. Fish meals, fats and oils, canned and dried fish are traded; fresh fish are chiefly consumed where they are landed.

It is of course deceptive to write about the demand for "fish." Although this item plays a very small part in the diets of most countries, it is yet hardly an item at all, but a catch-all term for a wide variety of products produced by fishing. By weight, 25 per cent of the yield is consumed indirectly, as feed for animals and as fertilizer; this component is growing much more rapidly than "food-fish." The remaining three-quarters of the catch consists mainly of a wide variety of inexpensive demersal (bot-

[2] Food and Agriculture Organization, *The Yearbook of Fishery Statistics* (Rome).

tom-dwelling) fishes such as cod, and to a smaller extent of pelagic (dwelling in the high seas, near the surface) fishes such as tuna and mackerel. In terms of value, however, the demersal staples are nearly equalled by the luxury fishes: salmon, tuna, halibut, crab, shrimp, and so forth. Notice that the luxury fish are not close substitutes for the staple fish in most peoples' diets. They are often processed and packed so that they are ready to eat; they are used in different parts of the meal — often side-dishes; and (either because of scarcity or high demand) they are more expensive per pound than other species of fish.

Therefore, it is taking some liberty with the way consumers exercise their choice to talk about a "demand for fish." But students of family budgets do not usually make more than one distinction, say that between canned and fresh fish. So, if we are to use the results of their studies, we must follow their lead. In any case, the expected increase in the world-wide demand for fish is overwhelmingly for staple food, not for luxury trimmings to large diets.

Another distinction is that between fresh-water and ocean fish. Biologically, the distinction is not particularly interesting. But the techniques of catching are quite different in the two environments. In many parts of the world, river, lake, and pond fisheries are already exploited to capacity. In other places, such as Africa and northern Canada, the rivers and lakes are expected to increase their yields in response to demand. Almost everywhere, pond culture is a possibility. But the potentialities of these sources under existing techniques and institutions are small relative to the demand and relative to the productivity of the ocean. Fresh-water fishing will be touched on later, in connection with fish culture; but the present discussion is confined to ocean and coastal fish. Suffice it to say that FAO reports that about 12 per cent by weight of the world's catch is now taken in fresh water. This fraction has not changed greatly in recent years.

Having, therefore, resolved to concentrate on the pseudo-commodity "fish," and to ignore fresh-water fish so far as is possible, attention may be given to demand and its growth.

To fix ideas, here are a few statistics. The world catch in 1961 was about 41 million metric tons, *live weight*. Of this, about 25 per cent is used for meal, etc. Of the remainder, an unknown amount (ranging from 5 to 50 per cent) is discarded at sea, in the port, or by the consumer. The discarded proportion not only varies among species, but among countries. In any case, the estimated consumption of fish, *edible weight* in 1958 was only 14 million metric tons. Because Mainland China and Japan are each believed to consume 2 million, Russia 1.2 million and the United States 0.9 million metric tons, these four countries can be said to comprise almost one-half the world's fish market.

A recent estimate of this total consumption in 1958 by regions was:[3]

	Thousand metric tons
Asia and Far East	
(excl. Mainland China)	4,200
Mainland China	2,000
Russia	2,000
Western Europe	2,400
Africa	1,200
United States and Canada	1,000
Latin America	600
Near East	150
Australia and New Zealand	40
Total (rounded)	14,000

Among these regions, there is immense variation in consumption per capita. In a few relatively poor maritime regions such as Iceland, it may be as high as 30 kilograms per year. In Japan and Portugal the figure is over 20 kilograms. But in the United Kingdom consumption is only 10 kilograms and in Asia, the Near East, South America, and North America it is 5 kilograms or less. Clearly, in areas where fish is scarce it is not eaten. Nor is it eaten in very poor countries, nor in very rich countries.

In certain parts of the world, of course, fish is brought from the sea only at great expense. (These countries may use local fresh-water fish which may be understated in the statistics used here.) They do not depend on fish at all for calories or for protein. Just as important, they have not developed a taste for fish. Therefore, it is exceedingly misleading to talk about their income elasticity or price elasticity of demand for fish; for them it will be an unfamiliar product. Indeed, for many countries the problem is not to produce a supply of fish, but to encourage a demand.

However, some work has been done on income elasticity. It appears to decline with the level of income, if cross-section studies can be trusted. It is about 1.0 in Southeast Asia and about 1.0 in Central Africa. It was thought to be as high as 0.5 in Europe just after the war, but for all Western Europe it is now 0.1,[4] and may well be negative for the countries of

[3] FAO, *Agricultural Commodities — Projections for 1970* (Rome, 1962), with additions and adjustments by F. T. Christy, Jr.
[4] P. Lamartine Yates, *Food, Land and Manpower in Western Europe* (London: Macmillan, 1960).

the European Economic Community (EEC). In any case, per capita consumption has declined significantly in the United Kingdom and France since 1938, and barely stayed constant in the United States, Germany, France, and Italy. Since the relative price of fish has changed in many of these areas, fuller information on price elasticities is needed before anything more precise can be said about income elasticities. But it is interesting that in those countries where fish has been a staple source of protein and of calories, and where its consumption has been encouraged by observation of religious customs and commandments, an increase in income need not automatically lead to an increase in fish purchases. Where consumption is already high, people may buy more fish out of increased incomes only if other proteins become significantly more expensive.

Such information, incomplete as it is, can be used to forecast the future demand for fish only if the forecaster has already taken a view on the probable increases in per capita income and in population. This is not the place to review the detailed and adventurous calculations that have been made by FAO (on food consumption and GNP) and by the United Nations (on population). We may, however, examine their results.

Whereas world population is growing at about 1.75 per cent per year compounded (faster in parts of Asia, Latin America, and Africa), the demand for food-fish is expected to rise at from 3 to 4 per cent per year for the next ten years. World population, then, may double in forty years, but the demand for fish may double in twenty-five years or less. This more rapid increase is due to the fact that the per capita increase in fish consumption is expected to be greatest where population growth is fastest and where present consumption per person is very low. In such circumstances, even a small increase in income per person can have very large effects on the demand for food-fish.

Even in the next ten years, this increase in demand is expected to bring about an appreciable redistribution of consumption by the regions. The Americas and Europe today consume about 30 per cent of today's fish; but in ten years this share may fall to 25 per cent. Most of the increase in share goes to Asia, Africa, and Russia.

The expected growth rate, 3–4 per cent, has been worked out only for the next ten years. To go further would be extremely risky, for much fish consumption depends on price, and price on technology and supply. If the relative price of fish falls, the expected rate of increase will increase — perhaps to 5 per cent per year. But if it becomes dearer, the rate may fall toward the rate of population increase, 1.75 per cent per year.

These estimates are for food-fish alone. Taken with fish meal and other non-food uses, their total increase will be between 4.0 and 5.5 per cent per year. This may be compared with the growth of total catch since the war, almost 6 per cent per year. An increasing proportion of this increase, however, has gone to reduction plants: for example, almost all of the colossal Peruvian increase (which has made that country the second fishing nation) has gone to fish meal. Consequently, the expected rate of increase in food demand for fish is very little different from what it has been in the recent past. The expected increase in demand for meal is closely related to the demand increase for meat, for which fish is a feed. (However, it appears to have made its way into world markets by a price reduction — and here we are really talking about supply.)

SUPPLY: INDICATED PRODUCTIVITY OF THE OCEAN

We have seen that demand is expected to increase rapidly to about 60 million metric tons, live weight, in ten years. What is the ocean capable of supplying? We turn to this question before inquiring what men are capable of supplying from the ocean.

Biologists, in using the word "productivity" of the sea, mean something like what farm experts mean by "yield" per acre, or forestry experts by "sustained yield." They are striving for some measure of the capacity of the oceans to produce protein steadily, without taking account of whether it would be economically profitable to attain this level. Yields in all kinds of production, however, depend upon some assumption about prevailing technology.

Fisheries being rather like agriculture in their capacity for sustained yields, it is tempting to compare yield estimates that have been made for both. But from many points of view, more can be learned by comparing estimates with those of reserves of minerals. Geologists make a useful distinction between (a) "proven" reserves, these being blocks of mineral to which they can move at present prices with present techniques, (b) "indicated" (probable) reserves, which describes mineral about which there is a fair degree of certainty, and (c) "inferred" or "possible" reserves, which describes ore or oil that has not been measured or blocked out at all. Clearly, this classification depends upon the confidence of the geologist in the amount of mineral he has estimated to exist. In addition, the geologist makes much of "potential" reserves or ores. Here the question concerns not the amount of mineral, but its grade. The lower the grade, the more costs will have to decline, technology improve, or prices rise before exploitation of the material can be worth while. "Potential" ore remains unusable until one of these conditions changes.

Estimates of the productivity of the sea, made by biologists, tend to be a mixture of these two dimensions of classification. The future harvest of the sea is partly a matter of learning where fish are that can be taken with today's markets and methods, and partly a matter of talking about "potential," with other "grades" of fish. Let us examine what can be expected from the ocean with both of these points of view in mind.

"Proven" and "Indicated" Reserves

Here the task is to move from what is known to what is likely. The estimator turns from those highly fished areas that are already being almost fully utilized to other areas with similar characteristics. Keeping in mind that only certain species of fish are commercially attractive today, and that there is a minimum density of fish per cubic mile of water below which fishing is unprofitable, he looks for similar bodies of water.

These bodies are usually on continental shelves or near to them. Either the water must be shallow enough that the local food chain can be based on food and light at the bottom, or there must be a "plowing up" of nourishment from the bottom by means of up-wellings.

Writing in 1957–58, "in the shadow of these limitations" (of species, methods, knowledge and facilities), Walford wrote ". . . it looks as though the total world production could increase in the natural course of events only by a factor of something less than two."[5] That would be an increase from 26 to 52 million metric tons per year.

A similar approach was used by Graham and Edwards in 1961.[6] Explicitly confining themselves to the continental shelves, paying little attention to pelagic fisheries on the high seas, and generalizing on the basis of 20 pounds per acre per year as the average catch on already intensely fished grounds, they arrive at a figure for 6 billion acres of about 55 million metric tons per year — very close to Walford's estimate.

These are sobering estimates. They imply that current methods could only just provide fish to supply the demand ten years hence. Clearly, either the world must turn from fish or some change must intercede, if

---

[5] Lionel A. Walford, *Living Resources of the Sea* (New York: Ronald Press, 1958), p. 289.

[6] Herbert W. Graham and Robert L. Edwards, "World Biomass of Marine Fishes," paper presented at FAO International Conference on Fish in Nutrition, Rome, 1961.

the ocean is to provide for its share of the population increase and improvement in the standard of living.

Possible or Inferred Reserves

To what extent is it possible that there are new fisheries, profitable at present prices and with current techniques?

Unless the experts mentioned just above are wrong in their calculations, additional help to supplies can come only from the high seas. It is precisely here that much exciting exploration is being done. The South Atlantic has already revealed stocks of tuna; the South Pacific is being searched for tuna and other species; and large-scale exploration of the Indian Ocean is now going on.

It is possible that these efforts (which have so far revealed fish of high value but not of high weight or volume) will in themselves reveal fisheries as abundant, say, as the new Peruvian fishery which has increased its yield 170-fold since World War II. But it must be recalled that present methods, tastes, and prices are adapted to the yield of the continental shelf. Even highly productive waters in the high seas are unlikely to be profitable without a change in one of these constraining conditions. Let us therefore turn to the "potential reserves" of the ocean.

SUPPLY: POTENTIAL PRODUCTIVITY

We may commence by examining the recent estimates of the potential of the oceans. They have been based on the concept of the "biomass," its size and accessibility.

Marine plants, such as kelp, are relatively unimportant parts of the biomass. Microscopic floating plants, the phytoplankton, depend upon the nourishing elements in the water and on sunlight. They are rarely found much below 300 or 400 feet of depth. They form the food of zooplankton, small floating animals. The zooplankton are too small to be used by any but the smallest fish, which in turn are the food of larger fish. Thus there is formed a food chain, in which the largest links are those caught by man. There are of course complex interconnections within the chain: whales actually can feed on zooplankton, as can herring and sardines. But as a general rule, the larger the fish and the more valuable it is to man, the higher it is in the chain.

Just as man makes relatively "inefficient" use of grass when he eats it through the agency of meat or poultry, so the fish food chain is more and more "wasteful" of the basic nutrients available to the phytoplankton. With some knowledge of the loss at each stage, and with some idea of the number of links in an average chain, experts have attempted to estimate what the potential harvest of the biomass might be. Before presenting them, two warnings must be given.

First, it is not certain to what extent plankton feed on the nutrients released by the decomposition of dead fish. If their dependence were high, then a more complete utilization of the biomass might soon exhaust the nutrients on which the food chain now depends. The estimates assume that relatively full utilization of the seas would not significantly alter the store of basic nutrients upon which the chain depends.

Second, each link in the chain is a population of fish. It is necessary to maintain these populations at an "optimum" level. If they are too small, their own reproduction rates will be affected. In economic terms, there is some optimum inventory of working capital required at each stage in the chain. Unless it is proposed to harvest plankton instead of, or at the expense of, larger fish, it is not practical to harvest the biomass between the fish actually caught by fishermen and the plankton. On the other hand, the more of these populations there are, and the larger each is, the more inefficient the chain is in transmitting the nutrients to the desired level.

One estimate has been based upon knowledge of the primary organic production of the sea. The total net production of carbon is estimated to range from 1.2 to 1.5×10^{10} tons per year. This is converted to the production of phytoplankton by multiplying by the factor of 37, leading to an estimate of about 50×10^{10} tons of phytoplankton. On the assumption that this net production is fully harvested by the herbivores (zooplankton), and that their efficiency of use is 20 per cent, this means an annual production of 10×10^{10} tons of herbivores. Assuming that the primary and secondary groups of carnivores each has a feed efficiency of 10 per cent, then net output would be of the order of 1 billion metric tons of bony fishes. This billion tons is supposed to be an estimate comparable with the 52–56 *million* tons explained in the previous section; it also excludes whales, squid, and so forth.

A second method begins not with carbon as a nutrient, but with sunlight as a source of energy. Tracing the transfer of this energy from link to link, one arrives at an estimate of 340 million tons, which must in this method be reduced to allow for the maintenance of basic stocks and for the whales and squid which are also in the estimate. The final figure is 115 million metric tons.

The "potential" catch therefore has a very wide range: from over 100 million to 1 billion metric tons per year. The least figure in the range is more than twice the "indicated" or "probable" figure derived earlier. It will be noticed that the method of estimation here pays almost no attention to the catching of fish. The sole concession to the realities of today's industry is that the chain is carried all the way to the bony secondary carnivores, which are large enough to be caught by present techniques and to be usable in food preparation. Also, the stock of each species is maintained at an optimum level.[7]

Apart from this concession, the "potential" is far beyond today's methods. To realize it, the industry must develop along lines radically different from those of the past. The yield of these new fisheries may be so dispersed that it would be impossible to find them or catch them by present techniques. They may be soft, bitter, poisonous, or transparent, bony, or otherwise unattractive to the cook. They may be inconveniently small. They may fluctuate greatly, species by species, in their annual abundance. All the calculations are suggesting is that somewhere in the ocean is the biomass of bony fish in the predicted weight and yield.

In my opinion, it is almost inconceivable that, with the present arrangements on the seas, much progress will be made in raising the world catch far above the 60-million-ton mark unless technology advances even more rapidly than it has so far. The steps that must be taken are outside the scope of the industry. Let us examine these steps. They include improvements in gear, preservation, and processing; and increasing the productivity of the ocean.

Fishing Gear and Equipment

It is often said that fishermen are conservative people, slow to adopt new gear. On the contrary, I believe that in most free-enterprise Western economies fishermen are unusually venturesome entrepreneurs, who gladly adopt promising new techniques. But they are confronted by many obstacles to radical innovation.

In the first place, the scale of the fishing boat is small relative to the biological scope of the fishery. At the most the fisherman is allowed to improve his method of hunting and catching. He cannot adopt the techniques of the farmer who keeps thousands of poultry in a single building under controlled conditions. He is more like a hunter who is allowed

[7] This account of the two estimates of potential productivity of the oceans owes much to F. T. Christy, Jr.

only to adopt new weapons for killing game birds on the wing. He is not justified in investing a great deal, for he has no control over the resource. His expensive capital investment may yield him no benefit if other equally well-equipped vessels forestall him in the catch. And because there are many vessels, his income is usually being forced down toward the opportunity income of fishermen in other jobs. He has therefore few sources of capital of his own, and little long-term credit standing.

Under such circumstances the fisherman is precluded from adopting innovations except those of a type that will enable him to forestall his rivals on the grounds, in finding the fish, or in getting back to port. Given the shortage of capital, the risks that even good inventions will not work, and the fact that none in the industry (except the equipment manufacturer) has an incentive to find new methods, it seems to me there is actually a rapid rate of adoption of new techniques. Within these narrow limits, even the most uneducated fishermen in the most isolated ports are willing to listen to new ideas.

Indeed, it is arguable that fishermen have an incentive to innovate *more* rapidly than farmers. The latter, in possession of their own skills, tools, and land, can use whatever rent, profit, or surplus they are receiving as a buffer which enables them to delay the introduction of an invention. Eventually the invention will lead to an increase in supply, force down price, and so induce them to follow others in the new technique. But till then, they may earn some profit or avoid loss while still using the outmoded technique. A fisherman usually cannot delay. Most new inventions are destructive of fish or lead to the fisherman being forestalled on the grounds. Once a few rivals have the technique, he is threatened with the loss of his catch. In other words, in addition to the general quest for maximum profits and the general pressure of falling prices, the fisherman has the additional special threat of lost resources to goad him into quickly adopting the new technique.

That this force is important in practice is difficult to demonstrate, but it is easy to show that many statements about conservatism are mistaken. On the one hand, the force of Luddite legislation which banned new techniques is both evidence that some fishermen were keen to try them and a partial explanation of the slowness of their eventual introduction. On the other hand, it is clear that the steam trawler was introduced as rapidly as steam was used in ocean navigation (with a lag to allow for the appearance of a satisfactory engine), and that the slowness of *some* fishermen to turn to gear that was more seaworthy, better powered, or more effective in intercepting fish is merely an indication that *other* fishermen (with whom they are compared) were more progressive. "Conservative"

Newfoundland or Scots fishermen are threatened by the innovations already adopted by the fishermen of other countries.

The technical literature is full of new ideas that are being tried out. Small vessels are being given better shapes, more power and protection, and stronger nets and lines. Vessels of all sizes are being fitted with means of communication and sounding that aid navigation, cut wasted time at sea, and lead to larger catches. And the new larger vessels and mothership fleets find it economical to employ many scientific resources to find fish, storing and processing them at sea, and to cut travelling time to and from port to a very low level per ton of fish.

The low incomes and excessive entry that are a feature of fishing everywhere have meant that much of the research and pioneering must be done by government, or with government assistance. Both in Europe and North America there are methods of subsidizing new vessels almost as lavish as the assistance to house building. Government departments, similar to those for farming, experiment with new hulls, engines, preservation methods, and catching gear.

Such assistance is of particular importance to the small inshore fisherman. Fishing in coastal waters is an easy industry to enter. The threat of new equipment, which might deter entrants and reduce the fleets, is reduced by conservation and other regulations that, instead, shorten fishing seasons and inhibit technical change. Incomes fall, venturesome men move to other fisheries or industries, and the fishermen become "conservative." If any change is to be brought about, the government must do it. In addition, local fisheries often object to new techniques (or new methods of organizing the catch) because increased catches would bring a lower price, or otherwise spoil the market. Conservatism is then a technique for exploiting a monopoly situation.

On the other hand, the high-seas fisheries are wide open both to competition for the catch and rapid innovation. The fleets of Russia and Japan are avoiding competition between their own vessels, but are increasingly running into difficulties with vessels from other nations. The philosophers of international law who originated the "freedom of the seas" doctrine would be amazed if they could see the traffic congestion in the ocean fisheries today, hear of the fears of depletion, and read about the new claims to ocean sovereignty. Speed, maneuverability, and size are the technical answers to this new competition, though they would appear to be self-defeating in the long run.

So far as we know, it is chiefly in Russia's own waters that a more rational pace of innovation has been adopted. The competitive race for vessels that will forestall other vessels has been avoided, but there is no tendency to outlaw effective new methods as they appear. Large-scale management would appear to be well adapted to the task of exploiting a geographically extensive resource. Research in gear and resource can go forward together.

Increasing the Productivity of the Oceans

But these improvements are all in what is basically hunting. Except in the fisheries protected by treaty, or in coastal fishing, the effort is rarely on the scale of the resource: the fish population (or the ecological complex of populations) on each fishing ground. There is little incentive for the vessel owner, fleet owner, or government to undertake research in the basic biology or cultivation of high-seas fish population (apart from treaty obligations, discussed below). This can be confirmed by consulting any of the many fine books popularizing marine biology or oceanography. Invariably there is a chapter on fish farming or fish culture. But the experiments discussed and the new ideas heralded are very limited. Some apply to fresh-water fish: fishpond culture, river and lake management, and salmon development. Others apply to beach, brackish-water, and estuary improvement, ranging from pollution control to ambitious plans for shallow-water enclosure, fertilization, seeding, and harvesting.

Unquestionably, there is much to be gained by this work. Walford and others have argued that many coastal marshes, tideflats and estuaries are capable of much higher production of shellfish and bony fish than they are of agricultural products if drained and "reclaimed." Such shallows are immensely rich in fish-food; they are frequently referred to as a biological soup, constantly enriched by material carried down rivers from inland and brought from the deeps by marine currents and tides. Walford writes:

> In many regions, fishermen treat the brackish inshore waters just as they do the open sea, hunting and gathering only the wild stocks. In doing this, they are making just as foolish use of environment as ranchers would if they were to use rich farmland for range country, or range country for hunting wild game.[8]

This is a useful analogue, both for the brackish coastal waters, and for the high seas. The essential steps have yet to be taken. Just as the range must be fenced, animals bred true, predators eliminated, and food provided to turn open grassland into farmland, so the oceans must be turned into producing units under *control* of managers who can select and improve species, eliminate their competitors and predators where

[8] Walford, *op. cit.* (Note 5), p. 134.

possible; and for this objective — with the conspicuous exception of the small staffs of scientists working on treaty waters and their fish population — almost everything remains to be done. Indeed, we should perhaps ignore also most present research, for it is confined to the present ecology of certain fishing grounds, not to the study of what could be there if fish culture were taken seriously. I do not criticize the present efforts, and I recognize that many of their results are necessary initial steps for whatever is to be done next. I merely wish to demonstrate the gulf that exists between today's marine research and what is necessary before fuller use is made of the seas.

What may be involved in this fuller use? The details of a thorough "agriculture" cannot yet be guessed. But the intervening phase, of a managed but wild fishery, has already been the subject of speculation.

a) Breeding fish is probably out of the question for a while. But it is possible to transplant desirable species to more favorable environments.

b) Feeding ocean fish is also unthinkable. But the creation or encouragement of rich up-wellings is well within the orbit of today's technology.

c) Fencing fish, for easier harvesting, may be possible through the use of curtains of bubbles, sound waves, or waves of shorter frequency.

d) The control of predators and competitors may have to take a large variety of forms. Experts in fish population dynamics are already studying desirable programs of fishing for almost valueless species that reduce the yield of desired species.

These are exciting possibilities. But it should be stressed that they are like gamekeeping in mediaeval Europe, which, while it provided better hunting, did not really lead to the revolution of high-yield agriculture for which the land was waiting. Beyond these four steps lies the real fisheries' revolution. When the wild fishery yields to controlled use of the oceans' energy and nutrients, the "potential" productivity of the seas recounted above may be approached.[9]

---

[9] Some idea of the stages through which natural resources pass, from hunting and collecting to controlled development, will be found in my "The Development of the Extractive Industries," *Canadian Journal of Economics and Political Science,* Vol. 28 (February, 1962). In that paper I stress particularly the resource industries' development of first "mechanical," then chemical, technology, and the relation of these changes to parallel property-concept developments. In the argument, the contrast between agriculture and fishing is exploited more fully than is possible here.

Under such circumstances, all will be changed. Different links in the food chain of the seas may be exploited; there is already much speculation about the use of algae or plankton. Alternatively, there may be concentration on the first or second carnivores: bony fish which, like herring and anchovies, may be used for fish meal or fish flour. Such changes require revolutionary alterations in the regime of the seas and in human eating habits. Fish flour, in particular, is unlikely to become an important source of protein until millions of families have been educated in its value and in ways to make it attractive.

Over-Fishing

In view of the dramatic increase in demand and the rather limited reserves that the world can infer from present performance, it is obvious that increased fishing effort may be applied to no effect. Fears that this may happen on the high seas are a recent idea; as recently as the end of the nineteenth century, such eminent biologists as Huxley argued that man could have no effect on the yield of the important ocean fish. Such claims, often expressed as "over-fishing is impossible," require a brief exploration. They have both a biological and an economic aspect.

Biology

This matter may be disposed of briefly. It is obvious that fish in a pond can be over-fished — indeed the population can be totally destroyed. Many fisheries are today just as vulnerable to modern technology. Superficially, they may be identified as those that are visible on the surface, like whales or Pacific oysters; or congregate to migrate or spawn, like salmon; or school or remain in a limited area, like populations of groundfish. Basically, however, it appears that apart from species like salmon, where it is conceivable that *every* female may be caught and so prevented from spawning, vulnerability is inversely proportional to the prolificity of females. Whales, with a long gestation period, can be wiped out relatively easily. To kill one of the stock of females is to reduce the power of the stock to produce young, and so to reduce the stock's yield of fat and oil. On the other hand, female herring produce so many eggs that it is almost unthinkable that one year's yield should have any relationship to the number of females caught the year before.

Consider the mackerel, for example. Every year these important food fish lay eggs by the billions. A relatively few adult fish would be enough to keep the species abundant if most of their offspring reached maturity. However, the mortality rate by the time the young fish reach a two-inch growth has been estimated at as much as 99.9996 per cent. The great mackerel fisheries may depend on the survival of a few ten thousandths of one per cent of the annual spawning. What is more, the difference between good and bad years as far as mackerel fishing is concerned may be a difference of only one or two ten thousandths of one per cent in that survival rate.[10]

Between the prolific and virtually indestructible herring, anchovies and mackerel, and the vulnerable and sensitive whale and salmon are those fish stocks which can be reduced by intensive fishing. Cod, sole, halibut, and haddock are much-studied examples. The stocks are numerous and the females are prolific. But the stocks can be reduced, and then the number of young (the yield of the fishery) are also reduced. Hence, while such stocks can scarcely be destroyed, they can be reduced to such a low level that their annual increment, or yield, is not worth fishing. This is a frequent phenomenon on "over-fished" coastal grounds.

It follows that there is some level of fishing effort which will maintain the stock and its yield at an "optimum" level. It is the object of much fishing regulation and of fishing treaties to reduce effort to this level by means of quota or closed season.

Finally, it follows that the world, in attempting to reach the "potential" catch, must not only eventually adopt the measures sketched in the preceding section, but also govern closely the intensity of fishing each year. Heavy fishing, by reducing the stock of many of the most valuable fishes, can actually reduce the catch in all subsequent years, unless by abstention the fishermen allow the stock to grow again to its "optimum" size.

It is worth noting that the degree to which a stock is exhausted depends upon economic considerations. When the stock is reduced, fishing becomes more expensive per ton, since fish are harder to find and their density in the water is reduced. The pressure of fishing then tends to decrease, although the smaller catches may bring a higher price that will work in the opposite direction and cause the fleet to redouble its effort. Consequently, fish that are cheap to catch (because they school or because they take bait willingly) or that have a high value per fish, may soon be over-fished below their "optimum" level. But less valuable fish may be kept by the industry at an "optimum" biological level without any regulation being necessary.

The whole topic of regulation is too complicated to go into here. It

[10] Robert C. Cowen, *Frontiers of the Sea* (New York: Doubleday, 1960), p. 247.

was recently the subject of an FAO conference, the proceedings of which have just been published.[11] It is sufficient to point out that the concept of a *biologically* optimum catch is meaningless, since biology cannot indicate any particular size of stock or yield as an objective or goal. This brings us back to economics.

Economics

Only in this century have economists made much of the fact that entry into the fishery is free. Alfred Marshall, in his examples taken from the fishing industry, in effect ignored this important characteristic. Indeed, it was not until after World War II that economics caught up to the biologists who had been stressing that "no-profit" (no-rent) was the rule in the fishery.

Grotius, in his sixteenth-century work on the law of the sea pointed out that the sea cannot be enclosed or appropriated. The sea is common property. Consequently there is no entrepreneur to limit the employment of labor and capital in any fishery to the point where their marginal product is equal to their alternative earnings in industry; that is, to the point where the rent of the fixed resource — the fish population — is maximized. Instead, fishermen enter until — if we ignore the differences between fishermen's skill, equipment, and luck — their alternative earnings are equalled by the *average* product of the fishery. In this sense, the fishery has too much labor and capital applied to it. There is no rent earned; it is dissipated among a large number of fishermen. The marginal product of the last vessel may be small or even negative (as in the salmon fishery).

If we apply A. C. Pigou's variety of welfare economics, we must condemn this "over-fishing." The marginal social product of labor and capital is less in fishing than it is in other industries. There is a *prima facie* case for limiting entry, turning the fishery over to a manager-owner, or running it publicly, and so raising the production of other goods.[12]

The marginal productivity of labor and capital within the fishery may also differ from ground to ground, since at the best fishermen tend to equalize average catches, not marginal products. Thus there is also a

[11] R. Hamlisch (ed.), *Economic Effects of Fishery Regulation* (Rome: FAO, 1962).

[12] H. S. Gordon, "The Economic Theory of the Common Property Resource: The Fishery," *Journal of Political Economy*, LXII (1954) 2. See also Anthony Scott, "The Fishery: the Objectives of Sole Ownership," *Journal of Political Economy*, LXIII (1955) 2; and Ralph Turvey and Jack Wiseman (eds.), *The Economics of Fisheries* (Rome: FAO, 1957).

prima facie Pigovian argument for dispatching fishermen to the various grounds, rather than letting them choose what ground they will fish.

Another aspect of the common-property fishery is that no one is responsible for *its* fertility. Just as no one has an incentive to prevent the waste of labor and capital mentioned above, so also no one has an incentive to maintain the stock. It may be over-fished in the biological sense, so that the returns of all fishermen decrease; yet it profits no man to reduce his own fishing effort until the damage is done. Again, no one is responsible for catching predator fish, or preventing the catching of fingerlings.

These fertility aspects of common property are frequently dealt with by government or treaty fishing regulations. But rarely if ever are the wastes of labor and capital dealt with. There is more than a little truth in the gibe that fish stocks are protected at the expense of human populations.

What is the relevance of these remarks on the efficiency of the fishery to economic development? They suggest that much of the increased yield of the oceans can be obtained with little or no real expansion in the fishery. It is entirely possible, to be specific, that the "inferred" yield of the Grand Banks or Georges Bank could be caught with fewer men and less capital than is now required, even without a change in technology.

This point in turn suggests that the fishery may easily produce its future share of the world's food without ever becoming a very large industry. It is not surprising that works on economic development make very little of the development of local fishing industries. Even in Peru, where the catch has increased over one-hundred fold since the war, the impact on the country has not been overwhelming. It is entirely likely that even in the Indo-Pacific area and on the coasts of Africa, the full development of the fisheries will produce only a small effect on the local economies of which they are a part.

As a world-wide source of food, the fishery will become important. But in most areas it is likely, as it develops, to release labor to other industries rather than to become an engine for over-all growth. In this respect it is perhaps more like the mining or the oil industry than like agriculture.

Of course, in local areas its growth and change will be important. Firth and others have already done excellent work on the anthropology of changing fishing villages in countries like Malaya.[13] Much remains to be said about the connection between inshore fisheries and the agricultural

[13] Raymond Firth, *Malay Fishermen: Their Peasant Economy* (London: Routledge, 1946).

pursuits that occupy such communities. Even with their present techniques they are capable of large increases in production, as is discussed in Bottemanne,[14] and has been shown by the excellent educational and planning support given by the fisheries division of the FAO. But the full development of these countries' coastal waters must proceed from large fishing ports. The recent changes in the Newfoundland and Japanese inshore fisheries show the kind of development that is needed for real increases in catch and labor productivity.

The chief exception to this statement is the farming of brackish waters. Throughout Asia, primitive fish-farming is already practiced. Scientists have given much attention to methods of improving the yields of these intensively worked ponds, irrigation ditches, and swamps. Such simple improvements as the erection of gates or pumps to govern the temperature, salinity, or fertility of the water can produce startling improvements. Selections of the fish to be reared and the exclusion of predators are also important. Feeding the fish directly has scarcely been attempted. In the Western world, this type of farming has been undertaken chiefly with shellfish: oysters and mussels. Startlingly high yields have been achieved — a Dutch establishment produced 6,000 pounds to the acre.[15] Clearly, this sort of farming, foreshadowed in the remarks of Walford quoted earlier, may eventually make a very large contribution to food production. Note that it is usually labor-intensive, at least at certain periods of the year, and may require a large investment in works and equipment.

PATTERNS OF INTERNATIONAL CO-OPERATION

Until the middle of the nineteenth century, nations competed for the rights to coastal fisheries as they did for territory. In effect, the law of the sea was a combination of the basic principle that waters within three-mile limits were territorial waters, closed to foreign fishermen, while the high seas without were open to all nations, with a vast body of treaties and legal decisions giving certain countries rights to fish in certain contested fishing grounds.

In the Baltic and the North Sea, however, certain arrangements about fishing rights were gradually combined with provisions about the intensity of fishing. At the turn of the century, with the advent of the steam trawler,

[14] C. J. Bottemanne, *Principles of Fisheries Development* (Amsterdam: North-Holland, 1959).
[15] F. G. Walton Smith and Henry Chapin, *The Sun, The Sea, and Tomorrow* (New York: Scribner's, 1954), p. 103.

Britain and her continental neighbors agreed to study the biology of the North Sea, with a view to discovering the effects of fishing on yield, and then perhaps to restricting fishing pressure. In this respect they were following the lead of the pioneering seal treaty in which the North Pacific fishing powers agreed to leave the harvesting of the seals to the United States and Russia; the proceeds to be shared among Japan, Canada, Russia, and the United States.

Soon after World War I some progress was made when the groundwork for the halibut treaty and the salmon treaty between the United States and Canada was laid. In the North Sea, the powers attempted to come to agreement on the mesh of trawls, and just before World War II Britain took the lead in increasing the minimum mesh size, thus allowing small fish to escape. The whaling industry came to some agreement on the total kill of whales, but its administration was marred by dissidents so that the stock was gradually reduced. Today the situation is much more formalized than was the case in 1939, but the threat of overwhelming fishing pressure is greater than ever. Three elements in the situation are worthy of note:

The Territorial Sea. Both by a series of decisions and by agreement among the signatories of the Fishing Convention resulting from the UN Law of the Sea conference in 1956, this has been effectively widened. Up to World War II it had been argued that the three-mile limit should follow the contours of the coastline. Today, however, nations are entitled to draw the boundaries of their territorial sea to join islands and across the mouths of wide rivers and inlets. Equally important, the great powers have (by treaty) bowed to the demands of Iceland and other countries for fishing zones twelve miles wide. Even the claims of Chile, Ecuador, and Peru to zones two-hundred miles wide have not been completely denied by the great fishing powers.

At the Law of the Sea conference, a majority of nations eventually favored either a twelve-mile fishing zone or else a six-plus-six arrangement, in which territorial waters were to be widened from three miles to six miles, and an additional six-mile zone for national fishing rights created. The claim for wider fishing zones was backed by the smaller and newer "coastal states," and opposed by the older fishing powers such as Britain. In the end, however, it proved impossible to obtain a sufficient majority for any proposal to become an agreed Convention, so that legally the three-mile limit presumably still holds.

In general, the tendency is for the high seas to shrink somewhat, and for a larger portion of the world's presently valuable fisheries to come under the national control of the coastal state.[16] Nations which have historically fished in waters that are now declared to be national fishing zones (such as Britain in the waters off Norway) have been excluded. Indeed, the Law of the Sea conference totally rejected the idea of "historic rights" as a qualification to the idea of extended territorial seas or fishing zones.

The Continental Shelf. We are not discussing minerals in this essay. To the extent that they are thought to be exploitable, they are on the "continental shelf," that part of the ocean that is less than 100 fathoms deep (200 meters), adjacent to the continents. Following wartime action by Britain and Venezuela in the Gulf of Paria, and the United States' Truman declaration, it was generally agreed that the exploitation of the earth in the shelf, and the life fixed to it (such as shellfish) was a right of the coastal state. This was confirmed by a Convention passed by the Law of the Sea conference. However, it is intended to have no bearing on fishing above the shelf.

Fishing Conservation Treaties. There are now some fifteen treaties between nations that have pretensions to do more than establish rights to fish. Like contracts in domestic law, they complement and substitute for general rules and laws. They are of three types:

> *a) Research treaties.* Most fishing treaties started as agreements to conduct research on the fisheries of particular regions of common interest to the signatories. The Mediterranean and the Indo-Pacific treaties, sponsored by FAO, are still of this type. They allocate research tasks and share results of their investigations.
>
> *b) "Species treaties."* This type undertakes to protect a particular fish population or species against over-fishing, usually by the imposition of a quota. The salmon and halibut treaties between Canada and the United States are important examples. The North Pacific seal treaty, the whale agreement, the tuna treaty and the Japan-Russia Northwest Pacific salmon treaty are also of this type, being effectively confined to one or a few species, often pelagic (that is, moving around from one region to another).
>
> *c) "Regional treaties."* These cover all the fish in a certain region of the ocean. There are three important examples: for the northeast Atlantic (North Sea); the northwest Atlantic (ICNAF); and the northeast Pacific.

[16] M. S. McDougal and W. T. Burke, *The Public Order of the Oceans* (New Haven: Yale University Press, 1962).

The first two of these regional treaties are concerned with a variety of fish species, usually demersal. Their main policy approach has been to increase the minimum mesh that may be used in trawling. The third treaty is a curious mixture. It is really an arrangement by which separate fish populations can be examined to see whether they are fully utilized and managed by Canada and the United States. If they are not, then they are open to fishing by Japan. Russia is not a member, but has so far respected those fisheries from which Japan must abstain. (The commission is now [February, 1963] attempting to convince Canada and the United States that Japan must be allowed to exploit certain herring and halibut stocks that have been under-utilized so far.)

The Law of the Sea conference approved these three types of treaties, though it had refused to recognize for general application the so-called "abstention principle" built into the northeast Pacific treaty. It proceeded to pass the Convention on the Living Resources of the Sea, which set up machinery by which nations interested in protecting certain fisheries can, in effect, force other nations to negotiate a conservation treaty and admit (or yield the initiative to) the coastal state in the region.

Of these three types, the "species treaty" has been by far the most effective. The regional treaty of the ICNAF type has moved very slowly. But the application of the species approach is rather limited, chiefly to valuable fish like halibut, tuna, and salmon, whose "welfare" has been promoted above that of the fish with which they compete. It has been workable when confined to two or three nations; in the multi-nation whaling treaty, it is not very effective. Indeed, it often applies chiefly in national waters, as with salmon and halibut. Its research tasks are clear and have been amply rewarded by important discoveries.

The regional treaty is more cumbersome. Its research effort is slow and discouraging, partly because it is diffused over a large area of the ocean, partly because it deals with many fish populations. Typically, it has many members, and entry to it is open. It finds it difficult to determine its objectives when there is a conflict of aims between members or fisheries. But in my opinion, the regional treaty, with all its shortcomings, is closest to the pattern of the future. In view of what has been argued in earlier sections, this pattern must include two things:

a) provision for making full use of the "potential" productivity of the ocean, from basic nutrients to final large fish; and
b) taking account of the cost of fishing on neighboring grounds, and the values of competing and predatory fish.

The ocean's productivity, in other words, must be exploited under conditions where both the ecology and the economy are heeded. The species treaty cannot do this, for it is charged with the conservation of a particular fish population, regardless of its relationships with other more or less valuable fishes, and regardless of the alternative fishing and land opportunities of the fishermen and their capital. I do not believe that much harm is done by today's species treaties which range over many fishing regions (apart from halibut, but the halibut regulations in the northern Pacific are under criticism for these reasons by the Japanese).

But it is clear that the full use of the oceans must be organized by the fishing powers in such a way as to make it possible to obtain the desired species in the proportion demanded by the members and their markets. The treaty commission must be able to determine quotas for the competing species, and the sub-areas in which they may be caught. It must be able to arrange for the suppression of predators. It must be free to undertake research into the catching and development of species now not utilized, or even known. The regional form of treaty is best adapted to these tasks.

Furthermore, in the search for economic efficiency, I believe it would be desirable to limit entry of vessels in some way that is equitable to the members. In this way, the economic efficiency of the world fishing industry can be increased *pari passu* with developments on shore. It may even be that these regional treaties and commissions can increase the productivity of the international fisheries *before* the same progress is made in national waters.

Political considerations point the same way. The task for diplomacy is to reconcile the interests of the chief fishing nations (Russia, China, Japan, the United States, Norway, Peru, Canada, and the United Kingdom) among themselves and with the smaller "coastal states." Only a truly regional body, with jurisdiction over large areas of the ocean, and with the problem in hand of studying and administering a complex ecological situation can, I suggest, deal with such powerful members. It is simpler to come to ad hoc arrangements about the sharing and conserving of a single species. But these species arrangements tend to ossify and to exclude more efficient approaches to exploiting the seas. The scientists of all the countries mentioned are already aware of the immense complexity of the ocean's biology and physical structure. They are aware that only limited progress can be made on a piecemeal basis, for the oceans and their fisheries are increasingly revealed to be unified. As a first step toward wider agreement, the recognition that fisheries management is indivisible may assist in setting up valuable patterns of co-operation.

Eventually, in the space age, it may be easy to form an "international fishing authority" minimizing the costs of obtaining the full potential food supply of the oceans. Till then, we must be content with our slowly developing regional treaties, accepting new members, new knowledge, and new tasks with increasing efficiency and productivity.

Note: I should like to acknowledge the assistance I have received from Francis T. Christy, Jr., with whom I am working on a longer study on some of the topics discussed here. Mr. Christy and I have received much help from numerous experts in fisheries, biology, and law. In addition, I have received valuable research assistance in my work on fisheries law and treaties from Frank Iacobucci. But none of these kind persons is responsible for anything in this essay.

Resources in Europe, Africa, and Latin America

Resource Development and Utilization in the Soviet Economy
DEMITRI B. SHIMKIN

Resource Relationships among Countries of Western Europe
P. LAMARTINE YATES

Resource Development among African Countries
ARTHUR GAITSKELL

Resource Aspects of Latin-American Economic Development
JOSEPH GRUNWALD

RESOURCE DEVELOPMENT AND UTILIZATION IN THE SOVIET ECONOMY

DEMITRI B. SHIMKIN

The pattern and extent of resource development and utilization in today's Soviet economy are significant in several respects. They have provided foundations for major military-economic capabilities and for moderate increases in living standards over the past generation. They represent the end products of large and diversified national efforts, some of which have taken decades to culminate. And the policies and administrative procedures underlying these persistent efforts have differed radically from the mechanisms characterizing Western market economies.

In the Soviet Union, State-set goals have largely replaced spontaneous and evoked consumer demands as economic prime movers. Political con-

---

DEMITRI B. SHIMKIN is professor of anthropology and of geography at the University of Illinois. From 1953 to 1960, he was with the U.S. Bureau of the Census; from 1948 to 1953, with the Russian Research Center, Harvard University; from 1947 to 1948, with the Institute for Advanced Study, Princeton; in 1946–47, with the National War College. Prior to the war he served a year with the Institute of Child Welfare, California, and for four years did ethnological and psychological research with the Shoshone Indians, Wind River Reservation, Wyoming. Mr. Shimkin is the author of *The Soviet Mineral-fuels Industries, 1928–1958: A Statistical Survey* (1962), *Soviet Industrial Growth* (with F. A. Leedy, 1958), *Trends in Economic Growth: A Comparison of the Western Powers and the Soviet Bloc* (with others, 1955), and *Minerals, a Key to Soviet Power* (1953). Mr. Shimkin was born in 1916. He attended the University of California, where he was a Johnson Scholar in 1937–38, a University Fellow in 1938–39, and received his Ph.D. in 1939.

trols and psychological pressures have promoted intense economic activity. This, in combination with maximal autarky, has led to the widespread employment of marginal as well as optimal manpower, other natural resources, and capital. Direct allocations and subsidies have insured the maintenance of such full and over-full employment, while minimizations of slack time, simplifications of jobs, types and uses, and standardizations of patterns and flows together have lessened the diseconomies inherent in marginal resource use. Abroad, exports of Soviet raw materials and skilled manpower have paid for key imports from Western Europe, aided the extension of Soviet influence in buffer and neutralist areas, and provided minimal support to the military capacities of satellite countries. For the future, the Soviet Union anticipates continuing rapid resource development and highly controlled resource utilization. Its apparent goals are national power, an internal transformation to a homogeneous, urban-type society, and an expansion, internationally, of trade and influence.

The novelty and evident success of the Soviet economic system, combined with widespread hostility towards capitalism, have aroused worldwide interest in Soviet planning and management techniques, notwithstanding their long association with political repression. At the same time, the advent of powerful logical and quantitative approaches to economics, especially game theory and linear programming, of techniques for rapid and reliable data procurement and of large-scale data handling has given some hope that the best features of Western and Soviet-type economics — of marginal utility and Marxist rationalizing — might be malleable into new, effective, and socially responsive means of resource development and utilization.

This paper seeks to outline the Soviet approach to resource use. However, a brief essay can deal only selectively and suggestively with the many facets and implications of Soviet resource management and use. This is particularly true because the very field of resource development must first be defined in appropriate form. With that done, the initial goal of this report is to sketch and evaluate the major instruments and procedures of Soviet resource development and allocation, especially as applied to manpower and agricultural land. The study then tries to explore the effects of Soviet management upon resources by a review of Soviet reserves, operations, problems, and plans in energy development, including current and potential international trade in fuels. Tentative observations on the utility of Soviet practices and experience to other countries, both undeveloped and relatively developed, replace conclusions for this paper.

What Is Resource Development?

Resource development is, in my view, a process in which the natural endowments of an area and of its populations are captured by appropriate management, productive skills, and technology for the end uses of household consumption, public service, defense, capital accumulation (including that of knowledge), and exportation. The aggregate of resources captured by an economy over a given time, expressed in monetary terms, is its national or regional product.

The term "natural endowments" is used here for the inventory, quantitatively expressed, of potential factors for generating economic product. Illustrations are as follows: given concentrations and quantities of various mineral elements; given quantities and patterns of precipitation, growing-season heat and evaporation in an area; and the numbers, age-and-sex compositions, and reproductive potentials of human and domesticated animal populations. Many natural endowments can be *upgraded* by exploration, improvement in accessibility, and processing; *exploited* at various levels of intensity and efficiency; and depleted through exploitation or *downgraded* through such agents of physical deterioration as pollution, erosion, and disease, or by economic displacement. Other distinctions between endowments are those of expendable flows — notably energy, as contrasted to recycled materials, such as metals; directly consumable versus initial-stage resources which must be transformed prior to use — for example, beef versus atmospheric nitrogen; and biological as opposed to physico-chemical resources. Plants and animals are themselves involved in complex ecological interactions — feeding, growth, reproduction, death — and generally less subject to human management than inanimate materials.

"Resource management" I would define as the combination of apperception of possibilities, goal definition, institutional arrangements, and controls utilized by a country's decision makers, great and small, to govern the physical aspects of economic activities. Innovations and communications; value systems; economic, educational and administrative organizations; and mechanisms of motivation and coercion enter into resource management. Moreover, the points and alternatives of decision involved in such management are multitudinous in all but the smallest and simplest economies. Maximum differences in returns per unit of effort may rest with scale, or efficiency of yield, or velocity of circulation, or in a total substitution of materials or processes. Changing distribution patterns to different end uses may be very influential upon returns from the same inputs. Beyond this, the results gained are often sensitive to the order of relationships examined, from single-stage to initial-terminal. The projections of relationships over time and for contingencies such as war and crop failure are particularly unreliable when concerned with key scarcities, large requirements, and long lead-times. Thus, the most strategic aspects of resource planning are precisely the least reliable in regard both to inputs and potential effects.

Two aspects of management need particular stress. First, multiple foci of decision making are present in every economy, no matter how totalitarian. Group and regional solidarities, mass food habits, and sexual mores are particularly intractable. When ignored or overridden, they generate higher-order effects, such as lowered productivity, which may require a series of unanticipated actions — labor recruiting, migration, heightened demand, inflation, etc. — often more costly in aggregate resource diversions than direct accommodations. Second, present mathematical systems, which are based ultimately on a binary or Boolean logic free of contradictions, cannot develop general and unconditional solutions for the multidimensional matrices of multi-valued components needed to describe economies fully and validly.[1] In economic programming, a concentration on gaining categorical decisions for particular situations, given a single objective, has obscured this cardinal fact. What is achievable at most (where general hierarchies of advantage and disadvantage can be stated for several dimensions) are probabilistic solutions.[2] In short, while objective criteria and procedures can be specified for short-term, microeconomic decisions, the greater strategies are still intuitive. These intuitions can be aided, however, by the systematic examination of alternative chains of possibilities rapidly processed by computers.

The concepts of "productive skills" and "technology" are no less complex than those of "natural endowment" or "resource management." Their nature and their economic roles are extremely fluid in the modern world. Both specialization and generalization are constantly operative; commercialization and self-service are also strong countercurrents.

[1] For an incisive discussion of consistency requirements in mathematics see P. Rosenbloom, *The Elements of Mathematical Logic* (New York: Dover, 1950), pp. 170–81. The complex, non-linear nature of realistic economic models has been imaginatively explored by A. Tustin, *The Mechanism of Economic Systems* (Cambridge: Harvard University Press, 1953).

[2] Valuable sources on the potentialities, techniques, and limitations of mathematical analyses of economic decisions and processes are R. D. Luce and H. Raiffa, *Games and Decisions* (New York: Wiley, 1957); and R. H. Howard, *Dynamic Programming and Markov Processes* (New York: Wiley, 1960).

Nevertheless, the skills underlying the broad gamut of today's occupations can be specified to include an awareness of time, place, number, and action; also, capacities for fine manipulations, functional literacy, conditional thinking and, above all, continuous learning. In technology, a number of broad trends are likely to continue. Among them are the shifts from custom to batch and then continuous-flow production, and from complex aggregates to assemblies of multipurpose units; the increasing substitution of mechanical and biological processes by hydraulic, chemical, and electrical means; use of an expanding range of pressures, temperatures, voltages, and velocities; expanding applications to radiation; and shorter fabrication chains.[3] In all, the viability as well as the inventory of immediately available skills and technology are essential components of contemporary capacities for resource development.

The scope and complexity of resource development as described here are enormous; the task is unending, while the procedures of development are nowhere free of fault. For these reasons, a survey of the practices, results, problems, plans, and alternatives of the Soviet Union in the field of resource development has general value for more and less developed countries alike. The U.S.S.R., as the oldest and most successful expounder of power-centered state management, provides many positive and negative lessons for every type of economy. This essay seeks to identify the salient features of, and the major lessons derivable from, Soviet experience, with particular reference to resource development in manpower, energy, and agricultural land.

Some Instruments and Procedures of Soviet Resource Development and Allocation

Specialized decision-making and administrative agencies, determined yet inconsistent efforts at resource assessment, systematic developmental

[3] The most important study of potential technological developments and their significance, particularly from the standpoints of materials extraction and use, is still President's Materials Policy Commission, *Resources for Freedom,* Vol. IV: *The Promise of Technology* (Washington: U.S. Government Printing Office, 1952). Process analysis has been greatly advanced in the study of the machinery industries of the United States (by the Division of Productivity and Technological Change, U.S. Bureau of Labor Statistics) and of the Soviet Union (by the Institute for Research in the Social Sciences of the University of North Carolina). See M. Boretsky, "The Soviet Challenge to U.S. Machine Building," pp. 69–143 of Joint Economic Committee, Congress of the United States, *Dimensions of Soviet Economic Power* (Washington: U.S. Government Printing Office, 1962).

hypotheses, and comprehensive mid- and short-term plans and controls constitute the major features of Soviet practice in resource development and allocation. The system has evolved over a considerable period and thus is colored by traditions as well as explicit rules. Cumbersome yet strong, costly yet vigorous, it requires careful, balanced evaluation.

Means of Decision Making and Administration

An extensive, central decision-making apparatus, local administrative agencies, and a limited yet influential popular autonomy interact in the Soviet Union today to govern the nation's resource activation and use. The State's decision-making apparatus comprises five institutional groups. Of these, the periodic *Congresses* and the standing *Central Committee* of the Communist Party together form the means of determining national socio-political, economic, and strategic goals, e.g., those for 1980; of guiding governmental agencies; and of ensuring policy implementations with the help of economic, psychological, and police pressures. Within the framework of the Party's goals, primary responsibility for the creation of broad developmental concepts covering particular economic sectors or geographical regions is held by the *U.S.S.R. Academy of Sciences,* especially the Council for the Study of Productive Forces. The Academy works closely with the State Planning Commission, the State Commission on Problems of Labor and Wages, the Central Statistical Administration, and other *staff agencies of the Council of Ministers of the U.S.S.R.* Through the Council, the Academy and the staff agencies can obtain specialized support from the Research Institutes of the civilian Ministries and regional Economic Councils. Finally, the Ministry of Defense ensures the adequacy of developmental hypotheses from the standpoint of various military demands and contingencies.[4] Developmental hypotheses, once they are approved by the Party, become the basis for increasingly detailed resource assessments, estimates of requirements, and finally, of development, operations, and allocations plans. In current practice, the regional Economic Councils and other local administrative agencies are important

---

[4] The broad-ranging concerns of the Ministry of Defence in provisions for military and industrial mobilization are well discussed in P. V. Sokolov, *Voyna i lyudskiye resursy (War and Human Resources)*, Moscow: Voyenizdat, 1961, esp. pp. 68–69. Military requirements involve personnel; specialized end-items produced by ministries under armed forces control (atomic materials, ammunition, ordnance, naval shipping, aviation, etc.); civil-type operations (for example, military farms) supporting combat forces; and civil capacity convertible to military use. The last also involves the setting of standards for civilian equipment, such as tractors, to maximize suitability for emergency military use. This often involves added costs, e.g., for heavier bearings, which are passed on to the civilian economy.

sources of information, operational co-ordinators, and adjusters of supply imbalances.[5]

The economic autonomy of the population is greatest in the countryside. In 1959, over one-third of the entire labor input of the collective farmers, and probably an equal proportion of that of the state farmers, was devoted to their private plots, livestock, and handicrafts. About a third of all energy consumed in rural areas in that year was self-procured. Almost all rural housing and a third of the livestock were held privately. Almost a quarter of the gross output of crops and livestock products in Soviet agriculture came from the private sector. Finally, since much fodder accrues as a payment in kind from the public sector, and since private livestock may graze on pastures, the impact of private holdings on Soviet agricultural-land use is far greater than suggested by the share of private plots, 1.5 per cent, in the country's farmlands.[6] City people are far more vulnerable economically than rural, and are also subject to special pressures such as the "anti-parasite" campaigns. Nevertheless, Soviet difficulties since 1958 in the build-up of a Siberian labor force suggest that today's controls are limited even in urban areas. Furthermore, Soviet experiments with public-opinion polls have publicized a widespread demand for better housing, more public child care, and other urban amenities.[7]

Resource Assessment

Within the central apparatus, resource assessment, planning and allocation procedures in the U.S.S.R. manifest many distinctive features. In

[5] See G. I. Grebtsov and P. P. Karpov, *Material'nyye balansy v narodnokhozyaystvennom plane* (*Materials Balances in the National-Economic Plan*), Moscow: Gosplanizdat, 1960, esp. pp. 13–28. The discussion pertains essentially to 1959–61; since then, considerable changes in administrative organization and procedures have changed specific features but not the basic system.

[6] The labor input data are from N. I. Shishkin *et al., Trudovyye resursy SSSR* (*Labor Resources of the U.S.S.R.*), Moscow: Ekonomizdat, 1961, pp. 90–91; on energy, Appendix Table 8, Note 7; on aggregate production, landholdings, and livestock holdings by sector see Ts.S.U. pri Sovete ministrov SSSR, *Sel'skoye khozyaystvo SSSR* (*Agriculture of the U.S.S.R.*), Moscow: Gosstatizdat, 1960, pp. 22, 124, 263–64. The materials on contributions from the public and private sectors to Soviet gross agricultural output are from V. Venzher, "The Auxiliary Economy —A Supplementary Source of the Production of Agricultural Products," *Voprosy ekonomiki*, 1962, No. 7, pp. 58–69. For an over-all survey see J. A. Newth, "Soviet Agriculture: The Private Sector, 1950–1959," *Soviet Studies*, 13:160–71, 1961. See also D. Gale Johnson's discussion of agriculture in the U.S.S.R., in the present volume.

[7] See V. Perevedentsev, "Problems in the Territorial Redistribution of Labor Resources," *Voprosy ekonomiki*, 1962, No. 5, pp. 48–56; and *Komsomol'skaya pravda*, October 7, 1960 (*Current Digest of the Soviet Press*, XII, 41, pp. 9–18); *ibid.*, December 17, 1961 (*C.D.S.P.*, XIV, 9, pp. 17–19).

general, the types, quantities, and qualities of data on natural endowments available to Soviet planners are not as adequate as those extant on major Western countries but are far better than the ones characterizing underdeveloped areas. But because the data are far more standardized and more systematically collated than in the West, analysis and interpretation are enhanced. Unfortunately, controls and measures of reliability are often lacking, while desire to excel often introduces major biases into Soviet reports on mineral reserves, crop yields, longevity, etc. No evidence of modern probability sampling has been found, although unsophisticated fragmentary surveys are common.

In manpower statistics, the excellent but limited population census of 1959 is the current landmark, supplemented by establishment statistics, school reports, annual household registrations, etc. The data appear to be qualitatively variable, worse for rural than for urban areas, and especially poor for the private sector and for adults not in the labor force.[8]

In contrast to demographic data, Soviet geological and geophysical surveys seem to be very good. The surface geology of the entire country has been mapped at a scale of 1:1,000,000, while the major subterranean structures west of the Yenisey have been revealed through extensive gravitational and seismological soundings, reinforced by selective deep drilling. A nation-wide mapping of surface geology at the scale of 1:200,-000, with ore-bearing areas at 1:50,000, is to be completed by 1965. Soviet prospecting has been generally successful, notably so for oil, natural gas, and diamonds. Ore shortages in phosphate rock and base nonferrous metals have, however, been recently noted. Soviet reserve-assessment standards and techniques have been substantially modernized over the past decade. In particular, factors of relative economic advantage, such as suitability for pillar-and-chamber or opencut operation (in coal deposits), are now being given much weight.[9]

---

[8] Shishkin, *op. cit.* (Note 6), pp. 149, 225–43; obsolescent but still valuable is A. Y. Boyarskiy and P. P. Shusherin, *Demograf-cheskaya statistika* (*Demographic Statistics*), Moscow: Gosstatizdat, 1955, esp. pp. 222–42. On the techniques of the 1959 census, the best summary is U.S. Bureau of the Census, *Materials on the Preparation and Conduct of the U.S.S.R. All-Union Population Census of 1959,* by J. F. Kantner and L. Kulchycka, Bureau of the Census Working Paper No. 8, (Washington, 1959). The basic source on Soviet labor force statistics is U.S. Bureau of the Census, *The Soviet Statistical System: Labor Force Record Keeping and Reporting,* by Murray Feshbach. International Population Statistics Reports, Series P–90, No. 12 (Washington: U.S. Government Printing Office, 1960).

[9] On Soviet geological-mapping plans see Ye. D. Shlygin, *Kratkiy kurs geologiyi SSSR* (*A Short Course in the Geology of the U.S.S.R.*), Moscow: Gosgeoltekhizdat, 1959, pp. 7–8. A representative modern geological study of the U.S.S.R. west of the Yenisey is V. G. Bondarchuk, *Geologiya Ukrayni* (*Geology of the*

Soviet materials on agricultural-land resources are very uneven. On one hand, Soviet agronomists are thoroughly conscious of the possibilities and value of modern ecological and edaphic measurements. Small-scale national maps have been published on such variables as the moisture reserves of the first meter of soil at the beginning of spring and the end of fall.[10] On the other hand, the basic observational network for soils is still too thin for modern needs. In A. V. Sokolov's words:

> A serious problem has been set in regard to large-scale soil mapping and assessment. Two methods of large-scale soil mapping exist. One is applied abroad — that is the agrochemical study of soils with the aid of mass determinations of P, K, and pH in soil samples taken from every two to four hectares of plowland. This method has been proven by practice; it permits the economic and effective use of fertilizers. The second method is applied in the U.S.S.R. — that is the investigation of the fields of state and collective farms with the goal of determining what types of soils are present. In this method, enormous areas (100–1,000 hectares) are sometimes characterized by the analysis of a few soil samples. This method is useful for the introduction of crop rotations, the organization of the economy, and especially the mastery of new lands . . . [but] is of little value in the practical support of fertilization. . . .[11]

The Soviet government uses agricultural-land productivity assessments as bases for differential pricing for crops bought by the State and for planning future production and input requirements. The regions established for pricing are very gross, e.g., seventeen pricing zones for grain in the entire U.S.S.R.[12] Even the production-planning data use single productivity coefficients for entire oblasts or provinces.

The assessment procedures and results, as officially reported by Sobolyev and Malyshkin in 1958, are based upon long-term grain yields for

---

Ukraine), Kiyev: Vid. Akademiy nauk Ukr. R.S.R., 1959. For Soviet prospecting in the fossil fuels see U.S. Bureau of the Census, *The Soviet Minerals-Fuels Industries, 1928–1958,* by D. B. Shimkin, International Population Statistics Reports, Series P–90, No. 19 (Washington: U.S. Government Printing Office, 1962), pp. 33–7, 153–63. See also Appendix Table 5. On nonferrous-metals reserves note B. Chugunov, "Non-ferrous Metallurgy and Technological Progress," *Voprosy ekonomiki,* 1959, No. 10, pp. 120–23.

[10] For example, Plate 40 of A. I. Tulupnikov *et al., Atlas sel'skogo khozyaystva SSSR (Atlas of the Agriculture of the U.S.S.R.),* Moscow: Glavnoye uprav. geodeziyi i kartografiyi ministerstva geologiyi i okhrana nedr SSSR, 1960.

[11] A. V. Sokolov, "Problems of Agronomic Chemistry in the U.S.S.R." *Pochvovedeniye,* 1959, No. 4, pp. 1–8, esp. p. 3.

[12] N. A. Tsagalov (ed.), *Zemel'naya renta v sotsialisticheskom sel'skom khozyaystve (Land Rent in Socialist Agriculture),* Moscow: Gosplanizdat, 1959, esp. pp. 95–100.

four periods.[13] These include peasant farming up to 1914; collective and State farms prior to 1941, and again, after 1947; and, finally, seed plots for fifteen to twenty years. Allegedly, the data from all sources showed high consistency in relative yields by area. The data from each sampling area were segregated by major groups (thirteen types for the U.S.S.R. excluding Central Asia and the Transcaucasus) and corrections were finally introduced for mechanical composition of the soil and for erosion.

Assessment investigations have continued since 1958. For example, more intensive work on Gorkiy Oblast, based on ninety-eight collective farms (187,000 hectares of plowland), divided into ten soil types, and utilizing 1953–55 yields, disclosed a 5 : 1 range in land productivity within that oblast.[14] Again, in Rostov Oblast, researches have demonstrated by graphic methods that soil fertility, soil depth, and humus content there correlate almost exactly. The range of grain yields, by type of soil, is fourfold (3.8 to 14.9 quintals per hectare) for state and collective farms, but threefold (10.0 to 29.9 quintals per hectare) on seed plots.[15] Finally, Cheremushkin's study of all areas but Central Asia and the Transcaucasus has used 1955–59 yields to assess the relative qualities of aggregate farmland, including hay meadows and pastures, and to evaluate plowland in terms of feed-unit and digestible protein yields.[16]

In general, Soviet agricultural assessments embody weak and scanty primary data handled by primitive statistical methods or even fully subjective means. They appear, in common with much of the manpower data, to be shaky foundations for precise planning. Energy data are better, while those on raw materials vary greatly in quality.

Developmental Hypotheses

From the time of the First Five-Year Plan, Soviet economic development has been structured by a limited number of general, economically strategic concepts. Among the more important of these were the Urals-Kuznetsk Combine, which built up large-scale steel capacity at both ends

[13] S. S. Sobolyev and M. N. Malyshkin, "Problems in the Qualitative Assessment (*bontirovka*) of the Soils of the U.S.S.R." *Pochvovedeniye,* 1958, No. 9, pp. 10–28.

[14] A. S. Fatyanov, "Agro-soil Regionalization and the Relative Evaluation of Soils," *Pochvovedeniye,* 1959, No. 6, pp. 16–22.

[15] F. Ya. Garrilyuk, "A Qualitative Evaluation of the Soils of Rostov Oblast," *Pochvovedeniye,* 1959, No. 11, pp. 1–7. The metric system is used throughout this essay. For purposes of comparison: 1 metric ton = 10 quintals = 2,204.6 lbs.; 1 hectare = 2.471 acres.

[16] Cheremushkin, "On the Rational Use of Land in Agriculture," *Voprosy ekonomiki,* 1961, No. 8, pp. 80–89.

of a long-range coal-iron ore exchange, and the Volga Basin project, which yielded hydroelectricity, urban and industrial water supplies, and improved waterways at great cost to Caspian Sea fisheries and navigation.[17] Some major undertakings, in contrast, were aborted after costly starts. These included the "Baykal-Amur Magistral" railroad, which was to parallel the trans-Siberian north of Lake Baykal, and the Turkmen Canal, which was to divert the Amu Darya into the Caspian Sea.

Within the past decade, procedures for generating developmental hypotheses (*nauchnyye gipotezy razvitiya*)[18] have been formalized as initial points for large-scale planning. Let us examine the nature, utility, and limitations of such hypotheses by reviewing the key points of two interrelated projects: the concepts for population structure and manpower use in 1980, and the long-term (1965–72) agricultural goals.

The 1959 Soviet census of population enumerated 209 million persons. It disclosed continuing influences from World War II. Survivors of births during the 1940's numbered only 32 million; also, in the population aged 35 years and over, which had been subjected to enormous combat losses, less than 27 million men were still alive while women of this age group numbered 46 million. In contrast to these adverse effects, the substantial educational efforts of the past twenty years had greatly increased average educational attainments. In 1959, 59 million persons, or about 45 per cent of those aged 20 and above, had at least seven years of schooling, while 3.8 million, or 2.9 per cent, had completed higher education. The comparable proportions in 1939 were 21 per cent and 1.6 per cent. Sixty-eight per cent of the Soviet population aged 16 years and over, or 99 million persons, were employed by the State and by co-operatives in civilian and military capacities. The corresponding fraction in 1939 had been 74 per cent, with the decline in labor-force participation being attributable largely to wartime losses of men and to urbanization. Over twenty years, the proportion in agriculture within State and co-operative employment had fallen from 50 to 39 per cent. At the same time, the share of industry, construction, transportation, and communications as an aggregate rose from 30 to 37 per cent; that of professional services (research, technical

[17] D. B. Shimkin, "Economic Regionalization in the Soviet Union," *Geographical Review,* 42:591–614, 1952; S. Yu. Geller, "On the Question of Regulating the Level of the Caspian Sea," *Soviet Geography: Review and Translation,* 3:59–66, 1962.

[18] A term used in I. P. Bardin *et al., Razvitiye proizvoditel'nykh sil Vostochnoi Sibiri, Rayonnyye i mezhrayonnyye kompleksnyye problemy (The Development of the Productive Forces of Eastern Siberia, Regional and Interregional Complex Problems)*, Moscow: Izd. akademiyi nauk, 1960, p. 188.

services, education, entertainment, propaganda, and health) increased from 6 to 10 per cent; and those of trade, distribution, and food services and of miscellaneous branches remained stable, at 5 and 9 per cent of the total, respectively. Rural-urban contrasts in educational attainments diminished. In 1939, only 1.3 per cent of the agricultural workers had seven years or more of schooling, compared to 7.8 per cent for other types of physical workers. By 1959, the figures had risen to 22 and 39 per cent, respectively. Extreme differences were still evident in the frequency of higher education, by economic branch. This ranged, in 1959, from 20.7 per cent in the professional services to 1.9 per cent in industry, and 0.2 per cent in agriculture. Finally, while the branches of high prestige — industry, construction, transportation, research, and technical services — had remained predominantly male, women made up the bulk of employment in all other activities.[19]

Starovskiy has recently summarized Soviet manpower anticipations for 1980.[20] By that time, the total population is projected to be 278 million persons, while the number in Soviet nominal working ages (16 through 59 for men, 16 through 54 for women) is expected to rise from 120 million in 1959 to 157 million in 1980. The goal for State and co-operative civilian employment is about 139 million, compared to 95.5 million in 1959. This disproportionate increase is to be accomplished by a total absorption into public employment of private economic activity, which had engaged 10 million individuals (largely women) in 1959, and by the heightened labor-force participation of mothers with young children. The goal, furthermore, is to be attained coincidently with universal eleven-year education and with a higher-educational enrollment of 8 million students. Together, these developments would increase the number of full-time stu-

[19] Data compiled from Ts.S.U. pri Sovete ministrov SSSR, *S.S.S.R. v tsifrakh v, 1961g* (*The U.S.S.R. in Figures for 1961*), Moscow: Gosstatizdat, 1962, pp. 29, 32–33, 37, 43, 48–56, 313; Anonymous, "Population Data by Occupations and Education," *Vestnik statistiki*, 1961, No. 1, pp. 58–71 (*C.D.S.P.*, XIII, 6, pp. 25–30, 45); and for detailed estimates of the composition of the 1959 population by age and sex, J. W. Brackett, "Demographic Trends and Population Policy in the Soviet Union," pp. 487–589 of Joint Economic Committee, *op. cit.* (see Note 3), esp. pp. 564–65.

[20] V. N. Starovskiy, "The Productivity of Socialized Labor and Problems of National Population," *Vestnik akademiyi nauk*, 1962, No. 5, pp. 43–53. His population projection corresponds closely to Brackett's for 1/1/1981 under Fertility Assumption B, with slightly higher adult mortality than indicated in Model 3 (see Brackett, *op. cit.* [Note 19], pp. 566–69). Data on 1980 economic and educational goals have also been drawn from *SSSR v tsifrakh, op. cit.* (Note 19), pp. 108–9, 168, 326 and 357, and from *Pravda*, 30 July 1961 (*C.D.S.P.*, XIII, 29, pp. 8–14).

dents older than 15 years from 5.8 million in 1959 to about 18 million in 1980.[21]

In general, even if the high 1959 labor-force participation rates for working-age males and for the elderly of both sexes are maintained in 1980, and even if the armed forces remain at 3.6 million men, about 85 per cent of all women aged 16 through 54 will have to be either employed or in school to meet the 1980 labor-force goal. The comparable proportion in urban areas in 1959 was only 60 per cent, although a smaller part of all city women were married than are likely to be in 1980.[22] Soviet working mothers today face a 13 to 14 hour day on the job and at home.[23] Without dramatic improvements in working and living conditions, the intensification of pressures to seek paid work may have major effects on morale, labor productivity, and fertility. Little public attention has been given such adverse possibilities.

The anticipated structure of civilian employment in 1980 differs markedly from that of the 1959 base.[24] As an aggregate: industry, construction, transportation, and communications are to employ 48 to 56 million persons, or 35 to 40 per cent of the total; agricultural employment is to fall to 21 to 24 million, less than half the 1959 number inclusive of workers on private plots; professional services and real estate are to use 30 to 36 million persons; employment in trade, distribution, and food services (branches scheduled for fivefold expansion between 1960 and 1980) would rise to 7 or 8 million, judging from Soviet hopes for gains in the productivity of industrial labor. The residual for other civilian and military branches would be from 33 million persons at a maximum to 15 million at a minimum. Thus a thorough mobilization of Soviet manpower would be enough to meet the daring goals of 1980 — provided annual la-

[21] For 1959, Shishkin, *op. cit.* (Note 6), p. 19. The 1980 estimate assumes an average start in school at 7 years 6 months, an average repetition of half a grade, 100 per cent attendance, and 50 per cent daytime enrollment of those in higher education.

[22] On labor-force participation, urban and rural, in 1959 see Table 1 of D. B. Shimkin, "Current Characteristics and Problems of the Soviet Rural Population," in R. Laird (ed.), *Proceedings of the Conference on Soviet Agricultural and Peasant Affairs* (Lawrence: University of Kansas, 1963). The estimated marriage rates for women are derived from estimates of the number of men aged 16 to 59 and application of the age-specific male marriage rates in Shishkin, *op. cit.* (Note 6), p. 21. They come to 70 per cent for Soviet urban women in 1959 and 85 per cent for all Soviet women in 1980.

[23] Shishkin, *op. cit.* (Note 6), pp. 147–52.

[24] For sources see Note 20. Labor requirements have been calculated from stated output and productivity goals for 1960–80.

bor productivity gains of 7.2 to 9.4 per cent per year can be maintained for twenty years. Another difficult task implied by the 1980 targets is very rapid urbanization, with city dwellers to number 210 to 230 million persons by that date, as contrasted with only 100 million in 1959 and 56 million in 1939. The rural population, which constituted slightly more than half of the national total in 1959, would be reduced to less than a quarter. Since the bulk of today's peasantry is non-Russian, the problems of mass assimilation in a tightly knit city culture might be severe.

Soviet agricultural goals for the period 1965–72 are dominated by the desire to improve the nutritional standards of a growing population, by interest in increasing agricultural exports, and by a continued heavy reliance upon cultivated fibers.

Soviet data indicate that in 1953 the gross supplies of human food per capita totalled almost 3,100 calories daily, close to the level of the United States (Appendix Table 1). But qualitatively the diet was like that of the Italian population in 1934–38, or a bit poorer than those of Yugoslavia and Greece in 1954–56. Flour, potatoes, sugar, and alcohol accounted for 78 per cent of the calories; fats consumption was only 59 grams per day, and that of animal proteins, 23 grams. By 1958, food consumption had risen to almost 3,200 calories, the proportion of major carbohydrate sources and alcohol had fallen to 72 per cent, and fats consumption had risen to 73 grams; that of animal proteins, to 30 grams per day. Qualitatively, Soviet rations approximated contemporary Italian standards.[25]

Physiologically rational goals, adjusted to the age and sex composition, the labor-force participation rates, and the occupational structures of the Soviet Union, with further allowances for its cold climate, have been devised by the Institute of Nutrition of the Academy of Medical Sciences of the U.S.S.R. and the Research Institute for Trade and Food Services of the Ministry of Trade of the Russian Republic, for implementation in 1972.[26] The 1965 goals constitute interim targets. These shorter-term objectives call for a caloric level of almost 3,500 per day, which only the Irish exceed. Carbohydrate sources, including alcohol, are to provide 60 per cent of this total; fats consumption is to be 108 grams daily, and that of animal proteins, 45 grams. Qualitatively, this would be like the French diet today and a little poorer than that of northwest Europe. The ultimate

---

[25] The Italian diet in 1934–38 comes from Food and Agriculture Organization, *Food Balance Sheets* (Washington, 1949), pp. 85–92; for postwar nutritional levels see United Nations, *Economic Survey of Europe* (Geneva, 1961), Chapter III, p. 30, and Food and Agriculture Organization, *The State of Food and Agriculture 1962* (Rome, 1962), pp. 187–92.

[26] P. S. Mstislavskiy, *Narodnoye potrebleniye pri sotsializme* (*National Consumption under Socialism*) Moscow: Gosplanizdat, 1961, pp. 141–42.

goal of 3,300 calories, with only 52 per cent from flour, potatoes, sugar, and alcohol, and with daily intakes of 117 grams of fats and 56 grams of animal proteins, would match current achievements in Finland and Ireland, but be more austere than contemporary Canadian or American diets.

Soviet production goals for 1972 are designed not only to provide rational diets but export surpluses and abundant industrial supplies as well. In animal products, a 20 per cent margin beyond human consumption is to be provided. In breadstuffs, allowing for 17 per cent seed retention and a milling ratio of 75 per cent, the margin, in flour equivalent, would exceed 60 per cent, compared to 43 per cent in the bumper-crop year of 1958 and approximate self-sufficiency in 1953. Potatoes would be used essentially for fodder, half the vegetable oil would go to industry and abroad, while surpluses would replace chronic deficits even for sugar and fruits (Appendix Table 1).

Academician V. S. Nemchinov has directed a considerable cycle of studies on ways of implementing these grandiose hopes. Ruzskaya's analysis of livestock potentials is a key part of this work.[27] Its methodology is based on an explicit assumption that processing facilities for edible and inedible products, refrigeration, and means of distribution will become available in sufficient numbers and proper locations to raw materials supplies. With this proviso, the work seeks to develop desirable and feasible standards of animal productivity, based on changes in breed compositions, herd structures and care; to estimate the gross output attainable; and to calculate fodder and labor requirements corresponding to desired outputs and modern technologies. For the sake of simplicity, Ruzskaya utilizes standardized coefficients, e.g., of food requirements for a given species, breed, and age. But she also examines the effects of variant herd structures. Much attention also is given to regional problems, from the standpoints of fodder resources, production requirements, climatic and other current conditions, and desirable goals. Over-all, her approach is detailed and quantitative, but the underlying coefficients are never critically examined, nor is the vast mass of statistics subjected to strict mathematical programming to determine various types of optimizations, e.g., for costs per gram of protein, or labor inputs, or fodder needs. Thus the study as a whole represents a set of intuitive judgments of feasible, but not necessarily optimal, courses of action in meeting Soviet goals for animal production.

[27] Ye. A. Ruzskaya, *Perspektivy razvitiya i razmeshcheniya zhivotnovodstva v SSSR* (*Prospectives for the Development and Distribution of Livestock Breeding in the U.S.S.R.*), Moscow: Izd. akademiyi nauk, 1959, esp. pp. 3–16.

Ruzskaya's substantive conclusions are nevertheless interesting. Total livestock numbers should rise from 94 million head (in cattle equivalent) in 1958 to 141 million head in 1972. Except for the anticipated reduction in horses and camels from 12.3 to 5.4 million head, the species composition would be little changed. The number of cattle would increase from 67 to 103 million head; of sheep and goats, from 130 to 212 million head; of swine, from 44 to 66 million head; and of adult fowl, from 400 to 660 million. The rise in numbers of productive livestock, by 62 per cent, and a 64 per cent increase in productivity per head would yield the desired increase in edible animal products, 1958–72, of 165 per cent.[28]

The feed requirements for all livestock would rise to 526 million metric tons of feed units (oats equivalent), compared to an actual supply of 196 million metric tons in 1958. For productive animals alone, consumption would come to 510 million metric tons, or 6.0 metric tons per head (in cattle equivalent). Thus each kilogram of oats equivalent would yield 253 kilogram calories of meat, milk, and eggs. In 1958, the corresponding figures were 169 million metric tons, or 2.0 metric tons per head, and 286 kilogram calories produced from each kilogram feed unit. The better finished animals of the future would be slightly less efficient feed users. The quality of their feed would also be better, with the proportion of grains and concentrates rising, in feed units, from 20 to 30 per cent of the total.[29] In addition, Ruzskaya's estimate of labor requirements for the care of the animals and the raising of fodder, and excluding overhead and indirect inputs, comes to 49.8 billion man-hours or 22.2 million man-years at 1960 work norms (280 days a year at 8 hours per day). The comparable figure in 1960 was 25.4 million man-years, and the implied gain in productivity is from 2.04 million kilogram calories to 5.81 million kilogram calories per man-year, or 185 per cent. Since livestock and fodder operations comprised only 63 per cent of Soviet agricultural labor inputs in the socialized sector in 1960, Ruzskaya's projection suggests that perhaps 35 million workers might be necessary to meet the agricultural goals of 1972. In all, Ruzskaya's estimates of labor productivity gains and of

[28] *Ibid.*, pp. 202–3, 218, 226 and, for coefficients converting to cattle equivalents, p. 209. For the livestock count in 1958 see also Ts.S.U. pri Sovete ministrov SSSR, *Sel'skoye khozyaystvo SSSR* (*Agriculture of the U.S.S.R.*), Moscow: Gosstatizdat, 1960, pp. 263, 301. For the caloric values of livestock products in 1958 (48.5 trillion kilogram calories) and 1972 (129.0 trillion kilogram calories), see Appendix Table 1.

[29] Ruzskaya, 1959, *op. cit.* (Note 27), pp. 214–15, 220. For feed in 1958, see D. Gale Johnson and A. Kahan, *The Soviet Agricultural Program: An Evaluation of the 1965 Goals*, Memorandum RM–2848–PR (Santa Monica, Calif.: The RAND Corporation, 1962), p. 97.

agricultural employment are difficult to reconcile with Starovskiy's model for 1980.[30]

Let us now examine the Soviet goals and planned means of implementation for crop production. Here the best basis is the year 1956, when the Virgin Lands project, which brought into cultivation some 39 million hectares of steppe land, had been first completed (Appendix Table 2). Between 1956 and 1972, the major anticipated increases are as follows: fodder, about 185 per cent (to 528 million metric tons of oats equivalent); wheat and rye, 94 per cent (to 121 million metric tons); cotton, flax and hemp for fibers, oils, and fodder, 126 per cent (to 12.4 million metric tons, gross); sugar beets, 165 per cent (to 86 million metric tons); and fruits, grapes, and berries, elevenfold (to 38 million metric tons).[31]

To effect these gains, the Soviet planners call for changes in land use, upgrading land quality, changes in acreages under particular crops and, above all, a ninefold increase in the use of mineral fertilizers. The land-use model for 1972 and the changes anticipated from practice in the winter of 1955–56 are as follows: total farmland, 581 million hectares (plus 5 per cent); intensively irrigated Central Asiatic lands, within the sown acreage, 5.8 million hectares (plus 93 per cent); clean, plowed fallow, 15 million hectares (minus 32 per cent); orchards, 5.5 million hectares (plus 157 per cent); and meadows and pastures, 320 million hectares (minus 4 per cent).[32] Almost a tenth of the meadow and pasture land is to be periodically cultivated, sown, and fertilized.

[30] The 1972 data are from Ruzskaya, op. cit. (Note 27), pp. 223, 226–27. Labor inputs into meat, milk, and eggs production, including fodder, as a total but excluding the private sector, are given in Starovskiy, 1962, op. cit. (Note 20). The same data, with the inputs within agriculture alone are also reported in Ts.S.U. pri Sovete ministrov S.S.S.R., Narodnoye khozyaystvo SSSR v 1961g. (National Economy of the U.S.S.R. in 1961), Moscow: Gostatizdat, 1962, p. 119. To expand the figure cited there, 16.8 million man-years, full-time equivalent, to a coverage including the private sector, use was made of the table in Shishkin, 1961, op. cit. (Note 6), p. 91 which gives 1959 data for collective farm labor inputs in both the socialized and private sectors, with livestock, crop, and overhead operations measured in each. The adjustment used adds on only direct livestock operations in the private sector, since virtually all fodder comes from the socialized sector. The estimate of livestock-products output in 1960 is the 1958 datum (Appendix Table 1) increased by application of the official index for 1958–60 (Nar. khoz. v 1961, op. cit., p. 293).

[31] Sources: Appendix Table 2; Sel'khoz, op. cit. (Note 6), pp. 202–3; P. M. Zemskiy, Razvitiye i razmeshcheniye zemledeliya po prirodno-khozyaystvennym rayonam SSSR (The Development and Distribution of Crop Cultivation by the National Economic Regions of the U.S.S.R.), Moscow: Izd. akademiyi nauk, 1959, esp. pp. 10–13, 26–29, 105, 114.

[32] Ibid., pp. 10–13, 26–29; and Ruzskaya, op. cit. (Note 27), pp. 210–15; for 1959 populations, the source is Ts.S.U. pri Sovete ministrov SSSR, Narodnoye khozyaystvo SSSR v 1959g (The National Economy of the U.S.S.R. in 1959), Moscow: Gosstatizdat, 1960, pp. 27–33.

Apart from irrigation and pasture improvement, upgrading projects are to concentrate on drainage and especially on the revival of eroded lands. Today, at least 10 per cent of the farmland area of the Soviet Union has been destroyed by water erosion; in the uplands of the Transcaucasus and especially Central Asia, 30 to 40 per cent of pasture land has been lost.[33] In European Russia the damming of gullies, reforestation, and allied measures are essential to reclaim 15 million hectares of eroded, rapidly wasting lands. Out of this, the Soviets hope to gain 6 to 8 million hectares of excellent pasture, 5 to 6 million hectares of plowland, 1.5 million hectares of forest, and about 16,000 ponds.[34] Beyond these tasks lies an immense problem of education and management to insure proper agronomical practices. These include, in Zemskiy's words:

> . . . correct and timely soil working, timely sowing, cultivation and harvesting, the full utilization of manure, the extensive sowing of clover in the podzolic areas of European Russia, and of alfalfa in Central Asia and southern Kazakhstan. . . .[35]

The Soviets plan only moderate changes in crop patterns. The most important of these is the increase in hay, silage, and root-crop feeds from 19 to 26 per cent of all sown acreage. Correspondingly, grain acreage would fall from 68 per cent in 1956 to 61 per cent in 1972. Within grains, wheat and rye acreage would fall by a fifth and corn (maize) would rise 75 per cent, to comprise 35 per cent and 8.5 per cent respectively of all sown acreage in 1972. The shifts toward higher-yielding species within grains would increase the average yield for all grains by 6.6 per cent. A 15 per cent increase in grain acreage and a 60 per cent increase in mean yield per species constitute the other components of the 96 per cent rise in grain output anticipated between 1956 and 1972.[36]

The use of mineral fertilizers in Soviet agriculture is to rise from 9.4 million metric tons in 1956 to 84.5 million in 1972. The nitrogen content of the fertilizer used would rise from 402,000 metric tons to 4,692,000, nearly twelve times; potash (K_2O), from 756,000 metric tons to 5,297,000, or sevenfold; and phosphoric oxide (P_2O_5), from 921,000 metric tons to 7,573,000, or more than eightfold.[37] The present practice of concentrating half the nation's fertilizer on the 3 per cent of sown acreage taken by fibers and sugar beets would be replaced by much more uniform

---

[33] Tulupnikov, *op. cit.* (Note 10), Plate 53.
[34] I. D. Bravde, "Agro-forestry Ameliorative Measures of Erosion Control in the European Part of the U.S.S.R.," *Pochvovedeniye*, 1959, No. 6, pp. 35–41.
[35] Zemskiy, *op. cit.* (Note 31), p. 227.
[36] *Ibid.*, pp. 99–158.
[37] *Ibid.*, p. 266 and *Nar. khoz. v 1959, op. cit.* (Note 32), p. 380.

distributions (Appendix Table 2). The Soviet literature also points out the need for eliminating today's transport and storage losses, which average 15 to 20 per cent, partly because of the shortage of containers.[38] Better fertilizers are needed, especially neutral and alkaline nitrates (carbomide, urea, ammonia) to replace ammonium nitrate, which is both unstable and unsuitable for acid soils.[39] However, these and allied aspects of chemical support for agriculture seem as yet to be the subject of qualitative discussion rather than detailed estimation and planning.

Soviet agronomists must consider in their planning hypotheses not only national production goals but also the effects of proposed shifts in the population, as related to agro-climatic conditions and land resources. The fodder production plans show the influence of anticipated population distributions. In 1959, the North Caucasus, Ukraine, Moldavia, and Belorussia as an aggregate accounted for 31 per cent of the Soviet population and 22 per cent of the fodder output. For 1972, the comparable proportions are to be 27 and 26 per cent. Similarly, the Baltic States, and Central and North Russia included 32 per cent of the people and only 23 per cent of the fodder production in 1956–59; the planned figures are 32 and 26 per cent respectively. For the Volga, Urals, Western Siberia and the north-central parts of Kazakhstan, the 1956–59 percentages are 19 and 33 per cent, while the targets are 20 and 30 per cent respectively. Southern Kazakhstan, Central Asia, and the Transcaucasus display a similar convergence: 12.6 per cent of the population and 14.5 per cent of the fodder in 1956–59; 12.3 and 12.0 per cent in 1972. Eastern Siberia and the Far East alone show a growing disproportion: their share of the Soviet population is to rise from 5.6 per cent in 1959 to 8.6 per cent in 1972, but their share in fodder output is to decline, from 7.6 to 5.9 per cent.[40]

---

[38] E. Savinskiy, "On the Wide Application of Chemistry in the National Economy," *Voprosy ekonomiki,* 1962, No. 6, pp. 16–29, esp. p. 20.

[39] P. Bobrovskiy, "The Economic Effectiveness of the Use of Chemicals in Agriculture," *Voprosy ekonomiki,* 1961, No. 1, pp. 134–40, esp. p. 136.

[40] See Note 32 for sources. The groupings used are in terms of the Soviet agricultural project divisions, see Ruzskaya, *op. cit.* (Note 27), pp. 17, 257–58:
a) North Caucasus, Ukraine (Steppe, Forest-Steppe, Polesye, Carpathian Mountain), Moldavian SSR, Belorussian SSR.
b) Lithuanian SSR, Latvian SSR, Estonian SSR, Northwestern, European North, Central Podzolic ("Non-Black Earth"), Northeastern Podzolic ("Non-Black Earth"), Central Black Earth, and Eastern Black Earth.
c) Southeastern, Central Urals, Southern Urals, Western Regions of Siberia, Altay-Kemerovo, Western Kazakhstan, Northern Kazakhstan, Central Kazahkstan, and Eastern Kazakhstan.
d) Southeastern and Southwestern Kazakhstan, Kirgiz SSR, Tadjhik SSR, Uzbek SSR, Turkmen SSR, Azerbaydzhan SSR, Armenian SSR and Georgian SSR.
e) Eastern Siberia and the Far East.

The unfavorable climate of these areas has been an undoubted deterrent to proportional expansion. (See Map 1.)[41]

Climate also has influenced Soviet anticipations in regard to future yields. The areas of severe drought between Orenburg and Barnaul, where dry farming is expected to persist, are expected to bear yields running not better than 80 per cent of the national average. In contrast, the greater warmth of Southern Kazakhstan, Central Asia, and the Transcaucasus, buttressed by irrigation, should support yields at least 70 per cent greater than the average for the Soviet Union.[42]

The feasibility of the plans may be briefly examined by reference to experience in the United States. Tabulating Soviet yields in 1958, the 1972 goals, and American average yields in 1956–60, we obtain the following:[43]

	Yields (quintals per hectare[1])		
Crop	Soviet, 1958	Soviet, 1972 goals	U.S., 1956–60
Wheat	9.7*, 16.2**	12.1*, 18.0**	15.8
Rye	8.8**	18.8**	10.5
Oats	9.0	18.0	13.3
Barley	13.1*, 15.5**	15.3*, 17.5**	16.2
Corn for dry grain	23.3	30.2	32.1
Rice	20.1	33.9	36.6
Cotton for fiber	6.8	10.9	4.9
Flax for seed	2.4	7.0	5.1
Sugar beets	218	268	392
Irish potatoes	91	186	205

[1] 1 quintal = 220.46 lb.; 1 hectare = 2.471 acres.
* Spring strains; ** winter strains.

For individual crops, the plausibility of the goals, considering American performances, anticipated increases in fertilizer inputs (Appendix Table 2), and 1958 yields, is quite variable. Those for wheat, barley, corn, sugar beets, and potatoes appear reasonable; those for rye, oats, cotton,

[41] Compiled from Tulupnikov, *op. cit.* (Note 10), plates 41, 46–47. The basic concepts of Soviet agro-climatic analysis are given in G. T. Selyaninov *et al.*, *Mirovoy agro-klimaticheskiy spravochnik* (*World Agro-climatic Handbook*), Leningrad: Gidro meteorologicheskoye izdatel'stvo, 1937, p. 412, esp. pp. 19, 23–25, 38, and 45–47.

[42] See, for example, Zemskiy, *op. cit.* (Note 31), p. 72.

[43] *Ibid.*, esp. p. 85; Appendix Table 2; for the United States, U.S. Bureau of the Census, *Statistical Abstract of the United States, 1962* (Washington: U.S. Government Printing Office, 1962), pp. 651–52, 667.

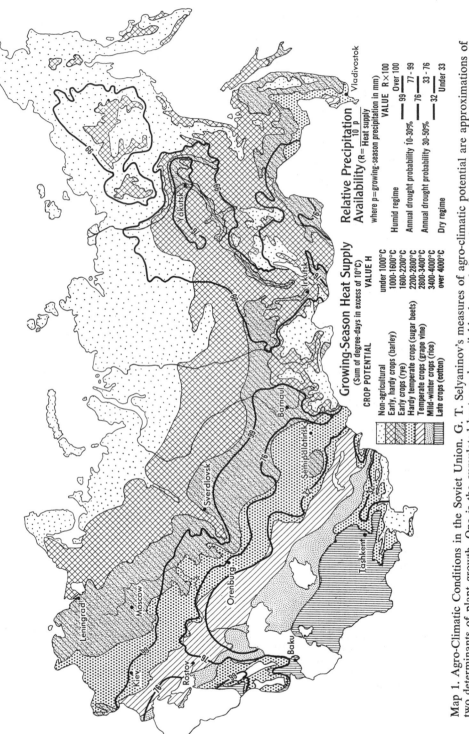

Growing-Season Heat Supply
(Sum of degree-days in excess of 10°C)

CROP POTENTIAL	VALUE H
Non-agricultural	under 1000°C
Early, hardy crops (barley)	1000-1600°C
Early crops (rye)	1600-2200°C
Hardy temperate crops (sugar beets)	2200-2800°C
Temperate crops (grape vine)	2800-3400°C
Mild-winter crops (rice)	3400-4000°C
Late crops (cotton)	over 4000°C

Relative Precipitation Availability
$(R = \dfrac{10 \, p}{H} = \text{Heat supply}$

where p = growing-season precipitation in mm)

	VALUE R×100
Humid regime	99 — Over 100
Annual drought probability 10-30%	76 — 77 - 99
Annual drought probability 30-50%	32 — 33 - 76
Dry regime	Under 33

Map 1. Agro-Climatic Conditions in the Soviet Union. G. T. Selyaninov's measures of agro-climatic potential are approximations of two determinants of plant growth. One is the cumulated heat supply available, beyond the maintenance needs, for growth, flowering and reproductions. The other is moisture supply during the growing season, related to heat.

and flax are hard to accept. Beyond these considerations are two partly offsetting forces. On one hand, the moisture and heat conditions encountered by Soviet crops are substantially poorer, for each species, than in the United States. On the other hand, Soviet plans call for a fertilizer input of 322 kilograms per hectare of sown land, 15 per cent higher than the American figure for 1960.[44] The over-all evidence certainly calls for a considerable deflation of Soviet anticipations, or at the least, an urgent call for the development of much more effective strains. Much more fertilizer also would be needed to gain the stated targets.

To sum up: The evidence on Soviet practice in the formulation of developmental hypotheses shows that these originate both from the availability of resources (manpower) and from demand (for food, exports, industrial materials). The hypotheses seek to solve general national problems in broad fashion, assuming the presence of appropriate pre-conditions. The basic technique used is the construction of multi-stage models qualitatively defining the systems of variables and quantitatively assessing requirements and potentials through the use of large masses of current and projected statistics. These statistics do not appear to be subjected to much critical analysis. The models, moreover, are intuitive; little evidence of the use of formal mathematical tests of systems consistencies or of programming for optimization of given variables has appeared.[45]

In general, while the developmental models certainly provide useful concepts for planning, they are definitely hazardous as quantitative, operational designs. Apart from ignoring the areas and magnitudes of probable error in their basic data, these models consistently overload the available resources and exaggerate attainable results. Cross-checks between hypotheses of different type (manpower and agriculture) appear to be feeble. Finally, little provision for the continuous re-examination of these models seems to be made. Rather, fragments from them are crystallized, all too often into Communist Party directives, which then assume an impact of their own upon the national economy that may be far removed from the original intents of these developmental models.

[44] *Ibid.*, pp. 628, 649.

[45] Interest in optimization techniques has developed in the Soviet Union since 1960. For example, see V. S. Dadayan and V. V. Kossov, *Balans ekonomicheskogo rayona kak sredstvo planovykh raschetov* (*The Balances of an Economic Region as a Means of Calculation for Planners*), Moscow: Izd. akademiyi nauk, 1962, esp. pp. 6–18. The pioneer studies of L. Kantorovich in this field, formulated as early as 1939, have yet to be systematically applied in the U.S.S.R. Kantorovich's basic report has been translated as "Mathematical Methods of Organizing and Planning Production," *Management Science*, 6:366–422, 1960.

Mid- and Short-Term Plans and Controls

The implementation of long-term developmental projects and response to unexpected civil and military developments comprise the major business of Soviet resource management. Characteristic approaches to these tasks are a sharp stratification of goals, with concentration — often, over-concentration — on those of highest priority, and with overriding emphasis upon reliable achievement rather than least cost in priority sectors; on least cost rather than reliability, in others, especially the sphere of consumption. The measures taken are limited in scope and extremely detailed in content. Planning gaps and inconsistencies commonly occur at operating levels, where lateral co-ordination is often most difficult. Command rather than persuasion predominates. While central authorities permit themselves many expedient changes, subordinates are supposed to follow orders and to exercise initiative only within prescribed bounds.

Data on mid- and short-term planning and controls in manpower, energy, and agriculture exemplify these generalizations.

In planning the use of manpower, economic targets and anticipated changes in productivity serve as the foundations. These are balanced against current employment, by establishment, class of worker and occupation, with adjustments for anticipated losses and absences. Deficits throughout the economy are met first by local recruiting and then by seasonal or permanent migration plans. Sources for labor include anticipated surpluses on collective farms and in other enterprises, young persons completing or dropping out of school, able-bodied persons working on private agricultural plots, and housewives and pensioners not in the labor force.[46]

Several aspects of manpower planning are especially noteworthy. Many plans which call for upgrading labor forces with new graduates of higher and specialized secondary educational institutions, as well as those for skilled craftsmen, require several years of lead time. These plans are essentially based on standard organizational tables, adjusted for changing technical demands. In order to ensure that numerical requirements are met, point by point, the Soviets employ a so-called "address" system. That is, ". . . the plan itself gives each regional Economic Council, Ministry, and Office having educational establishments assignments for the matriculation of students and the graduation of specialists in the corresponding planning period, while the specialist-distribution plan concretely directs the allocation of these graduates by regional Economic Council,

[46] Shishkin, *op. cit.* (Note 6), pp. 225–44.

Ministry, and Office."[47] It should be stressed that Soviet education systematically produces technical personnel far beyond calculable requirements in industry, construction, research, and other appropriate civilian assignments. Such over-production provides a leeway for qualitative selection but is especially a response to the current and mobilization requirements of the Soviet armed forces. According to official data, the current ratio of officers to men in the Soviet Army is 1 to 10–12, while the ratio of technical to command officers is now 1 to 1.5.[48] In the civilian economy, surplus technical people man innumerable positions requiring literacy, since alternative sources of educated persons are meager.

Another aspect of Soviet manpower planning, given the chronic overloading of agricultural labor, is provision for recruiting and drafting urban people — housewives, students, and even factory workers — for help at times of peak operation.[49] Conversely, most urban establishments must make provisions for a considerable burden of part-time workers, especially those taking higher and special secondary training by correspondence, and for periodic lay-offs because of materials or power shortages. Finally, once goals and allocations have been effected, the fundamental questions of control, motivation, and productivity present thorny problems for Soviet manpower management. These are at a maximum in rural areas, where a predominance of non-Russians, low educational attainments, indifferent health, traditional attitudes, an economy in kind, dispersed settlements, and poor communications combine to frustrate central authority.[50]

In current Soviet practice, 12.8 thousand commodities are governed by specific production and allocation plans. Among them are 437 types of metal ingots, castings, and rolled products; 112 types of solid fuels; 176 types of petroleum (and gas) products; 1,162 chemicals and rubber products; 393 kinds of wood and paper products; 408 types of textiles, furs, apparel, and footwear; 580 types of food, fats, and alcohol products,

---

[47] L. A. Komarov, *Planirovaniye podgotovki i raspredeleniya spetsialistov v SSSR* (*Planning the Preparation and Distribution of Specialists in the U.S.S.R.*), Moscow: Ekonomizdat, 1961, p. 60.

[48] D. A. Voropayev and A. M. Iovlev, *Bor'ba KPSS za sozdaniye voyennykh kadrov* (*The Struggle of the Communist Party of the Soviet Union for the Creation of Military Cadres*), Moscow: Voyennoye izdatel'stvo ministerstva oborony SSSR, 2nd ed., 1960, pp. 242. See pp. 6, 237.

[49] Shishkin, *op. cit.* (Note 6), pp. 97–114; Central Committee of the Communist Party, "On the request of some Union Republics for enlisting urban workers and employees for agricultural work on collective and state farms," *Pravda*, July 14, 1962 (*Current Digest of the Soviet Press*, XIV, 28).

[50] See Shimkin, 1963, *op. cit.* (Note 22).

and 9.4 thousand kinds of machinery, transportation equipment, metalwares, and instruments. The national and regional energy plans cover general fuels, light petroleum products (gasoline, kerosene including jet fuel, and light diesel fuel), and electrical power. General fuels are subdivided into solid fuels, including fuel wood; liquid fuels (fuel oils and diesel oil used for stationary engines); and gases (dry and wet natural gases, distilled gases, coking gas, blast-furnace gas, etc.). Lubricants, greases, paraffin, and asphalt are also included in the general sphere of energy planning.[51]

Soviet energy plans and allocations initially consider demand in caloric terms, i.e., standard fuel equivalents of 7,000 kilocalories per kilogram, and then by specific types and grades, down to individual establishments. In case the prescribed fuel, say peat, is unobtainable, temporary substitutions with least-cost modifications may be authorized. One consequence of this rigidity is the active mining and use of low-grade lignites, officially designated as local fuels, in such areas of superior fuel resources as the western Urals and Central Ukraine. The energy plans cover over 90 per cent of the national supply, including imports and stocks, in accord with extensive input-output standards, e.g., per metric ton of open-hearth steel; in part, on the basis of unit coefficients, e.g., for hours of bulldozer operation; and to a modest extent, by proportional allowances, such as those for evaporation losses. Standard allowances for urban household needs, based on space heating, cooking, and hot water requirements, have come into use only recently. Rural householders depend on self-procured, purchased, and stolen fuels.

Exports constitute a very important part of the energy allocation plans. In 1960, for example, the U.S.S.R. exported 4.8 million metric tons of light diesel fuel; this made up a sixth of the nation's total oil exports. Yet in the same year, an authoritative treatise by Grebtsov and Karpov complained that ". . . our petroleum industry is not yet fully ready to supply the needs of the national economy with diesel fuel of suitable quality; . . . new processes . . . will permit liquidating the temporary imbalance between resources of diesel fuel and requirements for it. Nevertheless, the further progress of dieselization must be implemented with allowances for the actual resources of diesel fuel. This fuel, presently in deficit, should not be used, . . . for example, . . . on low-powered tractors. . . ."[52] In short, export priorities are met, when needed, at the expense of other sectors,

[51] Grebtsov and Karpov, *op. cit.* (Note 5), pp. 20–22, 68–69, 98.
[52] *Ibid.,* p. 101.

especially agriculture, where small diesel-powered tractors would be a major advantage.

In the mid-range and long-range planning of energy production, optimal resources — major deposits of coking coal, large deposits of steam coal suitable for opencut operation, major pools of oil, large natural-gas deposits, and prime hydroelectric sites — provide the conceptual foundation. The questions of development policy are then concerned with the relative possibilities, direct investment costs, and production advantages of on-site industrialization or of supply to existing centers. Little consideration is given in these plans to social costs — housing, schools, etc. Preferences for maintaining and even expanding industry in established areas such as Central Russia, the Urals, and Central Kazakhstan markedly exceed those for plant location at more convenient new sites, such as Voronezh in the Black Earth region or Omsk in Western Siberia. Because of this, current Soviet practice and future Soviet plans involve enormous hauls of fuels, an increasing use of long-distance electric power transmission, and extensive water development. Among the most ambitious of such ancillary efforts are the Irtysh-Karaganda Canal, to bring water 300 miles west and 1,500 feet up for mining, metallurgical, and urban users. Another is the 800 kilovolt line between Central Siberia and the Urals, scheduled for completion during the 1970's.[53]

In general, the management of Soviet energy resources is certainly competent and comprehensive. The relative profitability of alternative courses enters into decisions, but is far outweighed by emphasis on reliability of supply to priority sectors of the economy. National strategic goals, the welfare of old, Great Russian industrial areas, and a keen eye for spectacular engineering also have their influences. At the same time, the vast scale of investment required for energy extraction, refining, transformation, storage, and distribution (almost 8 per cent of the nation's total fixed capital at the end of 1960), the long lead times of major energy projects, and the control imposed by energy requirements on all regional development lead to project simplifications. These tend to be accomplished by minimizing refining standards, by eliminating marginal claimants (such as irrigation in the Volga), and by reducing storage and distribution systems to skeleton layouts most adequate for large-scale use by key customers.

Agricultural-land management in the Soviet Union is dominated by the

---

[53] See, for example, L. A. Melentyev and Ye. O. Shteyngauz, *Ekonomika energetiki SSSR* (*Energy Economics of the U.S.S.R.*), Moscow: Gosenergoizdat, 1959, pp. 235–38, 303–8.

procurement demands imposed by the state to meet the needs of the Armed Forces, industry (fibers, fats, alcohol, leather, etc.), exports, current urban consumption, and emergency stocks. Soviet planners recognize that these demands, added to the internal needs of agriculture, will require, over the long term, both a substantial labor force and massive investments in agriculture. Short-term policies continue, however, to stress maximum output per acre of farmland at least cost. They attempt to offset through better techniques a diminishing farm manpower, limited inputs of chemicals (largely concentrated on fibers, sugar beets, and oil crops), moderate quantities of intensively used field machinery, and considerable proportions of poor, diseased seed and livestock.

Variations in natural endowments, which have been substantially downgraded by erosion in the Black Earth region and by salinization in the Central Asian lowlands, impede centralized planning and control in agriculture. Another local influence, imposed by the paucity of rural roads, storage and processing facilities, is the policy of developing circum-urban potato and vegetable cultivation, and dairying. Circum-urban agriculture operates under the aegis of city administrations, or specific civilian or military establishments, and is often heavily subsidized thereby. Another complication derives from the institutional distinctions between state and collective farms. In the former case, the government is both total owner and total risk-taker; staffs, other than specified temporary help, are permanent, and wages are fixed; profits accrue to the national treasury, which also disburses investment funds and subsidizes losses. In the latter case, which is legally that of a co-operative renting land from the state, the collective farm is not only responsible for all costs but must pay income taxes to the state. Apart from particular patronage relations found in circum-urban agriculture, the state's economic assistance is limited to the provision of higher prices for collective-farm than for state-farm procurements, to loans, and to permission to sell produce above state needs to the urban populace. The collective farm, as a firm, finances its own investments, including schools and maternity homes, its own salaries to Party-appointed management and technical workers, and its own social security, if any. Hours, working conditions, and medical care and veterinary inspections are also governed by local standards and resources. The rank-and-file collective farmer is purely a residual claimant who prospers under favorable circumstances and is reduced to dependence on his private plot and to off-farm work in hard times. The private plot and private livestock on both state and collective farms are of interest to Soviet planners only as sources of manpower or goods to reinforce faltering public operations. No counterpart exists to the family-level education in farm techniques and home management which has been, via county agents, so prominent in American agricultural development.[54]

Concrete illustrations of the Soviet approach to mid-term agricultural land planning are available in the published records of the 1958 farm-management conference in Novosibirsk Oblast, a key part of the West Siberian "Virgin Lands."[55] In the previous year, 625 collective and state farms in the oblast had operated 8.75 million hectares of farm land, including 4.14 million hectares of plowland, and 4.62 million hectares of pastures, hay meadows, and long-term fallow. Sown acreage totalled 3.49 million hectares. Of this, 57 per cent was in spring wheat, 20 per cent in other grains, 10 per cent in tame hay, 7 per cent in silage, 5 per cent in oil seeds, and 1.4 per cent in potatoes and vegetables. In 1957, grain yields were 10.5 quintals per hectare, 28 per cent over the 1950–57 average. Tame hay yields per hectare were about 10 quintals; silage, about 35 quintals; potatoes, a disastrous 50 quintals, and natural pastures and meadows, 9 to 12 quintals. Cattle on the land totalled 1.07 million head, with a third in private hands. Cows numbered almost half a million. Other livestock included 1.45 million sheep (38 per cent private), 0.49 million swine (45 per cent private), and 0.66 million fowl, including only the publicly owned. Animal products included a gross milk output of 950,000 metric tons, or about 1.950 kilograms per cow; roughly 15 per cent of this was consumed by calves and 46 per cent was delivered to the State. Aggregate meat and fowl production, in liveweight, was 160,000 metric tons (about half of this is edible product); wool sheared came to 3,600 metric tons, or 2.5 kilograms per head. Over-all, the 1957 gross output of Novosibirsk Oblast agriculture was distributed by value as follows: grain, 62 per cent; oil crops, 4 per cent; potatoes and vegetables, 4 per cent; cows' milk, 17 per cent; beef, 5 per cent; mutton and wool, 3 per cent; pork, 3 per cent; and poultry and eggs, 0.7 per cent. The peak labor force, in August, came to 1,037,600 workers; machinery included over 20,000 tractors, 11,000 combines, and 3,800 trucks. Feed and livestock operations were, however, almost totally manual. Grain cleaning and drying, encompassing 90 per cent of the harvest, also required much labor.

In order to achieve a 50 per cent increase in grain production, a rise of

---

[54] Shimkin, 1963, *op. cit.* (Note 22).

[55] I. I. Sinyagin (ed.), *O sisteme vedeniya sel'skogo khozyaystva v Novosibirskoy oblasti* (*On the System of Conducting Agriculture in Novosibirsk Oblast*), Novosibirsk: Novosibirskoye knizhnoye izdatel'stvo, 1958, p. 416.

250 per cent in milk output, one of 320 per cent in meat, and a tripling in wool, along with a 70 per cent decrease in peak labor input, the conference recommended a comprehensive program of investments and technical improvements. Salient features of the program were as follows. The tractor inventory would rise from 12 to 37 per cent. Increased power would permit better cultivation and a 19 per cent rise in plowland, with corresponding reductions in hay meadows and pasture. Systematic crop rotation, hitherto absent, would include clean summer or winter fallow, to reduce weed infestation and to increase moisture accumulation. Contour plowing and stubble planting would reduce wind erosion in semi-arid parts of the oblast. Fertilization, currently nominal, would employ fully local manure, compost, and peat resources; in addition, superphosphate in small quantities would be used as a starting fertilizer with seed. Hay fields would be rotated, plowed, fertilized, and reseeded every four years; controlled grazing would also be instituted. Selected seed, now used on only half the grain acreage, would become the sole type planted; special farms would have to be organized to grow select grass seed, now totally lacking. Corn and beans would provide abundant, high protein silage, in addition to a doubled grass output from improved meadows. This would permit a 130 per cent increase in cows, and a milk production of 3,000 kilograms per cow, with corresponding rises in other livestock. Stock would be improved by the control and gradual elimination of brucellosis and tuberculosis through quarantine, the timely removal of young and recovered animals from infected areas, and the strict isolation and ultimate destruction of diseased animals. The registration of stock would be introduced while the proportion of over-aged, barren stock and the large numbers of young that die would be reduced through contracting with private households for the supply of young meat and breeding animals. Finally, livestock operations would be mechanized, heated barns constructed, and allied capital improvements undertaken.

Agricultural education, improvements in rural living conditions, and better incentives to rank-and-file farmers fall outside the scope of this narrowly technological approach.

General Observations

This fleeting summary of Soviet problems in resource management indicates their diversity and the degree to which technical and human questions rather than economic policies alone have been involved. In Soviet practice, most attention has been paid to technical questions, less to economic ones, and least to human aspects.

Meeting operational demands has occasioned the organization of large and complex institutions with highly specialized staffs, and intricate data-gathering, communications, and procedural requirements. These facilities represent fruits not merely of the nearly half-century of Soviet rule but of extensive preparations from the middle of the nineteenth century onward. In the 1840's, Roderick Murchison had already collated extensive Russian geological work into a trustworthy summary of the geology of European Russia and the Urals. In the 1890's Sergey Witte, with the brilliant technical advice of D. I. Mendeleyev, had conceived and advanced greatly the systematic industrialization of Russia. Mendeleyev in particular expounded clearly the fundamental role of industrialization in economic development, the functions of expanding energy supplies (and the promise of the Donets Basin), and the qualitative problems of Russian manpower (from a meticulous analysis of the census of 1897). The studies of the Resettlement Administration brought out the immense promise of Siberia. Finally, World War I not only brought about the development of a variety of assessment and planning agencies, including the Council for the Study of Productive Forces of the Academy of Sciences, but revealed with tragic power the necessity of adequate means of control over the nation's resources.[56]

Old planning traditions have created both empirical wisdom and a variety of unanalyzed assumptions and rules of thumb. Market research, net rather than gross output analyses, and similar innovations are resisted; rigid ideals, such as the venerable housing norm of 9 square meters (96.8 square feet) per person, have persisted. Much else in Soviet planning is habitual; notably, a paternalistic, yet puritanical and class-conscious viewpoint on consumer needs.

The Soviet system of resource management is elaborate and costly but

[56] R. Murchison *et al., The Geology of Russia in Europe and the Ural Mountains,* 2 vols. (London, 1845). See also V. V. Tikhomirov, *Geologiya v Rossiyi pervoy poloviny XIX veka (Geology in Russia of the First Half of the Nineteenth Century),* Moscow: Izd. Akademiyi nauk, 1960, p. 228. On Witte, see Theodore H. von Laue, "The High Cost and the Gamble of the Witte System: A Chapter in the Industrialization of Russia," *Journal of Economic History,* 1953, pp. 425–46. Western biographies of Mendeleyev have disgracefully ignored his economic contributions. A representative selection of these studies has been reprinted in D. I. Mendeleyev, *Problemy ekonomicheskogo razvitiya Rossiyi (Problems of the Economic Development of Russia),* Moscow: Sotsekizdat, 1960, p. 616. The great publication of the Resettlement Administration of the Main Administration of Land Management and Agriculture (Glavnoye upravleniye zemleustroystva i zemledelye) was *Aziatskaya Rossiya (Asiatic Russia)* 3 vols. and Atlas, S. Petersburg, 1914. On the Russian economy in World War I, the fundamental sources are in the *Russian Series* of Carnegie's *Economic and Social History of the World War.*

immensely effective in mobilizing the country's strength and directing it down channels clearly visualized by strong national leaders. But its very responsiveness to central direction represents an inhibition of autonomous, spontaneous innovations. Fundamentally, Russia's leaders still borrow from the West rather than aiding native genius to come to flower.

The Soviet system today works under immense pressure, with consequent damage to low-priority and neglected sectors, especially rural consumers. Long-term downgrading through soil erosion, water pollution, and air contamination have been little checked, since the State has been both the police and the policed. Many problems have arisen from the burdening of modestly developed resources with enormous tasks of capital formation and armaments. Yet, paradoxically, these very burdens have eased other major requirements that Soviet planning is ill-prepared to meet — satisfaction of the many, varied, and changing desires of free consumers.

THE MANAGEMENT AND DEVELOPMENT OF ENERGY RESOURCES IN THE SOVIET UNION

The consequences of the Soviet system of resource management, applied to an excellent natural endowment, and under conditions of persisting high priority, are well shown in the current status and prospects of the Soviet mineral-fuels industries. Pertinent aspects include characteristics and trends in reserves, production, domestic distribution and transport, domestic consumption, and foreign trade. Comparisons with the United States help to sharpen appraisals, while detailed attention to foreign trade helps clarify political as well as economic phenomena, particularly Soviet anticipations vis-à-vis Western Europe.

The basic data underlying this discussion are from my recent monograph, which is the culmination of five years of research on the Soviet energy-producing industries at the U.S. Bureau of the Census and the University of Illinois.[57]

Reserves

The Soviet Union, because of its size and geology, has an enormous natural endowment of all fossil fuels and probably of fissionable elements.

[57] D. B. Shimkin, *op. cit.* (Note 9). Attention is also called to the following important studies: R. E. Ebel, *The Petroleum Industry of the Soviet Union,* American Petroleum Institute (Washington: Royer and Roger, 1961); P. Zieber, *Die Sowjetische Erdolwirtschaft* (*The Soviet Petroleum Economy*), Hamburg: Cram, De Gruyter & Co., 1962.

Water power, too, is abundant, albeit in areas remote from present-day industrial centers of prime importance. Fuelwood, heavily utilized in industry, households and agriculture, is a rapidly diminishing resource in European Russia but still plentiful in Siberia.

Vigorous exploration of all of these resources has long been underway. In recent years, the scale, co-ordination, and quality of Soviet geophysical mapping have been especially outstanding. This program has, in conjunction with systematic, deep-structural drilling and the collation of data from operational drilling, permitted the survey and broad volumetric assessment of the sedimentary cover of about half the Soviet Union, including most of the area west of the Yenisey River.[58]

As of 1958–60, the Soviet Union had ample measured resources — about 185 billion metric tons of standard fuel (7,000 C/kg equivalent) — to support rapid development in coal and lignite, petroleum, natural gas, and shale production. Its measured resources were about as great as those of the United States but with a somewhat different structure: more known petroleum, less known natural gas, shale, and coal (Appendix Table 3).

The magnitude of available resources of mineral fuels is promoting a departure from the extreme conservatism of resource use which has hitherto held back optimal energy development in the U.S.S.R. In contrast to the stress on maximum use of local fuels, even of the poorest quality, which was dominant between 1935 and 1950, and is still evident, current policies emphasize selective exploitation. In coal mining, present-day plans are oriented toward large-scale mining potentials, particularly suitable for pillar-and-chamber operation and for open-cut mining, even to depths of 1,200 feet.[59] Appendix Table 4 indicates the pattern of effort now underway in such selective development. It should be noted that mining for coking coal is to remain concentrated in the Donets, Kuznetsk, Karaganda, and Pechora fields; steam coal is to come increasingly from major open-cut operations in Kazakhstan and Eastern Siberia. In petroleum development, the enormous deposits of the Tatar Dome (Romashkino, etc.) and the mid-Volga (Mukhanovo, etc.) are the basis of production. However, since these crudes are heavy, sulfurous, and relatively

---

[58] An excellent illustration is A. I. Olli and V. A. Romanov, *Tektonicheskaya karta Bashkiriyi (Tectonic Map of the Bashkir ASSR)*, 1:650,000, with explanatory text (Ufa: Bashirskiy filial Akademiyi nauk SSSR, 1959).

[59] See notes to Table 4, and F. Ya. Kagan, "Once More on the Development of Open-cut Mines and the Complex Exploitation of Deposits in the Moscow Coal Basin," *Ugol'* 1961, No. 5, pp. 39–41; also, N. V. Mel'nikov, "Prospects of Developing Coal Extraction by Open-cut Methods," *Ugol'* 1961, No. 10, pp. 5–9.

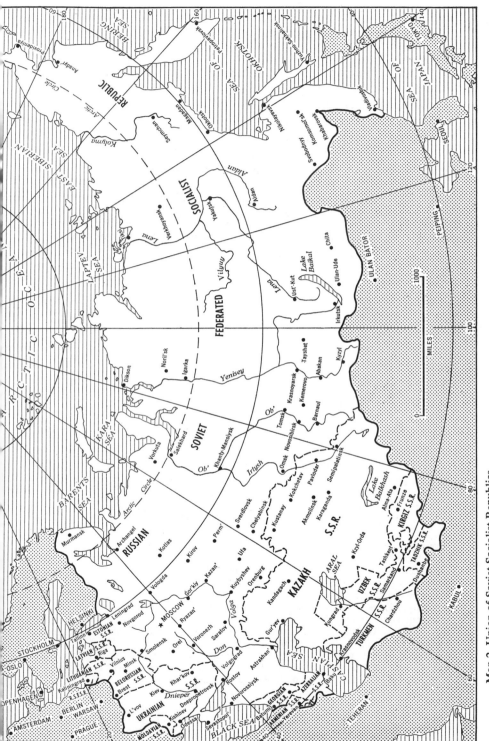

Map 2. Union of Soviet Socialist Republics

poor in aromatic hydrocarbons, developmental efforts for increasing the output of superior crudes in Perm and Volgograd Oblasts and in the Caucasus are continuing vigorously, as is the exploration in Western Siberia which is finally meeting with success.[60] Natural gas development is also based on a few large deposits in the North Caucasus, the Ukraine, and most recently, Uzbekistan. Shale is economically significant only in the Estonian-Leningrad area; other reserves are being conserved for the remote future. Peat, in contrast, is being rapidly depleted for fuel and especially agricultural purposes in the Baltic States, Central Russia, and the Urals, where alone it has much economic utility.[61] Finally, although reliable data are scanty, Soviet uranium development appears to be concentrated in Central Asia (the Karatau Range and the Fergana Valley). Imports from Eastern Europe are also apparently significant sources for the Soviet atomic energy program.

Production

With excellent resources which are increasingly well explored and with heavy investments of manpower and capital, the Soviet Union has been able to achieve a sevenfold expansion of energy production since 1928. In fact, by 1960, Soviet energy production (736 million metric tons of standard fuel) exceeded that of Western Europe (the OEEC countries) and was almost half as great as that of the United States (Appendix Table 5). Moreover, the structural changes in Soviet energy production since 1928 have been favorable. The share of oil and natural gas has risen from 17 to 36 per cent, and that of coals (excluding lignites), from 28 to 43 per cent, while fuelwood in particular has dropped in importance.

By 1972, the Soviet Union anticipates another 120 to 130 per cent increase in energy production.[62] By that time, nearly 60 per cent of all en-

[60] V. A. Kalmakarov, *Razvitiye neftyanoy i gazovoy promyshlennosti* (*Development of the Oil and Gas Industry*), Moscow: Gostoptekhizdat, 1961, esp. pp. 14–17.

[61] In 1956, Soviet peat output for fuel was 44.8 million M.T.; for fertilizer and livestock bedding it was 29 million M.T. By 1960, the output figures were 52.8 and 96 million M.T., respectively. Currently, the 1965 Plan calls for an aggregate production of 296 million M.T., including 81.0 million M.T. by industrial establishments (which will yield 57.4 million M.T. of fuel and 29.4 million M.T. of fertilizer) and 212.0 million M.T. by collective farms (largely for fertilizer and bedding). Thus, peat production as a whole is to increase fourfold in nine years, 40 per cent faster than petroleum. See Shimkin, 1962, *op. cit.* (Note 9), pp. 38–40, 69, 89; S. A. Tsuprov, "For the Development of Output and Complex Use of Peat in Agriculture and Industry," *Torfyanaya promyshlennost'*, 1962, No. 1, pp. 1–4.

[62] The higher goal is given by A. F. Zasyad'ko, *Toplivno-energeticheskaya promyshlennost' SSSR, 1959–1965* (*The Fuel and Electrical Power Industry of the U.S.S.R., 1959–1965*), Moscow: Gosplanizdat, 1959, p. 28.

ergy is to come from petroleum and natural gas, a pattern emulating U.S. energy production in 1955. Atomic energy plans, which earlier called for large contributions (10 to 15 per cent) to the national energy supply from this source by 1972, are now clearly in abeyance.[63] Shortages of ore and electrical power, competitive military demands, and unfavorable reactor economics have apparently led to this change.

An outstanding feature of Soviet energy production in the past (excluding the 1940's) and as planned in the future, is the anticipation of expanding net exports. By 1965 these are to approximate 150 million metric tons of standard fuel, mostly crude and refined petroleum. Thus, the 1960 level would be tripled in five years. Thereafter, exports are to rise more slowly, even under maximum production plans. In 1972, the anticipated level is 265 to 320 million metric tons.[64] Since Western Europe and the United States together may have a shortage of 500 million metric tons by 1975, the prospects of Soviet energy sales to the Western World seem excellent. This would be particularly true if demand rose sharply in other countries and if the rise of alternative suppliers in the Middle East, North Africa, and Latin America were impeded by anarchy and sabotage. In short, energy exports may well provide the Soviet Union with powerful levers in international economics in future years.

Output Technology

The prospecting, extraction, and refining of mineral fuels in the Soviet Union occupied about two million persons in 1960 and accounted for 4.6 per cent of the nation's fixed capital at that time. Electrical power plants and networks made up an additional 3.3 per cent of the fixed capital at the end of 1960. In general, labor productivity in the Soviet energy-producing industries is less than a sixth as high as in the United States; capital in these industries, as measured by power capacity per unit of energy produced, is also less effective.[65]

Basic problems in Soviet energy production are engendered by the maintenance of a very inefficient, albeit highly mechanized, peat extraction industry, by production of much low-grade lignite, and by inappro-

---

[63] On the earlier atomic energy plans see Melentyev and Shteyngauz, *op. cit.* (Note 53), pp. 43, 294–97.

[64] According to Zasyad'ko, 1959, *op. cit.* (Note 62), p. 28, energy output is to increase by 56–59 per cent between 1965 and 1972, while consumption is to rise 50–52 per cent. These data have been applied to the 1965 estimates given in Appendix Table 5.

[65] On U.S.S.R.–U.S. comparisons for 1954–55, see Shimkin, 1962, *op. cit.* (Note 9), pp. 53–58.

priate designs in underground mining. However, it must be noted that, since 1958, a fundamental reconstruction of Donets Basin mines has been underway. In mines producing 35 per cent of the Basin's output, chamber-and-pillar layouts, steel pit-props, simplified transportation schemes including gravity interchanges, and safety features such as automatic sprays to allay coal dust at faces had been introduced by 1961. Similar progress has been achieved in the Estonian shale mines.[66]

In the Soviet petroleum industry, all major field developments of the past decade have followed very careful designs based upon the dynamics and lithology of each deposit. Flooding has been instituted from the beginning while well spacing and flow have also been carefully regulated. This excellent practice has been partially offset, however, by continued waste of associated gas, 42 per cent of which was flared off in 1960. Furthermore, insufficient attention to the de-emulsification, desalting, and stabilization of crudes in the field has had varied consequences, including the substantial loss of lighter fractions, which have the refining difficulties inherent in high-sulfur crudes.[67]

Soviet petroleum products, other than in military grades, are poor. However, since 1957, somewhat higher standards have been required of products for export. Motor gasoline, tractor kerosene, light diesel fuel, illuminating kerosene, and spindle oil in these grades meet good standards of purity, volatility, etc. The residual fuel oil exported (ETU–638–57) is much worse, with 2.5 per cent sulfur, 0.3 per cent ash residue, 2.0 per cent water and mechanical admixtures, etc.[68]

Domestic Distribution and Transport

Nearly 40 per cent of all Soviet rail, river, and pipeline traffic is taken by mineral fuels. The railroads, in fact, carry over four-fifths of the ton-mileage of all mineral fuels transport. Even in the 1961 Plan, pipelines were to handle only 15.5 per cent of the crude oil and petroleum ton-

---

[66] See A. F. Serkin, "Sprinkle and Fire-fighting Water Piping in the Underground Works of Coal and Shale Mines," *Ugol'*, 1961, No. 1, pp. 46–7; A. S. Kuz'mich and S. B. Ostrovkiy, "Five Years on the Path of Technical Progress" (in the Donets Basin), *Ugol'*, 1961, No. 8, pp. 9–13; and V. A. Viylup and A. P. Semenov, "An Experiment in the Mines of the Shale Trust, *Estonslanets*," *Ugol'*, 1962, No. 1, pp. 13–17.

[67] Shimkin, 1962, *op. cit.* (Note 9), p. 41; Kalamkarov, 1961, *op. cit.* (Note 60), pp. 11–12, 43ff.

[68] I. Ye. Zhalnin *et al.*, *Tekhnicheskiye usloviya na nefteprodukty* (*Technical Standards for Petroleum Products*), Moscow: Gostoptekhizdat, 1960, pp. 15–17, 20, 21–23, 28, 49 and 105.

mileage of the U.S.S.R.[69] Since railroad transportation requires, according to Soviet 1956 data, 5.5 times as much labor and is 2.2 times as costly as pipeline use, the disadvantages to the Soviet economy resulting from these practices are considerable. Nevertheless, such practices have been characteristic for the past decade, and even the 1965 Plan is not designed to change them significantly (Appendix Table 6).[70]

The increasing pressures of the mineral fuels industries upon Soviet transportation since 1928 have developed despite an appreciable decentralization of coal production, a northward shift in the center of petroleum output, and the reduction of other gross disbalances between production and consumption. They have developed especially because Soviet industrial locational policies have remained insensitive to transport costs. For example, the Urals, which produce almost no coking coal, fabricate nearly one-third of the coke of the Soviet Union from materials hauled from Kazakhstan and Western Siberia. Similarly, the vast agricultural expansion in Kazakhstan and Western Siberia, begun in 1955, led immediately to major problems of petroleum products distribution. Nevertheless, the extension of pipelines eastward from the Urals, the opening of refineries at Omsk and Angarsk, near Lake Baykal, and vigorous drilling for oil in Western Siberia have been developments of only the past two years.[71]

These locational difficulties have been compounded by the rigidity of Soviet fuel allocations programs, which specify the sources and types of fuel to be used, establishment by establishment, and leave only a small proportion of the supply for free retail sales. These policies lead, for example, to a substantial degree of high-cost mining of very poor lignites in the Urals and the Ukraine, at the same time that these areas export large quantities of superior fuel, and even flare off over 40 per cent of their wet natural gas.[72] Moreover, investment limitations upon petroleum refineries impose needs for importing crude oil from the Caucasus to the central Volga area to improve the inputs, while Volga residual fuel oil is cross-hauled to the Caucasus.

Although current programs for facilitating energy transport in the Soviet Union are not sufficient to promise general improvement by 1965, they will provide relief to priority consumers. These measures include

---

[69] Kalamkarov, 1961, *op. cit.* (Note 60), p. 55.

[70] For a more extended discussion, see Shimkin, 1962, *op. cit.* (Note 9), pp. 29–33.

[71] See also Ebel, 1961, *op. cit.* (Note 57), pp. 141–153.

[72] Kalamkarov, 1961, *op. cit.* (Note 60), p. 43.

the completion of trunk petroleum pipelines from the Volga and Urals east to the refinery at Angarsk and west, via Mozyr' in Belorussia, to East Germany. The projected natural-gas pipeline from the large Bukhara fields in Central Asia to the Urals is also noteworthy.[73] Especially significant is the linkage, to be completed by 1965, of the Central Russia, Volga, Urals, and Ukrainian grids, by 400–500 kilovolt lines. The new unified system is to embrace nearly 50 million kilowatts of capacity, including the Soviet atomic energy stations at Voronezh in Central Russia and Beloyarsk in the Urals. The current status of the very ambitious Central Siberian electrical power system, designed to interconnect the Angara and Yenisey hydroelectric stations with large thermal ones in the Kuznetsk Basin of Western Siberia, is not certain.[74]

Domestic Consumption

Current and projected patterns of energy utilization within the Soviet Union can best be assessed by beginning with the rather complete and accurate data for 1955, then moving to comparative statistics for the United States in the same year. These materials illuminate Soviet plans for 1965, which in turn provide a basis for judging the successes and failures in energy supply achieved by 1960.

In 1955, the Soviet Union produced 520 million metric tons of standard fuel (7,000 C/kg equivalent), or 2.64 metric tons per capita. The largest single consumer of this energy was industry, including atomic energy. Industry took half the energy supply. Twenty-eight per cent of this industrial consumption was in the form of electricity and went especially to aluminum production, steel furnaces, metal working, and chemicals. Moreover, for 1955, input-output analysis using Soviet coefficients and production statistics yields, within industry, a residue of 3 to 5 billion kilowatt-hours which is ascribable to atomic energy. Fuel extraction and refining (predominantly coke manufacture and use), open-hearth furnaces and rolling mills, and cement mills jointly took 37 per cent of all Soviet industrial energy consumption. Within the remaining 36 per cent, the metal-working branches, including ordnance, were the largest users;

[73] The distribution of Soviet natural gas production and consumption, urban household use of natural gas, and pipelines in operation and under construction for 1959, 1960, and 1965 are all given in the annotated map, "The Seven Year Plan in Operation," *Gazovaya promyshlennost'*, 1961, No. 8, insert between pp. 28–29.

[74] For an authoritative review of Soviet electric-power plans, see D. G. Zhimerin, *Razvitiye energetiki SSSR* (*Development of Electric Power in the U.S.S.R.*), Moscow: Gosenergoizdat, 1960, esp. pp. 29–58, 302–23.

food and fats were also important consumers, for processing and for refrigeration (Appendix Table 7).[75]

Civil transportation, including operations and losses at tank farms, bunkers and other distributive installations, constituted the second largest share of total energy consumption. Its requirements were about 82 million metric tons of standard fuel, or 16.4 per cent of the national supply. Three-fourths of this was railroad consumption for freight, passenger, and terminal uses; railway shops comprised additional consumption within industry.

Agriculture was a much smaller consumer, taking 4.2 per cent of the Soviet total — half a metric ton of standard fuel per worker, or 120 kilograms per hectare. Tractors consumed about 12.4 million metric tons; other field machinery, around 1.9 million; and all other uses, especially grain drying, irrigation, power tools, and illumination, roughly 7.5 million. Net exports made up only half a per cent of the aggregate U.S.S.R. supply. Miscellaneous productive uses consumed about 63 million metric tons, or 12 per cent. These uses included construction, defense, various government services, municipal transport excluding buses, urban services such as water and public baths, and commerce.

In 1955, household uses took 16.3 per cent of the Soviet energy supply. Urban per capita consumption was about 460 kilograms of standard fuel; rural, about 400 kilograms per capita. Almost half of urban household consumption was for space heating; another quarter, for cooking. Other fuel uses, especially water heating, and electricity, largely for illumination, took the rest. In rural areas, food preparation (including bread baking, butter making, and preserving) and home industries were significant; space-heating and hot-water supplies were correspondingly austere.

Per capita, Soviet energy consumption in 1955 came to 30 per cent of that of the United States. In both countries, about half of the supply went to industry, including atomic energy. Although both atomic energy, which consumed 50 billion kilowatt-hours, and electrically purified chemical reagents were far more important than in the Soviet Union, electricity comprised only 23 per cent of American industrial consumption. High station efficiency (26 per cent greater than in the U.S.S.R.) and the more extensive use of internal combustion prime movers for power in mining

[75] For details and underlying calculations see Shimkin, 1962, *op. cit.* (Note 9), pp. 59–78. The basic source for American data is S. H. Schurr and B. C. Netschert, *Energy in the American Economy, 1850–1975* (Baltimore: Johns Hopkins Press for Resources for The Future, Inc., 1960).

account for this phenomenon. The fuel, steel, and cement industries took 39 per cent of American industrial consumption, a fact largely attributable to large inputs of natural gas for repressuring (as contrasted with the water flooding characteristic of Soviet oil wells). As in the Soviet Union, metal working dominated the remaining third of American industrial consumption. In general, input-output investigations show that American industry produced about 15 per cent more goods per calorie of input than Soviet industry. Soviet industrial workers, supplied with 30 per cent of the energy available to Americans, produced a quarter as much per man-year.

American agriculture used a quarter more energy than Soviet agriculture to produce about twice as much in crops and animal products. Tractors and other field machinery accounted for three-fourths of the American total, compared to two-thirds for the U.S.S.R. Most of the remainder went to irrigation and livestock operations. Miscellaneous productive activities consumed about an eighth of the national energy supply in both countries. However, it is believed that commerce and municipal services (water, sewerage, street lighting, etc.) made up a substantially larger part of this sector in the United States than in the U.S.S.R.

American transportation used a fifth of the country's energy supply, but almost half of this input went to private passenger cars, which accounted for 90 per cent of all U.S. passenger traffic. Commercial transportation was about 15 per cent more efficient, over-all, than in the U.S.S.R. The American preference for more costly and more flexible trucking largely offset two-to-one efficiency margins in rail and truck operations, taken separately.

Apart from private transportation, American household consumption came to 1.6 metric tons of standard fuel per capita, or 3.5 times as much as Soviet urban household use. Space heating alone used 940 kilograms per capita, or 4.4 times as much as for Soviet city dwellers — a reflection of 2.5 times as great a living space, a far lower proportion of multi-family housing, and inputs per square meter of comparable housing a quarter higher than in Soviet practice. The other major difference came in hot water availability. In general, physical mobility, more and better housing, and better sanitation represented the basic contrasts between American and Soviet urban living standards in 1955, insofar as these were reflected in energy consumption.

Soviet plans for energy supply and use in 1965 are predicated on an over-all increase of about 110 per cent, and a per capita increase of roughly 75 per cent, over 1955. These greater resources are to provide for a rapid rise in net exports — from 0.5 to 13 per cent of the national energy supply — and for a proportional expansion of energy consumption by industry. Other sectors are to expand energy use more slowly, at about the following rates of increase over the decade: agriculture, 80 per cent; households, 75 per cent (including 100 per cent for uban households and 50 per cent for rural ones); miscellaneous uses, 50 per cent; and transportation, 40 per cent.

Substantial technological changes as well as rises in levels of activity are subsumed within these plans. In industrial consumption, the share of energy consumed as electricity is to rise from 28 to 31 per cent, although anticipated economies in inputs per kilowatt-hour of electricity are 21 per cent as opposed to 13 per cent for other forms of energy. Almost certainly, exceptionally rapid rises in nuclear materials, in electrolytic products (elemental phosphorus, high-purity nonferrous metals, and rare earths), and in electrical metal working are anticipated. The fuel, steel, and cement industries are to retain the same share as in 1955, but that of other users is to fall to 33 per cent. This evidently reflects a slow growth in energy use by consumers' non-durables.

In agriculture, the Soviets hope to achieve rapid electrification, particularly in the livestock sectors. Consumption for field operations, grain drying, and other non-electrical uses is to rise 60 per cent over the decade. This increase would facilitate both better agronomic practices and additions to acreage, especially for tame hay. In miscellaneous productive uses, the major elements of rising demand appear to be construction, urban growth, and improvements in amenities, such as municipal transportation, water supplies, sewerage, restaurants, etc. In civil transportation and storage, input requirements per ton-mile are to fall more than a third between 1955 and 1965, through a shift from steam to electric and diesel locomotives, through greater efficiencies in trucking, and through improved storage. Finally, household consumption among urban and rural dwellers, separately, is to increase 50 per cent per capita. In the cities, better space heating from central steam sources, more hot water, and more electricity for appliances are foreseen.

Actual Soviet accomplishments in 1960 have shown both progress along, and divergences from, the planned courses of development. Energy output in that year, 736 million metric tons of standard fuel (Appendix Table 5), was about 5 per cent, or 40 million metric tons, short of that called for by the 1958–1965 Plan. Although petroleum production exceeded Soviet goals, a failure to meet the coal extraction target and a marked decline in the private procurement of fuelwood led to an over-all deficit. How was this met?

Nearly half the deficit in planned production was reflected in changes in stocks, which were reduced by about 5 per cent rather than rising at least 20 per cent.[76] Over 40 per cent of this deficit was made up by short-ages of fuel for rural households. Even with a generous allowance for thefts by and clandestine sales to rural people taken from the high "stor-age losses" reported by the Soviets, rural household consumption in 1960 was at least 10 per cent *below* that of 1955, rather than being about 25 per cent *higher* as anticipated by the 1958–1965 Plan. Finally, agricul-tural operations consumed about 4 million metric tons of standard fuel, or 13 per cent, less than planned. Shortages of tractive power in the fields, shortages of electricity, and disappointing crops led to this discrepancy.[77]

Other sectors fared better. Net exports, excluding indirect inputs came to 50 million metric tons of standard fuel, about 6 million metric tons more than indicated by an interpolation of 1958 exports and 1965 Plans. In industry, kilowatt-hour inputs both in 1960 (190 billion) and in 1961 (213 billion) increased in excellent conformity with the 1958–1965 Plan. Moreover, economizing proceeded more rapidly than planned — at 4.5 per cent per year rather than 2 per cent. As a result, industrial electrical power saved about 7 million metric tons of standard fuel. Between 1955 and 1960, the electrical power consumption of alumina-reduction plants and of steel furnaces rose about 60 per cent, compared to the 68 per cent rise in electrical-power use in all of industry. In metal-working, the input of steel rose 44 per cent over the same period, while electrical-power use

[76] In the primary source used, the statement on exports excludes fabricated fuels (coke, petroleum products) and hence indicates a slight rise in stocks through 1960 rather than the actual decline. See A. Riznik and S. Litvak, "The Fuel and Electrical-power Balance of the U.S.S.R. for 1960," *Vestnik statistiki,* 1962, No. 6, pp. 15–27, esp. p. 16.

[77] The Seven-Year Plan of the U.S.S.R. calls for a rise in tractive power in agriculture (tractor and combine engines, stationary prime movers, and electrical generators) of 87 per cent, from 74.5 million h.p. in 1958 to 134.2 million h.p. in 1965. In 1960, agricultural tractive power should have been 20 per cent higher than in 1958 by this projection, but was actually only 5 per cent higher. Similarly, electrical power inputs into agriculture were scheduled to quadruple, from 3.6 billion kw-hr in 1958, to 15.0 billion kw-hr in 1965. The interpolated value for the 1960 goal was a 50 per cent increase over 1958; the actual achievement was a gain of 30 per cent. See Appendix Table 7, Notes (*The Economy of the U.S.S.R. in Postwar Period*), Moscow: Sotsekgiz, 1962, pp. 273, 280.

probably rose somewhat more.[78] In general, an analysis of trends in industry's use of electricity leads to the estimate that allotments of atomic energy rose to 20–40 billion kilowatt-hours by 1960, compared to 3 to 5 billion in 1955. In the United States, the rise of AEC electrical-power consumption between 1950 and 1955 was from 3.8 to 50.1 billion kilowatt-hours. Over-all, the aggregate power input of the Soviet Union into atomic activities between 1950 and the end of 1961 was at the most a fifth of that of the United States; the relative supplies of nuclear materials are probably in proportion.

The industrial consumption of non-electrical energy rose in conformity to the 1958–1965 Plan, with economizing in the steel and cement industries also being satisfactory.

Even apart from extraordinarily large "storage losses" (20 million metric tons of standard fuel), Soviet transportation expended more energy than planned. Specifically, the Soviet railroads increased their ton-mileage by 15.5 per cent, rather than 10 per cent, between 1958 and 1960. In addition, economies per ton-mile hauled were 13 per cent, rather than the anticipated 22 per cent, over this period. Delays in the shift from steam locomotives, which hauled 56.8 per cent of the traffic in 1960 rather than 46 per cent as planned, accounted for this failure in economizing. Over-all, the Soviet railroads expended at least 10 million metric tons of standard fuel beyond the foreseen level.

In summary, Soviet patterns of domestic energy consumption in 1955 and 1960 have been distinguished by the following features:

First, in the U.S.S.R. as in the United States in 1955, about half the national energy supply has been devoted to industry, including atomic uses. Energy consumption per industrial worker was 32 per cent as high as in the United States in 1955, and had increased by a fifth by 1960. In 1955, the efficiency of Soviet industrial use of energy was about 85 per cent of the American level.

Second, Soviet inputs into atomic uses have climbed from 3–5 billion

---

[78] Between 1955 and 1960, the output of electric-furnace steel in the U.S.S.R. rose from 3.41 million M.T. to about 5.65 million M.T. Primary aluminum output was about 430,000 M.T. in 1955 and 700,000 in 1960. See Ts.S.U. pri Sov. Min., *Narodnoye khozyaystvo SSSR v 1958 g.* (*National Economy of the U.S.S.R. in 1958*), Moscow: Gosstatizdat, 1959, p. 189; Ts.S.U. pri Sov. Min. RSFSR, *Promyshlennost' RSFSR* (*Industry of R.S.F.S.R.*), Moscow: Gosstatizdat, 1961, p. 57; and Central Intelligence Agency, *Aluminum in the Sino-Soviet Bloc, 1950–65* (Washington, 1962), p. 6. See also Appendix Table 7, Note 1.b.5.

kilowatt-hours in 1955 to 20–40 billion in 1960. Aggregate inputs since 1950 have been 20 per cent or less those of the United States.

Third, transportation and storage consume about one-sixth of the Soviet energy supply, compared to a fifth in the United States. This reflects the virtual absence, now or in the planned future, of private cars in the Soviet Union. The efficiency of Soviet domestic commercial transportation in 1960 equalled that of the United States in 1955, thanks to partial shifts from steam to diesel and electric locomotives, and to austere use of flexible but costly trucking.

Fourth, Soviet agriculture now consumes slightly more energy than U.S. agriculture did in 1955. Inputs per cultivated acre are, however, only two-thirds as great.

Fifth, aggregate Soviet household energy consumption per capita failed to rise between 1955 and 1960, and was about one-fourth that of the United States, excluding fuel used by private cars.

And sixth, since 1955, a moderate under-fulfillment of energy-production goals, combined with accelerated exports and rigid allocation policies favoring industry, transportation, and the urban economy, have resulted in no less than a 10 per cent decline, by 1960, in rural-household energy consumption. This deficit, with its consequences for rural living standards,[79] has undoubtedly contributed to Soviet agricultural difficulties since 1958.

Foreign Trade

Since 1955, the Soviet Union has expanded its net exports of mineral fuels with great vigor. In particular, it has increased shipments of crude oil and petroleum products, directly and via its European satellites, to Western Europe. The major purpose of this drive has clearly been to provide an increasing share of the foreign exchange needed to finance Soviet purchases of machinery and materials, especially from West Germany, the United Kingdom, France, Italy, and Malaya. By 1961, mineral fuels comprised 22.5 per cent of the value of Soviet exports to all countries, excluding those to the Communist bloc and Cuba. The comparable figure for 1955 was 14.7 per cent, while in the prewar decade, 1929–38, mineral fuels comprised an average of 14.4 per cent of all Soviet exports, by

---

[79] For a general survey of current conditions in Soviet rural areas, see Shimkin, 1963, *op. cit.* (Note 22).

value. The prewar peak, 20.9 per cent in 1932, has now been surpassed.[80]

The Soviet dominance of mineral-fuel supplies in a number of neutralist and buffer states, especially Iceland, Sweden, Finland and Greece, has also served political and military ends. In Eastern Europe, the Soviet Union has acted as a middleman in transactions between satellites, but made no net contribution to their energy supplies. On the other hand, the Far Eastern satellites, including Mainland China, have received most of their petroleum products from the Soviet Union. Soviet exports of fuels to Cuba began in 1960 and comprised virtually all of that nation's energy supply in 1961.

Appendix Tables 8 to 11 provide statistical details on Soviet foreign trade in mineral fuels.

Appendix Table 8 shows that net Soviet exports of mineral fuels in 1961 were, in terms of heat value, 27 times as great as in 1955 and 9.5 times as great as the average for the prewar decade, 1929–38. As a proportion of mineral-fuel output, they had also risen from a half per cent in 1955 to 9.4 per cent in 1961, the latter proportion being higher than the prewar average. The coal and coke trade has swung from a net import balance of 1.2 per cent to a net export balance of 3.3 per cent of output, an increment of almost 16 million metric tons in physical weight, or 14.7 million metric tons in standard fuel. The growth of crude oil and petroleum products exports has been even greater, 34 million metric tons of physical weight or 48.6 million metric tons of standard fuel between 1955 and 1961.

Today, Soviet net exports of crude and refined oil constitute almost 23 per cent of the country's output, compared to 5 per cent in 1955 and 18 per cent, on the average, in 1929–38. Such an effort represents, not a true surplus but, as the previous discussion of domestic consumption has shown, a forced allocation at the expense of other economic sectors, particularly agriculture and rural households. It should be stressed that 14 per cent of the Soviet oil exports in 1961 were made up of light diesel fuels, officially reported to be in short supply within the U.S.S.R.[81]

[80] See Ministerstvo vneshney torgovli SSSR *Vneshnaya torgovlya SSSR za 1918–1940 gg.* (*The Foreign Trade of the U.S.S.R. for 1918–1940*), Moscow: Vneshtorgizdat, 1960; ibid., *Vneshnaya torgovlya SSSR za 1956 g.* (*Foreign Trade of the U.S.S.R. for 1956*), Moscow: Vneshtorgizdat, 1958; and ibid., *Vneshnaya torgovlya SSSR za 1961 g.* (*Foreign Trade of the U.S.S.R. for 1961*), Moscow: Vneshtorgizdat, 1962. Code Items 200–230.

[81] V. A. Kalamkarov, "Petroleum and Gas in 1959 and Tasks for 1960," *Neftyanoye khozyaystvo*, 1960, No. 1, pp. 1–12.

Furthermore, crude oil and residual fuel oils constituted 78 per cent of all petroleum exports in 1961, compared to 70 per cent in 1957, 93 per cent in 1955, and 41 per cent, as an average, in 1929–38. The Soviet Union thus is both placing stresses upon its internal economy and gaining low value-added through fabrication in its oil exporting programs. While these operations may be expedient in promoting high crude-oil production despite bottlenecks in refining and distributing capacity, and in providing the wherewithal for immediate technological, military or political goals, their utility for the long-term strength of the Soviet economy appears doubtful.

Appendix Table 9 delineates the distribution of total Soviet foreign trade in mineral fuels and, separately, those of coal and coke, crude and refined petroleum, in the typical prewar year 1934, in 1955, and in 1961. Prewar, almost half of the exports went to the Mediterranean, with the two largest customers, Italy and France, taking over one-third of the coal and coke exports, and almost one-third of the oil. The United States, Greece, and Egypt were other active buyers of Soviet coal, especially high-grade anthracite, which also was widely used for marine bunkerage. Major purchasers of Soviet petroleum apart from Italy and France, were Spain, Germany, the United Kingdom, and Japan. Soviet imports of mineral fuels were negligible.

For 1955, Soviet foreign trade in fuels must be examined separately for the European satellites and other countries. At that time the Soviet Union was a heavy importer of fuel from its areas of political control. It received coal from Poland, and crude and refined oil from Albania, Austria, and Rumania. In part, these imports were reallocated, as nominal Soviet exports, to other satellite states, especially the Soviet Zone of Germany. From Eastern Europe as a whole, the Soviet Union gained net imports of 6.5 million metric tons of standard fuel, 2.7 times as much as its net exports, worldwide.

Domestic resources and net imports from the satellites permitted the Soviet Union to export 8.8 million metric tons of standard fuels to the Far Eastern satellites and to non-bloc countries. Mainland China was the most important destination, receiving over 1.8 million metric tons; another 0.2 million metric tons went to North Korea. Northern and Western Europe as a whole took 3.1 million metric tons of standard fuel, almost 90 per cent of these imports going to Finland, Sweden, and Iceland. The Mediterranean, excluding Albania, also purchased 3.1 million metric tons. France, Yugoslavia, Egypt, and Italy accounted for more than three-fourths of the Mediterranean imports from the Soviet Union.

By 1961, the Soviet Union had become a net exporter to Eastern Europe as well as other major areas. The nominal re-exports of Polish coal to the Soviet Zone of Germany, and of Rumanian petroleum products to Bulgaria, Hungary, and Poland had to be supplemented by actual shipments from the Soviet Union. In all, the Eastern European satellites, excluding Albania, received 28 per cent of Soviet net exports or 22 million metric tons of standard fuel. This included 56 per cent of the coal and coke exports, and 21 per cent of those of crude and refined petroleum. The Federal Republic of Germany took 6 per cent of Soviet mineral-fuel exports, largely oil.

In the Mediterranean, Italy bought 14 per cent of Soviet net exports; other countries, notably Egypt, France, Greece, and Yugoslavia, 11 per cent. Elsewhere in Europe, Finland and Sweden were the Soviet Union's greatest customers for mineral fuels, each receiving 3.5 million metric tons of standard fuel, or more than 5 per cent of U.S.S.R. net exports in 1961. Cuba, with imports of 5.8 million metric tons; Japan, with imports of 5.2 million metric tons; and Mainland China, with imports of 4.0 million metric tons, were the largest importers in other parts of the world.

Over-all, the Soviet Union had re-established part of its prewar pattern of trade by 1961—namely to Germany, Italy, and Japan, the former Axis Powers; and to Egypt, France, and Greece. It also developed new markets within the Communist bloc, in Cuba, in Yugoslavia, and in Scandinavia. With many other countries it has maintained fluctuating trade.

Appendix Table 10 shows the redistribution of Soviet foreign trade in mineral fuels in terms of absolute increments or decrements in exports, between 1934 and 1955, 1955 and 1961, and 1934 and 1961. By these measures, the outstanding long-term developments in this trade have been the rise of Soviet exports to Germany as a whole, Italy, Czechoslovakia, Cuba, and Japan. The partial Soviet dependence upon imports from Rumania and Poland, significant during the post World War II decade appears now to be a transactional fiction.

The significance of trade with the Soviet Union in the energy balances of other countries can be assessed with reasonable accuracy for 1960. The statistics in Appendix Table 11 show that, as an aggregate, the Eastern European satellites produced 304 million metric tons of standard fuel, or 47 per cent as much as the Soviet Union. Their total consumption of fuels was 5 million metric tons less than their production, although for petroleum alone it was 3 million metric tons greater. About 2.6 million metric tons of this total consumption seems to have been used, not by individual countries, but by military forces of the Warsaw Pact nations as a bloc. Generally, the small share of petroleum in Eastern European consumption as a whole testifies to the modest military capacity and the aging capital structure of these countries. Soviet mineral-fuels shipments to this area provided about 70 per cent of the fuels exported, often after refining, by Eastern to Western Europe. Direct Soviet exports to the West were thus augmented by a quarter.

The Far Eastern satellite countries, largely Mainland China, received about 40 per cent of their new supply of liquid fuels of natural and synthetic origin from the Soviet Union. They consumed somewhat more than the visible new supply either by drawing on stocks or through unreported receipts, perhaps from non-bloc nations. As in Eastern Europe, the vast bulk of the energy produced and consumed was from domestic coal. Total fuel consumption approximated 444 million metric tons of standard fuel or almost three-fourths the Soviet figure.

In 1960, about half of Cuba's energy consumption came from Soviet oil, the rest being Venezuelan oil and stocks.

Eleven other countries were significant importers of Soviet and Eastern European fuels. Four of these nations, France, the Federal Republic of Germany, Italy, and Japan, may be categorized as major energy consumers. To augment their aggregate production of 310 million metric tons of standard fuel, they imported 220 million metric tons, which covered both consumption and gross exports, largely refined products, of 62 million metric tons. A third of their fuel consumption was in the form of liquid fuels; this compared favorably with a fourth in the U.S.S.R., 7 per cent in Eastern Europe, and 3 per cent among the Far Eastern satellites. Imports from the Soviet bloc constituted almost 12 per cent of Italy's gross supply of fuels, but less than 5 per cent for France, Germany, and Japan. Thus, while these countries are important markets for the Soviet Union and Eastern Europe, they are not seriously dependent today upon Soviet sources of supply. A similar situation, but with much greater dependence upon Soviet-bloc imports, applies to Austria, Sweden, and Yugoslavia. Seventeen per cent of Austrian gross supplies, 18 per cent of the Swedish, and 11 per cent of the Yugoslav, came from the U.S.S.R. and Eastern Europe. Among the minor energy consumers, Finland, Greece, and Iceland are heavily dependent upon imports from the Soviet bloc; Egypt, however, acts largely as a re-exporter.

Recent trends and future prospects in Soviet foreign trade in minerals may be summarized as follows:

First, since 1955, Soviet net exports of mineral fuels have risen very sharply. By 1961, they reached 66 million metric tons of standard fuel (7,000 C/kg equivalent), 27 times as high as in 1955. For 1965, the Soviet target is about 150 million metric tons; for 1972, 265 to 320 million metric tons.

Second, these exports are taking an increasingly large share of Soviet mineral-fuel output: 0.5 per cent in 1955, 9.4 per cent in 1961, with estimates of about 15 per cent in 1965 and perhaps 18 per cent in 1972.

Third, given Soviet plans for the continued maximization of military-economic strength rather than consumer welfare, the Soviet Union can export increasing portions of its mineral-fuel output only by severely restricting the use of private cars, housing space, single-family dwellings, hot water, and appliances. Pressures on residual claimants in rural areas are likely to intensify even further.

Fourth, mineral-fuel exports have served primarily to gain foreign exchange (and barter credits) for trade with Western Europe. Their share in the value of all Soviet exports outside the Communist bloc has risen from one-seventh to more than a fifth of the total. Shipments of mineral fuels to Western Europe via the Eastern European satellites and Egypt add at least another quarter to this value.

Fifth, the Soviet Union has supported its foreign marketing of mineral fuels by expanding its tanker fleet, beginning the construction of pipelines westward, and developing acceptable standards for export grades of petroleum products other than residual fuel oil. Nevertheless, since three-quarters of the Soviet oil is shipped as crude or residual fuel oil, the Soviet Union fails to maximize the foreign exchange returns on its resources by adding value through fabrication.[82] Moreover, its bilateral deals, although undoubtedly valuable in gaining particular scarce goods or achieving desired influences, are less effectual in larger markets.

Sixth, the Soviet Union has captured the energy markets of Iceland, Finland, and Greece, and is influential in Austria, Sweden, Yugoslavia, and Italy. Expanding Soviet sales to West Germany and Japan have as yet had minor impacts upon these large markets.

Seventh, Soviet exports to its Eastern European and Far Eastern satellites, transshipments apart, have been limited essentially to the support of moderate military requirements. In contrast, Cuba has become totally dependent upon the Soviet Union for its energy supplies.

[82] As Professor M. A. Adelman notes in his essay elsewhere in this volume, the basic profits in petroleum come from the extraction of crude, so that the national income of the U.S.S.R. (as opposed to foreign exchange alone) is being maximized in relation to factor costs by current Soviet policies of exporting crude and minimally refined products.

And eighth, future Soviet prospects for marketing mineral fuels in Western Europe will depend upon the magnitude of energy deficits in the Common Market and the United States, Soviet domestic capacities for restraining consumer demands, and the degree of viability of alternative energy sources in the Middle East, Africa, and Latin America.

THE SIGNIFICANCE OF SOVIET RESOURCE-MANAGEMENT TECHNIQUES

What is the general significance of Soviet practice, as it has developed, for other countries?

In my opinion, the crucial lesson of the Soviet record for more and less developed countries alike is the productiveness of planning and operations based on physical resources and requirements. Physical terms alone permit a full assessment of a country's potentials and needs; monetary models have value essentially as generalizing simplifications and initial guides. Monetary systems are invaluable servants of optimal resource management (as the United States learned in World War II) but very poor masters indeed. In an age of rapid population growth, enormous pressure on physical endowments, and exploding technological change, scientifically and technically blind economics is anachronistic.

The desirability of a systematic consideration of resource needs and availabilities in public and private economic activities does not mean adoption of the rigid and cumbersome Soviet system. Better, more flexible approaches testing the limits of certainty in knowledge and the consequences of alternative strategies are feasible — and essential for the experimentation underlying every free, dynamic, and pluralistic system. In developed countries, with strong information-gathering facilities, better collation, easier retrieval, and more analytical interpretation are the major needs. Careful attention is needed to the possible effects of disjunctive changes, as well as the linear growths in demand and capabilities all too commonly used. Qualitative factors, e.g., specified levels of skill, need far more thought than is often given. Finally, Western traditional concerns with demand must be better balanced with thorough assessment of potential supplies — lest the price of future energy or raw materials may be freedom itself.

For less developed countries, the Soviet system is a costly, antiquated luxury. Modern survey technology, probability sampling, and attention to domestic markets and demand can provide much more. The tasks are large, for each country is a unique configuration in which neither the experience of the West nor of the Communist bloc can be transplanted mechanically. Excellent hybrids appear to be the answer.

Note: I wish to acknowledge the editorial assistance of Edith M. Shimkin and Henry Eaton. Rainer Erhart prepared the basic map of agro-climatic conditions. The Aero-Space Information Division, Library of Congress, under the direction of George Pughe, helped me greatly in gathering data for the section on energy.

STATISTICAL APPENDIX

Table 1. Reconstructed Soviet Dietary Levels and Goals, Related to Domestic Food Production in Selected Years, 1953–1972[1]

Characteristic of the food supply units of consumption	Performance: 1953				Performance: 1958			
	Consumption			Related to domestic output	Consumption			Rela te dome outp
	Person per day	Total population per year			Person per day	Total population per year		
Units of measurement	Cal. (I) Gm. (II, III)	Tril-lion Cal.	Mil-lion M.T.	Per cent	Cal. (I) Gm. (II, III)	Tril-lion Cal.	Mil-lion M.T.	Pe ce
I. Total food supply	3,087	213.6	—	—	3,174	239.6	—	-
1. Plant products	2,550	176.5	—	—	2,479	187.0	—	-
a. Carbohydrate sources	2,368	163.9	—	—	2,260	170.5	—	-
Breadstuffs[2]	1,788	123.7	[3]35.1	63	1,663	125.5	34.6	3
Potatoes	336	23.3	34.0	47	292	22.0	32.1	3
Sugar	244	16.9	4.1	119	305	23.0	5.6	10
b. Other	183	12.7	—	—	219	16.5	—	-
Vegetables[5]	37	2.6	9.4	83	44	3.4	12.3	8
Fruits	(24)	(1.7)	(3.5)	(164)	35	2.6	5.4	1
Oils	121	8.4	0.9	67	140	10.5	1.2	5
2. Animal products	510	35.3	—	—	660	49.9	—	-
a. Meat, lard and meat products	201	13.9	5.9	102	241	18.2	7.6	9
b. Milk and milk products	276	19.1	[7]39.8	[7](100)	375	28.3	58.7	10
c. Eggs	16	1.1	0.8	86	22	1.7	1.2	9
d. Fish and other aquatic products	17	1.2	2.1	94	22	1.7	2.9	10
3. Miscellaneous products, largely alcoholic	(27)	(1.9)	8	(100)	35	2.6	8	(10
II. Total fats	59	—	4.1	—	73	—	5.5	-
1. Animal fats	41	—	2.8	—	21	—	4.0	-
2. Plant fats	19	—	1.3	—	52	—	1.6	-
III. Total proteins	84	—	5.8	—	88	—	6.6	-
1. Animal proteins	23	—	1.6	—	30	—	2.2	-
2. Plant proteins	61	—	4.2	—	58	—	4.4	-
IV. Indices, 1958 = 100								
1. Total food supply	97	89	—	—	100	100	—	-
2. Animal products	77	71	—	—	100	100	—	-
3. All fats	82	—	75	—	100	—	100	-
4. All proteins	96	—	88	—	100	—	100	-

1 metric ton (M.T.) = 2,204.6 lb.
— Inapplicable.　　n.a. Data not available.　　( ) Coarse approximations.
Sums may not add because of independent rounding. All calories are kilogram calories.

Plan: 1965				"Rational" (1972) Goals			
Consumption		Related to domestic output		Consumption		Related to domestic output	
Person per day	Total population per year			Person per day	Total population per year		
Cal. (I) Gm. (II, III)	Tril-lion Cal.	Mil-lion M.T.	Per cent	Cal. (I) Gm. (II, III)	Tril-lion Cal.	Mil-lion M.T.	Per cent
3,480	288.3	—	—	3,310	302.0	—	—
2,446	202.7	—	—	2,091	190.8	—	—
2,074	171.8	—	—	1,711	156.1	—	—
1,385	114.7	31.6	[4](30)	1,155	105.4	29.0	24
205	17.0	24.8	17	192	17.5	25.5	13
484	40.1	9.8	98–106	364	33.2	8.1	94
372	30.9	—	—	380	34.7	—	—
90	7.5	27.2	78–91	86	7.8	28.3	72
70	5.8	12.0	171	119	10.9	22.5	91
212	17.6	1.9	[6](71)	175	16.0	1.8	49
1,013	83.9	—	—	1,205	110.0	—	—
351	29.1	12.4	77	394	36.0	15.6	76
599	49.6	103.3	100	708	64.6	134.6	86
31	2.6	1.9	88	70	6.4	4.6	99
31	2.6	4.6	100	33	3.0	5.3	n.a.
21	1.7	n.a.	n.a.	13	1.2	n.a.	n.a.
108	—	8.9	—	117	—	10.7	—
80	—	6.7	—	94	—	8.6	—
28	—	2.3	—	24	—	2.2	—
96	—	8.0	—	99	—	9.1	—
45	—	3.8	—	56	—	5.1	—
51	—	4.2	—	44	—	4.0	—
110	120	—	—	104	126	—	—
153	168	—	—	183	220	—	—
148	—	162	—	161	—	195	—
109	—	120	—	113	—	136	—

Notes to Table 1

[1] Sources and general methodology for the table were as follows:

a. The structure of daily food consumption in calories is reported for 1958, and the 1965 and "rational" goals in P. Nazarov: "Increase of the Level and Change of the Structure of Food-Products Consumption in the U.S.S.R.," *Voprosy ekonomiki,* 1959, No. 11, pp. 110–19. The same source also indicates per cent changes, 1953–58, in the per capita consumption of all but two component categories. "Miscellaneous products" for 1953 were calculated from trends in per capita vodka and beer production (see notes 1.*e.* and 1.*i.*), "fruits" were a small, arbitrary estimate, while the total was the sum of all components.

b. Converting reported patterns of food consumption into caloric values (kilogram calories) began with data for 1958. First, Nazarov's (*op. cit.,* above) per capita output statistics were divided into aggregate production figures to yield his population estimate (midyear) of 206.8 million persons. See Ts.S.U. pri Sovete ministrov SSSR, *Sel'skoye khozyaystvo SSSR (Agriculture of the U.S.S.R.),* Moscow: Gosstatizdat, 1960, pp. 202–3, 333. Second, the caloric value of foodstuffs was estimated from Soviet flour consumption. This equivalence corresponds to Soviet practice, as shown by P. S. Mstislavskiy, *Narodnoye potrebleniye pri sotsializme (National Consumption under Socialism),* Moscow: Gosplanizdat, 1961, pp. 127–28. In 1958, flour production came to 35 million M.T.; with net exports being negligible, this closely approximated consumption. See Ts.S.U. pri Sovete ministrov SSSR, *Narodnoye khozyaystvo SSSR v. 1961g. (National Economy of the U.S.S.R. in 1961),* Moscow: Gosstatizdat, 1962, p. 263; and Ministerstvo vneshney torgovli SSSR, *Vneshnaya torgovlya SSSR za 1958g. (Foreign Trade of the U.S.S.R. for 1958),* Moscow: Vneshtorgizdat, 1959, Item 82. Third, the ratio of wheat flour to rye flour within the total was estimated to equal the average ratio of wheat to rye production, less exports of each, for 1957–58. This came to 81% wheat and 19% rye. Fourth, caloric values of 3640 C/kg for wheat flour and 3594 C/kg for rye flour were taken from R. Pearl, *The Nation's Food* (Philadelphia: Saunders, 1920), pp. 46, 100. And fifth, weighting wheat and rye flour to gain an average value of 3630 C/kg yielded, tentatively, a national breadstuffs supply of 127.0 trillion calories; hence, a national total food supply of 242.5 trillion calories, a daily per capita breadstuffs supply of 1,680 calories and a total daily per capita ration of 3,210 calories.

c. These calculations were verified and adjusted by relating the calculated food values of sugar, fish and other aquatic products, and dairy products consumptions to reported supplies. For sugar, Pearl's value of 4,100 C/kg indicates a consumption of 5.68 million M.T., compared to 1958's reported production of 5.43 million M.T. and net imports of 180,000 M.T. Similarly, using Pearl's recovery of 51.82% edible product for fish and other aquatic products and his caloric value of 1093 C/kg yields a consumption of 3.00 million M.T., the reported catch being 2.94 million M.T. For milk, Pearl's calculations, allowing an average butterfat content of 3.6% and deducting losses to animal consumption and waste of 4% of the fat and 50% each of the proteins and carbohydrates, give a net human-consumption value of 480 calories per kilogram. The resulting estimate of consumption is 59.6 million M.T., with output reported to be 58.7 million M.T. (See Pearl, *op. cit.,* pp. 45–6, 63–64; *Nar. khoz. v. 1961, op. cit.,* p. 263; and *Sel'khoz, op. cit.,* p. 329). In all, these checks indicate that the estimate gained from breadstuffs alone was slightly high, probably from rounding error in the output datum. Hence, the final figures adopted were 1.2% *lower* than the tentative estimates.

d. Soviet meat statistics alone present special analytical difficulties because of the inclusion of inedible offal (along with meat, lard, and edible offal) and because of the poor condition of the meat marketed. However, it is believed that acceptably reliable estimates can be made by multiplying Pearl's coefficients for caloric values and for fat content by 0.70, and his coefficients for protein content by 0.80, for each type of meat separately. Supporting data on these estimates are materials on meat recovered as a per cent of the live weight (*Nar. khoz. v. 1961, op. cit.*, p. 267); on live weight produced (*Sel'khoz, op. cit.*, pp. 328–29); on the weights of marketed animals, 1950–59 (*ibid.*, pp. 376–78); on the proportions of meat, lard, edible and inedible offal in cattle of varying fatness, and on standards of lean meat. These last items came from Ye. A. Ruzskaya, *Perspektivy razvitiya i razmeshcheniya zhivotnovodstva v SSSR* (*Prospectives for the Development and Distribution of Livestock Breeding in the U.S.S.R.*), Moscow: Izd Akademiyi nauk, 1959, pp. 46, 226. It must be stressed that Ruzskaya's general data on p. 226 cannot be used directly because they are for lean meats only, net of lard. Finally, the varying proportions of different meats in 1953, 1958, and 1972 have also affected average calorie fat and protein contents per kilogram. The proportions have been as follows by weight: 1953, beef, veal, horsemeat, camel meat and reindeer meat, 38.4%; pork and lard, 39.6%; mutton and lamb, 12.3%; chicken, about 7.9%; and ducks, geese, turkeys and hares, about 1.8%. For 1958, the corresponding per cents were 37.8, 42.4, 11.5, about 7.0 and about 1.3; for 1972, 35.0, 36.4, 14.8, 7.9 and 5.9. For 1965, the estimates have been interpolated between 1958 and 1972, in corresponding order, to be 36.4, 39.4, 13.15, 7.45 and 3.6. See Ruzskaya (*ibid.*), pp. 148, 226, 240–41; *Sel'khoz, op. cit.* (note 1.*b*.), p. 333.

  e. Pearl's data on cabbages were assumed to typify Soviet vegetables; those on apples, all fruits (*op. cit.*, p. 46). For alcoholic beverages, reported production in 1958 (excluding home brews for personal consumption) included 199.1 million decaliters of beer (1 decaliter = 2.64 gallons), 61.8 million decaliters of wines, and 145.4 million decaliters of vodka (*Nar. khoz. v 1961, op. cit.*, p. 263). Foreign trade was negligible. Use of a caloric value of 5,000 C/decaliter for beer and wines is suggested by data in *Bol'shaya Sovetskaya entsiklopediya* (*The Great Soviet Encyclopedia*), 2d. ed., 33:14–15, 1955. This further indicates an acceptable value of 9,300 C/decaliter for vodka.

  f. In summary, the following nutritional values have been uniformly adopted for the table:

		Content per Unit		
Food	Unit of measurement	Kilo-calories	Fats (Gm)	Proteins (Gm)
Wheat flour	kg	3,640	10	114
Rye flour	kg	3,594	9	68
Potato	kg	686	1	18
Sugar	kg	4,100	0	0
Cabbage	kg	276	2	14
Apple	kg	485	3	3
Vegetable oil	kg	9,118	980	0
Beef and veal	kg	(1,440)	(108)	(122)
Horse, camel, reindeer	kg	(1,440)	(108)	(122)
Pork and lard	kg	(3,625)	(396)	(79)
Mutton and lamb*	kg	(1,933)	(168)	(104)
Chicken	kg	(984)	(64)	(107)
Dairy products	kg	480	34	18
Eggs	kg	1,400	93	131
	10 eggs	795	53	74
Fish**	kg	1,093	38	172
Beer	decaliter	(5,000)	0	0
Wine	decaliter	(5,000)	0	0
Vodka	decaliter	(9,300)	0	0

  * Also an approximation of ducks, etc., as an aggregate.
  ** 51.82% of catch.

g. Domestic outputs in 1958 are from *Nar. khoz. v 1961, op. cit.*, p. 263 and *Sel'khoz, op. cit.*, pp. 202–3, 254, 328–29. The vegetable oil figure comprises commercial production plus 25% of the weight of the sunflower seeds retained in the household sector, or 1,465,000 M.T. plus 502,000 M.T. See *Nar. khoz. v 1961, op. cit.*, p. 270 and *Sel'khoz., op. cit.*, pp. 100, 202. Grapes are excluded from all data on fruit production and attributed to wines only.

h. For 1953 per capita consumption see note 1.*a*, above. The 1953 population estimated by Nazarov was recalculated from his per capita outputs divided into total production, to yield 189.6 million persons. This figure provided the base for the aggregate consumption calculations, and also for per capita alcoholic beverages consumption. By interpolation of 1950–55 vodka and beer statistics, and from data on grape crops, vodka consumption in 1953 is believed to have approximated 95 million decaliters, and beer and wine, 200 million decaliters. See Ts.S.U. pri Sovete ministrov SSSR, *Promyshlennost' SSSR (Industry of the U.S.S.R.)*, Moscow: Gosstatizdat, 1957, p. 372 and *Sel'khoz, op. cit.*, p. 256. It must also be noted that in 1953 the ratio of wheat to rye was 74 to 26% (*Sel'khoz, op. cit.*, p. 202); thus, the average caloric value of flour was lower than in 1958, i.e. about 3,528 C/kg (see note 1.*b*, above). The vegetable-oil estimate was calculated as for 1958 (note 1.*h*, above); that for meat used the reported structure of production (*Sel'khoz, op. cit.*, p. 333) for estimating the physical weight of the total meat supply.

i. Nazarov's data (see note 1.*a*) on 1958–65 planned increases in per capita consumption of eggs and fish, by 40%; of vegetable oils, by 60%; and of vegetables, by at least 100% are compatible with similar data in Mstislavskiy, *op. cit.* (Note 1.*b*), pp. 129–30, which report per capita consumption goals of 395 kg of dairy products and 41–44 kg of sugar. The two sources together coincide in showing the 1965 target to be 3,480 calories per person per day. However, not all goals cited by these authors are consistent: Nazarov's meat (plus 90%) and milk (plus 70%) goals are too high, and his sugar target (plus 50%) is too low. Mstislavskiy's meat target (plus 84%) also fails to fit. Despite these difficulties, the measure of agreement found, and important agreements between calculated total demand and output led to acceptance of the figure used. The 1965 population estimate derived from these authors from per capita and total production figures averages 227.0 million persons, with an absolute range of 225.4–230.0 million. For wheat, potatoes, vegetables, meat, dairy products, eggs, fish, sugar and vegetable oil Mstislavskiy, *op. cit.*, p. 123 cites the targets. However, the vegetable-oil figure covers State procurements only; it is assumed that the household sector is to rise proportionately. For rye, an estimate of 26 million M.T. has been interpolated between 1958 output and the 1972 target. See *Sel'khoz, op. cit.* (note 1.*b*), p. 209; and P. M. Zemskiy, *Razvitiye i razmeshcheniye zemledeliya po prirodno-khozyaystvennym rayonam SSSR (Development and Distribution of Crop Cultivation by Natural-Economic Regions of the U.S.S.R.)*, Moscow: Izd: Akademiyi nauk, 1959, p. 114.

j. Ruzskaya, *op. cit.* (note 1.*d*), p. 6, gives the population for the period of "rational" nutrition as 250 million persons, and annual per capita consumption to be 551.2 kg of dairy products, 62.3 kg of meat "in the raw" and 307 eggs. She also cites production goals (p. 7) of 156 million M.T. of milk, 20.4 million M.T. of meat, and 81 billion eggs (*ibid.*, p. 7). Her population figure corresponds to a geometrical interpolation for 1972 between Soviet projections for 1965 (note 1.*j*) and 1980 (see text); this has also been a reported target date for Soviet energy programs (see Table 5). The per capita goals yield slightly inconsistent results: from milk, a daily ration of 3,379–3,395 calories; from meat (see also note 1.*d*), 3,287–3,315 and from eggs, 3,110–3,262 calories. Nazarov's per capita data on 1972 (*op. cit.*, see note 1.*a*) are internally inconsistent, and may be separate norms for all persons and adult male workers. The figures and indicated rations are as follows: potatoes, 103 kg (3,309–3,367 calories); vegetables, 153 kg (4,366–4,536 calories); fish (presumably, edible portions only), 14.2 kg (4,050–4,476 calories, and meat, 85 kg (4,607–4,646 calories). The estimate finally used, 3,310 calories, is thus plausible but not certain. The crop targets are from Zemskiy, *op. cit.* (note 1.*j*); see also, Table 2. Sugar recovery from sugar beets has been estimated at 10.0% of the gross crop, as in 1958 (*Sel'khoz, op. cit.* [note 1.*b*], pp. 202–3, and *Nar. khoz. v 1961, op. cit.* [note 1.*b*], p. 264). For vegetable oils, the recovery estimates were also made in accord with 1958 experience (see note 1.*h*): 11.5% of unginned cotton, 30% of sunflower seed, and 15% of flax and hempseed.

² All flour, assumed to be produced from wheat and rye.

³ The figure of 27 million M.T. flour production for 1953 in Mstislavskiy, *op. cit.* (note 1.*b*), p. 128 apparently covers only State output, excluding collective-farm mills.

⁴ See note 1.*j*.

⁵ Excludes melons (*bakhchevyye*) in the production data; the relation of consumption to output therefore runs several per cent too high.

⁶ See note 1.*j*.

⁷ Reported production in 1953: 36.5 million M.T. of milk (Mstislavskiy, *op. cit.* [note 1.*b*], p. 123). The discrepancy is not explicable.

⁸ See notes 1.*e* and 1.*i*.

Table 2. Trends and Anticipations in Soviet Agriculture:
Plantings, Mineral Fertilizer Use, and Harvests[1]

| Trends in practice | | All sown land | Fibers and seeds | | Sugar beets[2] | Pota toe |
Year	Item		Cotton	Flax and hemp		
1956	Acreage (million ha.)	194.8	2.06	2.54	2.01	9
	Mineral fertilizers:					
	Input (kg/ha.)	47	1,020	⁵440	830	119
	Use (million M.T.)	9.2	2.11	(1.12)	1.67	1.
	Crops:					
	Yields (100 kg/ha.)	—	21.0	4.65	162	104
	Harvests (million M.T.)	—	4.33	1.18	32.5	96.
1960	Acreage (million ha.)	203.0	2.19	1.97	3.04	9.
	Mineral fertilizers:					
	Input (kg/ha.)	55	1,128	548	830	119
	Use (million M.T.)	11.1	2.47	1.08	2.52	1.
	Crops:					
	Yields (100 kg/ha.)	—	19.6	n.a.	191	92
	Harvests (million M.T.)	—	4.29	n.a.	57.7	84.
1965 Plan	Acreage (million ha.)	(214.2)	2.60	(2.2)	(3.9)	(9.
	Mineral fertilizers:					
	Input (kg/ha.)	(137)	1,128	(705)	(938)	(535
	Use (million M.T.)	29.3	2.93	1.55	3.66	4.
	Crops:					
	Yields (100 kg/ha.)	—	—	n.a.	205	(162
	Harvests (million M.T.)	—	(5.9)	n.a.	(80)	147
1972 Plan	Acreage (million ha.)	(233.3)	3.02	2.55	3.21	10.
	Mineral fertilizers:					
	Input (kg/ha.)	320	1,222	918	854	623
	Use (million M.T.)	75.1	3.69	2.34	2.74	6.
	Crops:					
	Yields (100 kg/ha.)	—	32.7	10.0	268	186
	Harvests (million M.T.)	—	9.87	2.56	86.1	190
Indices, 1956 = 100:						
Acreage:	1960	104	106	78	151	99
	1965P	(110)	126	(87)	(194)	(99)
	1972P	(120)	147	100	160	111
Fertilizer use:	1960	121	117	(96)	151	100
	1965P	318	139	(139)	219	447
	1972P	816	175	(209)	164	585
Harvests:	1960	—	99	n.a.	178	88
	1965P	—	(136)	n.a.	246	153
	1972P	—	228	217	265	198

1 hectare = 2.471 acres; 1 kilogram = 2.2046 lb.; 1 metric ton = 2,204.6 lb.
— Inapplicable or negligible.   n.a. Data not available.   ( ) Approximate.
P Planned or projected.

Vegetables (including melons)[a]	Corn for grain	Other grains	Fodder oil and other sown crops	Orchard crops	Cultivated meadows and pastures
2.38	9.30	119.0	48.26	[4]2.14	n.a.
180	37	12	21	(103)	—
0.43	0.34	1.43	(1.02)	(0.22)	—
[6]91	[7]12.1	9.7	[8]8.8	16.1	n.a.
[6]14.3	[7]12.5	115.1	[8]30.5	3.44	n.a.
2.1	11.2	110.5	62.9	[4]3.97	n.a.
180	37	16	22	71	—
0.38	0.41	1.78	1.39	0.28	—
[6]107	16.7	10.5	[8]11.7	12.4	n.a.
[6]16.6	[7]18.7	115.7	[8]51.4	4.94	n.a.
(2.5)	(20)	(111)	(62.9)	n.a.	n.a.
(685)	(102)	(72)	(73)	n.a.	—
1.71	2.05	7.94	4.62	1.67	—
(128)	(19)	(12)	n.a.	n.a.	n.a.
(32)	(38)	(134)	n.a.	13.9	n.a.
3.25	21.2	(123)	66.8	5.51	30.7
920	487	(179)	371	655	189
2.76	10.33	22.1	24.8	3.60	5.81
189	[7](28)	(15)	[8]33	69	n.a.
61.5	[7](58.7)	(189)	[8]163	37.8	n.a.
88	120	93	130	186	n.a.
(105)	215	(93)	(130)	n.a.	n.a.
137	228	(103)	138	257	n.a.
88	120	124	136	(127)	—
398	603	555	453	(759)	—
642	3,038	1,545	2,431	(1,636)	—
[6]116	150	101	169	144	—
[9]224	304	116	n.a.	404	—
[9]430	470	164	534	1,099	—

NOTES TO TABLE 2

¹ Sources and methods:

a. Data on acreages sown, in orchard crops and in cultivated meadows and pastures were derived, for 1956, from Ts.S.U. pri Sovete ministrov SSSR *Sel'skoye khozyaystvo SSSR (Agriculture of the U.S.S.R.)*, Moscow: Gosstatizdat, 1960, pp. 132–33, 251. For 1960, the statistics come from Ts.S.U. pri Sovete ministrov SSSR, *Narodnoye khozyaystvo SSSR v 1961 g. (National Economy of the U.S.S.R. in 1961)*, Moscow: Gosstatizdat, 1962, pp. 311–12, 376. The 1965 estimates were compiled as follows: the area of sown acreage was taken to be 5.5% greater than in 1960 in view of the 11% increase in plowland targeted for the decade 1960–70. This estimate may be slightly conservative in view of continuing Soviet reductions in clean fallow, which fell from 15.8% of all plowland in 1953 to 7.9% in 1960 (*Nar. khoz. v 1961, op. cit.,* p. 313). See E. Savinskiy, "On the Wide Application of Chemistry in the National Economy," *Voprosy ekonomiki,* 1962 No. 6, pp. 16–29, esp. p. 18. Targets of 2.6 to 2.7 million ha. for cotton and of 3.8 to 4 million ha. for sugar beets in 1965 are reported by P. Baranov, "Let Us Sharply Increase the Scale and Tempo of the Use of Chemicals in Agriculture," *Voprosy ekonomiki,* 1959 No. 12, pp. 18–26, esp. p. 21. The goal of 20 million ha. for corn harvested as grain is given by D. Gale Johnson and A. Kahan, *The Soviet Agricultural Program: An Evaluation of the 1965 Goals,* Memorandum RM–2848–PR (Santa Monica, Calif.: The RAND Corporation, 1962), p. 66. The vegetable acreage for 1965 is an interpolation between 1960 and the 1972 goal. For other acreages, the 1960 figures appear to be reasonable approximations. Finally, the 1972 targets were taken from P. M. Zemskiy, *Razvitiye i razmeshcheniye zemledeliya po prirodno-khozyaystvennym rayonam SSSR (The Development and Distribution of Crop Cultivation by the Natural-Economic Regions of the U.S.S.R.),* Moscow: Izd. akademiyi nauk, 1959, pp. 105–245.

b. Mineral fertilizers are reported, by Soviet convention, in equivalents of ammonium sulfate (14.9% N by weight), potash (K_2O) of 41.6% concentration; and super phosphates and ground phosphate rock of 18.7 and 19.0% concentrates, respectively (*Nar. khoz. v 1961, op. cit.,* p. 219). Mineral fertilizer inputs for 1956 came from P. Bobrovskiy: "The Economic Effectiveness of the Use of Chemicals in Agriculture," *Voprosy ekonomiki,* No. 1, pp. 134–40. The year referred to in this source is readily derivable from the pattern of cropland use given; however, this distribution times the reported inputs per hectare do not jibe with the over-all distribution of fertilizer use Bobrovskiy cites. That item may well refer to another year and has been disregarded. For 1960 the absolute quantity of fertilizer used has been reported in *Nar. khoz. v 1961, op. cit.,* p. 380; for 1965, in Baranov, *op. cit.* (note 1.*a*), p. 18. Fertilizer uses by crop for 1960 and 1965 are given in N. Baranov: "Economic Effectiveness of the Use of Chemicals in Agriculture," *Voprosy ekonomiki,* 1961, No. 9, pp. 102–110, esp. p. 108. The 1972 data are from Zemskiy, *op. cit.* (note 1.*a*), p. 266.

c. Yields and harvests in 1956 came from *Sel'khoz, op. cit.* (note 1.*a*), pp. 202–3, 208–9, 254–56. For 1960, the source is *Nar. khoz. v 1961, op. cit.* (note 1.*a*), pp. 300–303, 379. *Sel'khoz, op. cit.,* pp. 26–27, reports 1965 goals for cotton (5.7–6.1 million M.T.), sugar beets (76–84 million M.T.), potatoes (147 million M.T.), fruits and berries (7 million M.T., minimum), grapes (6.9 million M.T., minimum), and all grain (164–180 million M.T.). The central values have been used wherever ranges have been reported; for grain, the estimate has involved an adjustment for the increased acreage of corn. The vegetable target, which apparently includes melons, comes from Johnson and Kahan, *op. cit.* (note 1.*a*), p. 47n. All 1972 goals come from Zemskiy, *loc. cit.* (note 1.*a*).

² Reported in gross weight. The figures exclude beets raised for fodder only.

³ The figures exclude root vegetables and melons raised for fodder only.

[4] The acreage cited excludes a small area of cultivated berry patches (29,000 ha. in 1955, according to Zemskiy, *op. cit.* [note 1.*a*], p. 245).

[5] The input is reported for flax only.

[6] The yield and harvest data exclude melons.

[7] Soviet estimates of the grain equivalent of corn harvested ripe and in the waxy stage of ripening.

[8] The yield and harvest data include only cultivated perennial and annual grasses, including corn cut green.

[9] Slightly exaggerated, since the base figure excludes melons.

Table 3. Planning-Level Reserves of Mineral Fuels in the
U.S.S.R. and United States, 1958–1960

(Billion M.T. of 7,000 C/kg equivalent)

Fuel	U.S.S.R., 1958 "Balance" Reserves[1]		United States, 1960 Proven Reserves[2]	
	Quantity	Per cent	Quantity	Per cent
Total	(185)	100	223.2	100.0
Coal and lignite	[3](140)	76	194.4	87.1
Oil shale	[4]5.8	3	10.4	4.7
Petroleum and natural gas liquids	(15)	8	7.7	3.5
Natural gas	2.1	1	10.3	4.6
Peat	[4]22.8	12	n.a.	n.a.
Bitumin	n.a.	n.a.	0.4	0.1

1 metric ton = 2,204.6 lb.
n.a. Data not available.
( ) Estimated.
[1] Categories A + B + C₁, the last within prescribed proportions. For a detailed discussion see
D. B. Shimkin, *The Soviet Mineral-Fuels Industries, 1928–1958: A Statistical Survey*, U.S. Bureau
of the Census Series P. 90, No. 19 (Washington: U.S. Government Printing Office, 1962), pp.
153–67.
[2] U.S. Department of Labor: *Technological Change and Productivity in the Bituminous Coal
Industry 1920–60*, Bulletin No. 1305 (Washington: U.S. Government Printing Office, 1961), p. 75.
[3] Approximate heat equivalent of 179.0 billion M.T. of coal and lignite reserves.
[4] For 1955.

Table 4. Major Underground Coal Deposits under Construction or Selected for Development in the Soviet Union as of 1961[1]

Item	Total USSR	Donets Basin	Kuz-netsk Basin	Kara-ganda Basin	Pechora Basin
1. Number of deposits	142	47	63	23	9
of which,					
for long-wall mining	85	34	30	19	2
for chamber-and-pillar mining	57	13	33	4	7
2. Aggregate annual capacity (mill. M.T.)	319.6	68.6	189.9	34.4	26.7
of which,					
in long-wall mines	101.8	33.2	39.9	24.8	3.9
in chamber-and-pillar mines	217.8	35.4	150.0	9.6	22.8
3. Average annual capacity (thous. M.T.)	2,250	1,460	3,015	1,500	2,965
of which,					
long-wall mines	1,200	1,000	1,300	1,200	2,000
chamber-and-pillar mines	3,800	2,700	4,500	2,400	3,200
4. Total planned investment (bill. 1961 rubles)	38.2	9.55	20.81	4.27	3.43
of which,					
long-wall mines	14.1	5.00	5.36	3.16	0.57
chamber-and-pillar mines	24.1	4.55	20.81	1.11	2.86
5. Planned investment per M.T. of annual capacity (1961 rubles)	119.4	139.2	109.6	124.2	128.5
of which,					
long-wall mines	138.3	150.5	134.4	127.5	145.0
chamber-and-pillar mines	110.5	128.5	103.0	115.6	125.7
6. Planned employment (thousands of exploitation workers)	326.3	83.0	184.3	30.0	28.0
of which,					
long-wall mines	118.6	45.4	46.3	22.4	4.4
chamber-and-pillar mines	207.7	37.6	138.0	7.6	23.6
7. Annual productivity per worker in M.T.	979	827	1,030	1,159	954
of which,					
long-wall mines	858	732	862	1,106	888
chamber-and-pillar mines	1,049	942	1,087	1,264	966

1 metric ton = 2,204.6 lb.
Totals may not add because of independent rounding.
[1] *Source:* Y. P. Kalmykov *et al.,* "On the Effectiveness of Large Coal Mines with Block Development and Operation of the Coal Bodies," *Ugol',* 1961, No. 3.

Table 5. Energy Production and Self-Sufficiency, for Selected Past and Projected Years in the Soviet Union, United States, and Western Europe (OEEC)

Area and years	Energy output in million M.T. of 7,000 C/kg equivalent[1] of which						Self-sufficiency ratios[2] (production/consumption) including		
	Total	Anthracite and Bituminous coals	Lignite, peat and shale	Petroleum and natural gas	Hydro-electric power	Fuelwood and allied	Total output	Anthracite and Bituminous coals	Petroleum and natural gas
I. Soviet Union[8]									
1928	103	29	4	17	...	53	104	101	131
1933	168	62	10	32	1	64	105	103	128
1940	291	129	26	49	3	84	99	98	103
1950	353	173	49	61	8	62	97	96	97
1955	520	262	73	113	12	61	100	99	105
1960	[4]736	[4]316	[4]80	265	22	53	107	103	124
1965P	[4]1,098	[4]385	[4]100	520	43	50	115	n.a.	n.a.
1972P	[4]1,615	[4]553		940	82	40	n.a.	n.a.	n.a.
II. United States[5]									
1928	876	541	...	251	31	53	102	101	107
1933	688	360	...	251	26	51	105	104	107
1940	952	482	...	390	32	49	105	107	104
1950	1,284	527	...	658	57	42	102	113	94
1955	1,439	462	...	886	52	38	98	110	93
1960	1,541	409	...	1,035	62	35	93	109	88
1975P	[6]2,520	[6]815	...	1,595	85	25	93	[6]119	83
III. OEEC[7]									
1950	532	442	[8]25	7	40	[8]20	87	99	8
1955	603	477	[8]30	20	56	[8]20	78	94	12
1960	608	437	[8]34	36	81	[8]20	70	87	13
1965P	[9]690	460	45	55	95	[8]20	68	93	19
1975P	[10]850	465	60	105	140	[8]20	62	93	22

1 metric ton = 2,204.6 lb.
Data are partly estimated.
n.a. Data not available.
... Trifling output.
P Planned or projected outputs.

Notes to Table 5

[1] The energy-conversion coefficients follow the official practices of each area and thus embody very slight inconsistencies. In all cases, hydroelectric power has been credited with the energy equivalent of the input requirement for the same output reported for central thermal stations in the same area and year. In addition, all the figures on fuelwood and allied minor energy sources are estimates subject to large errors. Nuclear energy has been specifically estimated only for the 1965 and 1975 projections for the OEEC countries. For the United States, it has been included within the coal projection for 1975. A separate estimate for nuclear power in the Soviet Union has not been made, in view of the sharp reduction of Soviet plans in this sphere. See text.

[2] The ratio of production to apparent consumption (output less net exports or plus net imports), including bunkerage but without systematic adjustment for changes in stocks.

[3] *Sources:*

a. Energy output data for 1928–55 and the 1965 and 1972 plans are from D. B. Shimkin, *The Soviet Mineral-Fuels Industries, 1928–1958. A Statistical Survey*, U.S. Bureau of the Census, Series P–90, No. 19 (Washington: U.S. Government Printing Office, 1962), pp. 30, 67, 80, 85, 95. See also note 4.

b. Energy output data for 1960 have been calculated from A. Riznik and S. Litvak: "The Fuel and Electric-power Balance of the U.S.S.R. for 1960," *Vestnik statistiki*, 1962, No. 6, pp. 15–27, esp. p. 16; G. V. Krasnikovskiy, "Prospective Development of the Coal Industry of the U.S.S.R.," *Ugol'*, 1962, No. 3, pp. 1–6; Ya. M. Prudkin; "World Coal Output," *Ugol'*, 1961, No. 7, pp. 58–9; and A. Kortunov: "The Gas Industry on the Eve of the XXIId Congress of the Communist Party of the Soviet Union," *Gazovaya promyshlennost'*, 1961, No. 10, pp. 1–3, esp. p. 3. Note that two distinct values for 1960 centralized fuel production can be calculated: 681:6 million M.T. of 7,000 C/kg equivalent and 660.8 million M.T. The lower value, consistent with the revised series for 1958 and subsequently used by the Central Statistical Administration of the U.S.S.R. and in Riznik and Litvak's report, has been adopted. See also note 4. Riznik and Litvak give the hydroelectric power datum and an approximate figure for non-centralized fuelwood procurements.

c. Foreign trade data for 1928–40 are from Ministerstvo vneshney torgovli SSSR, *Vneshnaya torgovlya SSSR za 1918–1940 gg.* (*The Foreign Trade of the U.S.S.R. for 1918–1940*), Moscow: Vneshtorgizdat, 1960, Items 20–22. For 1955, the source is Ts.S.U. pri Sov. min. SSSR, Narodnoye khozyaystvo SSSR v 1958 g. (*The National Economy of the U.S.S.R. in 1958*), Moscow: Gosstatizdat, 1959, pp. 802–4. For 1955 and 1960 see Table 6; for 1965 Plan see Shimkin, 1962, *op. cit.*, p. 69.

[4]*a.* Revised values have been used for the heat value of Soviet coal and lignite production in 1960, 1965, and 1972. These lowered previous calculations by the Central Statistical Administration of the U.S.S.R. for coal and lignite energy equivalents by about 6%. The old values are still used in some current technical literature. See note 3*b*, above.

b. The figure for anthracite and bituminous coal production within the 1965 aggregate plan for coal and lignite has been calculated from two sources. One is the reported set of plans for 1965 output in the Donets, Kuznetsk, Karaganda and Pechora Basins, which together accounted for 82.8 per cent of Soviet anthracite and bituminous coal production in 1958. The estimate assumes these basins would produce the same proportion of bituminous coal and lignite in 1965. See Shimkin, 1962 *op. cit.*, p. 85; and A. F. Zasyad'ko *et al., Osnovy tckhnicheskogo progressa ugol'noy promyshlennosti SSSR* (*Foundations of the Technological Progress of the*

Coal Industry of the U.S.S.R.), Moscow: Ugletekhizdat, 1959, p. 34. The other is the ratio between heat equivalent and physical output planned for 1965, which is 0.735, compared to 0.722 in 1960. (See Shimkin, 1962 *op. cit.*, p. 67; and Zasyad'ko, 1959, *op. cit.*, p. 32). The two indications coincide.

⁵ Output and consumption data for 1928–55, with fuelwood interpolated for 1928 and 1933, are from S. H. Schurr and B. C. Netschert, *Energy in the American Economy, 1850–1975* (Baltimore: Johns Hopkins Press, 1960), pp. 497–98, 512–13. For 1960, the fuelwood estimate is a linear extrapolation from Schurr and Netschert, while other data are from U.S. Bureau of the Census, *Statistical Abstract of the United States, 83d Annual Edition* (Washington: U.S. Government Printing Office, 1962), p. 528. The 1975 projection is taken from Schurr and Netschert's consumption estimate modified as follows: The relation between consumption and output for each major energy source was calculated for 1926–30 and 1956–60. The arithmetic averages of the level of self-sufficiency in each energy source for each of these two periods were then linearly extrapolated to 1975. Finally, a 1935–55 trend in fuelwood output was linearly extrapolated to 1975 and added to the sum of the other estimates (*ibid.*, p. 239).

⁶ This figure includes nuclear energy which Schurr and Netschert, 1960, (*op. cit.*, p. 25) estimate at 68 to 102 million M.T. of 7,000 C/kg energy equivalent.

⁷ The data for 1950, 1955, and the 1965 and 1975 plans (central values of ranges) are from Austin Robinson *et al.*, *Towards a new Energy Pattern in Europe* (Paris: Organization for European Economic Co-operation, 1960), pp. 16–18, 59. For 1960, the data have been recalculated in OEEC (as opposed to UN). Coefficients from United Nations, *World Energy Supplies 1957–1960, Statistical Papers*, Series J. No. 5 (New York: United Nations, 1962). The OEEC includes the following countries and areas: Austria, Belgium, Denmark, France, Germany (Federal Republic), Greece, Iceland, Ireland, Italy, Luxembourg, Netherlands, Norway, Portugal, Saar, Sweden, Switzerland, Turkey, and United Kingdom.

⁸ Peat and shale are included with fuelwood.

⁹ Includes an estimate of 15 million M.T. of 7,000 C/kg fuel equivalent for atomic energy in 1965; 60 million M.T., in 1975. See Robinson *et al.*, 1960 *op. cit.*, p. 59.

Table 6. Transportation of Mineral Fuels in the U.S.S.R. by Rail,
River and Pipeline, Selected Years, 1928–1961[1]

Item	1928	1940	1950	1955	1961
Freight originated by mineral fuels, in million M.T.	45	202	341	542	838
Coal and coke	30	155	270	398	506
Oil and petroleum products	15	47	70	144	333
As a per cent of:					
Output of coal and crude oil[2]	102	118	153	156	154
All tonnage	26	30	36	37	36
Railroad freight originated by mineral fuels, in million M.T.	39	182	309	467	662
As a per cent of:					
All mineral fuels traffic	87	90	91	86	84
All railroad freight	25	31	37	37	33
Rail, river, and pipeline traffic in mineral fuels, in billion M.T./km.	30	160	249	402	637
As a per cent of all traffic	27	35	38	38	37
Average length of haul, in kilometers	663	793	730	741	760

1 metric ton = 2,204.6 lb.; 1 kilometer = 0.62137 miles.

[1] *Sources:* D. B. Shimkin, *The Soviet Mineral-Fuels Industries, 1928–1958: A Statistical Survey,* U.S. Bureau of the Census Series P–90, No. 19 (Washington: Government Printing Office, 1962), p. 32. Ts.S.U. pri Sovete ministrov SSSR, *Narodnoye khozyaystvo SSSR v 1961g.* (*National Economy of the U.S.S.R. in 1961*), Moscow: Gosstatizdat, 1962, pp. 204, 209, 477–78, 494, 500.

[2] Excludes lignite.

Table 7. The Structure of Energy Consumption in the Soviet Union 1955, 1960 and 1965 (PLAN), and in the United States in 1955[1]

(Except as otherwise noted, in million metric tons of 7,000 C/kg equival

	Soviet Union		
	1955		
Category	A	B	C
I. Domestic output	520	520	100.0
II. Net exports	2.5	2.5	0.5
III. Apparent consumption	518	518	99.5
1. Electricity	95	—	—
2. Other manufacturing, mining, energy production and factory repair; atomic industries included	190	262	50.4
a. Fuels, steel and cement[2]	97	—	—
b. Miscellaneous[3]	93	—	—
3. Civil transportation and storage losses[4]	(82)	(85)	(16.4)
a. Trucks and cars	(15)	(15)	(2.9)
b. Railroads	58	62	11.9
c. Losses and other[5]	(8.3)	(8.3)	(1.6)
4. Agriculture[6]	20	22	4.2
5. Households[7]	(78)	(85)	(16.3)
of which, urban	(33)	(39)	(7.5)
6. Construction, commerce, administration and defense[8]	(53)	(63)	(12.1)
IV. Consumption coefficients			
1. Industrial (Kg. per employee-year)[9]	860	1,190	—
2. Domestic commercial transportation (Kg. per 10,000 net M.T.-km. of freight)[10]	(720)	(740)	—
3. Agricultural			
a. Kg. per worker-year (including family workers)[11]	(460)	(500)	—
b. Kg per hectare cultivated per year	110	120	—
4. Household (Kg. per capita per year)[12]			
a. Including private transport	—	—	—
b. Excluding private transport	(400)	(430)	—

1 metric ton = 2,204.6 lb; 1 kilogram = 2.2046 lb.; 1 hectare = 2.471 acres.
— inapplicable or unavailable.   ( ) more approximate.
A with electricity unallocated; B with electricity allocated by end use; C per distribution of B.

Soviet Union						United States		
1960			1965 Plan			1955		
A	B	C	A	B	C	A	B	C
736	736	100.0	1,098	1,098	100.0	1,439	1,439	100.0
50	50	6.8	(146)	(146)	13.3	−4	−4	−0.3
686	686	93.2	952	952	86.7	1,443	1,443	100.3
136	—	—	230	—	—	274	—	—
259	360	48.9	378	550	50.1	530	691	48.0
132	—	—	(196)	—	—	272	—	—
127)	—	—	(182)	—	—	258	—	—
116)	(123)	(16.8)	105	120	10.9	289	292	20.3
(33)	(33)	(4.5)	45	45	4.1	213	213	14.8
(64)	70	9.6	31	42	3.8	29	32	2.2
(19)	(20)	(2.8)	29	33	3.0	47	47	3.3
(24)	(26)	(3.5)	(32)	(40)	(3.6)	(22)	(27)	(1.9)
(84)	(95)	(12.9)	(130)	(148)	(13.5)	206	268	18.6
(46)	(54)	(7.3)	(65)	(77)	(7.0)	—	—	—
(67)	(82)	(11.1)	(77)	(94)	(8.6)	122	165	11.5
,030	1,430	—	(1,350)	(1,960)	—	2,860	3,740	—
610)	(650)	—	(410)	(470)	—	650	660	—
540)	(600)	—	(700)	(870)	—	(2,600)	(3,200)	—
120)	(130)	—	—	—	—	(160)	(195)	—
—	—	—	—	—	—	2,100	2,400	—
390)	(440)	—	(560)	(640)	—	1,200	1,600	—

Notes to Table 7
[1] Basic data derived as follows:

a. For the Soviet Union, 1955 and 1965 Plan, and the United States, 1955, see D. B. Shimkin, *The Soviet Mineral-Fuels Industries, 1928–1958: A Statistical Survey,* U.S. Bureau of the Census Series P–90, No. 19 (Washington: U.S. Government Printing Office, 1962), pp. 61, 69, 95–96, 102–9, 144–51. Household consumption on p. 95 should be 33 rather than "3.3" million M.T. New data have permitted a slight revision of the Soviet 1965 Plan estimates for agriculture and for construction and allied. See note 6 below.

b. For the Soviet Union 1960 (see also Tables 5 and 8), the major sources are Anonymous, "Basic Indicators of the Fuel and (Electrical) Energy Balance for 1960," *Vestnik statistiki,* 1962, No. 5, pp. 86–92, and the associated analysis by A. Riznik and S. Litvak, "The Fuel and Energy Balance of the U.S.S.R. for 1960" (*ibid.,* No. 6, pp. 15–27).

(1) The input into electricity collates the reported fuel equivalent of hydro-electricity (*ibid.,* p. 17), the output of thermally produced electricity (p. 18), and the national average input per kw-hr (p. 26). The result for thermal electricity, 113.7 million M.T. of standard fuel, further cross-checks with a reported proportion of 18.7% devoted to this end, out of domestic fuel consumption less refining losses (which comes to 608.2 million M.T. of standard fuel of 7,000 C/kg equivalent). See pp. 21, 23.

(2) The gross output of Soviet electrical power in 1960, 292.5 billion kw-hr, can be allocated into 19.2 billion kw-hr of plant consumption, 17.6 billion kw-hr of transmission losses, and 255.6 billion kw-hr of supply to consumers. The last category is divisible into 190 billion kw-hr for industry (mining, manufacturing and repair), 10 billion kw-hr for construction, 15.8 billion kw-hr for transportation (including municipal mass transport), and 39.8 billion kw-hr miscellaneous. See Anon., 1962, *op. cit.,* p. 89; Ts.S.U. pri Sov. Min., *S.S.S.R. v tsifrakh v 1961g.* (*The U.S.S.R. in Figures in 1961*), Moscow: Gosstatizdat, 1962, p. 96; and United Nations, *Annual Bulletin of Electric Energy Statistics for Europe 1960* (Geneva: United Nations, 1961), p. 64. Comparison with 1958 national data and 1958–60 trends for the R.S.F.S.R. determined that the transportation total comprised close to 13.4 billion kw-hr of main-line and 2.4 billion kw-hr of municipal use, the latter being a category normally included in Soviet statistics within the "urban economy." See Ts.S.U. pri Sov. Min. SSSR, *Narodnoye khozyaystvo SSSR v 1959g.* (*The National Economy of the U.S.S.R. in 1959*), Moscow: Gosstatizdat, 1960, p. 150; and Ts.S.U. pri Sov. Min. R.S.F.S.R., *Narodnoye khozyaystvo R.S.F.S.R. v 1960g.* (*National Economy of the RSFSR in 1960*), Moscow: Gosstatizdat, 1961, p. 22. The aggregate of "urban economy, cultural and household uses" (Anon., 1962, *op cit.,* p. 89), including municipal transportation, comes to 35.1 billion kw-hr, while 4.7 billion kw-hr, the remainder, may be ascribed to agriculture exclusive of household uses. Each of the sectors supplied, from industry to agriculture, was attributed its proportionate share of the total input into electricity, 136.0 million M.T. of 7,000 C/kg equivalent, in column B.

(3) Riznik and Litvak's statements that 33% of the primary fuel resources were refined, with a recovery of 94% (1962, *op. cit.;* 16–18), yield an absolute aggregate input of at least 254.8 million M.T. of standard fuel for coking, petroleum and natural gas refining, and shale processing. On p. 27, they further indicate a value of 6.7 billion cu.m. for associated natural gas processed, equivalent to about 10.6 million M.T. of standard fuel. (Shimkin, 1962, *op. cit.,* p. 131, n.1.*b.*5). These data are consistent with reported 1960 outputs and 1954–55 coefficients: 1,257 kg of standard fuel input per physical M.T. of coke; 9% consumption of crude oil as such (apart from net exports); 21% processing loss of shale, as well as a slightly better recovery (about 88%) of crude oil and gas run to stills (*ibid.,* see also pp. 144–45,

note 5). Fuel-industry consumption in standard fuel equivalent includes all coking inputs (70.6 million M.T.), plus refining losses of 15.3 million M.T. It also includes extraction expenditure. These have been estimated at 1955 rates (petroleum, 1%; natural gas, 5%; peat and shale, 4%) except for coal and lignite. For coal and lignite, R.S.F.S.R. data for 1960 show a power capacity of 23.5 h.p. per M.T. (standard fuel) extracted, compared to 25.2 h.p. for the U.S.S.R. in 1955. Accepting this as a valid national indication yields a coefficient of 3.69%, 93% the earlier level (*ibid.*, p. 84; and Ts.S.U. pri Sov. Min. R.S.F.S.R., *Promyshlennost' RSFSR* [*Industry of the RSFSR*] Moscow: Gosstatizdat, 1961, p. 43). Aggregate extraction expenditures were thus estimated at 18.9 million M.T., including 13.7 million M.T. for coal and lignite; the grand total for fuels being 104.8 million M.T.

(4) Estimates for non-electrical energy consumption in open-hearth steel production, rolled iron and steel products, and cement manufacturers come from 1960 input coefficients given by Riznik and Litvak, 1962, *op. cit.*, p. 25; and from output data in *SSSR v tsifrakh v 1961, op. cit.*, p. 122 and P. V. Belan and I. M. Denisenko, *Perspektivy razvitiya chernoy metallurgiyi SSSR* (*Prospects for Development of the Ferrous Metallurgy of the U.S.S.R.*), Moscow: Ekonomizdat, 1962, p. 102. The resulting estimates, in millions of M.T. of standard fuel, are: open-hearth steel, 10.4; rolled products, 7.8; and cement 9.1; total — 27.3.

(5) The estimate for non-electrical energy consumption by industrial branches other than fuels, steel and cement stems, in the first instance, from the stable proportion that these major components take of all industrial non-electrical energy, namely, about 51%. (See Shimkin, 1962, *op. cit.*, pp. 106–7, n.5.c.3.) This gives an estimate of 259 million M.T. of standard fuel for total, and 127 million M.T., for miscellaneous, industrial non-electrical consumption. For the miscellaneous category, the figure represents an increase of 37% over the period 1955–60. The plausibility of this estimate can be assessed from data on trends in the group of machinery, transportation equipment, and metal-fabricating branches, including ordnance, which consumed, in 1955, at least 30 million M.T. of energy other than electricity (*ibid.*, pp. 60–62, 95). The basic measure of production and, correspondingly, of demand for energy in this group is the input of rolled iron and steel products, which can be closely approximated from national rolled products output less that of construction specialties (beams and channels, pipes and tubes, railroad rails, splice bars, wire rods, concrete bars, and roofing iron), and less net exports. The estimate for 1955, thus derived, is an input of 22.4 million M.T., while that for 1960 is 32.4 million M.T. or 44% higher. (See *ibid.*, p. 71, n. 21.) For 1960, the estimate of construction specialties, 16.8 million M.T., compared to 11.4 million M.T. in 1955, is a projection of 1959 data based on 1959–60 trends in the R.S.F.S.R. Total rolled products and net exports are reported. (The sources are *S.S.S.R. v. tsifrakh v 1961, op. cit.*, p. 122; *Nar. khoz. SSSR v 1959, op. cit.*, pp. 163, 166, 233; *Prom. R.S.F.S.R., op. cit.* pp. 59, 62, 194 and Min. vneshney torgovli SSSR, *Vneshnaya torgovlya SSSR za 1961g.* [*Foreign Trade of the U.S.S.R. in 1961*] Moscow: Vneshtorgizdat, 1962, Items 264–266lz.) A rise of 44% in steel inputs is compatible with a 37% rise in non-electrical energy inputs granting a reasonable 5% economizing in the years 1955–60. Therefore, the estimate of 127 million M.T. for miscellaneous industrial consumption has been accepted.

(6) The aggregate estimate for industrial energy consumption, including electricity, 360 million M.T. of standard fuel is not equivalent to the Riznik and Litvak datum of 404.4 million M.T. (1962, *op. cit.*, p. 23) which apparently reflects an institutional concept incorporating extensive repair, administrative, housing and probably other functions.

(7) The estimate for transportation and storage (123.5 million M.T.) includes four components: reported expenditures of, respectively, 70.5 million M.T. of standard fuel for the railroads, 27.3 million M.T. for other transportation, and perhaps

16 million M.T. for storage and transport losses (Riznik and Litvak, 1962, *op. cit.,* pp. 23, 27) plus an estimate of 9.6 million M.T. for agricultural transportation. The railroad figure undoubtedly includes electrical power expenditures, which may be estimated, from firm 1958 data and 1958–60 operations trends, at 11.9 billion kw-hr, or 6.3 million M.T. (*S.S.S.R. v tsifrakh v 1961, op. cit.,* pp. 271, 275, indicating a 66% increase in electric-locomotive operations; an intuitive 5% gain in efficiency, 1958–60; and base data from Shimkin, 1962, p. 107, n. 6.1.) Non-electrical railroad consumption thus approximated 64.2 million M.T., almost the 1958 level. Aggregating "other" and agricultural transportation, and subtracting 0.8 million M.T. electrical input [into storage] leaves an estimate of 36.1 million M.T. for the sum of motor-vehicle, shipping, aviation and pipeline expenditures. This comes to only 78% of the level required by the 1960 operations of these carriers at 1955 expenditure rates (*ibid.,* p. 148, n. 15.*b.* and *SSSR v tsifrakh v 1961, op. cit.,* pp. 271, 273). Such a rate of improvement in efficiency is doubtful and makes probable the assumption that part of the unbelievably large losses officially recorded (21 million M.T. compared to 5.4 million M.T. in 1955) are actually operating expenditures. At least 5 million M.T. of these losses must be regarded as thefts and diversions to rural consumption (see note 1.*b.* 9.6. below).

(8) The agricultural figure of 26 million M.T. includes a previous datum for electricity (see note 1.*b.*1 above) and component estimates totalling 23.5 million M.T. for tractor operations, combines, other field equipment, and miscellaneous consumption based on 1955 data, 1955–60 operating trends, less a 10% allowance for economizing. Tractor operations are believed to have comprised about 917 million hectares of soft plowing equivalent, judging from the 1960 inventory (1,985,000 in 15 h.p. units) and the average 1956–59 performance of 468 hectares per year. This was 24% more than in 1955, and is estimated to have taken 13.9 million M.T. of standard fuel. See Shimkin, 1962, *op. cit.,* pp. 134, 136, 8.*b* and 9.*c, SSSR v tsifrakh v 1961 op. cit.,* p. 198; and Ts.S.U. pri Sov. Min. SSSR, *Sel'skoye khozyaystvo SSSR* (Agriculture of the U.S.S.R.), Moscow: Gosstatizdat, 1960, pp. 409, 420. For combines, the operational estimate is 103 million hectares (or 85% of the grain acreage sown, as in 1956–59), 93% of the 1955 level. Requirements came to about 0.8 million M.T. of standard fuel. (Shimkin, 1962, *op. cit.,* p. 133, n. 6.*c. SSSR v tsifrakh v 1961,* p. 173 and *Sel'khoz. SSSR, op. cit.,* p. 123.) Other motor equipment excluding trucks and electrical generators, took, on the basis of relative power, about 10% as much as tractors and combines together, or some 1.5 million M.T. of standard fuel (*ibid.,* pp. 402, 428). Finally, other energy use has been most closely connected with fodder preparation, grain drying and allied functions. Since fodder preparation increased by about 40% between 1955 and 1960 (*SSSR v. tsifrakh v 1961, op. cit.,* p. 173), a corresponding rise (less 10% efficiency gains), to a level of 7.2 million M.T. of standard fuel has been estimated for these requirements. (See also Shimkin, 1962, *op. cit.,* p. 149, n. 16.*b.*) The total estimate for agriculture, 26 million M.T., is 11.6 million M.T. of standard fuel lower than that reported by Riznik and Litvak, 1962, *op. cit.,* p. 23, on an institutional basis. The difference is believed to contain two components: 2.0 million M.T. equivalent of electrical energy consumed by Soviet rural households (*Sel'khoz. SSSR., op. cit.,* pp. 428, 432, 436), and agricultural trucking, 9.6 million M.T.

(9) The Soviet aggregate of "(urban) economic, cultural and household needs" (Anon., 1962, *op. cit.,* p. 89) comprises urban services (utilities, municipal transportation, public baths, laundries, etc.); retail trade, food services, health, education and administration; urban households and the centrally (publicly) procured portion of rural household consumption. Evaluating this aggregate involves several analytic problems.

(9.1) First, it comprises 11.1% of all domestic fuel consumption "net of refining losses," plus 12.0% of all electricity, and 14.2% of the heat energy (steam, hot air) produced by power plants and allied installations in the U.S.S.R. The absolute value of domestic consumption "net of refining losses," given by Riznik and Litvak, 1962 (*op. cit.*, p. 20) as 608.2 million M.T. of standard fuel thus indicates refining losses of 43.5 million M.T. (*ibid.*, p. 23) rather than the 15.3 million M.T. calculable from the same source on p. 18. This apparent discrepancy may be accounted for by the inclusion of coking gas and non-combustible petroleum products such as lubricants, greases, and asphalt within the larger loss figure.

(9.2) Second, heat energy (16.5% of 608.2 million M.T.) produced at higher temperatures and pressures than in normal space-heating, has a thermal efficiency of about 85% compared to 50% for low-pressure, low-temperature furnaces. See L. A. Melentyev and Ye. O. Shteyngauz, *Ekonomika energetiki SSSR* (*Energy Economics of the U.S.S.R.*), Moscow: Gosenergoizdat, 1959, p. 193. Moreover, the heat energy produced in 1960, 14.2 million M.T. of standard fuel equivalent, constituted an increment of 10.6 million M.T. over 1955 (Shimkin, 1962, *op. cit.*, p. 148, n. 19) and thus represented an economizing, in the urban economy and in urban household space-heating, of about 7.4 million M.T. for 1955–60. This economizing has been distributed between the urban economy and urban household sectors in proportion to their space-heating consumptions in 1955, i.e., 28% for the former and 72% for the latter (*ibid.*, p. 150, n. 20.*a.*).

(9.3) Bases for calculating urban, non-electrical, energy consumption are U.S.S.R. urban housing-space data for 1955–60. Estimating living space at 71% of floor space, Soviet publicly owned housing (virtually all multi-story) approximated 414 million sq. m.; private housing (virtually all single-story), 266 million sq. m. The corresponding figures for 1955 were 306 million sq. m. and 148 million sq. m. For the former category the basic space-heating input by Soviet coefficients runs 3 M.T. of standard fuel per 100 sq. m. of living space; for the latter, 6 M.T. Thus, the unadjusted space-heating estimate for 1960 is 28.4 million M.T., compared to 18 million M.T. in 1955. With adjustment for expanded high-pressure, high-temperature, heat use, the estimate drops to 23.1 million M.T. For cooking and water heating, a 1960 input of 177.3 kg per capita has been interpolated between 1955 data and the 1965 Plan. This, with the officially estimated urban population of 106.0 million in mid-year 1960, yields a consumption of 18.8 million M.T. for cooking and hot water. Miscellaneous needs, excluding electricity, are believed to have run about 8.7% of space-heating, cooking and water heating needs as a sum, or 3.4 million M.T. The aggregate for non-electrical inputs into urban housing is 45.5 million M.T. of standard fuel. See Shimkin, 1962, *op. cit.*, pp. 63–5, 108 (n. 8) and 150 (n. 20). *SSSR v tsifrakh v 1961, op. cit.*, pp. 378–79, 382.

(9.4) The urban economy other than households consumed about 17 million M.T. of standard fuel, apart from electricity, in 1955. See Shimkin, 1962, *op. cit.* p. 149, n. 19, and Melentyev and Shteyngauz, 1959, *op. cit.*, p. 193. Close estimates of the rise in demand in this sector are not feasible. However, significant indications are the 123% increase of urban housing space provided with water, and the 135% increase in that provided with sewage piping in the R.S.F.S.R. in 1950–60 (*Nar. khoz. R.S.F.S.R. v 1960, op. cit.*, p. 545). Applied to the period 1955–60, this indicates about a 50% rise in demand, to a base level 25.5 million M.T. of standard fuel. A deduction for space-heating economies in public buildings (note 1.*b*.9.2. above) yields a 1960 estimate of 23.4 million M.T. of standard fuel.

(9.5) Electrical consumption by the urban economy and urban households totalled 19.4 billion kw-hr in 1955, split about equally between the two; in 1960, the aggregate was about 31.3 billion kw-hr. See notes 1.*b*.2 and 1.*b*.8, above; Shimkin, 1962, *op. cit.*, p. 96 (Table XXII). In urban housing, floor space, the fundamental component of demand under Soviet conditions, rose 50% between 1955 and 1960. For the remainder of the urban economy, the rise of electrical consumption by municipal transport, from 1.7 billion kw-hr in 1955 to about 2.4 billion kw-hr in

1960, or by about 41%, is the best available measure of trends in demand. A slight preponderance of urban housing is indicated in electrical consumption; hence, the estimated distribution is 8.5 million M.T. of standard fuel equivalent for housing and 8.2 million M.T. for other urban uses. Thus, the aggregate estimate for urban housing energy use in 1960 is 54.0 million M.T.; that for the remainder of the urban economy, 31.6 million M.T.

(9.6) Subtracting the urban economy and urban households from the total of "(urban) economic, cultural and household needs" leaves a remainder of 12.9 million M.T. of non-electrical energy for rural households. To this, Riznik and Litvak's figure of 21 million M.T. of decentralized (private) fuel procurement must be added (1962, *op. cit.*, p. 18). The total is only 33.9 million M.T., compared to 45 million M.T. for 1955 (Shimkin, 1962, *op. cit.*, p. 149, n. 18). This figure is almost certainly a major underestimate. As noted above (note 1.*b*.7), an arbitrary 5 million M.T. has been deducted from officially recorded "losses" and is ascribable to thefts by, and clandestine sales to, rural households. Thus a very approximate maximum estimate of 39 million M.T. of rural household non-electrical, plus the 2.0 million M.T. electrical calculated above (note 1.*b*.8), gives a sum of 41.0 million M.T. of standard fuel for aggregate energy used in this sector.

(10) The estimate for construction, commerce, administration and defense is the residual of total apparent consumption within the U.S.S.R. less other sectors, the urban economy other than housing excepted. That last category is partially comprised within industrial consumption as defined here (line III.2). Allocations within the residual are therefore not possible at present. Certainly, the 14.1 million M.T. of standard fuel attributed by Riznik and Litvak, 1962 (*op. cit.*, p. 23), to construction must be regarded to be covering only the direct uses of specialized building trusts; total construction demand is unquestionably much larger.

[2] Covers the entire input into coking, plus all fuel extraction inputs and refining losses in the petroleum, natural gas, and shale industries. Also covers energy consumption by open-hearth steel furnaces and iron and steel rolling mills, as well as cement plants. In modern industries this group embraces close to half of all non-electrical consumption by manufacturing, mining, gas works, repair plants, ordnance and atomic energy.

[3] All other branches, including atomic energy.

[4] Excludes municipal transport other than motor buses. See line III. 6.

[5] Includes marine and river shipping, aviation, oil and natural gas pipelines, and tank farm and bunker losses. Commercial, civilian non-commercial and private carriers are covered in so far as data permit.

[6] Operational consumption, excluding transportation. The 1965 estimates are a revision based on new information. The 1965 plan anticipates the following capacity in agriculture: tractors, 81 million h.p., combine engines, 39.4 million h.p., electrical generators and miscellaneous prime movers, 18.8 million h.p. Furthermore, agriculture is to consume 15.0 billion kw-hr for productive purposes, in addition to 12.5 billion kw-hr for rural household uses. See A. N. Yefimov, *Ekonomika SSSR v poslevoyennyy period* (*The Economy of the U.S.S.R. in the Postwar Period*), Moscow: Sotsekgiz, 1962, pp. 273, 280. Estimating that one-third of the miscellaneous power capacity can be attributed to electrical generators (see also *Sel'khoz. SSSR, 1960, op. cit.*, pp. 20, 428), gives an estimate of 132 million h.p. for 1965, compared to 53.8 million h.p. for 1955 and about 74 million h.p. for 1960 (Shimkin, 1962, *op. cit.*, p. 149, n. 17; *SSSR v tsifrakh v 1961, op. cit.*, p. 198; *Nar. khoz. SSSR v 1959, op. cit.*, pp. 415–416). At the same time, the non-electrical consumption of power by agriculture has been estimated (note 1.*b*.8, above) to have risen 18%, compared to 38% for power capacity, during 1955–60. Using the same ratio for 1960–65 yields the estimate used, 32 million M.T. of standard fuel. The estimate

for electrical inputs is at the standard conversion ratio for 1965, 504 gm of standard fuel per kw-hr delivered to final consumers, yielding 7.6 million M.T.

[7] The data exclude private transportation.

[8] A residual category.

[9] Man-year equivalents for total employment (workers, technical staff, and administrative employees). Data from Shimkin, 1962 (*op. cit.*, pp. 61, 69), except for
U.S.S.R., 1960. The 1960 employment estimate of 25.2 million persons derives
from a reported figure of 18,574,000 workers in State industry, including former
members of industrial cooperatives, but excluding employment in the industrial division of non-industrial establishments (e.g. repair shops). For that category an allowance of 12.2%, applicable to 1958, has been made, to yield a total for State
workers of 20.84 million. To estimate the industrial labor on collective farms, the
change in proportion of "cooperative" to "State" gross industrial output in the
R.S.F.S.R. between 1955 and 1960 was used — from 7.5% to 2%. In 1955, 11.8%
of the U.S.S.R. industrial workmen were in the cooperative sector; assuming that
the proportion was a quarter as great in 1960 yields an estimate of 640,000 persons.
Finally, the reported number of technical staff and administrative employees was
3,713,000, to give the total used. See *SSSR v tsifrakh v 1961, op. cit.*, p. 310; *Prom.
R.S.F.S.R.*, p. 10; and M. S. Weitzman and A. Elias, *The Magnitude and Distribution of Civilian Employment in the U.S.S.R.: 1928–1959*, U.S. Bureau of the
Census, Report Series p–95, No. 58 (Washington, 1961), esp. pp. 66, 69.

[10] The data attempt to exclude, both from operations and inputs, all non-commercial traffic and shipping to overseas ports. Otherwise, the consumption data are
global, while the operations are for freight only. This, in essence, attributes ware-
housing and passenger traffic to overhead. All data other than U.S.S.R., 1960, are
from Shimkin, 1962, *op. cit.*, pp. 61, 69. The 1960 statistics for freight operations
are from *SSSR v tsifrakh v 1961, op. cit.*, p. 271, with half of marine shipping deducted to yield a figure of 1,820 billion M.T.-km.; the consumption estimate deducts
both half of marine shipping and 13% of estimated truck and car consumption.

[11] The agricultural employment estimates here are approximately those for the
peak six months of the year; both the U.S.S.R. and the U.S. data include labor inputs into non-agricultural activities, as supporting and offseason operations. U.S.S.R.
1955 and U.S. 1955 estimates come from Shimkin, 1962, *op. cit.*, pp. 63–5. They
are based on Weitzman and Elias, 1961, *op. cit.*, p. 57. The 1960 estimate is derived
from the Weitzman and Elias estimates for 1958, extended by the 1958–60 ratios
for employment in State agriculture (an increase of 29%) and for households on
collective farms (a decrease of 9%). See *SSSR v tsifrakh v 1961, op. cit.*, pp. 201,
311. The absolute estimate is 43.6 million, a return to the 1955 level. The acreage
data are from *ibid.*, p. 173, and Appendix Table 2. Yefimov's data (1962, *op. cit.*,
p. 280) indicate an anticipated 2% rise, from 1958 to 1965, in employment in the
socialized sector of agriculture. Assuming this estimate applies to all agricultural
employment and utilizing the Weitzman and Elias base datum gives a 1965 estimate
of 45.5 million persons.

[12] Population estimates are as follows: U.S.S.R., 1955, 197.0 million persons;
1960, 214.2 million; 1965, 232.5 million; and U.S., 1955, 165.0 million. Sources:
Shimkin, 1962, *op. cit.*, pp. 104 (n. 8) and 108 (n. 8); and *SSSR v. tsifrakh v 1961,
op. cit.*, p. 29.

Table 8. Net Exports of Mineral Fuels by the Soviet Union,
by Commodity, 1929–38 Average and 1955–1961

Item	Measure
Net exports of mineral fuels	Thousands of M.T. of standard fuel (7,000 C/kg equiv.)[1]
Index	1929–38 average = 100
As per cent of output	Total mineral fuel output = 100[2]
Coal, coke and briquettes:	
Physical weight	Thous. of M.T.[3]
As per cent of output	Anthracite and bituminous output = 100[4]
Crude oil and petroleum products:	
Total, physical weight	Thous. of M.T.[5]
As per cent of output	Crude output = 100[6]
of which,	
crude oil	Thous. of M.T.
gasoline	Thous. of M.T.
kerosene	Thous. of M.T.
gas oil and diesel fuel	Thous. of M.T.
lubricants	Thous. of M.T.
fuel oils and other	Thous. of M.T.
Natural gas:	
Physical volume	Mill. cu.m.[7]
As per cent of output	Natural gas output = 100[8]

1 metric ton = 2,204.6 lb.; 1 cubic meter = 1.308 cubic yards.
( ) approximations converted from volumetric data.
Minus sign denotes a net import.

NOTES TO TABLE 8

[1] Sum of components, weighted as follows: coal, coke and briquettes, 0.92 times physical weight; crude oil and products, 1.43 times physical weight; and natural gas, 1.27 metric tons of standard fuel per 1,000 cubic meters. See also D. B. Shimkin, *The Soviet Mineral-Fuels Industries, 1928–1958: A Statistical Survey*, U.S. Bureau of the Census, Series P–90, No. 19. (Washington: U.S. Government Printing Office, 1962), p. 152, note 4.

[2] Prior to World War II, for 1930, 1933 and 1937 only. Data from Shimkin, 1962, *op. cit.*, Table I, p. 80, for prewar and 1955–57. For 1958–61, the revised, lower series of values has been used. Data are from Ts.S.U. pri Sov. Min. SSSR, *Narodnoye khozyaystvo SSSR v 1959g.* (*National Economy of the U.S.S.R. in 1959*), Moscow: Gosstatizdat, 1960, p. 176; A. Riznik and S. Litvak, "The Fuel and Energy Balance of the U.S.S.R. for 1960," *Vestnik statistiki*, 1962, No. 6, pp. 15–27, esp. p. 17; A. Kortunov, "The Gas Industry on the Eve of the XXII Congress of the Communist Party of the Soviet Union," *Gazovaya Promyshlennost'*,

Arithmetic average, 1929–1938	1955	1956	1957	1958	1959	1960	1961
6,960	2,419	7,572	20,275	27,291	38,080	50,284	65,837
100	35	109	291	392	547	722	946
(7.5)	0.5	1.6	3.7	4.7	6.1	7.6	9.4
1,644	–3,184	646	7,174	7,864	8,521	9,527	12,752
2.5	–1.2	0.2	2.2	2.2	2.3	2.5	3.3
3,814	3,616	4,759	9,412	13,842	20,950	28,820	37,595
18.0	5.1	5.7	9.6	12.2	16.2	19.5	22.6
(270)	2,341	2,387	4,592	8,014	11,402	16,659	22,501
(1,064)	–583	–580	–318	–206	392	644	1,809
(518)	92	252	614	496	562	788	803
(461)	696	1,317	2,400	3,035	4,285	4,823	5,432
(222)	43	66	115	230	235	272	293
(1,279)	1,027	1,316	2,010	2,272	4,073	5,633	6,757
0	139	136	170	206	222	242	272
0	1.5	1.1	0.9	0.7	0.6	0.5	0.5

1961, No. 10, pp. 1–3; and G. V. Krasnikovskiy, "Prospective Development of the Coal Industry of the U.S.S.R.," *Ugol'*, 1962, No. 3, pp. 1–6, esp. p. 1. The fuels include anthracite and bituminous coal, lignite, shale, peat, petroleum and natural gas.

[3] Data for 1928–38 and 1955–59 from Shimkin, 1962, *op. cit.*, p. 97. For 1960 and 1961, the source is ministerstvo vneshney torgovli, *Vneshnaya torgovlya Soyuza SSR za 1961g.* (*Foreign Trade of the Soviet Union in 1961*), Moscow: Vneshtorgizdat, 1962, Items 20,000–22,903.

[4] On bituminous and anthracite output 1929–59, see *Nar. khoz. v 1959, op. cit.*, p. 180; 1960 data are from Ya. M. Prudkin: "World Coal Output," *Ugol'*, 1961, No. 7, pp. 58–59; 1961 data, from A. A. Boyko, "Results of the Work of the Coal Industry in 1961 and Tasks for 1962," *Ugol'*, 1962, No. 1, pp. 1–6, esp. p. 4; and Ts.S.U. pri. Sov. Min. SSSR, *SSSR v. tsifrakh v 1961g.* (*The U.S.S.R. in Figures in 1961*), Moscow: Gosstatizdat, 1962, p. 122.

[5] See note 3.

[6] Data from Shimkin, 1962, *op. cit.*, p. 89; for 1959–61, *SSSR v tsifrakh v 1961, op. cit.*, pp. 122, 132, 136, 141, 148, 149.

[7] See note 3.

[8] See note 6.

Table 9. Per Cent Distribution of Soviet Trade in Mineral Fuels, by Destination: 1934, 1955 and 1961

Region and country	1934[1]			1955[1]			1961[a]		
	A	B	C	A	B	D	A	B	D
Total (million M.T. of 7,000 C/kg fuel equivalent)[3]	8.0	2.1	5.9	2.4	−2.9	5.2	65.8	11.7	53.8
Per cent distribution									
Total	100.0	100.0	100.0	100.0	100.0	100.0	100.0	100.0	100.0
European satellite countries[4]	x	x	x	−266.9	−149.8	−43.3	26.7	49.9	21.2
Far Eastern satellite countries[5]	x	x	x	91.2	−16.3	(51.9)	7.5	−1.2	9.4
Cuba	...	...	...	...	...	...	8.9	1.0	10.7
I. Mediterranean	47.6	55.4	44.9	122.5	33.0	38.6	25.7	22.4	26.6
Albania	...	...	...	−8.6	...	−4.0	−0.5	...	−0.7
Egypt	2.7	5.7	1.6	19.6	0.1	9.1	4.2	1.7	3.9
France	14.4	7.5	16.9	36.6	17.2	7.4	2.7	7.3	1.7
Greece	4.2	15.8	...	6.9	1.1	2.6	2.2	0.3	2.6
Italy	17.6	26.4	14.4	18.9	6.6	5.1	14.4	5.6	16.4
Spain	8.4	...	11.4	...	...	...	...	...	...
Yugoslavia	...	...	...	22.0	7.9	5.8	1.6	7.3	0.4
Other	0.4	...	0.6	27.0	...	12.6	1.0	0.2	1.2
II. Eastern and Central Europe	8.4	2.2	10.6	−288.1	−146.3	−55.3	33.8	57.7	28.3
Austria	...	...	...	−26.7	0.4	−12.7	0.5	6.4	−0.7
Bulgaria	...	...	...	7.8	0.6	3.3	3.3	4.8	2.9
Czechoslovakia	0.1	0.5	...	32.7	0.5	15.0	9.5	14.7	8.4
Germany, Federal Republic	7.8	...	10.6	3.5	2.7	0.1	6.0	1.4	7.1
Germany, Soviet Zone				136.2	91.6	11.8	14.8	53.6	6.4
Hungary	...	...	...	22.0	11.3	3.9	4.6	7.3	4.0
Poland	0.2	0.6	...	−277.7	−267.4	18.3	−0.4	−33.5	6.3
Rumania	...	...	...	−186.4	13.7	−94.9	−4.6	3.0	−6.2

[illegible]	[illegible]	2.9	21.0	[illegible]	22.2	48.0	[illegible]	12.7	13.0
Baltic States	1.0	0.9	1.0	x	x	x	x	x	x
Belgium	2.5	...	3.4	6.1	3.6	0.8	0.6	0.6	0.6
Denmark	2.8	...	3.8	0.3	0.1	0.1	1.3	4.4	0.6
Finland	0.4	...	0.5	48.6	10.2	16.9	5.4	5.7	5.4
Iceland	6	6	6	17.1	0.3	7.8	0.7	...	0.9
Netherlands	1.0	0.8	1.0	5.3	3.9	0.3	0.1	0.3	...
Norway	0.4	...	0.5	2.1	...	1.0	0.5	...	0.6
Sweden	3.7	1.2	4.6	47.8	4.0	20.1	5.4	1.7	6.3
United Kingdom	4.6	...	6.2	2.1	...	1.0	0.3	...	0.4
IV. Far East	7.9	8.7	7.6	(93.7)	–14.2	(51.9)	15.4	5.9	17.5
Jápan	6.8	8.7	6.2	2.5	2.1	...	7.9	7.1	8.1
Mainland China	0.9	...	1.2	(77.7)	–16.3	(45.6)	6.1	–1.5	7.8
North Korea	7	7	7	(9.8)	...	(4.6)	0.7	...	0.9
North Vietnam	x	x	x	...	...	...	0.2	...	0.2
Outer Mongolia	0.2	...	0.2	3.6	...	1.7	0.6	0.2	0.5
V. Western Hemisphere	4.5	17.1	...	...	...	...	9.9	1.0	11.9
Brazil	...	...	...	...	...	...	1.0	...	1.2
Cuba	...	...	...	...	...	...	8.9	1.0	10.7
United States	4.5	17.1	...	...	...	...	...	...	...
Uruguay	...	...	....	...	...	...	0.1	...	0.1
VI. Other (including bunkering of foreign ships and at foreign ports)	15.3	13.6	15.9	42.3	5.3	(16.8)	0.6	0.2	0.7

A = net exports of all fuels (coal, coke, petroleum and products, and natural gas) in 7,000 C/kg. fuel equivalent; B = net exports of coal (bituminous, anthracite, and briquettes) and coke in physical weight; C = net exports of petroleum and its products by volume; D = same by weight.

1 metric ton = 2,204.6 lb.; 1 cubic meter = 1.308 cubic yards.

Minus sign denotes net imports.

X inapplicable.

... less than 0.05%.

( ) estimated.

Totals may not add because of independent rounding.

NOTES TO TABLE 9

[1] Source: D. B. Shimkin, *The Soviet Mineral-Fuels Industries, 1928–1958: A Statistical Survey*, U.S. Bureau of the Census, Series P–90, No. 19 (Washington: U.S. Government Printing Office, 1962), p. 98.

[2] Source: Ministerstvo vneshney torgovli S.S.S.R., *Vneshnaya torgovlya S.S.S.R. za 1961g. (The Foreign Trade of the U.S.S.R. for 1961)*, Moscow: Vneshtorgizdat, 1962, items 20–22.

[3] Conversion equivalents from physical weight to standard fuel equivalent: coal and coke, 0.92 per M.T.; all petroleum and products, 1.43 per M.T. (0.185 per barrel); natural gas, 1.27 per 1,000 cu.m.

[4] Includes Albania, Bulgaria, Czechoslovakia, Hungary, Poland, Rumania, and Soviet Zone of Germany.

[5] Includes Mainland China, Mongolian Peoples' Republic, North Korea, and North Vietnam.

[6] Included with Denmark.

[7] Included with Japan.

Table 10. Absolute Increments or Decrements of Soviet Net Exports of Mineral Fuels, by Destination, 1934–1955, 1955–1961, and 1934–1961[1]

(In millions of metric tons of 7,000 C/kg fuel equivalent)

Regions and selected countries	Increment or (minus sign) decrement		
	1934–1955	1955–1961	1934–1961
Total exports	–5.6	63.4	57.8
European satellite countries	x	24.0	x
Far Eastern satellite countries	x	2.7	x
Cuba	...	5.9	5.9
I. Mediterranean countries	–0.8	13.9	13.1
of which, Egypt	0.4	2.3	2.8
France	–0.3	0.9	0.6
Italy	–1.0	9.0	8.0
Yugoslavia	0.5	0.5	1.1
II. E. and C. Europe	–7.6	29.2	21.6
of which, Czechoslovakia	0.8	5.6	6.3
Germany[2]	2.8	10.3	13.1
Poland	–6.8	6.5	–0.3
Rumania	–4.5	1.5	–3.0
III. N. and W. Europe	1.8	6.4	8.2
of which, Finland	1.1	2.4	3.5
Sweden	0.9	2.4	3.3
IV. Far East	1.6	7.9	9.5
of which, Japan	–0.5	5.1	4.7
Mainland China	1.8	2.1	3.9
V. Western Hemisphere and other	–0.6	5.9	5.3
of which, Cuba	...	5.9	5.9
United States	–0.4	...	–0.4

1 metric ton = 2,204.6 lb.   ... none or negligible; X inapplicable.
[1] For sources and compositions of regions see Table 8.
[2] For 1955 and 1961, includes both the Federal Republic and the Soviet Zone.

Table 11. Supply, Consumption, and Foreign Trade in Major Mineral Fuels for the Soviet Bloc and Selected Other Countries, 1960

(In million metric tons of coal equivalent)

Region and country	Gross supply excluding stocks		Domestic output		Gross exports	
	Total	of which, liquid fuels	Total	of which, liquid fuels	Total	of which, liquid fuels
I. Soviet Bloc	[2]1,455.2	[2]256.4	1,396.1	224.5	[2]103.8	[2]57.8
1. Soviet Union	664.1	205.6	652.4	199.2	61.3	46.3
2. European satellite countries:	[3](340.6)	[3](33.3)	304.1	18.5	41.4	11.5
Albania	1.0	0.8	0.9	0.8	0.4	0.4
Bulgaria	10.7	1.6	9.1	0.3	0.1	0.1
Czechoslovakia	69.5	3.7	63.5	0.2	4.5	0.2
Hungary	24.0	3.6	19.1	1.6	0.8	0.8
Poland	113.2	3.5	108.2	0.3	21.1	0.1
Rumania	33.9	15.3	32.9	15.3	8.8	8.6
Soviet zone of Germany	85.7	3.1	70.4	...	(5.7)	(1.3
3. Far Eastern satellite countries	444.9	12.0	439.6	6.8	1.1	...
4. Cuba	5.6	5.5	...	...	...	...
II. Selected Other Countries:	[6]606.5	[6]231.9	337.9	22.3	[6]65.3	[6]34.1
1. Major energy consumers	[6]530.0	[6]188.1	310.5	13.5	[6]62.0	[6]30.8
France	123.9	47.6	63.7	2.9	12.1	10.2
Germany, Federal Republic	233.5	49.1	181.2	7.2	34.5	5.3
Italy	66.6	46.6	12.4	2.7	14.6	14.5
Japan	106.0	44.8	53.2	0.7	[7](0.8)	[7](0.8
2. Midrank energy consumers	54.9	27.3	21.8	4.5	2.1	2.1
Austria	15.7	5.7	8.2	3.2	1.7	1.7
Sweden	23.5	19.5	0.3	0.1	0.2	0.2
Yugoslavia	(15.7)	(2.1)	13.3	1.2	0.2	0.1
3. Minor energy consumers	21.6	16.5	5.6	4.3	(1.2)	(1.2
Egypt	9.1	8.9	4.3	4.3	(1.2)	(1.2
Finland	(7.0)	3.7	...	...	...	...
Greece	4.7	3.1	1.3	...	...	...
Iceland	0.8	0.8	...	...	...	...

1 metric ton = 2,204.6 lb.
... under 0.05 million M.T.
( ) estimated.
Minus sign denotes net export.
Totals may not add because of independent rounding.

Domestic consumption including bunkers and losses		Net imports					
		From U.S.S.R.		From other Soviet-Bloc countries		From all other countries	
Total	of which, liquid fuels	Total	of which, liquid fuels	Total	of which, liquid fuels	Total	of which, liquid fuels
,353.2)	(193.6)	19.4	15.4	−19.4	−15.4	−45.1	−25.6
604.2	153.7	−49.5	−39.9	−19.4	−15.4	−30.1	−24.5
298.7)	[8](21.5)	11.7	7.5	[8]...	[8]...	−16.9	−3.8
0.5	0.3	−0.4	−0.4	...	...	...	...
10.6	1.5	1.3	1.2	(0.2)	(0.1)	...	...
64.2	2.8	4.6	3.5	−1.3	0.1	−1.8	−0.2
23.0	2.6	2.6	1.9	2.0	−0.1	−0.5	−0.5
91.9	3.2	−1.0	3.0	−6.0	(0.2)	−9.1	−0.1
25.6	7.3	−3.7	−4.2	−1.7	−1.9	−2.4	−2.4
80.3	2.1	8.5	2.6	4.2	−0.1	−3.1	[4](−0.6)
444.4	12.6	4.8	4.9	(...)	(...)	[5](−0.6)	[5](0.2)
5.9	5.8	2.9	2.9	(0.1)	(0.1)	2.5	2.5
550.3	200.9	26.7	22.1	(14.5)	(4.4)	162.8	149.7
477.2	160.3	14.0	12.3	7.7	2.8	136.7	129.7
108.2	35.7	1.9	1.2	1.1	0.8	45.1	32.5
204.8	43.6	2.8	2.8	(5.0)	(1.8)	10.0	32.1
56.8	36.8	6.9	6.4	1.1	0.2	31.7	22.9
107.4	44.2	2.4	1.9	[7](0.5)	[7](...)	49.9	42.2
52.8	25.4	5.1	3.1	(3.6)	(0.9)	(22.4)	(16.9)
14.1	4.2	0.3	−0.5	2.4	(0.6)	3.1	0.8
23.2	19.4	3.2	3.0	(1.0)	(0.2)	(18.7)	(16.0)
15.5	1.8	1.6	0.6	0.2	0.1	(0.6)	(0.1)
20.3	15.2	7.6	6.7	(3.2)	(0.7)	(3.7)	(3.1)
7.8	7.6	1.9	1.9	(0.6)	(0.6)	1.0	(0.9)
(7.0)	3.7	3.8	3.0	2.4	(0.1)	0.4	(0.1)
4.7	3.1	[8]1.4	[8]1.3	[8]0.2	[8]...	2.0	1.8
0.8	0.8	0.5	0.5	...	...	(0.3)	(0.3)

Notes to Table 11

¹ United Nations conversion coefficients: 1 kg of coal equivalent is 7,000 C/kg heat equivalent; 1 M.T. of coal equivalent equals 1.0 kg of anthracite or bituminous coal; 1.1 M.T. of coal coke; 0.77 M.T. of crude petroleum; 0.67 M.T. of petroleum products; and 750 cu.m. of natural gas. Data compiled from United Nations, *World Energy Supplies 1957–1960, Statistical Papers*, Series J, No. 5 (New York: United Nations, 1962); *ibid., Commodity Trade Statistics* Part I *Imports* and Part II *Exports*, January-December 1960, *Statistical Papers*, Series D, Vol. X, No. 4, Parts I and II, items 321, 331, and 332 (New York: United Nations, 1961). National sources used for amplification, verification, and rectification particularly included Ministerstvo vneshney torgovli, *Vneshnaya torgovlya SSSR za 1961g.* (*The Foreign Trade of the USSR for 1961*), Moscow: Vneshtorgizdat, 1962 (items 20–22). Also, Deutsche Wirtschaft wissenschaftlicher Forschungs-institut, *Untersuchung . . . in die Energie Wirtschaft der Bundesrepublik* (*Investigation . . . of the Energy Economics of the Federal Republic*), Berlin: Duncker and Humblot, 1962.

² Slightly overstated because of duplications.

³ Includes an excess of 2.6 million M.T. equivalent of total fuels (1.8 M.T. million of petroleum products) of reported exports over imports within the aggregate of European satellite countries. This excess probably constitutes part of the military consumption and stocks allotable to the Warsaw Pact nations as a bloc.

⁴ Exports to West Berlin. See Deutsche Wirtschaft Forschungs-institut, 1962, *op. cit.*, p. 290.

⁵ Probably understates imports from non-bloc nations, particularly petroleum products from Japan. See also note 8.

⁶ Slightly overstated because of duplications.

⁷ Probably understated; no inclusion for shipments to Far Eastern satellite countries.

⁸ Soviet shipments include 92,600 M.T. (physical weight) of Rumanian petroleum products shipped on Soviet account.

RESOURCE RELATIONSHIPS AMONG COUNTRIES OF WESTERN EUROPE

P. LAMARTINE YATES

Resources are what you make of them. Men discover or learn how to use the natural environment to further their purposes. Before discovery is made, the environment has no economic significance; afterwards the same material phenomenon becomes a valuable resource. Wind was of little use until someone invented the sailing ship and later the windmill. Coal had no real significance before the invention of the steam engine. Waterfalls have long been used to turn wooden mill wheels but became much more valuable when harnessed to generate electricity. A by-product of gold mining called uranium was thrown away as useless waste until a few years ago when it suddenly became immensely sought after, though not for long. In short, whether the natural object is a useful resource depends upon man's ingenuity or, in more sophisticated language, on the current level of technology.

P. LAMARTINE YATES is regional representative for Europe (Geneva) for the Food and Agriculture Organization of the United Nations. Prior to 1961 he was an adviser to the Mexican Government on regional economic development, associate director on *Europe's Needs and Resources* for the Twentieth Century Fund, controller of agricultural operations with the Colonial Development Corporation, London, and economist with FAO during its early formative years. During World War II he served with the Ministry of Economic Welfare and the Ministry of Agriculture, London, and from 1934 to 1939 was secretary of the Astor-Rowntree Agricultural Group, which published *British Agriculture*. Mr. Yates is the author of *Food, Land and Manpower in Western Europe* (1960), *Forty Years of Foreign Trade* (1959), *So Bold an Aim: Ten Years of FAO* (1956), *Food and Farming in Post-War Europe* (1944), *Commodity Control* (1943), and *Food Production in Western Europe* (1940). Born in England in 1908, he attended Cambridge University and did postgraduate work at Berlin University.

Nowhere has this been more true than in Europe which, for the past twenty centuries, has been the center of scientific and technical progress.

It was the Greeks and Romans who made the first beginning in modern mathematics, astronomy and engineering. It was Western Europe which cradled the agricultural and industrial revolutions of the eighteenth and nineteenth centuries. It was also Western Europe which first provided the educational and training facilities to transform her plentiful resource of ignorant manpower into an elite of skilled workmen. With so much history in learning how to make use of resources, Europe is naturally acutely aware of today's problems of optimum resource utilization.

In embarking upon an analysis of resource utilization, it is necessary to establish some agreed definition of terms. The word "resources" can be used in either a wide or narrow connotation. Different definitions will be appropriate to different parts of the world. For example, in most of the underdeveloped countries, the known resources consist of the land and the almost entirely unskilled manpower. Little is yet known about the availability of minerals and there is an acute shortage of capital and "know-how" for exploiting these and other natural resources. In advanced countries, there are not only land, minerals, and largely skilled manpower, but also much more. Many people would count the steel industry as a resource, and the chemical industry. But if the whisky industry is also a resource — and why not since it earns valuable foreign exchange for certain countries — where does one stop? It is admitted that skilled labor is a resource. Then what about technical colleges, universities, laboratories, and research institutes? If one accepts all these extensions of the definition, one is led into a discussion of virtually all the equipment and institutions of the modern world. Clearly there must be some rigorous exclusion in order to focus attention on a manageable bundle of ideas.

It is also necessary to determine the geographical area to be discussed. Europe may be regarded in some geography books as the whole western peninsula of Asia extending from the Ural Mountains to Portugal and Ireland. However, since another paper in this symposium will be concerned with resource utilization in the Communist countries, the present study can at least be confined to non-Communist Europe. Since, furthermore, a major aspect of our proposed analysis concerns the probable effects of the establishment of the European Economic Community (EEC) on resource utilization, it might be argued that the analysis should be limited to the six member countries of the Common Market. However, at the time of writing it is completely uncertain how large the membership of that Organization will be in two or three years' time.[1] Greece has already negotiated an agreement for associate membership; all the seven members of the European Free Trade Association have applied for either full or associate membership; Ireland has applied for full membership and, finally, Finland, Spain, Cyprus, and Israel are discussing the possible advantages of association. Under these circumstances of long-drawn-out uncertainty, it seems prudent to include the whole of non-Communist Europe in the present discussion, making special reference as occasion requires to the six founding members of the European Economic Community.

As for the definition of resources, it is essential, if only for reasons of space, to adopt a narrow definition excluding such subjects as fisheries, since fish can be and are caught far outside European waters, and likewise excluding all industries and institutions, since to these there is no end. The discussion will therefore be limited to manpower, agricultural and forest land, and energy.

The analysis will be directed to considering the role of resources in the current economic development of Western Europe, the possible effects of the EEC on resource utilization, and the consequence of all this on the economic relationships between Western Europe and the rest of the world.

RESOURCE INVENTORY

Manpower

Western Europe has just over 300 million people or 10 per cent of the world's population. Of these, nearly 45 per cent constitute the labor force; or, if one considers exclusively the population of 15 years and over, then nearly 59 per cent are active. Compared with other regions of the world, the European labor force contains a relatively large proportion of females. Over half the females in the 15 to 19 age group are at work and about 40 per cent of those in the age group 20 to 64.[2] Alto-

---

[1] Since this was written the negotiations between the Six and the United Kingdom have broken down and other countries have withdrawn their application for membership. In spite of this an enlargement of the Community at some future date is by no means excluded.

[2] For statistical information on manpower, see J. Frederick Dewhurst, John O. Coppock, and P. Lamartine Yates, *Europe's Needs and Resources* (New York: Twentieth Century Fund, 1961), Chapter III.

gether, females account for nearly one-third of the total labor force.

During the past century, the demand for labor in industry and in the services sector has grown unceasingly, while the labor required in agriculture has declined until, in the mid-fifties, the proportions were as follows for Western Europe as a whole:

Industry	38.4%
Services	34.2%
Agriculture	27.4%

This average disguised wide differences between countries. For instance, in Greece and Portugal nearly half the working population is still engaged in agriculture but in the United Kingdom the percentage is less than 4.5. The transfer of manpower from agriculture to the other sectors is, of course, one of the salient characteristics of economic progress, and the problems connected with this transfer are, as will be seen later, among the most important yet most difficult of the problems of economic expansion in Europe in the nineteen-sixties.

Western Europe's working population is well cared for in regard to primary education. Between the ages of 6 and 14, school attendance is almost 100 per cent except in the Mediterranean countries where the legal requirement is less and where, in practice, attendance may be maintained for no more than six or even only four years. The record is much less satisfactory in respect to secondary education whether general or technical; only about 16 per cent of the 15 to 19 age group enjoy full-time education compared with over 70 per cent in the United States. As to higher education, only 4.5 per cent of Western Europe's 20 to 24 age group are enrolled in full-time education, and even in such educationally advanced countries as Denmark and Sweden the proportion is under 7 per cent.

However, although a great majority of European children leave school for good between the ages of 13 and 15, a considerable number of them continue with some vocational education or technical training on a part-time basis. According to the best available estimates, something like one half of the 15 to 19 age group is enrolled in part-time technical education in Germany and the United Kingdom and something of the order of 30 per cent in Austria, Denmark, Ireland, and Switzerland. The system of in-plant training, or apprenticeship as the Europeans call it, dates back many hundreds of years and is still governed by a complete hierarchy of rules and regulations concerning the duties of the apprentice and the obligations of the master craftsman to whom he is contractually assigned. This system remains important in the German language countries covering, for example, as much as 30 per cent of the 15 to 19 age group in

Germany and Austria and 35 per cent in Switzerland. In Belgium and France, by contrast, this type of technical training is carried out in workshop schools or *Centres d'Apprentissage* rather than in the factory. In these schools pupils enter at the age of 14 and take a three-year course. In the United Kingdom most technical training is on a part-time basis: the so-called "day release students" who are given time off from their factory employment to attend prescribed classes.

The six countries of the Common Market possess 54.5 per cent of Western Europe's population. The labor force in these six countries represents almost exactly the same proportion of the total population as in Western Europe as a whole. Likewise, the proportion between males and females is very similar, though France and Germany have substantially more and Italy substantially fewer females at work than the European average. The labor distribution by sector in EEC is similar to that of Western Europe, but again there are internal differences, parts of Germany having a higher than average proportion working in industry while Italy has a much higher than average proportion working in agriculture.

The educational status of the labor force in the EEC is neither better nor worse than in the whole region but, with the exception of Italy, the level of technical training is relatively high.

Agriculture and Forestry

In Western Europe land is indeed a scarce commodity. Europe had its population explosion in the nineteenth century so that today it is the most crowded of all the continents. Per head of population Western Europe has 1.2 hectares (3.0 acres) of land compared with 1.5 hectares (3.7 acres) in the Far East and 12 hectares (29.7 acres) in North America. Her population density is thus ten times that of the United States and Canada combined. Yet, although land is scarce in Europe, a high proportion of it is usable and productive. For instance, Western Europe's cropland comprises 26.3 per cent of its total land area compared with 10.8 per cent in North America and 15.7 per cent in the Far East. Of course, if one disregards Canada and Alaska with their vast areas of waste land and if one compares Western Europe only with the continental United States, the difference largely disappears; both areas have about one quarter of their land classified as arable.

Another comparison may be made, namely between Western Europe and India which are almost equal in total land area. In 1960, India had a population of 433 million against just over 300 million in Western Europe. Nearly half of India's land area is classed as arable but so much of this lies fallow in any one year that the area actually cropped closely approximates the cropped area of Western Europe. The cropland resource per inhabitant may be expressed briefly in figures as follows:

Western Europe	0.31 hectares (0.77 acres)
India	0.37 hectares (0.91 acres)
	including fallow
U.S.A.	1.2 hectares (3.0 acres)

The forest land of Western Europe is extensive but unevenly distributed. Most of the forests lie in the northern parts of Scandinavia and these account for a major part of the timber production. Important forests are also found on the highlands of France, Germany, Austria, and Switzerland. The northern forest stands are almost exclusively conifers, those of central Europe are partly conifers and partly hardwood while the more modest forest areas in the Mediterranean countries are composed chiefly of hardwood species. Considering only the accessible forests, the total area in Western Europe almost exactly equals the area under crops. Per head of population there are 0.32 hectares (0.79 acres) of available forest compared with 2.0 hectares (4.9 acres) in the U.S.A. and 0.14 hectares (0.35 acres) in India. Europe must be regarded as fortunate in having much less than its share of totally unusable land in the shape of deserts or frozen tundra.[3]

Although Western Europe is short of land, the land which it does possess is extremely productive. Crop yields are far higher than in any other area of comparable size in the world, while the annual growth of forests is significantly above the world average. Partly, this results from the possession of favorable soils and a favorable climate. But this represents only part of the truth. It would be more correct to say that the Europeans have made outstanding progress in learning how to get the most out of the soils and the climate with which they were endowed. In previous civilizations it was the riverlands, for instance of the Euphrates and the Nile, which people found most easy to cultivate. The Assyrians and the Egyptians, with the techniques then at their disposal, could have made nothing of the forest-covered and rain-soaked soils of northwestern Europe. What has happened is that as a result of careful observation of nature handed down from one farming generation to another over the centuries, and as a result of organized scientific research over recent decades, the Europeans have learned how to obtain the maximum output from the resource at their disposal. They have adapted crop varieties to suit the special conditions of particular districts; they have developed livestock

[3] For data as to land areas under crops, forests, and in other uses, see Food and Agriculture Organization, *Production Yearbook*, Vol. 15 (Rome, 1961).

European Crop Belts. (Map by courtesy of Dudley Stamp and
The Geographical Magazine, London)

breeds, likewise for special environments; they have studied cultivation practices, fertilizer responses, drainage problems, animal nutrition and animal health. In the long run it is the level of technical knowledge more than any particular combination of climate and soil which determines the productivity of the farmland of the region.

The agricultural output per hectare in Western Europe is the highest in the world. In the late nineteen-fifties, it ranged between $450 and $500 per hectare ($180–$200 per acre) in the Netherlands, Belgium, and Switzerland but was as low as $100 per hectare ($40 per acre) in Portugal and Spain.[4] The high figures achieved in the first three countries result partly from high per-hectare output of crops, but partly also from the large quantity of productive livestock maintained by farmers in those countries. The Mediterranean countries' crop yields are much lower and there are far fewer meat and milk producing animals.

The six countries of the EEC have almost exactly the same share in Western Europe's land area as they have in its population, namely 54 per cent. However, they have as much as 68.8 per cent of the arable land. This is because they do not include the vast forest and rough grazing areas of northern Europe. The productivity of this arable land falls somewhat below the regional average owing to the low level of yields in Italy. Consequently the Six between them produce about 60 per cent of Western Europe's cereals, meat, and milk.

The EEC has only 26 per cent of Western Europe's forest area, but from this produces 40 per cent of the total cut due to the fact that in France and Germany the annual growth of forests is much above the European average. Nevertheless, the Common Market is much more dependent on imports of forests products than imports of foodstuffs.

Energy

Coal has for the past two centuries been Western Europe's chief energy resource, having ousted wood as the principal means of domestic heating and having fired the boilers of the industrial revolution. A belt of coal deposits, extending to a depth of some 6,500 feet, stretches from Scotland through England and Wales, Belgium, northern France and the south of the Netherlands into Western Germany. The known resources of this great coalfield, together with a few quite minor isolated fields in Spain and elsewhere, are estimated at 370 billion tons and of these some 163 billion tons are considered exploitable. About 35 per cent of the exploitable reserves are located in the United Kingdom and 55 per cent in

---

[4] P. Lamartine Yates, *Food, Land and Manpower in Western Europe* (London: Macmillan, 1960), p. 155.

Western Germany. However the term "exploitable" may be subject to various interpretations and may well change as the years pass. When it is remembered that the greater part of Europe's coal is at present being produced at a financial loss, it is reasonable to ask what "exploitable" precisely means. Western Europe has long since extracted all its most easily accessible coal and is now operating on deposits which are much more awkward to get out than those being exploited currently in the other great coal producing areas of the world.

Natural gas is a quite new energy resource. Large deposits have been found in recent years in southwest France, in southern Italy, and in the Netherlands. Additional supplies are located in Germany, Austria, and northern Italy. Since natural gas constitutes one of the cheapest forms of energy, prospecting is being pursued with vigor and further finds may be expected in the next few years. There is also a project to bring natural gas to Western Europe by pipeline from Algeria.

The hydroelectricity potential of Western Europe is estimated at 500 billion kwh, nearly half of which is located in Norway and Sweden. Unfortunately, these supply sources are at such a great distance from the major centers of industry that transmission costs would be inordinately high. At present the preferred policy is to establish industries which require large amounts of energy in the northern districts themselves. Italy and France are the two largest producers, with 36 million and 32 million kwh respectively in 1958. Hydroelectricity production has expanded at great speed during the past fifteen years but it still accounts for less than 7 per cent of Western Europe's energy supply.

Minor sources of energy include fuelwood, peat, and geothermal energy (in Iceland), lignite, crude oil, and atomic energy. Fuelwood, peat, and geothermal energy have only quite limited uses; lignite requires to be used close to the centers of its production. Oil is expensive to produce from shale, as has been done in Scotland, but it is always possible, though unlikely, that in addition to the modest supplies available mainly in Austria and Italy, important petroleum reserves may yet be located somewhere in Europe. Atomic energy has not yet become a serious economic proposition.

If all the commercial resources of energy are added together and expressed in their calorific equivalent of electricity, then Europe has 4.6 million kwh per person compared with 21.5 and 20.7 million for the U.S.S.R. and United States, respectively. Within Europe the range extends from 0.02 million kwh per person in Denmark to 30.5 million in Norway.

The Common Market countries in 1958 were producing 53 per cent of Western Europe's energy (in terms of hard coal equivalent) and consumed 54 per cent. Taken together, the Six produced 70 per cent of their total energy requirements.

THE ROLE OF RESOURCES IN RECENT ECONOMIC DEVELOPMENT

Since the end of World War II, the economy of Western Europe has shown a remarkable capacity for growth. With the invaluable assistance of the Marshall Plan, so generously offered by the United States at that critical moment in 1947, the Western European countries were able to organize a recovery more rapidly than anyone had anticipated. By 1950, or soon after, most of the countries had regained their pre-war level of production. The Organization for European Economic Cooperation (OEEC) had been set up and was working purposively to liberalize trade and to eliminate progressively the various difficulties in member countries' balance of payments, while on the political front more stable governments were establishing themselves. The stage was set for an advance towards a new prosperity.

Between 1950 and 1960 the boom was indeed spectacular. The gross national product of Western Europe expanded at an annual compound rate of 4.7 per cent which was more than twice as fast as during any previous comparable period in Europe's history.[5] The star performers were Western Germany, with a growth rate of 7.7 per cent, and Italy, with 5.9 per cent. The weakest were the United Kingdom, with 2.6 per cent, and Belgium, 2.9 per cent. The evidence so far in the nineteen-sixties suggests that expansion is continuing, probably at a somewhat slower rate than in the fifties but still much more rapidly than in any previous epoch.

It is reasonable to ask how far resources have contributed to this economic achievement. Were they themselves one of the motivating forces? Have they acted as a brake on progress or have they had little influence one way or the other? Beyond these questions lies a question for the future, namely, to what extent will the availability of resources stimulate or retard development during the coming decade?

Manpower

One of the major contributions to an increase in GNP can be an increase in the number of man-hours worked. Since in these days the working week tends to become shorter rather than longer, the increase has to be derived from an increase in the size of the working population. In Western Europe the rate of natural increase in the population has been

[5] A. Maddison, "Growth and Fluctuation in the World Economy, 1870–1960," *Quarterly Review Banca Nazionale del Laboro,* vol. 61 (June, 1962), p. 17.

very small, fluctuating between 0.7 and 0.8 per cent per annum; neither has there been any substantial change in the proportion of the population which is actively at work. The only other source of increase has been the massive immigration into Western Germany from Eastern Europe which, over the period 1948 to 1960, totalled some 12 millions and represented an addition to the region's population of some 0.3 per cent per annum. However, this influx was more than offset by emigration from Western Europe to overseas destinations.

Within Western Europe there has been some redistribution of labor force as a result of internal migrations. For example, during the nineteen-fifties some 20,000 Italians were moving each year into France, a similar number into Switzerland, and smaller numbers into Belgium and the United Kingdom — these being permanent settlers as distinct from seasonal immigrant workers. More recently, the flow of Italians has been increasingly into Germany. In addition, some 25,000 Irishmen were moving into the United Kingdom. The free flow of labor permitted among the Scandinavian countries resulted in an immigration into Sweden approaching 10,000 annually, chiefly from Finland. Some immigration has developed from Spain into France, Switzerland, and Germany. The only countries whose labor force has been substantially augmented by these movements are Western Germany, where immigration has added nearly one-third to her total population, and Switzerland, where one-quarter of the labor force consists of foreigners. Taking the Western European region as a whole, it is clear that the over-all increase in labor supply has been very modest and has made little contribution to the great increase in production. The outlook for the rest of the nineteen-sixties is for an even slower increase in labor supply. The natural growth of population will certainly not be accelerated and may even diminish somewhat, the supply of refugees from the east has been largely brought to a standstill but the emigration to overseas is likely to continue, even if on a reduced scale. Hours worked per annum will gradually decline further. The combination of these several trends will produce a rather static input of manpower.

The internal redistribution among Western European countries will undoubtedly continue and may well be intensified as the barriers to movement within the EEC are progressively removed, and this could be all the more important if the EEC becomes enlarged.

The immediate cause of the rapid economic growth has therefore been an increase in the productivity of labor rather than in the quantity of labor. This productivity increase was due, in the first instance, to the large-scale re-equipment of industry which had suffered material damage during the war and, in the second place, to maintenance as an objective of government policies of a high level of consumer demand. In short, there was at one and the same time great scope for the modernization of European industry and a great incentive to do so provided by the strong and expanding domestic market.

A supplementary and important method of increasing the average productivity of the labor force was the transfer of labor from low productivity occupations, especially agriculture, to high productivity occupations. Throughout the nineteen-fifties the demand for labor in industry and commerce continued to be so strong that these inter-sectorial transfers of manpower reached surprising dimensions. It is estimated that during the decade some 5½ million workers or 18 per cent of Western Europe's labor force transferred from agriculture to other occupations. In spite of this, the rate of transfer was insufficient to keep pace with the demand for labor in the expanding sectors, so that employers, bidding against one another, forced up wages faster than the increase in labor productivity, thus causing an inflationary erosion of the value of money; when, towards the end of the decade, inflation was damped down by governmental action, the same cost-push proceeded to start an erosion of profits.

Because the outlook in the coming years is for no material increase in the volume of labor, it becomes more important to secure a continuing increase in productivity. European governments are searching for appropriate growth policies, wage policies, and income policies, and for techniques of co-ordinating these so that expansion can continue at a regular rhythm without having to be periodically halted in an effort to reestablish equilibrium.

A contribution to higher productivity can also be secured from the side of labor, especially by a modernization of technical training. The system of apprenticeship, so traditional in many European countries, has become increasingly criticized as being poorly adapted to the requirements of modern industry. The period of apprenticeship prescribed in the craft regulations is often unnecessarily long and ill adapted for the task of preparing workers for work in mechanized modern factories. The system also tends to excessive differentiation between the skilled craftsman, who has passed through his apprenticeship, and the unskilled workers who have never had that training, whereas the reality of industrial life requires mobility between the different grades of employment and even between occupations. If vocational training can be recast to suit contemporary needs and if trade unions' regulations and practices can become more flexible, an important contribution will be forthcoming towards further improvement in labor productivity.

One further question is to what extent can Western Europe continue to squeeze underemployed labor out of agriculture? Undoubtedly there remains much that could be done. It has been estimated that if the six countries of the Common Market could organize their farms as farms are organized today in Denmark, they could manage with 40 per cent fewer farmers than they now have; nor need this be the limit since Denmark, too, is engaged in further rationalization and is encouraging the regrouping of small farms into larger production units. Nevertheless, since substantial institutional and other obstacles impede any rapid reform of the structure of farming, it may have to become one of the objectives of governments' manpower and agricultural policies to organize more deliberately than hitherto the mobility of labor from low to high productivity sectors.

Agriculture and Forestry

During the past fifteen years, European agriculture has been called upon to make a major effort in adaptation. The sector whose production cycle is the longest, whose activities are most limited by the physical environment, whose modes of thinking are the most conservative, suddenly found itself face to face with an economic environment more dynamic than at any time for more than a century. Long-held principles of agricultural policy had to be re-examined, the justification for the rural way of life came up for questioning and the role of farming in a full-employment economy had to be redefined.

On the whole, the response of agriculture and of the farming community was reasonably creditable. During the nineteen-fifties, the gross output of agricultural products rose at a cumulative rate of 2.7 per cent per annum while food consumption was rising at less than 2 per cent per annum. This meant that food imports declined and that food exports increased. For example, in 1959–61 imports of wheat into the United Kingdom represented 62 per cent of total supplies compared with 75 per cent in 1934–38; imports of eggs, 2.3 per cent compared with 29 per cent. There have, of course, been some exceptions to this trend. Thus, in the Federal Republic of Germany and in Switzerland the consumption of eggs and poultry meat has risen much faster than production. Likewise, the output of livestock products in Italy has not expanded fast enough and imports have increased. But generally speaking, Western Europe is coming closer to total self-sufficiency in those products which she can produce.

This increase in production has been achieved with very little, if any, increase in the input of resources. There has, for example, been virtually no change in the quantity of land devoted to agricultural production. Indeed, in some of the more densely populated countries there has been a decline owing to the requirements for land in road building, airport construction and new housing. The quantity of manpower used in agriculture fell by some 18 per cent during the nineteen-fifties and is still falling.

What really brought about the increase in production was the successful application of science and technology to crop and livestock husbandry: the wider utilization of machinery, fertilizers, pesticides, and herbicides; the improvements in animal breeding, animal nutrition, and so on. The extension services, which before World War II had been on a rather modest scale in most of the countries, were greatly expanded and succeeded in persuading farmers to modernize their practices in all branches of production. The advance was perhaps most striking in the Mediterranean region where the technical efficiency of farming had previously been low. On the other hand, there were a few countries in which progress could have been more rapid but for the difficulties encountered in finding export markets for the increased output.

Comparing 1950–52 with 1957–59, the Western European average yield of wheat increased from 15.6 to 19.2 quintals per hectare (23 to 28½ bushels per acre) and of barley from 19.4 to 22.7 quintals (36 to 42 bushels). Over roughly the same period, the consumption of fertilizers and pesticides in twelve northwest European countries increased by 43 per cent and the consumption of fuel and electricity on farms by 52 per cent.[6]

The economic climate was favorable to the modernization and expansion of farming. In many countries, agricultural prices were supported by governmental action, either through frontier protection measures or by means of direct subsidies to farmers. Generally the objective was to maintain prices at levels which would assure an acceptable income to the reasonably efficient small-scale farmer. Additional measures of all kinds were used to assist farmers in especially remote areas or those engaged in the production of especially risky or unremunerative products.

Much has been written about the advantages and disadvantages of the agricultural price policies of European governments. One thing, however, is clear, namely that the support extended to small farmers was never on

[6] ECE/FAO, *Towards a Capital Intensive Agriculture* (Geneva, 1961).

such a scale as to deprive them of the incentive to move to other occupations where opportunity offered. Wages in industry, even for unskilled workers, have continued to be higher than the wages of farm laborers while, of course, the conditions of work and other amenities of urban life proved a strong attraction. In fact, as mentioned above, the rural exodus has continued at a brisk pace. Moreover, even if the level of agricultural price support had been lower one cannot, with any certainty, conclude either that production would have been lower (and consequently imports higher) or that still more people would have left the land. It is true that the level of prices influences the volume of output and the level of wages the supply of labor, but the functional relationships between these elements are a complex matter that has been insufficiently studied.

It is sometimes argued that the policy of agricultural support as pursued in Europe meant more expensive food for the urban consumer. However, in most of the continental European countries, the proportion of food which is imported and, as such, may be subject to import duties represents a tiny fraction of the national food supply while, on the other hand, the domestic production of the basic food stuffs, such as cereals, meat and dairy products, has been becoming more and more efficient and low-cost so that in several of the countries, and in a number of commodities, the prices which farmers receive do not differ greatly from those received by farmers in overseas exporting countries. The United Kingdom is the only European country in which imports represent as much as half of the food supply, and here the government has operated its system of deficiency payments to farmers, thus subsidizing them directly from public funds while leaving to the consumer the benefit of cheap imported food.

Altogether, the record of the agricultural sector in Europe in recent years constitutes a remarkable example of improved resource utilization. The increase of nearly 30 per cent in the productivity of land and of over 50 per cent in the productivity of labor compares very favorably with what manufacturing industry was able to accomplish during the same period.

Looking toward the future, one may expect recent trends to continue regarding both the demand for and the supply of food. With population increasing slowly and no reason to expect major changes in the dietary habits, except possibly in the lower income groups in the Mediterranean countries, the over-all demand for food will expand very little but will be stronger for products such as meat, eggs, and fruit, and much weaker for bread and potatoes.

On the production side, there is now a built-in capacity for technical progress, and indeed the extension workers are busy teaching every small farmer how to produce more from his land and his animals. In a recent Food and Agriculture Organization (FAO) publication,[7] the growth of output was projected at a ten-yearly rate of 24 per cent. On this basis, the output of a number of commodities would, unless checked, seriously outstrip demand before 1970.

Apart from the United Kingdom and one or two small countries, Western Europe is already so nearly self-sufficient in major foodstuffs that there remains little scope for expanding output at the expense of imports. Moreover, the scope for substitution may not in reality be as great as appears. For example, European soft wheat is not regarded by the milling industry as an acceptable substitute for Canadian hard wheat. The United Kingdom continues to be the most important market for the agricultural exports of non-European countries and the modest increases that may be expected in the output of British farming would not basically affect that position.

In respect to grains, the FAO projections to 1970 indicate the total import requirement as being little changed from the period of the later nineteen-fifties. Wheat imports would decline very sharply but would be counterbalanced by an equivalent increase in the import of coarse grains for livestock feeding. Sugar production may well increase rapidly and imports are projected to fall.

Meat is one of the items for which demand is projected to increase quite significantly, especially the demand for beef and poultry. It seems as if production increases could cover all the expected consumption increases, leaving imports in 1970 at about the level of 1960. However, all these projections are based on the assumption of constant prices, and meat is a commodity particularly sensitive to price changes, so that the demand level and the volume of production might deviate substantially from the present projections.

Milk goes mainly to liquid consumption, to butter and to cheese-making. Demand for liquid milk is not expected to increase much except in the Mediterranean countries where it is still low. The European butter market already is in surplus but butter consumption might be artificially stimulated if taxes were imposed on margarine or the raw materials of margarine. Milk production can expand extremely rapidly as improved dairying techniques continue to be adopted and many countries are likely to have to devise policies for dealing with surpluses. There may be scope

[7] FAO, *Agricultural Commodities: Projections for 1970* (Rome, 1962).

for disposing of milk powder to the developing countries; there may be attempts to limit the imports of butter and cheese from overseas but ultimately it is the European production which will have to be adjusted to the market demand.

Summing up the outlook for individual products, it appears that by 1970 the production of several commodities could easily exceed the European demand, while for most of the remaining commodities the same position could be reached a few years later. At the core of the farm problem in Western Europe there is an economic and social tangle which can be briefly stated in the following terms: Governments are pledged to take care of the income of what they call a reasonably efficient farmer. They have used their extension services to make sure that almost all farmers are reasonably efficient; they have used price guarantees and price supports to provide the necessary level of income; yet, already to some extent now and certainly still more in the years ahead, they will be facing a double dilemma. As gross national product increases so also does the public concept of what is an acceptable level of income and, if incomes are rising in other sectors, farm incomes must rise *pari passu*. Unless agricultural prices are to rise continuously, which governments are naturally reluctant to permit, then farmers can increase their incomes only by reducing their inputs (for which the scope is strictly limited unless, and until, farms become larger) or by increasing their output. In practice they all strive to increase output and are so remarkably successful that they are beginning to embarrass their governments with unmarketable surpluses. But unless the number of farmers, and probably also sooner or later the amount of farmland, can be reduced the output will continue to grow larger and larger as farmers chase the objective of higher incomes.

It is argued in some quarters that the situation would right itself if governments would only withdraw all artificial support from agriculture and leave market forces to operate freely. This argument ignores the difficulties that, in the case of food, lower prices do not materially increase consumption, that price reduction may not diminish output, at least not in the short run, and that it is socially and politically unacceptable to exert a downward pressure on farm incomes sufficiently intensive to drive people out of farming.

The way out of the tangle and the way to achieve a more rational utilization of resources must be sought in two directions simultaneously, the first having as its objective the slimming down of the agricultural sector to a size commensurate with present-day requirements, and the second being the working out of policies designed to safeguard the income and welfare of the redundant farm labor force. It is worth considering briefly some of the means which might be employed to bring about these changes.[8]

It is not difficult to describe the sort of agriculture appropriate to a rapidly growing full-employment economy. It is one in which the average productivity of labor and capital as nearly as possible equals the average productivity of these two resources in the other sectors. Since in the European setting the minimum operating unit may be said to be one farm family and one tractor, the farm should at least be large enough to provide full employment to both these elements. The actual size in acres will vary according to district and type of farming, but the objective remains as the optimum utilization of the basic inputs.

To reach this objective will require a radical reform of the agricultural structure in Western Europe, where the great bulk of the farms are at present much below the minimum size as defined above. Various techniques are already being employed, for example: programs to effect the consolidation of fragment farms (i.e. one farmer having plots scattered in all directions outside the village); revision of inheritance laws which, in some countries, still require an equal distribution of land among all the heirs; programs to facilitate the amalgamation of farms, for instance by offering credit to farmers who wish to buy additional land or by the government acquiring land from retiring smallholders and making it available for the enlargement of neighboring farms. In Sweden, for example, programs along these lines have been initiated, the objective being to create farms of about 50 acres as being a minimum viable unit.

The creation of physically larger units will not in itself be sufficient to make the family farm an economic proposition. The farmer himself needs assistance to make him a more efficient "entrepreneur." Owing to the increasing technical complexity of farming operations, the farmer whose schooling ends at the age of, say, 14 is ill equipped to take advantage of all the "know-how" which the extension services make available. In some Western European countries junior agricultural schools exist for young people in the 14 to 18 age group while, in some, vocational training is available in short courses for adult farmers. Yet, even with better education, the typical family farmer can hardly be expected to have a thorough knowledge of the latest techniques in each of the various departments of his business. Largely for this reason, they are more and more seeking ways of obtaining expert advice and management by delegating some of

[8] For more detailed discussion see FAO, *Agricultural Policies in Europe in the 1960's* (Rome, 1962).

their activities. Not only through co-operatives in their traditional form but also through new forms of marketing arrangements, farmers attempt to improve efficiency by shortening the line of distribution between themselves and the consumer. Another example is the so-called "vertical integration," notably in the broiler industry where an industrial firm will provide the farmer with the capital to build poultry houses and will sell him feedingstuffs and give him technical advice while guaranteeing to buy the end product at fixed prices. In Germany, government subsidies are given for the establishment of centralized machinery stations which supply farm equipment on loan to co-operating farmers. In the Netherlands, in some districts farm workers are hired by a group of farmers acting jointly, which permits a fuller utilization of the hired men. In Denmark and Sweden, co-operative milk parlors exist in which a group of small farmers combine to keep their cows all together at one place where they are fed and milked more efficiently than they could be on the individual farms. These are just a few examples of the ways in which farmers are trying to overcome the disadvantages of small-scale enterprises and of insufficient technical knowledge.

The other direction in which governments can help is by granting assistance to farmers who wish either to give up farming or to transfer to another occupation. In several countries the early retirement of elderly farmers is encouraged by special schemes of old-age pensions. Such early retirement can speed up the process of farm amalgamation and, by opening the way for younger men, can speed up modernization. In the Federal Republic of Germany such a pension scheme has been introduced and has greatly increased the number of farms changing hands.

Governments can facilitate a more rapid movement of labor out of agriculture in a number of ways: for instance, by increasing the training facilities in non-agricultural occupations for which otherwise farm workers are poorly qualified; also by providing information in rural areas of job opportunities in urban centers. Beyond this, much could be done to stimulate a greater volume of employment in the predominantly rural areas, for example by measures encouraging the decentralization of industry and by the introduction of facilities which promote tourism. Several countries, indeed, have now evolved special development programs for their more backward regions.

Finally, it has to be recognized that however great may be the efforts directed towards farm modernization on the one hand and improving the mobility of labor on the other, there will remain for a number of years a great number of farm families which cannot benefit from such programs.

It is these which justifiably qualify for measures of income support designed to maintain their living standard until either they can obtain a more satisfactory farm or they can be transferred to another form of employment. In Denmark and Sweden the governments operate systems of cash payments to small-scale farmers which are entirely divorced from the volume of their output. In several countries governments give grants to farmers in remote regions in order to discourage depopulation as, for example, in the mountain regions of Switzerland. In some quarters there is discussion of an acreage subsidy which would be substantial for the first few acres and diminish rapidly as the size of farm increases.

It will be seen that in many countries attempts are being made to evolve new agricultural policies which will discourage the emergence of unusable surpluses while at the same time safeguarding and even improving the income of the farming community. All these attempts have in common the principle of divorcing income support from price support so that prices can be used for their traditional purpose of adjusting supply to the requirements of the market. As yet these programs are either still in the discussion stage or have only recently been put into operation, and it is not yet possible to say how far they will prove successful in bringing into existence a more modern agricultural structure and encouraging a more efficient deployment of resources.

What is likely to be the effect of these various developments on Western Europe's trade in agricultural products? It has already been noted that agricultural production is increasing faster than consumption of the products coming from farms so that in these commodities the volume of imports must be expected to diminish. This will apply to all the major products with the probable exception of cereal feedingstuffs. The actual rate of decline of imports will depend on the speed at which Western Europe's farmers improve their techniques and this in turn will, of course, be influenced by the nature of the agricultural policies pursued by governments. However, one cannot be too dogmatic about the precise way in which policy influences technical innovation. Some people argue that the maintenance of high support prices strongly encourages technical progress, whereas others maintain that a policy designed to encourage larger farms, even if combined with lower prices, would equally stimulate improvements. What can be said with certainty is that Western Europe possesses a combination of natural resources and technical knowledge which could provide it in the near future with most of its requirements at a production cost level comparable to that prevailing in most countries from which it could obtain imports.

As regards the tropical and subtropical products that are not produced in Europe except to a limited extent on the Mediterranean fringe, the FAO projections indicate that, even on favorable assumptions regarding the growth of per capita income, the imports of these commodities are not expected to increase by more than 2 per cent a year during the nineteen-sixties. The highest rates of increase are likely to occur in cocoa and coffee, the smallest in tea and jute, while imports of sugar might decline. Several countries still impose import duties and excise taxes on a number of these commodities and, if these imposts could be reduced or removed, demand would be appreciably stimulated — probably by some 11 per cent in the case of coffee and citrus fruit, and 8 per cent in that of cocoa, assuming total abolition of the taxes.

In respect to forest products, the research and projections for the future show quite a different picture. In this group of commodities consumption has been increasing faster than production and imports have been rising. Between 1950 and 1960, Europe's[9] consumption of forest products rose from 165 million m³ to 235 million m³ (5.8 to 8.3 billion cubic feet) in terms of roundwood equivalent. This was an increase of 42 per cent compared with an increase in GNP of 66 per cent during the same period. The increase was especially due to a great expansion in demand for woodpulp and for plywood and veneers.

Meanwhile, Europe's forest output rose only from 167 million m³ to 217 million m³ (5.9 to 7.7 billion cubic feet). This increase was accomplished because in several countries it was found that the annual net growth of forests had been underestimated so that it became possible to raise the levels of permissible cutting.

During the decade, the net trade balance in all forest products combined changed from a net export of 5 million m³ (1949–1951 average) to a net import of 11 million m³ (1959–1961 average) in roundwood equivalent (0.2 to 0.4 billion cubic feet). The increase in imports consisted largely of sawnwood from the U.S.S.R., hardwood logs from the tropical countries, and woodpulp from the United States.

Looking a decade ahead, these several trends may be expected to continue. The consumption of forest products will increase but at a less rapid rate than the increase in GNP but nevertheless perhaps by as much as 33 per cent. The demand for woodpulp and for particle board will expand much more rapidly than that for sawnwood. On the production side, there remains scope for some modest expansion of output, partly by further

[9] The figures cited in this section on forest products refer to Western and Eastern Europe combined.

upward revisions of the permissible cut, but more importantly by an expansion of plantation forests composed of quick-growing species.

However, the cumulative effect of consumption rising faster than production implies a deficit in the early nineteen-seventies substantially larger than the present one. This could be made good by a further increase in imports from the U.S.S.R., from North America, and from the tropics. Taking an even longer view, there is scope for a substantial expansion in Europe's own output if the area under quick growing species (notably poplar) is extended. It might well become desirable to retire some land from agricultural production, whose output threatens to become excessive, and plant it with forests which would mature in a period of fifteen years. Thus the difficulties of agriculture could partly be resolved by programs which at the same time would contribute to reducing the deficits in forest products.

Energy

The demand for energy expanded during the nineteen-fifties rather faster than the demand for food and even than the demand for forest products. This reflected the unprecedented outburst of activity in manufacturing industries, as well as the substantial development in transport, especially road transport.

In the mobilization of its own energy resources, Western Europe faced greater and greater difficulties. In spite of offering substantial wage increases, the coal industry found it impossible, during an era of full employment, to keep a sufficient labor force. Large sums of money had to be invested in mechanization in order to economize labor, and in modernization in order to make work in the pits somewhat more attractive. The combination of these heavy investments on the one hand and the competition of cheap American coal plus the products of imported petroleum on the other, has meant that most collieries have been running at a loss. Western Europe's coal production has, indeed, hardly increased at all since 1950.

In other directions Western Europe's domestic sources of energy have increased. During the nineteen-fifties, substantial additions were made to hydroelectric installations, both in the Alps and in northern Scandinavia. Furthermore, rather extensive deposits of natural gas have been located, the latest being the considerable gas field in the Netherlands. However, even at their present greatly increased levels of output, hydroelectricity and natural gas together represent barely 6 per cent of Western Europe's energy production. Thus the increase in the requirements over the past decade has been met chiefly by massive imports of petroleum, both crude and refined.

It was the mineral wealth of Europe, especially coal and iron ore, which gave it that commanding advantage during the first century of the industrial revolution. Yet this mineral resource base is now becoming so costly to exploit that it is unable to support any further expansion of industrial production. The new workshops of Western Europe are powered by imported mineral fuels which are costly in terms of foreign exchange and vulnerable in the event of war.

In the years immediately ahead the same trends are likely to persist. Coal production must be expected to decline rather than increase. The hydroelectric resources have mostly already been brought into use except in the extreme north of Europe where remoteness makes the transmission of power rather expensive. Further deposits of natural gas may be located and gas supplies may be brought by pipeline from North Africa. But virtually all of the future increase in energy requirements will have to be covered by imports, mainly of petroleum, but to some extent also of coal.

REGIONAL INTEGRATION AND RESOURCE USE

It has been seen that the tremendous economic upsurge in Western Europe during the past fifteen years has in no way been hampered by lack of resources. There appears to be plenty of fertile agricultural land to meet current food requirements. It has forests whose output has almost kept pace with the rising demand for forest products, and it is only in regard to energy that Western Europe has been constrained to look abroad, but fortunately at a moment when petroleum supplies were becoming abundant in many parts of the world.

A new economic factor has, however, made its appearance, namely the movement toward regional integration culminating in the European Economic Community. It is pertinent to ask what effects this new grouping will have on the utilization of Western Europe's own resources and on the extent to which she relies on the resources of other continents. Will the Common Market bring about profound changes in resource allocation or will the tendencies which manifested themselves during the nineteen-fifties continue to determine the evolution of supply/demand relationships? Is the Community something which will radically change the economic configuration of Western Europe or is it something within the framework of which the inevitable long-term trends will continue to exercise their influence?

The European Economic Community, about which so much is written today, was not the first move toward economic integration within Western Europe. Already, during World War II, not to go further back in history, the Belgian and Dutch governments, in exile in London, had entered into negotiations which led to the formation, in 1948, of a customs union known as Benelux comprising Belgium, the Netherlands, and Luxembourg. Following the initial abolition of customs duties between the territories (between Belgium and Luxembourg there had been economic union in 1922) import quotas were soon abolished and gradually in the succeeding years the movement of capital and of labor was freed. However, it cannot be maintained that integration proceeded very rapidly in the manufacturing industries of the members of Benelux, while in regard to the intra-trade in agricultural products serious difficulties persisted.

The next step was the creation, in 1952, of the European Coal and Steel Community which established for Benelux, Germany, France, and Italy a common market for coal, iron ore, scrap iron and steel products. Finally, in 1957, these same countries signed the Treaties of Rome, one creating a new specialized community, the Euratom, while the other created EEC, both Communities coming formally into existence on January 1, 1958.

The basic principles of EEC were fourfold: the first was to establish free movement of goods by the removal of duties and quantitative restrictions on trade between the members and by erecting a common tariff in respect of imports from the outside world. The second was to promote free movement of persons, services, and capital within the Community. The third was to establish a common agricultural policy, and the fourth to bring into existence a common transport policy, with common rules applicable to international transport and no discrimination on transport within the Community. Besides these basic principles, provision was made in the Rome Treaty for common action in other directions. For example, in order to promote free competition, regulations would be made concerning cartels, dumping, and government subsidies. Provision was made for the co-ordination of economic policy with a view to avoiding or removing balance-of-payments disequilibrium. Differences in national laws would be removed insofar as necessary to implement the common policies. A European social fund was to be created to assist the employment of workers without discrimination on ground of nationality. Likewise, a European investment bank was to be set up to promote economic expansion. Finally, arrangements were made for the association of the dependencies and former overseas colonies of member countries.

The institutions of the Community are an Assembly of 142 members nominated by the six respective parliaments (France, Germany, and Italy — thirty-six members each; Belgium and the Netherlands — fourteen, and Luxembourg — six); a Council of Ministers composed of seventeen members; a Commission of nine permanent officials with a Secretariat; and lastly a Court of Justice.

The integration of the economies of the six founding members is to be achieved in three stages of four years each from 1958 to 1970. Already, however, the removal of duty on trade between members is ahead of schedule, the tariffs on most manufactures having been reduced already by 50 per cent and those on most agricultural products already by 35 per cent by the middle of 1962.

The aspect of the treaty which most particularly concerns us here is the provision that member governments shall work out a common agricultural policy which shall have as its objectives:

a) to increase agricultural production by developing technical progress, ensuring the rational development of agricultural output and maximum utilization of the factors of production, especially manpower;
b) to ensure in this way a fair standard of living for the agricultural population, in particular by increasing the individual earnings of agricultural workers;
c) to stabilize markets;
d) to guarantee supplies;
e) to ensure reasonable prices for deliveries to the consumer.

These objectives will be sought through a common organization of marketing, through a common policy regarding agricultural structure, and through a common social welfare policy.

The marketing system can be illustrated by the arrangements that have already been made between the Six in regard to wheat. Within the Community, the national wheat price will, by stages, be brought to a common level which, in this case, will lie somewhere between the relatively high German price and the relatively low French one. This will be called the target price within the Community, but some 5 to 10 per cent below it there will be an intervention price at which the authorities will intervene to support the price if, for any reason, it temporarily weakens. These prices will be reviewed annually.

On imports of wheat from third countries a levy will be imposed equal to the difference between the importing country's domestic price and the lowest prevailing import price at the point of entry. Starting in 1970 when all the member countries' domestic wheat prices will have become identical, the levy will be the difference between the import price and the Community's target price.

As for trade in wheat between members of the Community during the transition period, this will also be subject to a levy, but at a lower rate than on imports from outside and moreover a rate which diminishes during the transition period as the differences in the domestic prices of the member countries gradually disappear. In other words, the member countries enjoy a special preference within the Community until such time as their trade with one another becomes absolutely free on the basis of absolutely uniform prices.

The system of protection by levy, instead of by import duty, is one which gives no opportunity to the overseas exporter to penetrate the European market by reducing the price of his product since to do so would merely increase the levy. The volume of imports at any particular time will therefore depend on the extent to which, at the target price, the Community production of wheat falls short of the Community's requirements.

This system, with adaptations, is to be applied to all agricultural products produced by member countries — principally cereals (wheat, coarse grains, and rice), sugar beet, beef, pig meat, poultry meat, eggs, milk and other dairy products (mainly butter and cheese), fats and oils, tobacco, fruit, vegetables and wine. But while the methodology of the internal price fixing and of frontier protection has been determined, the actual levels of target prices have got to be worked out, and likewise the length of the stages through which these levels are to be reached.

As for tropical agricultural products not produced in member countries, the exports of the associated territories will have free entry into the Common Market whereas similar products originating elsewhere will be subject to the Community tariff. The extent of the preferences enjoyed by the associated territories will therefore depend on the height of the tariff for each particular commodity. During the negotiations with the United Kingdom it was agreed that Commonwealth countries in Africa and the Caribbean together with almost all the remaining dependent British territories would become eligible for association.

The prospect of dividing the tropical product exporting countries, nearly all of them in early stages of economic development, into two categories namely those which have privileged access to the Common Market and those which do not, raises numerous practical difficulties. At its inception the plan was intended to cover the case of the ex-French territories which had developed rather high-cost export crops for the sheltered market of France and which could not suddenly face full competition with other suppliers. It is suggested in some quarters that the status of association might be merely a transitional arrangement until such time as all developing countries can be treated on an equal footing. Alternatively, the objections would be mitigated by fixing the Community's tariffs on tropical products at low levels, or at least progressively reducing them.

The other principal question mark hangs over the future volume of imports of temperate agricultural products into the Community. This is a matter of considerable commercial interest to North America, Oceania, Argentina, Uruguay, and certain other countries. The problem is frequently posed as being simply one of prices: if the Community's internal prices for these products are sufficiently reasonable, then, so it is argued, the volume of trade will be maintained and perhaps in some products even expanded. However, the real situation is more complex than this and since the future evolution of European agricultural policies may have important consequences for exporting countries in other continents, it is worth examining the problem in somewhat greater detail.

Western Europe's farming, as already noted, is entering on a phase parallel to that embarked on by United States farming some fifteen or more years ago. That is to say, production expanding faster than demand, import requirements falling, and export availabilities increasing. These trends will continue and become aggravated. In such circumstances the role of price policy needs re-examination as suggested above. For instance, it is not certain that farmers would respond to moderate reductions in agricultural prices by reducing their output. Many past instances suggest that they might instead increase their output in an effort to maintain their incomes. Nor is it likely that the Community could contemplate really large price reductions since such action would create major social difficulties among farmers.

About one-fifth of the working population of the Community is occupied in farming, the great majority working on farms of less than 25 acres in size. Their incomes average half to two-thirds of those of unskilled industrial workers. To reduce substantially the prices of agricultural products in the six member countries would cut the incomes of these people to the subsistence level or lower.

The situation will, of course, be partially relieved by the rapid movement of labor out of agriculture into other occupations. Yet assuming this trend continues and assuming even that it is accelerated, it will not by itself reduce the volume of agricultural output. It does not reduce the number of acres under crops nor the number of cows giving milk. Indeed, the modernization and mechanization of agriculture may well stimulate further increases in yields per acre and in milk per cow.

What complicates the problem for governments is that hitherto they have sought to support farm incomes by supporting farm prices. They fixed prices at levels which would provide a reasonable income to the reasonably efficient average farmer and, be it noted, under European conditions an average farmer means a small farmer. Nevertheless, even if in the new agricultural policy of EEC price support can be divorced from income support, while this will have a favorable influence on the redistribution of manpower, it is unlikely to do anything much to check the expansion of agricultural production. It would appear, therefore, that whether the Community opts for relatively high or relatively low agricultural prices may not have too great an influence on the volume of production, which is destined to increase anyway, and consequently may have little impact on the trend in the volume of imports.

The energy policy of the Common Market countries is determined by three organizations: Euratom, the Coal and Steel Community and, in respect to petroleum, by the EEC.

The policy for atomic energy is one of continuing experimentation to seek solutions to both the engineering and the nuclear-physical problems before launching out into investment in nuclear power stations as a commercial proposition.

The coal policy of ECSC consists chiefly in persuading the member countries to co-operate in trying to resolve their structural problems rather than exporting their difficulties to each other. To a substantial extent this has been achieved though not without going through certain crises such as the excessive stockbuilding during the 1958 recession. Progress has been made with the closure of high-cost mines, notably in Belgium where, in fact, the redundant labor has been absorbed into other occupations more easily than anticipated.

There remains the political decision of how far to let European coal compete freely with imported petroleum (and perhaps coal) and how far to protect or subsidize coal production as an insurance against the danger of being cut off from external supplies of energy. Until the members of ECSC take some definite decisions on this question it is difficult for them to determine what volume of investment is appropriate for the maintenance and modernization of the mines — and merely for maintenance the needed investment will be large.

An oil policy formulated by an inter-authority working party envisages the attainment by 1970 of free movement of petroleum and petroleum products within the Community. There would be a gradual reduction and harmonization of internal taxes on petroleum products as well as common rules regulating competition. The governments would consult together regarding their oil industries and particularly on their investments. The Community's external tariff on petroleum products would be quite low while crude petroleum would be imported free except that a quota is being suggested on imports from the U.S.S.R. This policy has not been accepted, at least for the present, by the ministers of the Six, and the whole matter has been deferred.

It will be noted that the policies of the Community for atomic energy for coal and for oil are being shaped by three different bodies and that as yet no over-all energy policy has been formulated which would give general guidelines as to the roles of the individual fuels. The Six are fully aware of the need to co-ordinate their energy policies and in the event of an enlargement of the Community this need would become much more urgent.

GENERAL CONCLUSIONS

We have now passed in review the current state of resource utilization in Western Europe as a whole as well as the particular policies of the EEC in the most relevant fields, namely in agriculture and in energy. It may be asked how far and in what directions the fact of economic integration is likely to change the pattern of resource utilization. Will there be major new departures which might have repercussions on the economic interests of third countries?

In considering this question the first uncertainty concerns the eventual size of the Common Market group. Will the Community become an eightsome or a ten or twelvesome? Or will it remain a sixsome? While the application of the United Kingdom had the greatest political and economic significance, the future character of Western Europe would certainly be affected according as the three neutrals — Sweden, Switzerland and Austria — were brought in or left outside.

Another uncertainty relates to the speed at which the group will move toward final political and economic integration. The Action Program published by the European Commission in November 1962 suggests ambitious targets and a rapid timetable. It envisages the attainment of a common monetary policy and fixed exchange rates among members (unilateral devaluation would become unthinkable); it proposes confrontation of national budgets and co-ordination by the Commission of planning for economic growth. It asks that the date of final abolition of tariffs between the member states be brought forward from 1970 to 1967. These proposals have yet to be discussed by governments and doubtless will be modified in many respects before they are finally adopted.

Another doubt hangs over the shape which the common economic policy of the group may eventually take. Internally, will it promote real harmony and healthy competition or will members succeed in protecting their favorite industries with hidden subsidies and other devices? Externally, will emphasis be placed on promoting trade with the outer world or on protecting the Community's producers against foreign competition? Certainly the Commission feels a deep sense of responsibility to the outer world and particularly toward the developing countries. At the same time, some of the member governments evince anxiety lest any sudden readjustments be required of the weaker sectors in their economies.

Yet though it be true that because the Community is young these uncertainties exist, in another sense they are rather superficial doubts. Thus the question of the Community's move toward closer integration is one of timing. There can be no doubt that the members will step by step move into a more intimate association; how fast will be the tempo is the only significant speculation. Likewise in trade relationships with third countries, it is only a matter of the time required to establish the appropriate world marketing arrangements for primary and other products.

Moreover in sectors where basic resources are involved, e.g. in agriculture and energy, the inevitable facts of the situation impose themselves so strongly that the Community would have no great scope for adopting any startling policies. In agriculture, as has been seen, the Community possesses an excess of resources. The task for the group, whatever its size, will be to adjust the volume and composition of the agricultural output to the requirements of the market, including therein both the commercial market and deliveries for food aid programs. The endeavor must be to produce those quantities with the most economic utilization of resources possible — meaning resources of land, manpower, and capital. This in turn will involve pushing ahead with all the modernization programs mentioned earlier.

The self-sufficiency of the Community in terms of forest products will depend on whether the Six negotiate some status of association with the Scandinavian countries. Yet whether the Community be enlarged or not two facts remain certain: first, Scandinavia will continue to be the main supplier of the rest of Western Europe, and secondly, these supplies will fall short of the expanding requirements so that larger imports will be needed from the outside world.

The policy for energy will likewise be a difficult one, but for different reasons. Here there can be no question of an over-all surplus, merely a possible excess of one less wanted form of energy, namely coal — as if in agriculture too many potatoes were being grown. It is perfectly clear that most, if not all, the net increase in energy requirements must be met by imports of petroleum at least until such time as nuclear energy becomes sufficiently cheap.

Within the framework of these over-all developments the impact of the Common Market organization may be felt in three principal fields. First, if a result of integration will be more rapid economic growth than otherwise, then demand in general, and for basic resources in particular, will rise. This could well be significant for forest products and for total energy requirements but would be less important for agricultural products, most of which have a rather low income-elasticity of demand. Secondly, the free movement of goods between the Common Market members will favor actual and potential exporters. In fuels this freedom will probably not alter appreciably the existing patterns of trade, but in farm products it may well favor France with her large export potential, while in forest products it will favor Austria, Norway, Sweden, and Finland, if they obtain associate status. Thirdly, in international trade there may well occur some diversion percentage-wise from third-country sources of supply of foodstuffs to Community sources, but this could be concomitant with an increase in the absolute quantities of food and feeding stuffs imported. Herein lies the major benefit of regional economic integration. A united and rich Europe, even with some agricultural protection, will offer a better market than a divided and poor Europe to the export products of third countries, including the United States.

The conclusion emerges that the physical facts of Western Europe, its agricultural surplus and its wood and fuel shortages, will prove more influential than economic integration on the evolution of resource utilization in the coming years. However, in the longer run, the successes of integration may give the European Community such improved economic strength that it will be far better equipped to play its role in world affairs, and especially in helping forward the economic growth of the developing countries.

RESOURCE DEVELOPMENT
AMONG AFRICAN COUNTRIES

ARTHUR GAITSKELL

This essay is divided into two parts, Background and Foreground. There are, however, one or two introductory cautions to make as to its limitations. First, Africa has, of course, immense diversity both in natural phenomena and human attitudes. Rather than attempt to catalogue this diversity the paper merely deals with features which seem to apply fairly widely.

Secondly, the essay deliberately concentrates more on the problem of the human conditions of development than on an analysis of what countries have good resources and what countries lack them. The latter con-

---

ARTHUR GAITSKELL, C.M.G., has had wide experience with African affairs, which in recent years has been placed at the service of organizations working toward development of African countries. Since 1955 he has been member of the board of the Commonwealth Development Corporation. He has also been consultant to the UN Special Fund, Sudan; The Ford Foundation, Nigeria; the Mitchell Cotts Company, Ethiopia; the KANU African party, Kenya; and the Food and Agriculture Organization, Tanganyika and Ruanda-Urundi. He was the nominee of the International Bank on the Food and Agriculture Commission of Pakistan, 1959–60, and a lecturer at the Economic Development Institute, Washington, D.C., in 1963. From 1956 to 1959 he was a Research Fellow of Nuffield College, Oxford. Earlier in the fifties Mr. Gaitskell was member of the board, Tanganyika Agricultural Corporation, British member on the Committee of Experts on the Development of Africa, Council of Europe; and member of the East African Royal Commission on Land. From 1923 to 1952 Mr. Gaitskell first served with the Sudan Plantations Syndicate in the Gezira Scheme, and later was chairman and managing director of the Sudan Gezira Board, member of the Executive Council of the Sudan, and chairman of the Council of Khartoum University. Mr. Gaitskell was born in England in 1900 and educated at Winchester College and Oxford University.

271

trasts might be overcome if Africa, like Europe, moves towards closer internal association. The former problem is of particularly vital importance because it forms part of the key question of relationships between the more developed and the less developed parts of the world.

A third limitation is that the essay is mainly based on experience in British Africa although, in the author's opinion, many of the conclusions therefrom have application throughout the continent.

A fourth limitation is that the essay interprets the situation in Africa from a background of European and Western World culture. It speaks of investment, labor, capital, land tenure — all Western World concepts. This is not entirely valueless, because African political leaders place a higher standard of living as one of their major objectives and the Western World still forms the major source of aid and trade for the continent and these are indispensable to that objective. But the essay inevitably is deficient in expression of the viewpoint of Africans themselves. This deficiency is very prevalent in all discussions about Africa which tend to take place in separate compartments, the Africans in their various orbits and the Western World in its various orbits. A forum for more joint exchange of views might do something to reconcile viewpoints and to evoke better machinery to develop resources for the future in Africa. Perhaps the United Nations Economic Commission for Africa will come to develop such a forum. But in the end the future of Africa is going to depend on the desires and will power of Africans themselves.

BACKGROUND

Geography

Geography and history chart our endeavors like the Fates. We cannot escape them. Geographers nowadays include everything in their portfolio. Africa perhaps more than any other continent vindicates them, for there man is dwarfed by the immensity of nature on a scale that still dictates his history. "Miles and miles of just Africa," is a comment often made by travellers who journey there. Generalities usually obscure the truth but in Africa distance and size give them a certain validity. Looked at on the map, the continent itself is huge, a fifth of the world's land surface. Looked at within, the traveller is proved right. This is no land of rapidly changing scene. Climate and geography control on a continental scale and man merely fits in.

The Sahara stretches from the Red Sea to the Atlantic and its fiery dryness dictates a climatic battle fought in the skies over the width of

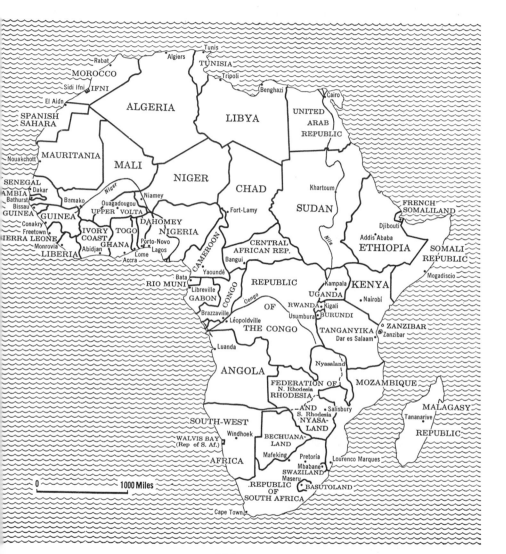

Africa

Africa below it. Southward, the pattern of rainfall gradually and jerkily increases. Grass begins to grow and then trees. But it is a continental pattern imposing bands of similarity from the Ethiopian foothills to Nigeria. Next come the rain forests, fringing the west coast with a deep belt and straddling the center of the continent for hundreds of miles. On the east, to break the picture, rises the high mountain land of Ethiopia with its fantastic scenery of deep gorges, but south of it a huge band of dry low-rainfall country stretches from Somaliland to Uganda. Sweeping around the highlands of Kenya, the dry land extends down through the heart of Tanganyika, giving way only in the interior to the lush climate around the great lakes of the Rift valley which link up with the forests of the Congo. South again of all this primeval scenery, the continental pattern is repeated. Another huge band of thinner bush country runs from the coast in Southern Tanganyika across Northern Rhodesia to the coast in Angola. South Africa itself completes the picture with subtropical Natal on the east but the skeleton coast on the west chilled to desolation by a polar current.

Of course there are exceptions to these generalities, but even the particular in Africa is on a giant scale. The Nile swamps in the Southern Sudan are the size of England. Lake Victoria is the size of Ireland. Mt. Kilimanjaro near the Equator lifts its snowy cap to 19,000 feet from the dry plain in a mass 100 miles wide and the Mountains of the Moon that bastion the Congo rival it. The eastern Rift valley with its occasional steep walls, its tall extinct volcanos, and its wonderland of game makes a cut in the earth's crust 500 miles long. Away in the Southwest the bushy Kalahari desert, where no surface water lies, is 500 miles long and 300 wide, and the Okavango River disappears into it in a delta swamp the size of lower Egypt. Even the well-known rivers, the Nile, the Niger, the Congo, the Zambezi, follow the pattern. They were never highways. Protected by cataracts they were for centuries mysteries emanating from heaven knew where in the unknown.

Africa, in short, with its great deserts, its huge forests, its vast horizons of savannah and miles of bush, its gigantic swamps, its wild animal life, its strange mountains and mighty rivers is the untamed continent par excellence. Hence its past allure for the explorer and, one may expect, its future allure for the tourist and the developer.

History

These descriptions matter because they condition human history in Africa right up to our own times from within and from without, and it is upon that base that any resource development now has to start.

From without, men found it difficult to get in until superior firearms gave them advantage over those within and until the invention of steam and railways enabled them to conquer distance. Only in the late nineteenth century did this combination coincide. It was a time when Western Europe led the world in material power and when its nations fought to extend their rival empires. The rapid carve-up of Africa into colonial appendages of Europe followed, and this so recent predecessor of our times enormously affects the setting of our efforts for development there today.

From within, what could humanity do cut off amid such formidable natural phenomena? On the whole, three activities to keep alive: irrigate with water wheels and flood from the rivers; graze with sheep and goats and cattle backwards and forwards according to the grass as the incidence of rain, water, and the killer tsetse fly permitted; and cultivate, mostly on high land where streams and rain and good soil were in combination, or in the forest belts. The immensity of distances, the huge barriers of mountain, swamp and dry waterless bush, wild beasts, the paucity of the soil compared with much of Europe and America, the irregularity of rainfall, and dangerous diseases like malaria, yellow fever and sleeping sickness, discouraged conquest of empty land, and people remained in general in isolated tribal communities fighting each other for the precarious viable portion they had acquired. Except at trading posts on the coast and inland markets on caravan routes, where one could gain from selling slaves, gold, and ivory, there were no large towns, not very much cohesion into countries.

These conditions also are only a short time behind our era, and for the vast majority they still dictate the needed pattern of developments: irrigation and improved water supplies wherever possible; rationalization of grazing and of cultivation on a stable, more productive basis; conquest of distance by better communications of all kinds, as much as a counter to famine as an outlet to trade and an inlet to new ideas; conquest of disease, for inadequate diet and exposure to sickness in many forms greatly impair human endeavor in Africa, and greatly impair the contribution of livestock to the economy; co-operation instead of fighting. Finally something that the external world wants has to be found in place of slaves, gold, and ivory, something in minerals and in products of the land to exchange for the imports needed for development. Only from this base can the almost universal poverty be raised and Africa begin to develop its own internal purchasing power and then turn to satisfy it with its own industries.

This order, placing priority on primary products and through them developing an internal market, is the logical sequence of this geography and history. Africa as a continent is not overcrowded and its peoples have not as yet the skills that justify giving priority to export industries which have to compete in world markets with lands more materially advanced and much more advantageously placed.[1] Surveys to find the best places for resource development, research to find the best methods, pilot schemes to find the best social forms for using them, and contacts to find markets for the products are priority preludes to any hope of "take-off."

Colonialism

What then happened in the colonial era if all this yet remains to be done? Of course the colonial era broke the isolation of Africa and in it began many of the development needs just listed. But the incidence of its impact has been curiously varied and limited because it fell in an age in world history when colonialism itself began to lose its prestige. As regards economic development by Africans this impact has only been very recent indeed and it would be true to say that colonialism had just begun to turn its attention to this objective as a priority when as an instrument for development it was fading out. This faltering nature of colonialism can be illustrated by three different aspects of it, the Indirect Rule aspect, the European Immigrant aspect and the Independence aspect, each of which has left prominent effects upon our development problems in Africa today.

The Indirect Rule Aspect of Colonialism. Taking the first of these aspects, there are many countries in Africa where European settlement was either unattracted or actively discouraged. In such countries, right up to the outbreak of the Second World War, active planned development was rarely regarded as a desirable thing by colonial governments. This was partly because there was no money and very unattractive prices for primary products, but more so it was a matter of administrative policy. The ideology of colonialism was indirect rule through local tribal chiefs. The preservation of peace was certainly a priority, but so also was the retention of customary ways against any upset by modernity. Many colonial

---

[1] Energy development, particularly water power is likely to be very important in Africa south of the Sahara where little oil has yet been discovered and little coal except in South Africa. Petroleum imports are expensive but, in the continent's present consumer poverty, so also is hydroelectric power. Development of the latter in Africa could be an important field for international and inter-state co-operation, for some countries have no energy resources. At present the high cost of power is discouraging to industry except in locations (e.g., the Copper Belt and European communities) where concentrated offtake is available.

administrators regarded themselves rather like game wardens in a garden of Eden. Such development as occurred was left to expatriate private enterprise and watched with some suspicion as liable to swindle the inhabitants of the garden. European, Levantine, and Asian traders might buy for export the local products, the palm oil, cotton, cocoa, coffee, oil seeds, groundnuts, grain and livestock, and sell in exchange imported manufactured products. Expatriate companies might open mines or estates and employ local people as labor, but the idea that the local people themselves should or could develop their own economy in a rational modern way hardly existed.

Only since the Second World War did colonial administrative policy swing right round to active government encouragement of local development, a change materially encouraged by the large funds accumulated by marketing boards set up to stimulate supplies for the war and by the higher world prices prevailing for colonial products. But hardly has this change come when colonialism itself has come to an end and its executive officials have departed.

In point of fact, the dual system of colonial paternalism and laissez-faire private enterprise had effects which put an end to the Garden of Eden picture of preserving everything as it was, and has by now led in many parts of Africa to rapid deterioration in the use of land, and to some extent in the whole structure of society. This statement needs some technical explanation which must now be considered.

The Priority Agricultural Problem in Cultivation and Pastoral Areas. Before the colonial era, for cultivating tribes, the method of land usage under tribal customs was a bush rotation. The land was held to belong to the ancestors and descendants of the tribe, and families in the current generation simply had the usufruct of a holding according to their subsistence needs. Under the method, a family obtained from their chief the right to cut out a holding from the bush and planted their crops thereon for perhaps three years, by which time the land had lost its fertility. Another holding was then cut out and so on until after ten to twenty years the family returned to the original holding. The family animals merely grazed in the bush with those of their neighbors and were not integrated in any way with the cultivation. The fertility lay in the bush rotation. The system suited a society wanting only subsistence when land was plentiful and when the hazards of disease, tribal raids and the slave trade kept the numbers of people and the stock small.

But after colonialism, with improved security and health, people and stock have gradually multiplied, while, stimulated by trading demands, land has come to be wanted for money crops as well as for subsistence — without, however, any thought-out plan as to how they can best fit in with each other. Under the dual pressure and prevented by the administration from invading their neighbors, many tribes have begun to find their portion of viable Africa uncomfortably overcrowded.

It is important to understand just what this means in the end to the land and to the society. In the first place, the bush rotation can no longer be preserved and land which ought to be lying fallow to regain fertility has to be allocated to someone to use. The yield naturally falls. As the pressure gets more extreme there can be no fallow. The land is then under continuous cultivation which, in sloping country, presents a great erosion hazard. The animals have no bush to graze in and climb the hills, destroying the tree and grass cover and increasing the erosion. In the next stage not only are the yields low but the family holding itself begins to be fragmented, so that after a while a typical holding is no longer in one place but a series of small patches scattered over quite a distance. It ceases to be a manageable farm at all. Finally some families have no land at all in a continent where land is the only security against starvation. It may well be imagined that somewhere before this stage is reached every individual will be desperate to hold his bit of land and may well lose it by litigation.

Two deductions logically fall from this dead-end picture. First, something is needed long before this state of affairs is reached; instead of the custom of bush rotation, some system of farming which retains a unit in one place where a permanently satisfactory rotation can keep up the fertility of the land. The first thought naturally turns to discouraging the habit of turning animals loose in the bush for grazing and instead to using their manure for crops by planting grass in the rotation to feed them. A next stage is to fence in the holding so that, by separation from neighbors' scrubby herds, improved stock can be carried and protected from disease, and an addition to income earned from dairy products. In such a system the cash crop, instead of being a chance appendage to subsistence with no plan to produce it to best yield and quality, would take its place in a rotation or, if a tree crop, as a fixture which could be well looked after near a homestead.

The second deduction is that the owner of such a unit (which technically could be individual or communal if preferred) needs some kind of title, stronger than mere allocation tradition from a chief, which will give him enough sense of security to invest in improvements.

Upon such a stable base can then be applied measures to control erosion, such as contour and tie ridging, with a direct sense of individual benefit. And to such a base can also be supplied as a package deal those factors which have so revolutionized Western World farming, namely, machinery to end hand drudgery, high-quality seed, artificial fertilizer, pest control, credit and marketing facilities.

Something of the same deteriorating nature has also been happening in the great pastoral areas of Africa since the advent of colonialism. Under the colonial shield and with improved veterinary control, herds have increased and the pressure of humans and animals has begun to have the same devastating effect on land as in the cultivation areas. Indeed in many parts of Africa the destructive effect of excess herds in the drier pastoral country has been more dangerous, for the disappearance of grass and tree cover has changed perennial streams to intermittent torrents and turned many a pastoral landscape to desiccation. One may rightly remember the once fertile shores of the Mediterranean and their change into the deserts of today. The risk is increased by the conservative nature of pastoral tribes where, as in the Bible, a man's prestige is reckoned in numbers not in quality of stock and where often a dowry has to be paid in stock.

As with the cultivation areas, something is needed, long before desiccation sets in, which can turn these pastoral lands, no worse than Queensland or Texas, into modern productive units. Rotational grazing, planting of selected grasses, control of stock numbers to the carrying capacity of the land, new water points, marketing facilities, and ultimately fencing, enabling thereby improved breeding, could increase livestock products from many of these areas on a far bigger and better scale than present methods permit. The descent to desert can be arrested and the contribution of these huge regions to national incomes enhanced.

But, both in the cultivation and pastoral areas it is quite clear that merely leaving matters to laissez-faire evolution is useless and dangerous. To introduce stable units for satisfactory future production throughout the whole range of agriculture will require extensive government initiative and investment in a number of fields. Other reasons for its priority importance in development in Africa, which may seem exaggerated here to Western World economists, are discussed later in this paper.

Although the dead-end stage described above has only been reached so far in certain warning examples, the rapidly increasing population and desire for money is leading to the penetration of remaining virgin areas of Africa on the same unplanned traditional system, and after the Second

World War colonial powers in certain places woke up to the seriousness of the situation. In the British sphere the most famous example is that of the Swynnerton Plan in Kenya. The purpose of this plan was to change a deteriorating region (that of the Kikuyu tribe) into individual consolidated holdings with title and to integrate in these stock, subsistence, and cash crops in the manner indicated above so as to give a very considerably enhanced family income in place of universal rural poverty. The cash crops might be tree crops like coffee and tea, or field crops like pyrethrum and pineapples, or merely livestock, dairy products, grain or vegetables, or combinations of these according to location. The essential points lay in registration of title, a sound rotational unit, insistence on high cultural standards through a quadrupled extension service and farm institutes, credit loans, and marketing organization. This scheme has now begun to acquire momentum and has been extended to other parts of Kenya. The demand for consolidation and farm planning has in fact outstripped the resources in staff and money to satisfy it, and undoubtedly this pattern is one of great significance elsewhere in Africa.

Another example in the British sphere of a more particular nature is that of the huge Gezira irrigated area in the Sudan with its standard unit holdings, planned rotation, and package deal services to farmers. This scheme has been the central dynamo of economic development in the Sudan, and this pattern also has features of important application to other regions of Africa.

One of the most advanced examples of planned land usage both in cultivation and pastoral areas is that introduced by the Belgians in the desperately overcrowded mandated territory of Ruanda-Urundi.[2] The *paysannat* (planned peasant family holdings) started in French colonial countries and the native land units in Southern Rhodesia are further examples of the search in colonial times for a new African land use system. With the coming of independence in so many African countries a new emphasis on this paramount problem is increasingly evident, as the need for more foreign exchange, more food, more avenues of employment, and more internal purchasing power became apparent with the responsibility of self-government. But this calls for comment at a later stage.

The European Immigrant Aspect of Colonialism. In other colonial territories the emptiness and nature of the land did attract European immigration, and it was encouraged. The reference here is to countries like Algeria, Tunisia, Kenya, Southern Rhodesia, and South Africa. The ef-

---

[2] Now the independent countries of Rwanda and Burundi.

fect of European immigration on such lands has been varied. One marked effect has been to accentuate the agricultural problem of African land use just described. With a large portion of often the best land devoted to exclusive European ownership, the pressures of population on the restricted African lands have come to the forefront much more prominently; hence, in the British sphere, the initiative shown in Kenya and Southern Rhodesia to deal with it. The worst results in this respect are visible in South Africa where only 13 per cent of the land has been left for 12 million Africans and 87 per cent reserved for 3 million Europeans. As against this, employment opportunities have been increased both on European farms and in the increased economic activity which European immigration stimulated. A benefit of more potential value to Africans has been the discovery by European pioneers of the best way to use land under African conditions, the introduction and breeding of improved stock, and the systematic production of crops like coffee, tea, sisal, tobacco, pyrethrum, citrus, and others with world market value.

There is no doubt at all, also, that while the Europeans were there and had confidence in the future, their development of the land with their own capital, and the impetus to ancillary commercial and industrial activities which their much higher spending power sparked off, raised the African standard of living in many cases above that obtainable in purely African countries. Apologists for South African methods can legitimately claim a higher African standard of living and services than in most of the continent in spite of the manifest injustice which most of the world sees in them.

It is, however, precisely the sense of injustice engendered by the allocation to Europeans of large estates in land adjacent to African "reserves" — where most holdings are by comparison tiny and many have no land at all — and the allied claim to political and social superiority by immigrant Europeans, which has in our age made the position of the latter untenable except by force. It is perhaps this fact more than anything else which differentiates African development in the future from any comparison with places like America and Australia. The age of nations going into other parts of the world with their own capital and "know-how," helping themselves to land and developing their own economy, has ended in Africa. The much more difficult age has begun wherein the Africans themselves, without money and technical knowledge, have to find their own solution to development with what help they can get from outside. Helping Africans to do this is likely to be more costly and difficult than doing it ourselves for our own benefit and using them simply as labor.

Meantime, one added difficulty in countries where European immigration was once the accepted policy but has now faltered — like Algeria, Kenya, and the Central African Federation[3] — is that many of the beneficial economic activities which provided employment and encouraged savings and trade have quite suddenly ceased. In such lands the European sector was the main contributor both to export earnings and taxation. The loss of these direct revenues, and of indirect revenues due to sudden stagnation in European demand, has left these countries in difficult financial circumstances. When flight of capital has been added, the inheritance taken over by Africans looks anything but a windfall.

It remains to be seen whether after the shake-out which has followed the failure of European immigrant groups to establish political control over the countries they settled in, some new acceptance can be found, both on the European and African side, whereby some of the advantages which the local European presence brought to the economy can yet be retained. It remains to be seen, also, whether in those areas of Africa where Europeans are still in control — such as in the Portuguese colonies, Southern Rhodesia and South Africa — force is to be the only solvent or whether here, too, some new acceptance can be found which can preserve the economic benefits the European could bring but give the African the sense of human dignity he seeks. Were such a thing possible, the European immigrant contribution could be a core of significant economic advance. But on present showing this solution looks utterly unlikely and these lands remain the cancer and the Achilles heel of the continent.

The Independence Aspect of Colonialism. The European immigrant problem must, however, be looked at in perspective. There never were more than about 5 million Europeans in a continent of about 150 million (?) Africans. It is undoubtedly with the latter and with their now numerous independent countries that the external world is far more prominently concerned. It is perhaps worth while recollecting one or two points about the achievement of independence from colonialism.

The first point is that no one ever expected this to happen so quickly. Probably except for the Second World War this would not have been the case. The war hastened independence on both sides. On the African side a great many Africans joined the forces and, after seeing the rest of the world, returned as an influence more sophisticated and less content to live under indirect rule and colonial paternalism. The European side was probably more important. Ever since World War I colonies had become

---

[3] Northern Rhodesia, Southern Rhodesia, and Nyasaland.

thought of less and less as imperial possessions and more as mandates with the ultimate objective of self-rule. The Second World War took the word "ultimate" from European minds. In a desperate fight against a recrudescence of imperial pretensions by Germany, Italy, and Japan, and with a slogan broadcast every day that the purpose of the allies was liberty and democracy, a denial of this purpose to the very people called upon to help in the cause seemed, at any rate in British spheres of influence, an impossible inconsistency. In United States spheres of influence, where colonies were anyway anathema, the case for independence was even stronger. India's case was early granted and gave an immediate precedent to the small educated class in Africa to press their claims. In such an atmosphere these fell in Britain on sympathetic ears and, although even then a more protracted period was contemplated to admit more time for experience, there was no desire to compel such a period by a use of force which would have forfeited the co-operation essential to make such a period fruitful. A galloping finish to the independence front then became contagious.

Certain results followed from this situation. As may be imagined from the earlier part of this essay, the number of educated people in Africa, by great contrast with India, was remarkably few. The great bulk of Africans while ready enough to back what was obviously going to be the winning horse, had hardly changed their lives from the days of native law and custom, indirect rule, and European paternalism. Neither they nor even the educated were really in a position suddenly to take over the development of a modern economy. Yet this in fact is what has happened to them. Even the educated had been given, and indeed claimed, only the arts kind of education of the superior administrative class in colonialism. That great bulk of scientific, technical, and craftsman class whose skills support our modern society is thus absolutely missing in these countries. Missing also is that other great pillar of our life, the manager and operator in commerce for, as related above, almost all commercial life in the age of colonialism was in expatriate hands.

Two other points of importance must be recollected. The first of these is that, with the stage of development described, for most people the standard of living in terms of money is extremely low. It follows that savings hardly exist and that African independent governments are likely to be very poor.

The second point is that there has not been much time in this race for independence for these countries to establish a sense of national cohesion. As countries they were simply lines drawn on a map by competing colonial powers. Often the lines cut right through tribal boundaries. Within the lines during indirect rule, tribe has lived isolated from tribe and pastoralist from cultivator. Only in the latest years have political parties and the elements of local and national parliamentary government brought them together. Nationalist leaders have shown no desire at all to alter the artificial boundaries which history has bequeathed to them. But the withdrawal of the colonial power does lay bare risks of dissension unless some cohesive force keeps the differing elements together.

As against these handicaps from which Africa suffers as a late starter in development, the continent has one great advantage for this very reason over continents like Asia and South America or indeed the poorer surrounds of the Mediterranean. No rich African class has yet collared most of the land or made a monopoly of industrial life or education. Those vested interests which so hamper or distort development in many other parts of the world have not yet arisen. African political leaders, with access nowadays to all the world's experience, may well tread warily to avoid losing this advantage.

FOREGROUND

From the above assessment of the background which Africa has inherited, one must turn to the foreground and hazard some opinions as to the future possibilities of development in the continent. It will already be clear that economic development cannot usefully be thought about in a separate compartment. All the time political and social problems get entwined with economics. It is proposed, therefore, to consider the matter here in the form of two main questions: first, "What is the African attitude to development?" and second, "Can the Western World fit in with this attitude?"

African Attitudes to Development

It is obviously risky to speculate about other people's opinions but from general circumstances the following five main objectives seem likely to be prominent in the minds of African political leaders.
1. Running one's own show.
2. Raising the standard of living in income, education, and health.
3. Establishing a fair society.
4. Carrying the people with the government, so that the sense of enthusiasm generated by independence can continue as a participating force in development.

5. Remaining "neutral" as far as external forces, and particularly the cold war, are concerned.

One outstanding characteristic about these objectives, which will confront both the external world and Africa, is that although they may be reasonable in the long run, in the short run it will not be easy to keep them all going together in harmony as they tend in present circumstances to conflict with each other. This fact may well explain many of those apparent changes of policy in African independent countries which cause uncertainty and discourage foreign aid and investment.

Running One's Own Show. It is quite clear that this is the essence of nationalism and that until political independence has been achieved no one can get ahead harmoniously with economic development. But even after independence one of the strongest emotions confronting us is the desire of African leaders to be in control of their own show economically. This does not mean that they are not perfectly able to appreciate that all nations today are economically interdependent. The cry "Neo-Colonialism," which is apt to puzzle and annoy when political independence has already been granted, reflects a very real feeling of continuing resentment at the sense of still being subordinate in much of the profitable production and trade of one's own country. The resentment may be directed against the continuing commercial permeation of the old colonial power or against a repetition of subordination to new expatriate business investment. Both suggest exploitation in the interests of foreigners rather than nation-building by controlling one's own economic destiny, and it seems probable that there will be no real contentment psychologically until the degree of local and national economic enterprise reaches the stage when nobody really minds whether a business is foreign-owned or not.

Raising the Standard of Living. This objective, which is likely to come to the top very quickly after independence, brings up the first example of potential conflict with the objective of running one's own show. As stated before, African countries are poor, many of them have exhausted government reserves in trying to expand their basic needs in education and communications and find a great difficulty now in balancing their expanded budgets. Some, to emphasize for their people the reality of independence, have spent resources on prestige investments which give no income return. Local capital is totally insufficient to provide the large sums needed nor is there mechanism for mobilizing private investment. Moreover, the prices of primary export products, on which such countries depend for revenue, have fallen to levels which make revenue collection by export taxes and marketing board surpluses liable to deter farmers' incentives to improve production just when the main need is to stimulate them.

All this adds up to the fact that however much these countries want to run their own show economically, they cannot raise their standard of living without the help of foreign capital. On top of this, in their present stage of development, they often need both foreign "know-how" in the techniques of business and foreign links to introduce them to markets. Finally, as with the rest of us, these markets are other people's markets and dependent on other people's demands. Whatever aid one may get or give for development, the ultimate answer depends on foreign trade. A compromise has therefore to be made in order to get the help of some external interested party, and the problem is how far one can get this without sacrificing too much of one's primary objective of running one's own show.

The problem is all the harder in countries with European immigrants. Here the antipathy to foreign control is concentrated on the European community which forms a double target as the opponent of political independence and the acquirer of much of the country's land. Yet in such countries it is the European sector which is at present the main contributor to revenue and employment. If some of this could be held until African participation in the economy has been built up, it would be invaluable for raising the standard of living, while its sudden elimination would be certain to depress it. In these cases the African nationalist has not only to persuade his constituents that the main focus of their antipathy could be a useful ally but to persuade the Europeans that they have a worthwhile future as a minority under an African government. The degree of compromise to attain is far harder than that of expatriate aid and investment, because for the European the desire to control politically has to be given up, land appropriations connected with this have to be surrendered, and life under an African government rather than a European way of life in Africa has to be considered as a permanent personal decision.

Whatever the outcome of the European immigrant problem, it must be confessed at the moment that its main significance is the damaging effect it has of drawing African and European apart just when new ties to help economic development are needed between Africa and the external world in the aftermath of colonialism. But whether the European immigrant plays a part or not, the main question is how Africans themselves can best start to raise their standard of living. As with other developing regions, the first inclination among African leaders has been to start up industry. This is partly a reaction to a suspicion that colonialism deliberately neglected industry in order to secure primary products for its own industries. It is also for the obvious reason that countries with the highest energy per capita appear to be the richest in the world. Nevertheless, there are signs in many African countries that, without this objective being discarded, the priority need to develop agriculture is being increasingly appreciated, as it is in other developing regions of the world.

The reasons for this switch of attention to making agriculture the spearhead are varied and often urgent. Some of them have already been given in the Background part of this essay. Some countries have no basis anyway in discovered minerals or oil, and these have usually been the spearhead of industry. But, even where they have, the investment cost per person employed is high so that precious government capital (and in Africa there is little else yet locally) goes a very little way. Some of the investments made in the enthusiasm for industry, with ample encouragement from external agencies wanting to sell their machinery, have not been profitable from lack of experienced management or skilled labor, or from lack of cost and market surveys. Apart from these reasons which have led to a pause for thought, the employment ratio in modern industry is low. At best it can cater for tens of thousands, but with increasing population pressure the problem of employment and standards of living covers hundreds of thousands. In most of Africa 85 per cent of the population is rural and at a very low subsistence level. Unless their purchasing power is raised there will be no internal market anyway for industrial products. In many African countries this general situation is made more urgent by increasing underemployment on land and by the continual stream of young school-leavers who, seeing nothing but low incomes and stagnation in rural areas, flood the towns in search of nonexistent jobs and form a dangerous focus of delinquency and discontent.

Although generalization in such a subject must be qualified in degree according to the circumstances of each country, the picture of future development tending to appear is one of agriculture and industry moving forward complementary to each other, industry being stimulated to supply the services needed by improved agriculture and the consumer goods for increased incomes derived from the rural areas, and agriculture being stimulated to supply many of the raw materials for industry and the food for those not engaged in growing their own. An additional stimulus to this pattern of using local products for local needs comes from the desire to save foreign exchange for essential imports to build up the development. This concept may be too cozy to work out as nicely as it sounds, but there seems little doubt that, economically speaking, a search for this kind of pattern for raising the standard of living will largely confront us. To help it to work out nicely three main features would seem important: the carrying through of an agrarian revolution of the nature referred to above under the heading "The Priority Agricultural Problem"; satisfactory trade outlets for export products which are the fundamental basis of improved rural and general incomes; and rational selection and competent administration of the requisite industries.

Establishing a Fair Society. A desire and respect for equality seems to have a greater appeal today than that for individual liberty. This is sometimes evident in our own society; in developing countries it is conspicuous in their relationship to the external world. Colonialism implied inequality politically, socially, and economically, and a determination to correct this is at the base of most of their attitudes and policy. But internally, also, a desire for development to end in a fair society is very prevalent. In Africa it is partly rooted in tradition, as can be seen in the customary allocation of land according to need. Large European estates, as noted before, are apt to appear conspicuously unfair and the same sense of inequality underlies the criticism of expatriate monopoly of trade and industry, whatever debt is owed to expatriates for starting Africans on the development road at all. Apart from this, the dangers of inequality in development are very evident in many parts of the world and put African leaders on their guard as to how best to change from traditional to modern methods. These dangers are felt to be especially relevant in land acquisition when, as in Africa, land offers the only form of social security.

Something of this feeling underlies the aversion not merely to foreign-owned plantations but even to nationally owned ones, for a system of management and workers, leaving the rest of the rural areas in stagnation, is felt to be less valuable, socially, than the upgrading of a peasant proprietor community throughout the countryside. Mention has already been made of standard family units in Kenya, the Sudan, and Ruanda-Urundi, and of the French *paysannets* pioneered under colonialism. Independent Nigeria is now particularly anxious to promote smallholders specializing in cash crops like palm oil, rubber, cocoa, and citrus, which can bring them reasonable incomes on top of subsistence. A particularly popular feature of all these smallholder schemes is the organization through a co-operative framework of supply of services, processing, and marketing, and it is quite clear that the co-operative is thought of both for the sense of equality which it brings and as the major method in which Africans can get control of their own economy. One of the most conspicuous examples of this attitude to co-operatives is their extent in the production, processing, and marketing of coffee and cotton in Tanganyika. A most important reservation should, however, be made here. For these schemes to be a success in an extremely competitive world market, high yields, high quality, and competent business management are recognized to be quite essential. Israeli experience in this field is widely sought after in Africa as a successful example of many African aspirations.

It is possibly this desire to plan for a fair society within a nation-building objective which makes socialism in varying degrees so obviously popular in Africa. Even in colonialism the State was the initiator of all infrastructure, and the first steps towards African economic development were taken through the funds of State marketing boards. In independence, the State provides the composite solution of a national protection against foreign economic control, a national arbiter between citizens against excessive acquisitiveness, and an instrument to administer undertakings when no individual group of citizens can yet do so. Co-operatives provide the ultimate alternative to the State, but their success depends initially on a great deal of State initiative and indeed direction. African attitudes to socialism, however, seem less matters of ideology than of practical solutions to their experience and objectives; and the pattern which seems to be emerging is one of State responsibility for all infrastructure and major land development schemes, State ownership of essential defensive industries, encouragement of private share capital in other industries if available but State participation in the meantime, and encouragement of co-operatives. In terms of practical solutions to objectives, the offer from the Communist world of loans at low rates of interest to install for the State modern tanneries, canneries, sugar factories, grain and milk processing plants, or any industry which directly improves the value of local products, and to allow the cost to be repaid in cotton, coffee, or any major export crop which is difficult to sell, has obvious attractions. This need not necessarily mean an intention to adopt any ideology; and if State management proves inefficient, transfer to private enterprise or to co-operatives, when available, is by no means excluded.

Nevertheless, the principle of equality does raise some difficult questions for some African leaders. Should one encourage the enterprising but acquisitive type in agriculture and industry or should one spread the opening wider in the interests of settling more landless people? Is there not a risk of too much equality resulting in universal poverty with no purchasing power and no capital savings? Where does one set the compromise? For without concentrating on the most productive use of resources the road to a higher standard of living will be longer. The problem arises again in the choices of what and where to develop first when everyone and every place is claiming an equal chance in developments. To satisfy equality, should one continue universal primary education without regard to the country's employment potential, or should one cut down the primary so as to give a smaller cadre the greater secondary and technical education which can improve that potential instead of leaving it to foreigners? And as between the regions, should one concentrate on spearhead productive zones which can give bigger results quicker, or diffuse development everywhere in the interests of equality?

Carrying the People with the Government. It is not at all easy to answer such questions and the answer may vary with the importance the speaker attaches to one rather than the other of these objectives. African leaders must find it extremely difficult not only to know what they think is the best answer but to what extent their followers will support them in their choices. As far as external aid and investment are concerned, this support is clearly quite vital, because without it one takes a much bigger risk on stability. As far as the African government is concerned, it is usually their main problem.

Potential opposition is very likely to arise after independence owing to misconceptions about the need to compromise if the objectives referred to above under the heading "African Attitudes to Development" are to be attained. Many will expect that independence ought to mean no more expatriate officials, and this belief will be encouraged by pressure to provide jobs for locals whether they are competent or not. Many will certainly expect a reduction, if not complete deletion, of European landed estates where these exist, and of European and Asian control of basic industry and commerce. Many will have been told for political reasons not to obey the technical instructions of expatriate agricultural officers, and it may be difficult after independence to reverse this attitude and impress upon rural people that, without compliance with such instructions, the country has no hope of the high yields and qualities which it vitally needs in a competitive world for the basic priority of all its development. Many will demand equality of opportunity, and all will expect an automatic rise in the standard of living with little conception of how these aspirations conflict with each other. The sophisticated may disagree about the degree of State control or private initiative or liberty that ought to be encouraged, and those of them who fail to get positions of authority or creative employment may challenge those who have done so. The unsophisticated may fear that their tribal or regional independence is threatened by those tribes or races or parties which gain control of the central government.

The history of Tanganyika since independence, which gave a shock to external confidence in what was thought to be a reasonable African government, is a conspicuous example of these difficulties, but they can equally be seen in Ghana, the Congo, Nigeria, Uganda, Kenya, and the Sudan, and are probably universal. They do underline the immense importance to the government of a developing country of having an adequate system of conveying to the people the objectives and compromises of government policy. They probably also explain why so often other alternatives are chosen, such as rule by one party with a dominant leader, suppression of press freedom, intolerance of any opposition and, finally, take-over bids by army officers.

Equally important to the government of a developing country is an adequate system of external public relations, for the external world whose help is needed is apt to be put off by the conflicting statements on policy attributed to individual ministers.

These twin difficulties of carrying one's own people and at the same time the external world as allies in development, reveal the absolute need for a definite national policy which puts an end to fears of a continuing colonial image internally but offers sufficient basis for co-operation with essential external capital and "know-how." It is perhaps in the evaluation and understanding of this policy that the core of the problem of co-operation between developing and developed countries lies.

Neutrality. Without such a firm national policy, from the moment of independence if not before, a developing country enters the jungle of conflicting ideologies unarmed. A great deal of Western World aid has of course been motivated by defense against Communism, and Communist aid has ideological objectives the other way. It would appear, however, that most developing countries in Africa want to make their own choice of what they think suits their circumstances and for this purpose to have a look at the Communist World as much as the Western World. This does not necessarily mean that they prefer the Communist ideology. What they are looking for is some pragmatic answer to their own particular and urgent circumstances.

It would seem important for us to understand the desire for neutrality,

and linking aid to the fight against Communism misses out in such understanding. So to some extent does excessive anxiety about democracy
which, however desirable, is not easy to work with perfection in Africa,
or about private enterprise which to many Africans has dangers and connotations of expatriate exploitation. For the governments of developing
countries in Africa, the real subversion risk lies in the coming generation
in their own countries if conditions continue to lead to frustration from
landlessness, unemployment, low incomes and no rise in the standard of
living, from corruption and dissension, from the lack of a solution to the
school-leaver problem, and from continuation of the image of colonialism. It is upon these frustrations that Communist infiltration thrives. To
avert failure and collapse of hopes may be far more important than to ask
for or to spread anti-Communist fervor. If this is true for us in the
Western World we must consider urgently whether we can fit in, and
want to fit in, with these main objectives in African leaders' minds.

Can the Western World Fit In with African Objectives?

Characteristics of Previous Economic Development. Before independence, expatriate private enterprise mainly concentrated on investment in
what seemed the easiest profitable openings, and these fall into three categories. One category has been investment by and to meet the needs of the
European minority. These, where they existed, had the large land holdings, their own capital and "know-how," and the purchasing power. It
was natural that their demands and accustomance to business methods
should make a spearhead for private enterprise investment to utilize. A
second main category for investment has been in extractive enterprise
for export, whether in minerals or in plantation crops like tea and sisal.
The third main category has been in the import and export trade and all
the ancillary services associated with it. This category has, of course,
been concerned with the profitable supply and purchase of African needs
and products as well as European.

While private enterprise went for these opportunities, the economic
infrastructure has usually been the responsibility of the colonial government and so has the development of any African participation in economic life apart from those who formed the working class of expatriate
private enterprise. Home governments have contributed since the war to
infrastructure costs, but on the whole these countries have had to meet
most of them from their own meagre resources, so the amount of infrastructure developed has been very limited, except where a large European element has provided both a stimulus and a contribution. In par-

ticular in communications it has been mainly directed to export outlets to the home country rather than between African countries themselves.

Implications of the New Situation. The most obvious characteristic of the situation after independence is that the categories of investment which expatriate private enterprise has so far favored are likely to be just those most exposed to latent hostility. However much, in their own search for profit, they may have contributed the major part of scarce revenues and introduced Africans to external trade, they are bound to appear to Africans as one of the main impediments to the concept of running's one's own show.

A second obvious characteristic is that the amount of money hitherto available for infrastructure will seem to Africans totally insufficient to modernize their countries at a pace which they feel appropriate to their needs. Moreover, after independence they can get better access to international and bilateral funds and personnel, although at the same time they may lose some of the advantages in this respect which they used to get from the colonial power.

In sum, therefore, the new situation implies for us, if we are going to fit in with it, the consideration of two major objectives: first, deliberately helping Africans to participate in and control their own economy instead of just picking individual plums for expatriate private enterprise investment; and, secondly, contributing much more than before towards infrastructure. We may feel at times that Africans expect much too much too quickly. We may feel that they give insufficient regard to the benefits and concentrate only on the inequality of the colonial era. We may feel inclined to leave them to it and let them see what they can get from others. But, if we are going to fit in, it does raise the major question of whether our economic theories and practices can be adjusted to meet the above situation, and to what extent African policies can be adjusted to meet our ways.

The Infrastructure Problem. Some people dislike the word "infrastructure," but it is difficult to find an equally short substitute to express all that basic element in development without which it is not easy for a country to stand on its own feet and without which public and private enterprise is much more difficult to get going. Infrastructure is considered here in two respects, that concerned with education and that concerned with physical works, the former being important in the new context of a country standing on its own feet and controlling its own destinies, the latter being essential to any destiny worth controlling.

Education. There is, of course, a tremendous demand for formal education, and this is needed to provide enough well-educated people and enough universal literacy; but many developing countries, having made a considerable start with formal education, are now worried about how to get the product creatively employed. Formal education, understandably in the circumstances, tends to suggest a brief-case job in the towns. Higher education for leadership in all aspects of national life is, of course, essential, but a balance is necessary to avoid creating a big gap between the leaders and the bulk of the people, such as has happened in the Middle East and Latin America. What is needed is much more supplementary education for development. A drastic shortage of trained manpower faces industry, where training at all levels from bottom to management, in craftsmanship, machine management, accounts, sales and finance, is a prime necessity. Very, very few trade schools yet exist and the absence of an experienced commercial and industrial cadre tends to make industry expensive and potential investors look elsewhere. The priority subject of agriculture is even more important. Agricultural and veterinary colleges, farm institutes, extension training centers, research establishments, and specialist institutions for teaching co-operative and community development personnel are all needed if a drive for better land usage is to succeed, and the rural areas where most people live are really to get a sense of participating in progress.

There is a parallel need for education in medicine and in the art of administering the government services efficiently. In many cases a small start has been made under the colonial regime, but with the departure of many expatriate teachers a very big gap is apt to be left. This is all the more difficult to fill because the bias in future needs to be in the training of scientific and technical skills for which teachers are already short in the Western World itself. Nevertheless, unless help can be given from experienced countries other aid and investment is exposed to much bigger risk, for the developing country has then either to rely on expatriate personnel, which is expensive and tends to perpetuate the colonial image, or will have to use untrained personnel, which is liable to lead to gross inefficiency.

The supplying of teachers for all aspects of development has the advantage that it is less exposed to hostility than many expatriate activities, because the personnel involved are not staying but are positively putting successors in a position to replace expatriates. One gets the impression in Africa that there is considerable resistance to advice and that the position of an "adviser," even on such an important matter as the formation of a national plan, is a very delicate one, but a man who can serve in the bureaucracy and transmit some new knowledge or skill appropriate to African needs and then go back to his home country is a very welcome ally. Contacts of this kind, and parallel secondment to our own universities and institutions for those experienced enough to benefit from it, do encourage potential new life-lines which may contribute on both sides to a new sense of international civilization in place of colonial paternalism.

Physical Infrastructure. Communications of all kinds, harbors and port facilities, railways, main roads, and minor roads have usually been and still are the first bottleneck of development. There are basic needs like watershed control to stop desiccation, management of river systems for irrigation and power, planned water development for resettlement, ecological, soil, and mineral surveys (the latter particularly sought by outside private enterprise), and research to discover the best land use pattern for both cultivation and pasture. There are later other needs: pilot schemes to test new methods in association with the people, extension services to persuade them to change to new patterns, and an efficient organization for supplying better seeds, stock, fertilizers, pesticides, processing and marketing facilities, and credit.

With the departure of the colonial power there is a serious risk that the beginnings made in tackling many of the infrastructure needs may falter when the immediate need is to extend these activities much more widely and thoroughly. One of the important problems is that a great deal of this infrastructure work is not applicable to bankers' loan terms. It was largely grant-aided in colonial days. It needs more grant-aid or, alternatively, undated low-interest-loan aid, on a much bigger scale today. And investment in this infrastructure is quite essential if the level of African incomes is to reach the point where private enterprise investment can usefully be expanded as an ally to the public sector.

The Private Enterprise Investment Problem. If the situation outlined as confronting us is generally true, fitting into it would seem to imply two main policy changes in the attitude of expatriate private investment. One involves a deliberate switch from relying chiefly on European to relying chiefly on African purchasing power and therefore deliberately encouraging development of the latter. The other involves acceptance of the fact that concentration on extractive and plantation industries is liable to be a major target for national antagonism, as also will be any monopoly of import/export trade and its ancillary services.

Recognition of these probabilities faces the private enterprise operator with a difficult choice of alternative. Should he defend his existing interests as citadels and wait for the worst? Should he gradually liquidate his interests and switch his investment to safer more profitable countries? Or can he achieve a new, mutually profitable arrangement with the new Africa?

Something of the same choice, however, also faces Africans. Should they take the attitude that government ought to undertake everything itself and that foreign private enterprise can never mean anything but exploitation? Or should they believe that foreign private enterprise could be a dynamic ally in raising the standard of living, providing scarce capital, continuing access to improvements in "know-how," and easier contacts with markets? But if they took the latter view, how could they control foreign private enterprise and how gradually build up their own private and public enterprise until these are so dominant in the economy that dislike of foreign investment disappears?

Searches for a Mutual Objective in Economic Development. In this situation, a number of examples are evident in many parts of the world which illustrate how expatriate private and public enterprise is trying to adjust itself to fit in with local objectives and where local governments are trying to modify their approach in order to get the benefit of external help.

Joint Capital Structures. One of the commonest examples is the joint capital structure system. This may take the form of arranging for part of the capital to be subscribed by the local government, or local development corporation, with the idea of giving local people a feeling that it is as much their show as that of outsiders. One of the great problems in these examples is that of management control. Expatriate capital is reluctant to concede majority holding for fear that decisions may be forced on them which are not businesslike. On their side, the locals often fear that if they concede majority control the expatriate partner will concentrate entirely on profit to the complete exclusion of social and political objectives. Being very sensitive to equality, they also fear that they may be treated in an offhand manner as if explanation of the accounts and working of the undertaking were too difficult for them to fathom.

There is clearly no uniform solution to these problems in an atmosphere so dependent on psychology, but two points seem valid. The first is that no one gains anything from an undertaking which is commercially a failure, a point increasingly realized as capital gets shorter and managerial ability more appreciated. The second is that remoteness on either side is likely to be worse in breeding suspicion than genuine close contact in encouraging dissension.

Another difficulty about the joint capital structure is that often the locality cannot find the money to put up its share of the capital. One of the most remarkable instances of overcoming this difficulty was that of the Williamson diamond mine in Tanganyika. In this case the Anglo-American corporation not merely agreed to a 50:50 capital structure with the government, management being conceded to the corporation, but actually loaned to the government the capital to subscribe its share and repay out of its subsequent profit. It may not be easy to imitate this example, but rather than start enterprises all over again entirely with foreign capital it would seem worth considering whether organizations like the International Bank could not specialize more in loaning their local capital subscription to local governments, particularly if the enterprise is in partnership with some firm which has business ability and market contacts. Expatriate development corporations, like the British Commonwealth Development Corporation, operate as policy tripartite capital structures with local governments and professional partners. This type of instrument can be helpful because when the business gets established successfully the Corporation's capital stake can be sold to the locality and the money turned over for investment elsewhere.

Another form of local capital participation is that of share subscriptions offered not merely to the local government but to local private subscribers. People are too poor in most developing countries for much money to be raised at first in this way, but where it can be done it often gives a much closer sense of association than does government subscription. Sometimes more local private capital is available than is generally believed, as was demonstrated in Latin America by the remarkable initiative of the Kaiser Company in deliberately offering shares for sale by touring the rural market towns. The same company now makes a principle of accepting only minority shareholding itself in undertakings which it stimulates in developing countries. There is at a certain point in development, in this respect, a great need to develop machinery for a local capital market. The formation of local industrial and commercial banks, staffed at first with competent expatriate professionals and with proper market survey facilities, can be of great assistance to encouraging investment of private savings, as they arise, into productive industry. The promotion of local private enterprise by such institutions, in co-operation with expatriate private enterprise capital and "know-how," reduces the dependence on the public sector and naturally swells the available funds for development.

An outstanding example of an expatriate company encouraging local industrial development is that of the Sears Roebuck Company in Mexico. Handicapped by shortage of foreign exchange from importing from traditional sources the goods needed for its stores, this company practiced import substitution and encouraged the promotion of local industries to meet its needs from local products. As and when pension funds begin to emerge, the creation of local building societies is another useful instrument for diversion of local savings into badly needed housing improvements, while undoubtedly lotteries are not to be despised as one way, outside taxation, of getting the public to contribute to social expenditure.

It is not so easy to see how expatriate capital and knowledge can be applied to agriculture as to industry, yet industrial development itself is going to be dependent on flourishing agriculture. Expatriate capital can finance major works like dams, and expatriate contracting firms can construct them and can carry out ecological and soil surveys, but the real problem is getting the land use improved. This is obviously a matter for the government, and one of the biggest needs is to get personnel to regard service in rural areas as a prestige occupation instead of the last choice as it commonly is now. This implies a priority investment of government monies in better pay and conditions and much more staff as a basic infrastructure there.

There is, however, one aspect in which expatriate capital can help. That is in the creation of nucleus plantations having as their objective the sparking off of efficient smallholder cash crop producers. The nucleus plantation in such a concept forms a focus of commercially managed business, a training ground for both peasant settlers and extension staff supervisors, and a processing center. Projects of this kind are already being run in different parts of the world for crops like sugar, palm oil, rubber, and tea, where the whole success depends on introduction of the best stock and the best methods of production. The antipathy to foreign plantations could undoubtedly be reduced if they could be viewed as valuable allies, in this respect, to local producers' co-operatives. It is no less possible that if European farmers — through their co-operatives (as some are in Kenya), and by interesting themselves in competent African settlement in some of their lands — could further this aim, they might begin to break down the greatest of all antipathies — that against a caucus of European resident settlers.

Africanization. Of all the tendencies which confront expatriates probably nothing is so strong as the desire for Africanization. This is partly due to local pressure for profitable jobs, but it is also very much a reflection of the emotion for equality in place of colonial inferiority and a demonstration that one is master in one's own land. Many expatriate firms have long since had programs for training local men for positions of responsibility, but some have been slow to do this, and in some countries frustration and political pressure on this issue have led to government legislation laying down that certain percentages of the payroll and upper posts must be in local hands and refusing immigration and residential permits to expatriate personnel. This is the worst of all solutions because it bears no relation to the competence of local candidates and risks the efficiency of development. Nevertheless, this is likely to be the solution adopted unless genuine practical programs are put into action by expatriate concerns, not on the standard method of working up slowly from the bottom of the ladder, but with much more of the deliberate emergency initiative which we ourselves applied to training within industry during the war. There seems little doubt that this is the kind of problem where risks will have to be taken on the ground that a good continuing relationship of "fitting in" may be more important than obtaining the last cent in efficiency.

The whole problem of Africanization following independence applies, of course, to an even greater extent to the government services and thereby reacts on the environment for aid and investment. In this respect the educational infrastructure previously referred to is exceedingly important to the satisfactory follow-up of external help, for at the start a tremendous burden is carried by the few trained men. But in many countries the fears of the colonial powers that the local people as yet were unfit to manage have proved excessively conservative. Without a doubt, responsibility has evoked capacities and people which were not thought to exist. Additionally, local capacities have often been measured by some imaginary yardstick of honesty and efficiency instead of being compared with current conditions in most other countries in the world, not excluding our own. If this yardstick is dropped and genuine training plans are widely used, it will be all the easier for African politicians to resist their relations and party supporters.

Time Limits. If it really is their economic development which is the objective, the question arises as to how long foreign capital and management is necessary. This may seem a revolutionary question to those who invested in some mine or plantation and imagined it would be for ever. Nevertheless it is a question which has to be faced. Association with foreign capital and management would seem far more tolerable, if not positively welcomed, if some kind of time limit could be envisaged when the undertaking would be in local hands. This is particularly true of major assets which dominate a country's revenues. The alternative has so often ended in nationalization.

If the Western World is going to fit in with developing countries' aims it is essential to ask ourselves whether there is any need for permanency. There must be instances on innumerable occasions in our own business life when an enterprise has been transferred from one collection of shareholders to another. It is usually a matter of trying to arrange fair terms, and after the deal the departing capital is employed in other directions. It is not impossible for such terms to be thought out in advance and, with the help of accountants and estimates, for the terms of transfer of assets to be laid down. It is not impossible to forecast the period needed to get a reasonable return on money invested and repayment of the capital. Nor is the risk of being wrong in such forecasts so obviously greater than the risk of nationalization and the risk of insecurity of government when issues like this are left uncertain. It would seem well worth investigation both in new and existing expatriate enterprises just how important permanence is. A deliberate program for termination over a period would avoid also the fall-off in efficiency which has so often resulted when an undertaking has been summarily nationalized. Apart from major undertakings which may merit such an arrangement with the local government, an alternative method would be to convert the initial foreign capital to local capital by selling shares to the local public over a period and to reinvest the monies paid in other enterprises in the country.

Transfer of Investment Interests. Parallel with the problem of termination there arises the question of whether expatriate concerns, which have in the past established extensive interests in the export and import trade, should deliberately get out of some lines of business and take steps to put local people into these lines instead. This is not a matter which can usefully be left to abdication on one side and clamor without knowledge of business on the other. To take an example, if an expatriate firm is importing motor cars and getting a trade discount therefrom from sales to African clients, the latter are apt to think that nothing more is involved than owning a shop and drawing the profit. It is not long before political pressure is exercised to license such activities to locals only. Sometimes it is only when that point has been reached that it is realized that to supply this service properly to the community requires a large amount of capital in spares, a competent storekeeping system, and an efficient maintenance section, and none of the locals have these requisites. The illustration is applicable to many other expatriate activities. To avoid this ultimately futile position expatriate firms might consider selecting local men and assisting them with capital and "know-how" until they can ultimately run such an agency effectively as their own business. If such a firm then uses the capital repaid for investment in other needs in the local country its acceptability is obviously enhanced. Of course this is not a new idea. There are firms which have long since decentralized processing plants and retail agencies to local people and helped them to succeed in the business, but a much more extensive application of this principle may help to reduce the antipathy and misconception about foreign trade monopolies.

The Quid pro Quo Position. If economic development could be approached anew with much more combined effort to contribute to infrastructure and with consideration given to a mutual "fitting in," as illustrated by some of the examples above, it might not only give a better follow-up to such international and bilateral aid as is now put into Africa but might also enable, in return, a better quid pro quo for the security of investments there. The sort of points needed are:

1. Agreement to the employment on adequate terms of expatriate personnel indispensable to efficiency.
2. Agreement to the regular transfer of dividend earnings and capital on termination.
3. A fair and equitable attitude to nationalization.
4. A businesslike attitude to Africanization, so that it is directed to real competence.

Theoretical investment charters have usually been drawn up by the lenders without much thought of change in their current habits. The reasonableness of African governments to see our viewpoints will depend on our vision of their objectives and our capacity to fit in with them. As at present most of the economic tools, except labor, are in expatriate hands, this task involves a real effort to build up a new balance in economic power in their favor, and a belief that our long-term interest lies in increasing their purchasing power and their control of their own economy.

Foreign Trade. This essay makes no attempt to deal with this intractable subject, which is dealt with elsewhere in this book. It would be difficult, however, to exaggerate its importance. Practically every African country is dependent on the overseas sale of some major product and a few minor products for any hope of improving its internal purchasing power, starting industrialization, or extending on its side any counterpart infrastructure for development.

So far in Africa only a few regions like Katanga, Rhodesia, South Africa, Liberia, and Mauretania have discovered minerals as a major prime mover for development. The rest, as has been very much emphasized in this essay, will be largely dependent in any hope to raise living standards on an expanding market for agricultural products. As much of Asia and Latin America appear to be faced with the same prospect, the discovery of sufficient market offtake at reasonably remunerative prices is rapidly becoming the most urgent and intractable of world problems. Rock bottom prices are no spur to development, and aid to be effective must be accompanied by trade. Unfortunately there seems at the moment to be little prospect of expanding the market in the Western World where agricultural protection, synthetic substitutes, and quotas and tariffs tend to restrict demand. The alternative of trading with Communist countries is thus attractive if not imperative to many developing countries, but is also not necessarily reliable.

These circumstances naturally incline developing countries to use as much as they can of their own materials to satisfy their own needs rather than import them from outside, so that some degree of internal industrial processing and a policy of import substitution may mitigate the foreign exchange problem. But this degree is limited by the purchasing power of the internal market which in turn largely derives from the sale of export agricultural commodities.

It may be that in time the rapid increase in world population may iron out the present time-lag in demand, and that this may be made easier by concentration in this period on investment in infrastructure and in all the preparation for efficient production rather than on increasing production itself, so that over-supply is avoided until supply and demand are in better adjustment. It may be that the rate of growth in developing countries cannot be as great as in developed countries and that the rich must get richer before the poor get richer, but this is hardly a tolerable conclusion for the poor. Whatever way out is suggested, this trade problem forces recognition that the world is rapidly demanding mutual human ingenuity to solve it.

Do We Want to Fit In with African Objectives?

The answer to this question seems open to some doubt. International agencies are undoubtedly playing a big part in helping to build up infrastructure. Bilateral aid is doing the same often with ideological and trade promotion motives. But foreign aid is not as popular as it was, both from financial stringency at home and doubts about its effectiveness either to gain friends or build up nations. With the exception of the French, the colonial powers, on the departure of so many officials and some European immigrants, are going through rather a withdrawal reaction, and by other Africans the ex-French territories are still thought of as appendages of France. With the exception of construction companies who get the benefit of foreign aid loans and clear out when their contract is completed, Africa is rather shunned as a bad risk by private enterprise. Few investment trust managers would include it in their portfolios. Unless some new enthusiasm for the continent can be developed it is unlikely that any but the big international companies already there will enter the field.

As far as private enterprise is concerned, the core of the difficulty is that our traditional economic principles which have evolved from our own experience are linked to making the most profitable openings for our shareholders. These loyalties come first, and although many companies now combine with this principle a sense of responsibility to the public, a deliberate policy of investing to build up the standards of developing countries only comes in incidentally. Moreover, there are very significant deterrents to such investment. There is the immaturity of the new governments, the inadequate administration and the corruption, the latent psychological antagonism to expatriates, the difficulty of getting expatriate personnel nowadays who can tolerate the changed conditions which no longer offer them prestige and who can fit in personality-wise with local habits. Even if the man does, so often his wife cannot and certainly his children's education worries him. There is the tendency to state ownership and arbitrary dictation. There is the insecurity of the local government, the risk of ineffectiveness through tribal jealousies and of subversion through discontented younger challengers. Finally there is anyway small profit, and the much pleasanter, less risky, more paying alternative of investment in our own Western World developments. There is also the doubt of whether or not we really are wanted in Africa by Africans themselves. Moreover one cannot escape the feeling that in the end everything depends on African will-power itself. Our enterprise was built up by ourselves. Can one really build up other peoples?

From a wider angle one has to consider what is likely to happen if development towards higher standards of living fails in Africa. There is first the general prospect that if other people's standards are not raised we will not in the end have an expanding market for our own products. And this must be put in a world context where two-thirds of the world's population are much poorer than the rest and where humanity is likely to be doubled in the next forty years. This in turn does raise the question of the effect on Western World security of increasing poverty in so much of the world around us. It is rather like facing on a world scale the situation of too many depressed areas within our own countries. However much as individuals we may find our private enterprise principles hard to adjust to such claims, as indeed we found in the "depressions" in our own society, we can not escape the fact that the economic philosophies with which we live are on trial today, not for their theoretical advantages connected with liberty and democracy, but as a practical solution to developing countries' urgent problems. If they are getting nowhere and we cannot help them they must try other alternatives, and Communism, in spite of its unattractive features and own modicum of success, is everywhere advertising itself as an interested ally. We do not enquire much into the huge sum we spend on physical armaments as a defense against Communism. We just have a vague confidence that they will see us through. But do we examine enough the suitability of our traditional principles and the strength of our effort to match the needs of developing countries where the highest losses to the Communists may well in the end be located? So much of our time as individuals and business firms is preoccupied with our own routine compartment that the wider problems of a much more definite plan to put developing countries on their feet is always somebody else's business.

Some Concluding Thoughts on the Economic Future

If we did turn our attention to a more comprehensive approach to the economic future in Africa I suggest that the following points should have a high place in any such plan.

1. Closer perspective planning between the infrastructure expenditure and the public and private enterprise which follows it.
2. Closer co-operation between international and bilateral agencies, private enterprise, and national and local capital to ensure the execution of the follow-on from infrastructure. Such co-operation should aim not only at education for leadership but at the creation, through training and experience, of competent cadres at all levels so that implementation by local personnel may follow aid and investment satisfactorily.
3. Acceptance that the main objective is the development of the country to stand on its own feet, not defense against Communism.

4. A proper national plan of development which can integrate and control competing and conflicting offers of aid.

5. A new approach by expatriate public and private capital to the problems of mutual co-operation, particularly in regard to joint capital structures, Africanization, time limits, and diversification of capital investment.

6. Examination of what steps can be taken to widen the markets for African products.

7. Encouragement of inter-African co-operation.

8. A forum for frank discussion of these problems with African leaders.

9. Much more publicity in the Western World to the importance and implications of our relationship with developing Africa.

It is clear that many of these points must be the kind of subjects discussed between the European Economic Community and their associated territories but most other African territories are afraid of the Common Market, partly because of the suspected subservience to France of the existing associated territories but more from fear of being overdominated by Europe in foreign policy and trade. Moreover, the issues involved here really concern the free world approach to civilization as a whole and not merely the future of Europe. Wider discussion of them among ourselves and with African leaders might well be of good value. Hostility and indifference are so easy to succumb to in Africa today. It needs real new effort to achieve a sympathetic but realistic understanding with its peoples and for them to do so with us in the Western World.

RESOURCE ASPECTS OF
LATIN-AMERICAN
ECONOMIC DEVELOPMENT

JOSEPH GRUNWALD

Latin America is no exception to the usual pattern of early development among the emerging countries: economic growth has generally been re-source oriented.[1] The surprising thing, perhaps, is that this region could have advanced to the extent that it has primarily through the exploitation of natural resources for export. After all, among the developing areas of the world Latin America is comparatively far ahead on an economic

---

JOSEPH GRUNWALD, who until recently was director of the Institute of Economics of the University of Chile, has been visiting professor of economics at Yale University since 1961. Prior to 1954 when he went to Chile, he was economic adviser to the Government of Puerto Rico and also acting director of the Economic Division of the Puerto Rican Planning Board (1950–1952). During the Second World War, he served as economist with the Military Government and as editor with the Psychological Warfare Division, U.S. Army in Europe. He later taught at Rutgers University, Columbia University, and the City College of New York. He has served as an adviser to the U.S. government and private organizations. His writings include, in addition to matters relating to the Latin-American economies, subjects on economic planning and problems of economic development in gen-eral. Mr. Grunwald, who was born in Vienna, Austria, received his B.S. degree from The Johns Hopkins University and his Ph.D. from Columbia University.

[1] In order to measure the role that natural resources play in the economic growth of Latin America, the resource sector is defined here as agriculture, forestry, fishing, mining, etc. This definition suffers from the difficulty of isolating the precise contribution of natural resources before any other value is added. Thus, "agricul-ture" is obviously not a natural resource; it comprises the products of the natural resource which is land. But we have no way of measuring the value of this re-source except in terms of its output. Similarly, minerals are measured at some stage of processing. Therefore, the following analysis deals with "resource industries" rather than "natural resources" per se.

scale, with the highest per capita income country reaching the levels of European industrial nations. Even the countries with lowest per capita income, such as Haiti and Honduras, maintain levels above those of South and Southeast Asia.

In recent years, however, there have been increasing signs that Latin-American economic development cannot continue its erstwhile pattern. Economic growth has depended chiefly upon exports. Natural resources have been exploited for foreign markets and generally only a small fraction has been absorbed in the domestic economy. Thus, in 1957 Brazil consumed only 15 per cent of its coffee production, Chile only 5 per cent of its copper output, Mexico only 10 per cent of its cotton production, and Venezuela only 7 per cent of its petroleum output.[2] Export-oriented growth, depending upon extractive industries including agriculture, has created an economic and social structure ill-prepared to cope with the exigencies of modern industrial development.

STRUCTURAL FACTORS IN RESOURCE EXPLOITATION FOR EXPORTS

There are four major structural aspects inherent in natural resource exploitation for exports. One is that not all of the export proceeds are returned to the country. This refers primarily to mineral exploitation. Since resource development, particularly of minerals, usually takes large amounts of investment, it is natural that foreign capital has played a major role in this activity. This has meant that profits have to a large extent flown out of the country. Even where the resources were exploited by domestic private capital, as tin was in Bolivia prior to the revolution, profits found their way into foreign bank accounts more often than into internal investment.

In Chile, for instance, an average of almost one-quarter of the country's export value due to mining exports by foreign-owned companies never reached the economy in the form of foreign exchange earnings during the nineteen fifties.[3] It constituted those companies' profits, amortization and depreciation charges, and that part of their cost of production

[2] United Nations, Economic Commission for Latin America (ECLA), *Inflation and Growth* (Santiago, Chile, 1961, mimeo.), Table II–1.

[3] Instituto de Economía de la Universidad de Chile, *La Economía Chilena en el Periodo 1950–1961* (Santiago, 1962, mimeo.), p. 396. If only copper exports are considered, this proportion was almost half of the total copper export value during the late fifties. There has been a tendency for this share to decline over the last three decades. See C. Reynolds, "Development Problems of an Export Economy," Doctoral Dissertation, University of California, Berkeley, 1962 (mimeo.).

Latin America

which consisted of purchases outside of Chile and which were retained abroad (mostly in the United States). Only the taxes on the profits collected by the Chilean government are "returned" to the country. The rest of the returns consists of the mine wage bill and purchases of local supplies and equipment, a factor which only recently gained some significance.

While a greater proportion of total export value was taken out in the case of other countries, there are several countries in Latin America where foreign companies played a lesser role in the exports of natural resources. Argentina is probably the outstanding example, but mining has been insignificant in its economy. Bolivia already has been mentioned as a case where "domestic" private capital owned and operated the tin mines before the 1952 revolution but where the profits did not tend to be repatriated. Although precise data are lacking, there is little doubt that a smaller proportion of total export value was returned to the country than in Chile.

In general, however, foreign capital has permitted the exploitation of resources in Latin America which might otherwise not have been developed.

The second important factor of a country's dependence on exports of natural resources is that the economy develops a special infrastructure. Railroads and highways are built primarily from the mine or plantation to the sea, and ports are developed for raw material exports. In short, the transportation and communications system will tend to be outward oriented. Energy development and even basic "social overhead capital" such as hospitals and schools are geared to the mine or plantation. Such an infrastructure is not adapted for economic development through industrialization. The development of industry requires not only a transportation and communications network which connects the centers within the country but also a more general increase and balance in "overhead capital" in order to maximize the mobility of the factors of production.

Furthermore, one of the characteristics of mining operations and plantations is that they are often located in geographically isolated regions. Because of the high productivity existing in this sector, the proportion of the total labor force employed there is usually small (see Appendix Tables 9 and 10). In Chile, for instance, the most productive sector is copper mining. Its exports constitute well over 10 per cent of the country's gross domestic product, but it employs less than 1 per cent of all production workers (*obreros*).[4]

[4] Instituto de Economía de la Universidad de Chile, *Desarrollo Económico de Chile 1940–1956* (Santiago, 1956), p. 231.

In addition, a characteristic often connected with natural resource exploitation is that the economic linkages have been very weak. In mining and plantation agriculture in particular, the requirements of supplies from the domestic economy have been relatively small. On the other hand, however, the resource products — with the possible exception of oil — usually have played a minor role as inputs for domestic production.

These factors — that only part of the export product accrues to the country, the special infrastructure, and the weak economic linkages — cause the spill-over effects of natural resource exploitation for exports to be comparatively small. Even though wages in mining or plantation activities may be much higher than in other sectors of the economy, the miners constitute a small part of the country's work force and they are usually cut off from the rest of the country. Thus, extreme poverty and economic stagnation can exist side by side with relatively well-to-do, modern export sectors.

The fourth major structural factor is the nature of the demand for raw materials. There are short-run and long-run aspects of this problem. The short-run characteristic is instability. That raw material demand tends to have a relatively low price-elasticity on the world market is fairly well established.[5] As can be seen from the Appendix, Table 1, this makes for highly volatile prices. On the other hand, demand for minerals is rather sensitive to international business cycles, that is, to changes in the level of economic activity of the raw-material consuming countries. This, and the fact that supply tends to fluctuate within individual countries (see Appendix Table 2), causes the value of production to be highly unstable.[6]

These vicissitudes are a serious matter for a country whose economic advance has greatly depended upon raw material exports. First of all, foreign exchange earnings fluctuate widely. The average yearly fluctuation was more than 20 per cent in the case of Chile during the nineteen fifties.[7]

Secondly, a good part of public revenue derives from taxes on raw material exports — usually on export profits (see Appendix Table 3). Because exports fluctuate, public revenues will fluctuate and therefore the

---

[5] See, for instance, United Nations, *Instability in the Export Market of Underdeveloped Countries* (New York, 1952), and *International Compensation* for *Fluctuations in Commodity Trade* (New York, 1961); also General Agreement on Trade and Tariff (GATT), *Trends in International Trade* (Geneva, 1959).

[6] As Bela Balassa points out in a forthcoming book, in the case of agricultural products supply fluctuations tend to be greater than demand fluctuations because of climatic conditions, while in the case of mining products demand fluctuations exceed those of supply. ("Trade Prospects for the Developing Countries," Yale University Growth Center.)

[7] Instituto de Economía de la Universidad de Chile, *La Economía Chilena . . . 1950–1961*, Table 115.

government has great difficulty in planning its expenditures. The average annual percentage fluctuation of government revenues deriving from exports over the 1948–58 period was 26 per cent in Colombia, 25 per cent in Chile, 13 per cent in El Salvador, 18 per cent in Mexico, and 26 per cent in Venezuela.[8] To a great extent this factor is responsible for the chronic budget deficits because there is considerable rigidity downward in current public expenditures. Governments in Latin America usually will not find it politically feasible to reduce operating expenditures or social security contributions even when they are confronted with declining revenues due to a drop in foreign trade.

The long-run aspect of the nature of the demand for raw materials is that the possibilities for export expansion appear to be limited. There are indications that the income elasticity of demand for raw materials is low relative to the income elasticity of processed goods. It might imply that the terms of trade tend to worsen for the raw material exporter over the long pull (see Appendix Tables 4 and 5). This has been argued for some time now and it has given rise to controversy. The matter has been dealt with at length elsewhere[9] and need concern us here only in its implications for the region's export possibilities for raw materials. That an expansion of these exports to the more developed areas of the world is limited has now been generally recognized.

In discussing the special nature of the demand for raw materials, however, it must not be overlooked that in many instances export expansion in Latin America has been limited not by the weakness of external demand but by the problems of internal supply. This has been particularly true of agricultural products whose exports, with the major exception of coffee, probably could have increased substantially were it not for the failure of supply to grow sufficiently.

[8] ECLA, *op. cit* (Note 2), Chapter IV, Table 12.
[9] ECLA, *The Economic Development of Latin America and Its Principal Problems* (Santiago, Chile, 1950). R. Prebisch, "Commercial Policy in the Underdeveloped Countries," *American Economic Review, Papers and Proceedings,* May 1959. G. Haberler, "The Terms of Trade and Economic Development" in *Economic Development and Latin America,* Howard S. Ellis, ed. (Rio de Janeiro: The International Economic Association, August 1957). K. Kindleberger, *The Terms of Trade, A European Case Study,* (New York: The Technology Press and John Wiley, 1956); "The Terms of Trade and Economic Development," *Review of Economics and Statistics,* Supplement February 1958; and "Terms of Trade for Primary Products" in this volume. D. Seers, "A Model of Comparative Rates of Growth in the World Economy," *The Economic Journal,* LXXIII, 285 (March 1962). H. Singer, "The Distribution of Gains between Investing and Borrowing Countries," *American Economic Review, Papers and Proceedings,* May 1950. W. Baer, "The Economics of Prebisch and ECLA," *Economic Development and Cultural Change,* X, 2 (January 1962).

The Importance of the Resource Sector

Contribution to Gross Product

Regardless of the validity of the long-run terms of trade argument, the fact of the matter is that raw material exports of all Latin-American countries collapsed during the Great Depression of the nineteen thirties and, with the exception of Venezuela, the per capita purchasing power of exports has not recovered its pre-depression levels since then (see Appendix Tables 4 and 5).[10] This dramatic experience with their exports of natural resources shocked the Latin American countries into an awareness of the need for diversification of their structure of production. While the smaller countries had little choice in the matter because of the limitation of their markets, the larger ones embarked upon, or accelerated, a process of industrialization through import substitution. That this process had some success can be seen from Appendix Table 6. The relative contribution to gross domestic product in Latin America of the combined natural resource sector consisting of agriculture, livestock, forestry, fishing, and mining, declined from about 36 per cent before World War II to 27 per cent in 1960, while the share of manufacturing industry increased from 15 per cent to over 21 per cent in this period. However, the major portion of this structural change occurred during the nineteen forties.

The contribution of agriculture (including forestry and fishing) has been declining consistently in most countries of Latin America but a leveling off can be noted in recent years (see Appendix Tables 6 and 7). In some countries, particularly in Mexico, the agricultural share has increased in the postwar period because of gains in productivity and incorporation of new lands for agricultural exploitation (see Appendix Table 7).[11]

Mining has been the fastest growing sector in Latin America until very recently, quadrupling its output since the thirties and therefore its contribution to gross domestic product has increased. This has been due principally to the rise in petroleum output, particularly in Venezuela where the size of the mining sector overshadows this sector in other countries and where its share in gross product increased from roughly one quarter to almost one-third (see Appendix Table 8). In most of the other countries of the region the mining contribution to gross domestic product de-

---

[10] The concept of the "purchasing power of exports" takes into consideration the terms of trade by deflating export value by an index of import unit value.

[11] See also Food and Agriculture Organization (FAO), *Production Yearbook 1961*, Vol. 15 (Rome, 1962).

clined (see Appendix Table 8). In a few countries the mining sector gained additional importance with the discovery and development of new natural resources. In some instances better agreements were exacted from the foreign mining companies often through giving them production incentives, which increased the returned value to the country in the form of taxes, payroll, and domestic purchases.

Employment

Employment in the resource industries has been shrinking relative to other sectors (see Appendix Tables 9 and 10). Agriculture and mining together accounted for about two-thirds of the labor force before World War II. This proportion has since declined to one-half of the labor force.

In general, employment in mining is negligible in Latin America. Even in Chile, the largest mining employer, less than 5 per cent of the labor force is in this sector (see Appendix Table 10). For the region as a whole it is only about 1 per cent and still declining (see Appendix Table 9). This has been due principally to two factors: first, the introduction of labor-saving mechanization and new techniques, second, production shifts within the mining sector from one resource to another. Thus, the rise in copper production relative to nitrate in Chile meant that while the value of total mining output increased, the modern United States copper companies operated with a much lower labor-output ratio than the highly labor-intensive nitrate exploitation. The decline of nitrate often produced unemployment in the mining areas because the mobility of miners has always tended to be rather low. This is contrary to the case in agriculture where migration to the cities, as indicated below, produced unemployment in the urban centers.

Employment in agriculture as a proportion of total employment in all Latin-American countries has been diminishing continuously. Productivity increases have played a lesser role here than in mining. Large portions of what are defined as agriculture for census and national income purposes consist of non-market oriented subsistence farms. In this respect there probably has been little "hidden unemployment" in the strict sense but, considering productivity levels, there has been substantial underemployment when compared to the other sectors of the economy (see Appendix Table 11).

Because of the existence of agricultural underemployment and because of increasing labor mobility through better transportation and other social overhead capital, the industrialization effort in the major economies has put into motion a migration from the rural sections to the urban centers. This outmigration has continued even though only a small proportion of the immigrants could be absorbed by the manufacturing industry. While many found employment in services (most often, partial or underemployment), a serious problem of unemployment developed in the cities. Nevertheless, nearly half of Latin America's labor force is still in agriculture.

It is noteworthy, but not surprising, that the greatest agricultural producer in Latin America, Argentina, employs the smallest proportion of the labor force in this sector (see Appendix Table 10). Venezuela employs over one-third of its economically active population in agriculture, an unusually large proportion considering that this sector contributes only 7 per cent to the country's gross domestic product. This is an indication of the vast difference in productivity between agriculture and the extractive industries (see Appendix Table 11). It is also evident that there are at least as great differences in productivity within the agricultural sector — between the highly commercialized export-oriented and the subsistence portions — as exist between the agricultural sector as a whole and the other sectors of the economy.

Exports

Yet, in spite of the attempt at diversification and the industrialization process, Latin America is still highly dependent on the exports of raw materials (see Appendix Tables 12–14). The export of natural resource products comprises well over 90 per cent of most countries' total exports and there has not been any significant decline in this share, except in the cases of Brazil and Venezuela during the late nineteen fifties. This was due partly to a relative increase in the exports of manufacturing industry, and in the case of Brazil also to the decline in coffee prices.

With the exception of Peru and Mexico, the countries fall neatly into two distinct groups: the agricultural and the mineral exporters. Argentina, Brazil, Ecuador and Uruguay belong in the first group, Bolivia, Chile and Venezuela in the second (see Appendix Tables 13 and 14).

On the other hand, there have been shifts in the composition of resource exports. For instance, there has been a sharp increase in the importance of agricultural exports in Mexico in the postwar period. In 1948 the share of minerals and fuels in the total exports of that country was almost as high as agricultural exports (42 per cent compared to 49 per cent respectively), but by the end of the nineteen fifties, minerals and fuels declined to less than one-quarter and agricultural products rose to nearly two-thirds of total exports (see Appendix Tables 13 and 14). Cotton and also coffee principally accounted for the increased importance of agricultural exports.

In the Chilean economy, the role of nitrate has been steadily declining while copper and, more recently, iron exports have been increasing. Just before the First World War, the bulk of the country's foreign exchange earnings was derived from nitrate exports and the nitrate boom supported many other economic activities. Today, the contribution of nitrate to gross domestic product is less than 1 per cent and it contributes only about 6 to 8 per cent to Chile's foreign exchange earnings. Copper replaced nitrate after the First World War as the country's major export item and still constitutes close to two-thirds of total exports. In recent years, iron exports have grown rapidly and now, constituting over 10 per cent of Chile's exports, iron has become a greater foreign exchange earner than nitrates.[12]

The change within the resource sector in Peru was equally sharp. Around the middle of the last century that country's economy was based upon guano. In the eighteen sixties, guano constituted over 90 per cent of all Peruvian exports and over 80 per cent of all government revenues were derived from it.[13] By the end of the last century, the boom had collapsed. Production and export of guano is negligible in Peru today.

In this century, Peru has been able to diversify its export sector more than Chile, despite, or probably because of losing the War of the Pacific with Chile (as a consequence of which the country had to cede vast nitrate fields to its southern neighbor). Today there is no one product in Peru which overwhelmingly dominates as a foreign exchange earner. Copper, cotton, and sugar are all important and in the last few years fishing has become a major industry which threatens to overshadow the other natural resources in production and exports. Within hardly half a decade, the country rose from an insignificant position to the second fishing nation in the world (in terms of weight).

Government Revenues

In addition to their contributions to gross domestic product and to foreign exchange earnings, the third basic economic impact of natural resources is through their contribution to government revenues. This is particularly true for mining products, including petroleum, whose export profits are taxed heavily. In spite of the fact that the exports of these products have increased and that their proportion in total exports has not declined, their share in government revenues generally has diminished

[12] Banco Central de Chile, *Boletin Mensual*, Aug.–Sept., 1962, p. 925.

[13] J. Levin, *The Export Economics* (Cambridge: Harvard University Press, 1960), p. 95. The first part of this book contains an excellent account of a country's nearly exclusive dependence on one specific resource (Chapter II, pp. 27–123).

(Chile is a case in point; see Appendix Table 3). While in absolute amounts government revenues deriving from production and export of natural resources have risen, Latin-American governments have been able to enlarge their tax base and yields since the last war, principally through the imposition of excise taxes, so that the relative importance of natural resource revenues has declined. Yet, in many countries these taxes still yield amounts considerably larger than the total capital budget of the public sector.[14]

RESOURCE DEVELOPMENT FOR FURTHER INDUSTRIALIZATION

Latin-American Attitudes and Foreign Investment

The Latin-American countries are firmly convinced that their future lies with industrialization and therefore they are inexorably committed not only to continue but to accelerate their industrialization effort. That this involves a strong need for the development of natural resources is less readily recognized. Because of their past experience with the uncertainty of the markets for their resource products, these nations have become wary of their dependence on raw material production and exports. This is particularly so because, in comparison with the rest of the world, Latin America has not been doing well as a primary products exporter, as the following figures show:[15]

	Percentage Change	
	1928–1955/57	1948–1955/57
Volume of world exports		
Total	55	76
Primary products	32	44
Manufactures	103	95
Volume of exports of Latin America		
Total	28	15
Excluding Venezuela	−1	3

Note: Percentages represent changes in physical quantity only and do not incorporate price changes.

[14] An important factor is that these taxes are usually collected in the form of foreign exchange, which can be used not only to defray the government's external and internal costs but also to subsidize high priority imports.

[15] UN, *World Economic Survey 1958* (New York, 1959); and ECLA, *op. cit.* (Note 2), Table II–8.

These data indicate that the volume of Latin-American exports has grown less than the world raw material exports particularly in the postwar period. Excluding Venezuela (and therefore petroleum), the difference becomes much larger. The deterioration of Latin America vis-à-vis the rest of the world is even more dramatic on a per capita basis because the population increase in Latin America has been far above the world average since the war.

More recent figures confirm this trend. While world exports outside the Communist bloc increased by about 18 per cent, Latin-American exports stagnated between 1957 and 1961. A great part of this is due to a deterioration of Latin America's export prices. The unit export value for Latin America declined by 5 per cent between 1958 and 1961 compared with no over-all change of the unit export value for the world outside the Communist bloc.[16]

These factors, compounded by a growing nationalism, have given rise in Latin America to the emergence of a certain prejudice against great emphasis on resource development, especially since so large a part of the region's resources has been exploited by foreigners. Recent data on U.S. investment in Latin America mirror this attitude. New net direct investment plus retained earnings of U.S. companies in the mining and smelting industries of Chile and the petroleum industry of Venezuela decreased from a yearly average of more than $177 million during 1950–58 to a net yearly outflow of $32 million during 1959–61. In other words, while U.S. capital in the resource industries of Chile and Venezuela increased by nearly $1.6 billion between 1950 and 1958, in subsequent years this turned into a net repatriation of capital from these countries back to the United States. On the other hand, net new U.S. investment plus retained earnings in the manufacturing industries of Argentina, Brazil, and Mexico increased from a yearly average of less than $98 million during 1950–58 to over $130 million per year during 1959–61. These trends contrast with U.S. investment in Africa where the situation is reversed. Net new investment plus retained earnings of U.S. companies in mining, smelting, and petroleum in that continent have nearly tripled since the early nineteen fifties, but U.S. net investment (including retained earnings) in the manufacturing industry of Africa has disappeared completely.[17]

Thus the prejudice against resource exploitation has led to a certain

[16] Organization of American States (OAS) and UN Economic Commission for Latin America (ECLA), *Economic and Social Survey of Latin America, 1961* (Washington, 1962, multi.).

[17] Information from the U.S. Department of Commerce.

neglect of the resource sectors and has contributed to the slowing down of raw material exports of Latin America.

Attitudes, however, have varied in the different Latin-American countries and these differences are reflected in changes of resource output. In respect to copper, for instance, Chilean policies discouraged an expansion of mine output from about World War II up to 1955,[18] but Peru provided incentives which contributed to a dramatic upsurge of copper production in recent years. Chile was the second largest copper producer in the world until the postwar period. Since World War II, Chile's share of the world market has declined and the country has fallen to third place. During the 1941–45 period, Chile produced about 20 per cent of the world output[19] but, even though Chilean production increased significantly in the last decade, in 1960–61 it was hardly 12 per cent. Yet, in the most recent years, Latin America as a whole increased its share in world copper output, rising from less than 16 per cent in 1957 to over 18 per cent in 1961.[20] The rise in total Latin-American production was exclusively due to the jump in Peruvian output. Peru more than quadrupled its copper production between 1957 and 1961, and its share of the world total increased from about 1 to 4 per cent in this period.

New Resource Needs and Potentials

It has been demonstrated that import requirements do not diminish in the process of industrialization, even though industrialization may be based upon the substitution of imports through domestic production. To the contrary, most often imports will have to increase in total as well as in per capita terms.[21]

[18] In 1955 the Chilean government passed a "New Deal" copper law which consisted primarily of a revision of the tax system applying to the foreign-owned copper companies. A sliding scale was introduced so that marginal tax rates would diminish as production went up. While the "New Deal" did not stimulate an increase in output and new copper investment, Chile has not been able to recoup its former position in the world market. This was due partly to the fact that the U.S. copper companies wanted but failed to obtain further assurances from the Chilean government before undertaking massive investments, and partly to international commitments among copper producers to curtail output after 1956 in order to put the brakes on skidding prices. While Chile complied with these informal agreements, Northern Hemisphere and African producers did not. On the other hand, because of serious balance of payments problems, in 1961 Chile imposed additional "temporary" taxes over and above the "New Deal" tax system so that in 1962 the effective tax rate for at least one U.S. copper company exceeded 80 per cent of profits.

[19] M. L. Bohan and Morton Pomeranz, *Investment in Chile* (Washington: U.S. Department of Commerce, 1960), Table 63.

[20] OAS and ECLA, *op. cit.* (Note 16), Table I–30.

[21] See, for instance, ECLA, *op. cit.* (Note 2), Chapter 3.

Import substitution, at least in the first stages, will diminish consumer goods imports but will raise the proportion of capital goods and intermediate goods import requirements in order to feed industrialization.[22] A very important role in this new import picture is played by resource imports, particularly petroleum.

Because in most Latin-American countries export earnings could not keep up with the new import demands, foreign indebtedness has risen dangerously in that region. Therefore, in spite of any negative attitudes, pressures have built up in Latin America to put renewed emphasis on the development of traditional and new natural resources, not only in order to increase export earnings but also to facilitate the import substitution process.

Petroleum. In the beginning of the decade of the nineteen fifties most countries in Latin America with the major exceptions of Venezuela, Colombia, and Mexico, had to import nearly all their oil requirements. In the less industrialized countries this did not matter very much, but in Argentina and Brazil this amounted to about one-fifth of total imports.[23] Expansion of petroleum production was quite drastic in that decade. While in prewar years the value of oil production was little more than half of the total value of all mineral output, it now constitutes well over three quarters of the value of total mine output (for detailed sources, see Appendix).

These were also the years when, because of industrialization and the increasing use of the automobile, oil consumption jumped sharply. In Argentina the rise in output could not keep up with the rate of increase of internal demand up to 1957 (7.3 per cent annually).[24] In 1958, the government concluded agreements with private foreign firms for drilling and operations, and production nearly doubled between 1957 and 1960. By 1961, the industry was not only able to supply the entire internal demand for crude oil but also had exportable surpluses.

Production from oil deposits in Brazil, all of which are exclusively government owned and operated, was insignificant prior to 1950. Since then it has grown faster than internal consumption, so that dependence on foreign sources of supply could be reduced appreciably. By 1961, domestic output could supply over one-third of internal demand for crude oil, compared with less than 1 per cent in the early fifties. Chilean produc-

---

[22] *Ibid.,* Table III–52.
[23] *Ibid.,* Vol. II, p. 268.
[24] OAS and ECLA, *op. cit.* (Note 16), p. 330.

tion, also in the hands of a government corporation, showed sharp increases too. The country is now nearly self-supporting in crude oil.

In comparison, the traditional producers and exporters registered only moderate growth rates in the fifties. Although Venezuela's production nearly doubled in this period, almost all of the increase in output took place before 1957. Since then, growth has been rather slow and in 1961 production of crude oil was less than 6 per cent above the 1,015 million barrels produced in 1957.[25] While exploration by the private companies fell off during the late fifties, a government oil corporation was established in 1960 and was given exclusive drilling rights outside zones occupied by existing concessions. Drilling started in the middle of 1961 and by the end of that year the company had achieved a significant daily capacity.

In Mexico and Colombia there have been more moderate increases. Production in both cases was about 50 per cent higher at the end than at the beginning of the last decade. With increasing industrialization, domestic consumption is absorbing a larger share of output so that exports have not risen during the last few years. In the smaller traditional producers, Peru, Ecuador and Bolivia, production has also leveled off in recent years due to the fact that the private companies have made little new productive investments. In Peru there is a possibility that this situation will improve in the near future as a result of new agreements reached by the government and the producers in 1960 which are intended to provide investment incentives.

Comparative Advantages. Latin America has obvious comparative advantages for the production of certain primary products. The cost of copper production in Chile, for instance, varies between a minimum of 15 cents and a maximum of 18 cents per pound compared with from 18 cents to 28 cents in the United States. While the production costs in Africa are lower than in Chile, fluctuating between 13 cents and 15 cents a pound, the world's lowest cost producer is now Peru with an 11 cents per pound cost at the Toquepala deposits where mining operations were begun in 1960.[26] Appendix Table 15 shows that, except for Oceania, Latin America has the smallest proportion of land area under cultivation of any major region in the world. About three quarters of its agricultural land is used for pasture, which is an unusually high proportion consider-

[25] *Ibid.,* p. 328.
[26] The deposits at Toquepala are calculated at 1 billion tons of ore, with the high copper content of 1.67 per cent. (*Ibid.*)

ing the fact that only 23 per cent of its area is used for agricultural purposes. On the other hand, almost half of the total area consists of forests.
This is the highest ratio listed in Appendix Table 15. The one billion
hectares of forest land in Latin America is nearly seven times Europe's
forest area and about a third more than the forest land of the United
States and Canada combined.

While it is obvious that the characteristics of the world's land areas
vary widely from one place to another, the data of Appendix Table 15 do
suggest strongly that Latin America has a great potential in expanding
agricultural production and in exploiting its forest resources. There is
hardly a country in the region where considerably more land cannot be
brought under cultivation. While, in some cases, the opening up of new
lands will require enormous outlays for infrastructure investment, in
other cases relatively little expense is involved in increasing the acreage
for agriculture.

Uncultivated land in Latin America falls roughly into two major categories: the unused land in the old settled regions and the new lands of
the frontier regions. In most countries both categories exist side by side.
Using the Chilean case as an example, there are large tracts of unused but
arable lands in the oldest settled part of the country, the Central Valley
(and much of it in the surroundings of Santiago, the capital). On the
other hand, there is the province of Aisén, a frontier region in the true
sense of the term, with largely unexplored but usable land (principally
for livestock production). The Central Valley has roads and other overhead capital which are almost completely missing in the frontier regions
such as Aisén.[27] Therefore, there are important cost differences for bringing new lands under cultivation.

New infrastructure investment is unavoidable for large-scale forest exploitation. Several countries have both natural and artificial forests. Some
overhead capital is usually existent in the areas where artificial forests are
planted, but the natural forests are most often highly inaccessible. Again
turning to Chile, it would take relatively small capital expenditures to exploit the artificial pine forests planted on the coastal regions between
Valparaiso and Puerto Montt. Many of these forests consist of trees approaching the age class most efficient for cutting. It seems logical that
they should be exploited first before an attempt is made to tackle the natural forests with their high capital and infrastructure requirements.

[27] R. Brown and C. Hurtado, *Aisén* (Santiago: Instituto de Economía, Universidad de Chile, 1959).

Agricultural Development and Policy. Increases in agricultural production in Latin America have been due mostly to extension of the land area rather than to higher yields. Because of the large reservoir of unused lands, new acreage is continually being brought into cultivation, and in the decade of the fifties alone the area planted to cereals increased by about 30 per cent. More than two-thirds of the rise in cereal output in Latin America during the last decade is due to the increase in acreage.[28]

Of course, there are important differences among countries in this respect. While in Brazil, for example, nearly all of the substantial increase in cereal production was due to an extension of cultivation, more than half of the addition to output in Mexico was due to more intensive cultivation or increased yields. Within the cereal group, wheat registered little productivity change while corn yields improved significantly. Contrary to some of the cereal crops, higher yields played an important role in nearly all the cotton-producing countries. This is true for such a traditional producer as Mexico, which doubled output but increased acreage only by less than one-third in this period, and for a comparatively recent upstart such as Colombia, which was able to increase production sixfold while cultivating only two and one-third times as much land in cotton as before.[29]

Despite the potentials, the performance of Latin-American agriculture as a whole has been disappointing. Agricultural production hardly kept up with population growth since the nineteen thirties, increasing only 2 per cent on a per capita basis. Per capita output of livestock actually declined and in 1960–61 was almost 20 per cent below the yearly average for 1934–38. Only crop production increased faster than population, but even there per capita output rose only 7 per cent over the twenty-five year period.[30]

There has been a recent trend in Latin America for governments to attempt to redress the balance between agricultural and industrial development. Past economic policies, particularly in the area of foreign exchange, trade and price controls, favored industry, and agriculture appeared neglected. Since the middle of the last decade some governments have made conscious efforts to stimulate agricultural production. Thus, in Peru, the proportion of public investments devoted to irrigation and other

[28] FAO, *Production Yearbook 1961* (Rome, 1962).
[29] *Ibid.*
[30] ECLA, *Economic Bulletin for Latin America,* Statistical Supplement, 1963 (mimeo., to be published).

agricultural projects increased from 16 per cent in 1959 to 28 per cent in 1961.[31] In Brazil, about 35 per cent of Bank of Brazil loans to the private sector were granted for agricultural purposes (including livestock) in 1960 compared with about 28 per cent in 1956.[32] Private commercial banks in Brazil have followed a similar pattern (although there, of course, personal loans play a greater role). In Argentina price policies have changed in favor of agriculture particularly since the fall of Peron but, because of structural rigidities in this sector, there has been relatively little expansion of agricultural output.[33]

It takes more, however, than the simple striving for higher productivity to achieve sound agricultural development. It is obvious that the objective cannot be just to release a part of the labor force for industrial development. Open unemployment and underemployment are widespread and, while an acute shortage of trained and skilled manpower exists in nearly all countries, there is no dearth of unskilled labor. The problem is often the other way around: how to put the brakes on the mass migration from the country to the urban centers. In Latin America, as in most regions of the world, higher productivity in agriculture must be accompanied by substantial expansion in the non-agricultural sector of the economy. On the other hand, there are structural factors in agriculture in most of the countries of the region, which often make for a low responsiveness to price stimuli and therefore a low rate of adoption of new techniques.

Latin America is notorious for its highly unequal distribution of land ownership (see Appendix Table 16). This leads to the *latifundia* and the *minifundia* systems, both of which signify inefficient modes of agricultural organization and imply also a lack of strong ties to the land on the part of the rural population. Agrarian reform through land distribution would be one of the means of giving the rural population greater stability. Advocates of land reform claim that while in the short run output may not expand significantly, a rational redistribution will provide incentives and a more propitious setting for future productivity increases. In any case, there appears to be much room for expansion of agricultural output by bringing into more intensive cultivation the insufficiently exploited lands present in the majority of the *latifundias*.

Regardless of the form which land reform takes, it is also true that in general the infrastructure which is essential for agricultural improvements

[31] OAS and ECLA, *op. cit.* (Note 16), Table VI–9.
[32] *Ibid.*, Table III–18.
[33] See the chapter on Argentina in ECLA, *op. cit.* (Note 2), Vol. IV.

is greatly inadequate. Significant portions of Latin-American agriculture are of a non-market oriented subsistence character. The transportation system is lacking. The rural populace is generally the least educated of the region's population. Institutions to facilitate the training of these people and to aid in the transmission of new methods and techniques are sorely needed, as are the means to finance them.

CONCLUSION

It is a fact that today's levels of economic development of the various Latin-American nations derive largely from their individual natural resource endowments. It is no coincidence that the land-rich countries of Argentina and Uruguay, mineral wealthy Chile and, more recently, Venezuela are relatively high on the economic ladder in the region. Great natural resource endowment often also has attracted high-quality manpower which has reinforced economic development.

Yet in more recent times it has become evident that the benefits of natural resource endowment depend heavily upon forces outside of the individual economies. Dynamism in economic growth has become more related to factors other than the mere existence of natural resources. The countries of the region with high standards of living, Argentina, Chile, and Uruguay, have been close to economic stagnation for some years now. Industrialization has become the password to economic growth. The objective is to get away from natural resource dependency and to bring greater flexibility into the economy.

What has not always been recognized in the region, however, is that a vigorous development of natural resources will make the economies of Latin America more viable, and that expansion of resource output on a diversified basis will be a *sine qua non* for the region's accelerated industrialization and economic growth. One of the major roles of natural resources must continue to be to provide the bulk of foreign exchange. But in the present, already more advanced stage of economic development of Latin America, this role must be expanded to the point where natural resource development directly furnishes essential support for industrialization. This support is in terms of direct inputs of raw materials for manufacturing, as well as providing the ingredients for an expansion of the necessary infrastructure. Great advances already have been made in several countries, particularly in petroleum and water resource development.

The relationship between resource development and industrialization has not always been very direct in Latin America. If resources provide foreign exchange earnings, these will be converted into general economic growth only insofar as the government provides adequate orientation through exchange and import policies and to the extent that public revenues accruing from such exports are devoted to productive investments. Sometimes resource discovery and exploitation will stimulate the development of new industries.

In general, however, industrialization efforts precede the development of specific resources as manufacturing inputs. In other words, resource development for industrialization has been largely demand-determined in Latin America, contrary to the primary supply-determined resource exports. In many cases an industrialization undertaking will lead directly to an expansion in resource production, as when a food packing industry will furnish new techniques, improved seeds, and other "know-how" for the production of the required crops.

In the final analysis, however, the speed and soundness of resource development in Latin America will depend upon further progress in the economic integration of the region. Individual countries with their limited markets cannot provide the stimulus for costly projects. Industrialization will receive a tremendous impetus from an effective functioning of the two "common market" arrangements now existing in Latin America.[34]

As industrialization accelerates, new demands for natural resources will be created and rational resource planning and development on a region-wide scale will become inevitable.

Note: This essay is part of a more extensive study which is supported by a grant from Resources for the Future, Inc. A discussion of water and energy resources, omitted here for brevity, will be dealt with in the full study. In the preparation of the statistical material I have had the assistance of John M. Davis. I am grateful to Bela Balassa who made helpful suggestions.

[34] The "Central American Common Market" which started to function recently and the "Latin America Free Trade Association" which came into being in 1961. The latter is a very loosely knit trade organization of nine countries open for membership to all countries in Latin America.

STATISTICAL APPENDIX

*References for National Income Data of Latin-American Countries
and Sources for Appendix Tables 6–8*

Note: Appendix Tables 6–8 were elaborated on the basis of special compilations made by the UN Economic Commission for Latin America, using the references listed below. Certain adjustments were made in the country data in order to attain comparability.

Argentina: *Producto e Ingreso de la República Argentina, 1935–54;* and various issues of *Boletin Mensual,* Banco de la República. Data at factor cost at 1950 prices.

Bolivia: *Planeamiento,* Revista Trimestral, Junata Nacional de Planeamiento, No. 3–4–5, Sept. 1961. Data at market prices in 1958 prices.

Brazil: *Revista Brasileira de Economía.* Data at factor cost in 1950 prices.

Chile: *Cuentas Nacionales de Chile 1940–54; Cuentas Nacionales de Chile 1950–60;* CORFO, 1957 and 1960. Data at factor cost in 1950 prices.

Colombia: *Cuentas Nacionales 1950–60,* Banco de la República, Bogota 1962. Also "Inflation and Growth," Volume II, Chapter III, ECLA; Data at factor cost in 1958 prices.

Costa Rica: Estimates by ECLA Regional Office, Mexico City. Data at market prices in 1950 prices.

Ecuador: *Contabilidad Nacional del Ecuador 1939–49,* Banco Central del Ecuador, 1955. Also National Accounts Questionnaire supplied to Statistical Office, United Nations, 1950–60. Data at factor cost in prices of 1950.

Guatemala: Estimated by ECLA, Regional Office, Mexico City. Data at market prices in 1950 prices.

Honduras: *Cuentas Nacionales 1925–55;* Banco Central de Honduras 1957; *Cuentas Nacionales 1950–60.* Data at factor cost in 1948 prices.

Mexico: Estimates by ECLA Regional Office, Mexico City. Data at factor cost in 1950 prices.

Panama: 1945–49: *El Desarrollo de Panamá,* UN Mexico; 1950–59, *Ingreso Nacional,* Estadistica Panameña, Serie C, Año, XVII and XX. Data at factor cost in 1950 prices.

Paraguay: Information from Banco Central de Paraguay and *Yearbook of National Accounts Statistics, 1961,* UN, New York. Data at market prices in 1956 prices.

Nicaragua: Banco Central de Nicaragua. Data at market prices in 1958 prices.
Peru: *Renta Nacional de Perú, 1950,* data elaborated by Statistical Office,
ECLA, Santiago. Data at factor cost in 1950 prices.
El Salvador: 1945–57: *El Desarrollo Económico de el Salvador,* UN, Mexico,
1958. 1958–59: *Yearbook of National Account Statistics 1961,* UN, New
York. Data at market prices, in 1950 prices.
Venezuela: *Memoria,* 1959, 1960, 1961, Banco Central de Venezuela. Data
at factor cost in 1957 prices. Also *Inflation and Growth,* 1961, Vol. II, Chapter III, ECLA, Santiago, Chile.

Table 1. Percentage Deviations of Prices of the Principal Export Products
from Average of Specified Period 1951–1959

Year	Copper	Tin	Cocoa[1]	Coffee[2]	Lead	Zinc	Sugar[3]	Wool[4]	Cotton[5] (Deviations from 1951–59=100)
	(Deviations from 1948–59=100)				(Deviations from 1950–59=100)				
1951	–4	41	0	6	53	70	43	86	47
1952	13	26	2	6	29	48	5	–8	14
1953	11	–4	–1	14	–14	–26	–14	–8	0
1954	8	–6	58	54	–8	–23	–18	–4	3
1955	53	–3	3	12	0	–10	–19	–15	–2
1956	43	3	–28	14	9	–3	–13	–21	–11
1957	–5	–1	–13	12	–8	–19	30	2	–11
1958	–14	–4	23	–5	–31	–35	–12	–22	–15
1959	4	3	1	–27	–33	–19	–25	–26	–25
Average fluctuation for period specified	22	12	20	20	19	27	20	21	14

[1] Bahía cocoa in New York.
[2] Santos 4 coffee in New York.
[3] Cuban sugar sold on free market.
[4] Uruguayan wool in Boston.
[5] Mexican cotton in Liverpool.
Sources: UN, *Monthly Statistical Bulletin* (New York), various issues, and ECLA, *Inflation and Growth* (Santiago, Chile, 1961, mimeo.), Table II–4.

Table 2. Percentage Fluctuations in Coffee, Sugar, and Cotton Fiber
Production, Selected Countries, 1957–1961

		Percentage change in production			
Country	Raw material	1957/58	1958/59	1959/60	1960/61
Brazil	Coffee	32	42	−32	27
El Salvador	Coffee	450	7	−7	−50
Dominican Republic	Sugar	0	−3	38	−14
Mexico	Cotton fiber	11	−28	20	−10

Sources: OAS and ECLA, *Economic and Social Survey of Latin America, 1961* (Washington,
1962, multi.), Chapter IV, Tables IV–1, IV–2, IV–3, IV–4.

Table 3. Government Revenues Derived from Exports as a Percentage
of Total Tax Revenues, 1937–1958

Year	Argen-tina	Brazil	Colom-bia	Chile	El Sal-vador	Mexico	Vene-zuela
1937/38	24	—	38	47	69	—	82
1949/50	3	5	17	28	63	39	86
1957/58	7	2	16	25	68	33	85

Source: ECLA, *Inflation and Growth,* Vol. III, Chapter IV, Table 10.

Table 4. Indices of Purchasing Power of Exports, Latin America
and Selected Countries, 1928–1959

(1955=100)

							Latin America	
Year	Argen-tina	Brazil	Chile	Colom-bia	Mex-ico[1]	Vene-zuela	Includ-ing Vene-zuela	Exclud-ing Vene-zuela
1928/29	242	78	123	49	75	14	71	87
1932	148	44	23	38	24	16	39	46
1940	112	42	64	42	39	19	45	53
1950	154	113	76	80	81	71	97	105
1958/59	128	100	93	[2]86	[2]86	[2]106	105	97

[1] Includes net earnings from tourist trade.
[2] 1958 only.
Source: ECLA, *Inflation and Growth,* 1961, Tables II–9, II–10, II–11.

Table 5. Indices of Per Capita Purchasing Power of Exports,
Latin America and Selected Countries, 1928–1959

(1955 = 100)

							Latin America	
Year	Argen-tina	Brazil	Chile	Colom-bia	Mex-ico[1]	Vene-zuela	Includ-ing Vene-zuela	Exclud-ing Vene-zuela
1928/29	405	140	195	86	137	26	123	152
1932	228	73	35	62	41	28	63	75
1940	151	60	85	59	58	30	63	75
1950	171	127	84	89	93	82	109	118
1958/59	119	91	86	[2]80	[2]79	[2]97	96	93

[1] Includes net earnings from tourist trade.
[2] 1958 only.
Source: ECLA, *Inflation and Growth,* 1961, Tables II–9, II–10, II–11.

Table 6. Latin America: Value Added in Agriculture, Mining and
Manufacturing as Per Cent of Gross Domestic Product[1]

Sector	1936–37	1940–41	1945–46	1950–51	1955–56	1959–60
Agriculture[2]	32.2	30.5	25.6	22.4	21.8	21.1
Mining	4.0	4.3	4.8	5.1	5.6	6.0
Resource sector total	36.2	34.8	30.4	27.5	27.4	27.1
Manufacturing	15.0	16.2	18.2	18.8	19.4	21.1
Other sectors	48.8	49.0	51.4	53.7	53.2	51.8
Gross domestic product	100.0	100.0	100.0	100.0	100.0	100.0

[1] Percentages based upon dollar data at 1950 prices.
[2] "Agriculture" includes forestry and fisheries in all tables unless otherwise stated.
Sources: See Appendix, p. 327.

Table 7. Value Added in Agriculture as Per Cent of Gross Domestic Product[1]

Country	1939	1945–46	1950–51	1955–56	1959–60
Argentina	23	20	16	17	17
Bolivia	—	—	32	29	[2]35
Brazil	38	33	28	28	25
Chile	[3]18	15	17	15	13
Colombia	46	43	40	36	36
Costa Rica	—	—	41	34	[2]39
Ecuador	33	31	39	37	36
El Salvador	[4]48	47	42	37	[2]37
Guatemala	—	—	51	43	[2]34
Honduras	60	56	53	48	47
Mexico	23	18	20	21	20
Nicaragua	—	46	44	40	39
Panama	—	22	27	26	26
Paraguay	—	—	46	46	40
Peru	—	33	33	29	[2]27
Venezuela	14	9	8	7	7

[1] Includes forestry and fisheries. Percentages based upon national currencies in constant prices.
[2] 1958–59.
[3] 1940.
[4] 1943.
Sources: See Appendix, p. 327.

Table 8. Value Added in Mining and Smelting
as Per Cent of Gross Domestic Product[1]

Country	1939	1945–46	1950–51	1955–56	1959–60
Argentina	1.1	1.1	1.0	1.1	1.6
Bolivia	—	—	15.5	16.7	[2]13.5
Brazil	0.4	0.4	0.4	0.3	0.5
Chile	[3]9.8	5.5	6.4	6.0	4.6
Colombia	3.2	2.2	3.9	3.6	4.1
Ecuador	[4]3.8	3.0	2.2	2.3	2.2
El Salvador	0.7	0.6	0.6	0.4	[2]0.4
Honduras	2.0	1.6	1.6	1.2	1.1
Mexico	7.9	5.4	4.6	4.1	4.4
Nicaragua	—	2.9	2.5	1.5	1.6
Peru	—	6.5	6.6	7.2	[2]7.3
Venezuela	25.6	31.1	31.6	30.7	31.0

[1] Includes petroleum. Percentages based upon national currencies in current prices.
[2] 1958–59.
[3] 1940.
[4] 1943.
Sources: See Appendix, p. 327.

Table 9. Latin America: Percentage Distribution of Labor Force, by Sectors

Year	Agricul-ture	Min-ing	Manufac-turing	Construc-tion	Serv-ices[1]	Other	Total labor force
1940[2]	60.4	2.0	n.a.	n.a.	n.a.	n.a.	100
1945	56.2	1.2	13.9	3.1	23.2	2.3	100
1950	53.0	1.1	14.5	3.7	25.3	2.4	100
1955	50.7	1.0	14.7	3.7	27.6	2.4	100

n.a. not available.

[1] Includes government employment.

[2] The 1940 figures were calculated using data for Argentina, Brazil, Chile, Columbia, Guatemala, Mexico, Nicaragua, Panama, Peru, and Venezuela. The population of these ten countries was approximately 83% of the total population of Latin America in 1940.

Sources: 1940: International Labor Office, *Yearbook of Labor Statistics,* 1949–50 (Geneva). 1945, 1950, 1955: ECLA, *Economic Bulletin for Latin America,* Vol. II, No. 1 (1957).

Table 10. Percentage of Labor Force in Agriculture and Mining[1]

(Total labor force = 100)

Country	Year	Agriculture (per cent)	Mining (per cent)
Argentina	1900–04	39	—
	1925–29	36	—
	1940–44	33	—
	1955	26	—
Brazil	1940	67	3
	1950	[2]61	
Chile	1930	39	6
	1940	36	6
	1952	30	5
Colombia	1938	73	2
	1951	54	2
Costa Rica	1927	63	—
	1950	55	—
El Salvador	1930	75	—
	1950	63	—
Guatemala	1940	71	—
	1950	68	—
Mexico	1930	68	1
	1940	65	1
	1950	58	1
	1958	58	1
Nicaragua	1940	73	1
	1950	68	1
Panama	1940	53	—
	1950	50	—
Peru	1940	62	2
	1955	59	2
Venezuela	1941	51	2
	1950	41	3
	1959	34	2

[1] Agriculture includes forestry and fisheries; mining includes petroleum and quarrying.
[2] Includes the agricultural and mining labor force; thus the 61% for 1950 corresponds to 70% for 1940.

Sources: ILO, *Yearbook of Labor Statistics* (Geneva) for 1940, 1950, 1955. Argentina: UN, *The Economic Development of Argentina* (Mexico), 1959. Peru, 1955: UN, *Industrial Development of Peru*, 1955.

Table 11. Latin America: Output and Employment by Sector in 1950

Sector	Total output (billions of dollars) (1)	Labor force (millions of persons) (2)	Output per capita (dollars) (1) ÷ (2)
Agriculture	8.2	28.3	288
Mining[1]	1.8	0.6	3,040
Manufacturing	7.2	7.7	937
Construction	1.5	2.0	757
Other[2]	19.0	14.8	1,284
All sectors	37.7	53.4	706

[1] Including petroleum.
[2] Including all activities not specified above.
Source: ECLA, *Inflation and Growth*, Table I–4.

Table 12. Latin America: Percentage Composition of Exports[1]

Product group	1934–38	1946–51	1952–53	1955–56[2]	1959–60[2]
Agricultural products	66	70	64	52	44
Minerals and fuels	33	28	34	44	49
Total exports of natural resources	99	98	98	96	93
Manufactured products	1	2	2	4	7
Total	100	100	100	100	100
Total exports of Latin America in billions of current dollars	1.9	6.1	7.3	8.3	8.5

[1] Percentages are based upon data in current U.S. dollars. About 10% of the exports could not be classified and were distributed over the three categories on a pro rata basis.
[2] Data calculated on basis of ten countries which constitute over 85% of all Latin-American foreign trade (see *Sources* below).
Sources: 1934–53: ECLA, *Study of Inter-Latin-American Trade,* 1957. 1955–60: official statistics of ten countries — Argentina, Bolivia, Brazil, Colombia, Chile, Ecuador, Paraguay, Peru, Uruguay, and Venezuela.

Table 13. Agricultural Exports as Per Cent of Total Exports, Selected Countries

Country	1948	1950–51	1955–56	1959–60
Argentina	94	94	95	95
Bolivia	1	2	3	6
Brazil	86	93	92	83
Colombia	82	81	86	80
Chile	14	14	7	6
Ecuador	81	85	93	93
Mexico	49	58	70	63
Peru	28	44	37	29
Uruguay	97	98	99	99
Venezuela	4	2	2	2

Note: Percentages based upon data in current dollars.
Sources: UN, *International Trade Yearbook* (New York), various issues. For Mexico: ECLA, *Inflation and Growth*, Vol. V.

Table 14. Mineral and Fuel Exports as Per Cent of Total Exports, Selected Countries

Country	1948	1950–51	1955–56	1959–60
Argentina	1	1	1	1
Bolivia	99	97	96	93
Brazil	3	3	3	8
Colombia	17	17	13	19
Chile	81	76	86	85
Ecuador	5	4	1	1
Mexico	42	32	23	24
Peru	44	37	46	46
Venezuela	96	96	97	94

Note: Percentages based upon data in current dollars.
Sources: UN, *International Trade Yearbook* (New York), various issues. For Mexico: ECLA, *Inflation and Growth*, Vol. V.

Table 15. Estimated Percentage Distribution of Total Land Area
by Major Use in the 1950's

Region	Arable land[1]	Perma-nent pas-tures	For-est	Other[2]	Total area Per cent	Total area Billions of hec-tares
Latin America[3]	5	18	48	29	100	2.1
North America	11	13	35	41	100	2.2
Soviet Union	10	17	39	34	100	2.2
Far East[4]	18	13	23	46	100	2.1
Near East	7	15	11	67	100	1.2
Africa	9	23	25	43	100	2.5
Oceania	3	53	6	38	100	0.9
Europe (excluding U.S.S.R.)	31	16	28	25	100	0.5
World	10	19	30	41	100	13.7

1 hectare = 2.471 acres.
[1] Includes land under tree crops.
[2] Built-up areas, waste and barren land, inland waters, etc.
[3] Includes all Caribbean islands and mainland colonial territories.
[4] Includes Mainland China.
Source: FAO, *Production Yearbook 1961,* Vol. 15 (Rome, 1962), pp. 3–7.

Table 16. Indicators of Land Tenancy in Latin America

Country	Date	Percentage of total land held by per-centage of owners listed in col. 2 (1)	Per cent of owners hold-ing land in col. 1 (2)
Bolivia	Prior to 1953 land reform	99.6	30.0
Brazil	1940	48.3	1.6
Chile	1955	61.6	0.7
Colombia	1954	40.2	0.8
Venezuela	1950	90.5	0.9
Latin America	1950	[1]64.9	[1]1.5

[1] 64.9% of the total land area was concentrated in 1.5% of all farms. This 1.5% constituted farms in excess of 1,000 hectares.
Sources: ECLA, *Inflation and Growth,* Vol. II, pp. 106–7, and sources cited therein; Thomas F. Carroll, "The Land Reform Issue in Latin America," in *Latin American Issues* (New York: The Twentieth Century Fund, 1961), p. 165.

Problems, Situations, Processes

Terms of Trade for Primary Products
CHARLES P. KINDLEBERGER

*Potentials and Hazards of Direct International Investment
in Raw Materials*
CHANDLER MORSE

International Transfers of Knowledge and Capital
EGBERT DE VRIES

TERMS OF TRADE FOR PRIMARY PRODUCTS

CHARLES P. KINDLEBERGER

In the early part of the fifties, there was a sharp division of opinion over the outlook for the terms of trade between primary products and manufactures or, in some contexts, for those between underdeveloped and developed countries. Prebisch, Singer, and Myrdal, on the one hand, believed that the terms of trade were turning increasingly against primary products and underdeveloped countries.[1] Their complaints were dismissed by theorists such as Haberler and Viner;[2] and counter-assertions that

CHARLES P. KINDLEBERGER has been with the Massachusetts Institute of Technology since 1948, first as associate professor and, since 1951, as professor of economics. From 1945 to 1948 he was with the Department of State, and during World War II was with the Office of Strategic Services. He was economist for the Board of Governors of the Federal Reserve System (1940–42), with the Bank for International Settlements (1939–40), and with the Federal Reserve Bank of New York (1936–39). He is the author of *Foreign Trade and the National Economy* (1962), *Economic Development* (1958), *The Terms of Trade* (1956), *International Economics* (1953, 1958, 1963), *The Dollar Shortage* (1950), and *International Short-Term Capital Movements* (1937). Mr. Kindleberger was born in New York City in 1910. He received his M.A. and Ph.D. from Columbia University.

[1] Raul Prebisch, *The Economic Development of Latin America and Its Principal Problems* (New York: UN, Economic Commission for Latin America, 1950); Hans W. Singer, "The Distribution of Gains between Investing and Borrowing Countries," *American Economic Review, Papers and Proceedings*, XL, 2 (May 1950), 473–85; Gunnar Myrdal, *The International Economy: Problems and Prospects* (New York: Harper, 1956), Chapter 13.

[2] Gottfried Haberler, *International Trade and Economic Development* (Cairo: National Bank of Egypt, 1959), and his "Terms of Trade and Economic Development," in H. S. Ellis and H. C. Wallich (eds.), *Economic Development for Latin America* (New York: St. Martin's Press, 1961), pp. 275–97; Jacob Viner, *International Trade and Economic Development* (Glencoe, Ill.: Free Press, 1952).

the terms of trade would develop adversely for developed countries were put forward by Clark, Lewis, and Aubrey,[3] on the basis of econometric models, a priori reasoning, or extrapolation from the sharp if short-lived rise in commodity prices induced by the Korean War.

In the event, the fears of the heretics have been more nearly fulfilled in the decade of the 1950's than the reassurances of the orthodox theorists or the predictions of the scientific forecasters and projectors. By 1960, the terminal date chosen by Clark and Lewis, export prices of the less developed countries had risen less or fallen more (depending upon the starting point) than those of developed countries. Nor had prices of primary products kept pace with those of manufactures. The returns are not yet in for 1975, for which Aubrey made his projections, but time has not validated his analysis which called for large increases in imports of primary products into the United States, and higher prices (and virtually no change in manufactured imports). The terms of trade of the less developed countries declined gradually from the early 1950's, after having shaken down from the Korean flurry of 1950–1952. Taking 1953 to be 100, the terms of trade of Latin America and Africa in 1961 and 1962 are in the 85–90 range; those of the primary producers, Australia and New Zealand, where the price of wool had not fallen by 1953 to its post-Korean level, at 66 and 84. The United States and Europe show an improvement in terms of trade of more than 10 per cent. Primary producers in Asia and the Middle East recorded over-all a slight improvement in terms of trade of 6 per cent in the first instance and 2 per cent in the second. This result gave little ground for satisfaction, however, since it rested on efforts at price maintenance (oil, jute, and burlap), the long-run success of which is open to considerable doubt.

Among primary products as a whole, indeed, heavy supplies accumulated by various authorities and agencies make clear that the problem is more serious than the recorded statistics of relative prices demonstrate. In two commodities in particular, coffee and petroleum, maintenance of the present price structure is regarded less as an economic problem than as a political necessity, owing to the strategic importance of a number of

---

[3] Colin Clark, *The Economics of 1960* (London: Macmillan, 1942), and his "Halfway to 1960," *Lloyds Bank Review*, No. 24 (April 1952), 1–13; W. A. Lewis, "World Production, Prices and Trade, 1870–1960," *Manchester School*, XX, 2 (May 1952), 105–38; Henry G. Aubrey, "The Long-Term Future of the United States Imports and Its Implications for Primary-Producing Countries," *American Economic Review, Papers and Proceedings*, XLV, 2 (May 1955), 270–87, and his *United States Imports and World Trade* (London: Oxford University Press, 1957).

the producer countries and the vulnerability of their social, political, and economic structures to losses of income from further price decline.

The importance of the terms of trade for economic development is virtually self-evident. Other things being equal, that is, assuming no changes in productivity in primary production nor compensating expansions in export volume, a reduction in the terms of trade reduces the capacity of developing countries to import. These countries have taken on the "Trade not Aid" slogan evolved in Europe in the days of the Marshall Plan, and insist that the choice of the developed countries is between commodity price stabilization and economic aid. Like the American and the European farmer, moreover, the less developed world prefers price supports to income subsidies.

The problem is divisible into two related parts: the elimination or moderation of short-run instability in commodity prices, and the correction of the long-term downward trend. The interactions between short-term fluctuations and trend are many and complex. In particular, attempts to correct short-term instability typically have an effect on the trend. This essay, however, is concerned only with trend and not with instability. This is not to deny that short-term instability would still present a problem if a solution could be found for the trend. If the long-run terms of trade of primary-producing countries were stabilized, there would still be need to discuss international commodity agreements, buffer stocks, buffer funds, and the like. There is, however, a basic asymmetry between the two problems: measures designed to correct the trend will contribute to the solution of short-run instability, whereas the reverse is untrue. Our concern is thus with the trend.

A SUMMARY OF EARLIER FINDINGS

The terms of trade have received so much attention, both empirical and analytical in recent years[4] that it may be in order to summarize the position with minimal explanation.

The Factual Position to About 1953

Prebisch's statistical demonstration that the terms of trade moved against underdeveloped countries, based on the inverse of the British

[4] C. P. Kindleberger, *The Terms of Trade: A European Case Study* (Cambridge: Technology Press and Wiley, 1956), and his "The Terms of Trade and Economic Development," *Review of Economics and Statistics*, XL, 1, Part 2 (Supplement, February 1958), 72–85.

statistics between 1870 and 1938, is unacceptable. The decline of transport costs relative to commodities improved the terms of trade both in Britain and abroad. Comparison beginning in the 1870–73 expansion and ending in the 1938 recession mixes cycle with trend. The terms of trade between manufactures and primary products are not identical to those between developed and underdeveloped countries, because of exports of primary products — coal, wheat, cotton, lumber, woodpulp, etc. — by developed countries, and of manufactures — cotton textiles and burlap — by underdeveloped. A considerable number of underdeveloped countries are so specialized, further, that they import foodstuffs, especially rice in the Far East. Nonetheless, the evidence points to the conclusion that from about 1870 to 1952, the merchandise terms of trade have tended to move in favor of developed and against underdeveloped countries, despite the Korean War and a peak of commodity prices in 1951. It is not so clear that they have moved against primary production and in favor of manufactures.

This tendency in merchandise trade has been offset in part by a change in the terms of trade on services, including not only transport, insurance, interest on long-term loans, but also and especially the rate of profit on direct investment. Transport, the price of which has fallen relative to merchandise, is typically a service provided by the developed countries. The long-term rate of interest on international loans has fallen. Significantly, the division of profits between direct investor from the developed countries and the host country levying taxes has altered substantially. While Chile's merchandise terms of trade declined from 100 in 1925 to 65 in 1955, its terms of trade on "returned value," i.e., the value of copper exports returned to Chile in the form of domestic expense and taxes, improved over the same period from 100 to 300.[5]

Demand and Supply Characteristics

In international trade, demand and supply are inextricably linked, as the excess demand of the importing country represents the net of total demand and domestic supply, whereas the excess supply offer of the exporting country is derived from total supply and domestic demand. Nonetheless, an arbitrary division of the discussion is possible. The issue is whether the deterioration of the merchandise terms of trade between de-

[5] Clark W. Reynolds, "Development Problems of an Export Economy: The Historical and Developmental Relationships of the Copper Industry to the Economy of Chile" (unpublished doctoral dissertation), University of California, Berkeley, 1961 (Statistical Appendix, p. 19).

veloped and underdeveloped countries is ascribable mainly to the conditions of demand, or to those of supply.

Short-term price instability is the result of short-term inelasticity of demand and supply with respect to price, of short-term shifts of supply in agricultural products, and of short-term speculative shifts of demand in minerals. Responsibility for the adverse trend in the terms of trade can be assigned to demand or supply only by assuming that other things are equal. Given parallel growth in the productivity of primary products and manufactures, the terms of trade of primary products tend to worsen because of Engel's law — the tendency for manufactured goods to incorporate more and more manufacturing labor and machine time per unit of initial primary-product input — and because of synthetic innovations which substitute the abundant capital of the developed countries for the relatively scarce land of the underdeveloped. Or conversely, given the demand conditions, the terms of trade tend to move against underdeveloped and in favor of developed countries, because developed countries reallocate their resources to expand output of those products in brisk demand, and to cut down on products for which demand is flagging. In underdeveloped countries, on the other hand, there is a basic asymmetry. Supply increases in foodstuffs and in raw materials in brisk demand, to hold down price increases; but supply is inelastic with respect to price decreases in lines of lagging or declining demand, which permits prices to fall substantially.

That the price inelasticity of net demand in international trade is greater for the output of underdeveloped countries than for that of the developed arises in part from the fact that underdeveloped countries tend to be more specialized in production. Fewer of their exports are consumed at home or produced abroad in the importing country, which reduces the elasticity of net supply in the exporter and of net demand in the importer. The thirty countries where, in 1953, more than 50 per cent of the value of their exports were represented by a single commodity are all underdeveloped.[6] Where the exports of underdeveloped countries meet local competition in importing countries, the local produce is frequently — in such lines as cotton textiles and petroleum products — highly resistant to price decreases and, owing to economic weakness or political strength, is able to protect itself by import restriction. On occasion, as in Turkish tobacco and Argentine linseed oil, or again in cotton textiles and petroleum products, the products will prove highly elastic in supply in the im-

[6] P. Lamartine Yates, *Forty Years of Foreign Trade* (London: Allen and Unwin, 1959), p. 180.

porting country, preventing undue price increases. This behavior in the importing country will set price ceilings, but not floors, on the exports of underdeveloped countries. The virtual unanimity of advice — from the General Agreement on Tariffs and Trade (GATT), its 1958 panel of experts, from the United Nations, and the Organization for Economic Cooperation and Development (OECD)[7] — that developed countries resist the temptation to impose limitations on imports of manufactures from the underdeveloped countries, takes cognizance of the lack of floor under the prices of such exports, but fails to notice the existence of the ceiling.

If it be necessary for operational purposes to distinguish between demand and supply in assigning responsibility for the movement against underdeveloped countries of long-run terms of trade, it seems more reasonable to regard the demand characteristics of Engel's law (increasing efficiency in the consumption of raw materials in manufacturing, and the development of synthetic substitutes for scarce materials) as immutable, and to focus on supply. The fact seems to be that in developed countries entry and exit are relatively easy for manufactures and primary products; in underdeveloped countries, entry is easy for primary products, particularly of agriculture, but exit is difficult. And entry is difficult in complex manufactures. When a price falls, supply fails to contract; when price threatens to rise, supply expands if it is a primary product but not if it is a manufactured import. This then provides a strong basis for the tendency of the terms of trade for underdeveloped primary producing countries to worsen. A young Swedish economist has pushed somewhat further this view that the capacity to transform is the secret of the terms of trade, and has suggested that some underdeveloped countries expand output in some sectors without regard to price. According to Burenstam Linder,[8] population and capital located in a staple export sector may expand through natural increase and retained profits, respectively, and have no choice but to stay in the sector, for lack of training, capital markets, technology entrepreneurship, and so on, which would make the switching of resources possible. In this circumstance, expansion of exports may continue until the returns become negative and even beyond.

As a corollary, it follows that when a developed country is engaged in

[7] GATT, *International Trade, 1961* (Geneva, 1962); GATT, Panel of Experts (Haberler Report), *Trends in International Trade* (Geneva, 1958); UN, *World Economic Survey, 1961* (New York, 1962), pp. 50–51; OECD, *Europe and the World Economy,* Eleventh Annual Economic Review (Paris, 1960).

[8] Staffan Burenstam Linder, *An Essay in Trade and Transformation* (New York: Wiley, 1961).

primary production — as, say, France in the production and export of iron ore and bauxite — this is not a weakness, as the Economic Commission for Europe has contended, but, since the resources are capable of being redirected into other activities, a sign that this is an appropriate use of the resources.

Monopoly?

Prebisch and Singer argued that the tendency for the terms of trade to turn against underdeveloped countries exporting primary products has been the result of monopoly in developed countries, both in goods and in factor markets. Manufacturers control output, particularly by reducing it in response to a fall-off demand, rather than lowering prices. Supply expands inadequately to increases in demand, thus leading to higher prices and wages. In particular, the fruit of technical progress is retained in developed countries through monopolistic restraint of the producing factors, rather than yielded, through competition and price reduction, to the buyer.

The converse of this argument applies only partly to primary production. Agriculture is highly competitive until government intervention occurs. But mineral production is typically dominated by large companies which work to order, vary supply, and maintain prices. An industry such as oil has succeeded in maintaining the structure of posted prices, with, to be sure, the help of the Texas Railroad Commission and not without increasing difficulty as a result of new entry encouraged by the margin of profit available at posted prices.

Monopoly exists on both sides in the important area of direct investment in primary production in underdeveloped countries. Here the investor typically has availability of capital, technical capacity, access to foreign markets, or some other advantage which gives him a monopoly rent over the new and independent entrant. But the underdeveloped country has sovereignty over the necessary materials in the crude state. As noted, the merchandise terms of trade are less significant than the total terms on which the mineral deposits are worked, including the national regulations governing taxes, labor laws, training of local staff, purchase of local supplies, and so on. Much, and in some cases all, of the monopoly advantage which initially accrued to the foreign direct investor because of his unique and necessary contribution to the operation may be gradually taken from him, after the investment is committed, by a government which exercises its short-run monopoly advantage. A government interested in stimulating additional investments in the long run, however, will find it useful to apply restraint in maximizing its short-run gains. On this account the existence of monopoly, and especially of bilateral monopoly, is uncertain in its effects on the terms of trade.

The presence of monopoly elements in developed-country industry is equally indeterminate in its impact on the terms of trade. Monopoly may push prices up. Often, however, with a view to the long run, monopoly may hold prices down. Changes in the length of the order book and competition in delivery dates are increasingly substituted for changes in prices in equating supply and demand in the short run. This may be the result of the statesmanlike recognition of the potency of long-run competitive forces even where these are weak in the short run. Or it may be a response to stickiness in other parts of the market. The wage-push from the side of labor is now met with the administered-price drag, with adverse effect on profits, because of fear of long-run international and interproduct, if not intranational and intra-industry, competition among firms.

International and interindustry competition, moreover, is beginning to steady the prices of manufactured and primary products in developed countries, without regard to industrial pricing policies, as excess capacity arrives in such products as petroleum, heavy chemicals, and steel, and as competition intensifies in automobiles, electrical equipment, and other durable goods. The early years after the war, in which European and Japanese prices were low, but with long delivery dates and poor, if any, credit terms, have given way to years of widespread availability of manufactured goods, discounts, dumping, underselling, not to mention intense competition in the provision of credits. It may look as though export prices have not changed or have even risen gradually since the early 1950's. But in fact, the terms on which the manufactured goods are made available to customers with good credit ratings have changed substantially, though to an unquantifiable extent.

Moreover, competition is making a comeback. The creation of the Common Market in Europe testifies to a new faith in competition and readiness to face its consequences, which replaces the old system of the large firms holding a price umbrella over the small. Tight factor markets in labor and capital and rising factor returns have kept a heavy pressure upward on prices, but increased productivity and willingness to compete have provided a nearly complete offset.

The effort to extract monopoly advantage from the market is less important than the conditions of entry and exit which make it successful if the effort is made. In developed countries there may or may not be monopoly, and it may or may not seek to maximize short-run profits. To the extent that labor exercises its monopoly restraint, the wage creep sustains the prices of manufactured goods. Limits are set by new entry, however, as the U.S. steel companies are finding out from European and Japanese competition.

When underdeveloped countries attempt to maintain prices, the results typically are unsatisfactory. Not every potential competitor is covered in the agreements. Acreage controls leave room for expanded output through increased productivity per acre. New entry is easy. Stocks accumulate. The price is set too high; or, with the certainty given by price maintenance, costs fall. Before very long the attempt to maintain prices is abandoned. Hope springs eternal, and new attempts to maintain prices are made. They uniformly end badly because they encourage production which cannot be marketed at the prices set. Thus the conditions of entry and exit are more important than the geographical incidence of the instinct to monopolize. These conditions are the major factor accounting for the tendency of the merchandise terms of trade to turn against underdeveloped countries that are exporting primary products.

COMMODITY DEVELOPMENTS IN THE LAST DECADE

It is well to recall that most broad generalizations about commodity prices and terms of trade rest basically on one or two commodities which dominate the indexes, and that for every general rule there are major and minor exceptions. It is useful then to look at the data. In this section we refer to the price behavior since Korea of some forty commodities, and the detailed terms of trade by broad geographical areas. Most of the data come from the data of dollar relatives collected by the International Monetary Fund and published in *International Financial Statistics*. The commodity data are set out in the appendix to this essay, Table 1, on a 1953 base.[9]

To group commodities, it is handy to use the breakdown provided by GATT in its annual report and in the 1958 report of its Panel of Experts.[10] These show all primary-products prices at 93 in 1960, 91 in 1961 and 90 in the first quarter of 1962, on the basis of 1953 as 100,

[9] The IMF changed from the 1953 to the 1958 base only in 1962. The 1953 base is a good one for most commodities, though in some products, like wool, which were still affected by their Korean War highs, the use of the early base makes relatives at the end of the decade seem very low.

[10] GATT, *op. cit.* (Note 7).

while manufactures prices rose from 107 in 1960 to 109 in 1961 and maintained this same level in the first quarter of 1962. Within primary products, foodstuffs were the lowest in relation to 1953, declining from 88 in 1960 to 85 in 1961. Agricultural materials held somewhat higher but with a declining trend: 96 in 1960, 92 in 1961, and 90 in the first quarter of 1962.

The commodities can also be grouped by exporting area, as is done by the International Monetary Fund. Indexes are available for Latin America, Asia, and Australia on a weighted basis, and have been converted to the 1953 base:

Weighted Export Commodity Averages
(1953 = 100)

	1951	1958	1959	1960	1961	1962	
Latin America[1]	n.a.	91	86	86	86	85	(March)
Asia[2]	130	97	105	109	103	98	(April)
Australia[3]	130	67	73	72	71	n.a.	

[1] Cocoa, coffee, copper, cotton, meat, petroleum, sugar, wheat, wool.
[2] Burlap, coconut oil, copra, cotton, jute, rice, rubber, sugar, tea, tin.
[3] Butter, wheat, wool.

THE TERMS OF TRADE

The International Monetary Fund also furnishes aggregated export and import price or unit-value indexes from which continental terms of trade can be derived. These, again on a 1953 base, further show the impact of the downward drift in most primary-product prices.

Terms of Trade, 1953 = 100
(Export/import prices [in unit values])

	1951	1958	1959	1960	1961
United States	94	106	107	107	112
Canada	82	96	100	99	97
Europe	92	103	101	102	114
Latin America	106	88	85	85	85
Middle East	113	110	107	103	102
Africa	109	94	98	94	89
Asia	118	100	107	110	106
Australia	120	64	68	66	66
New Zealand	114	81	93	90	84

The surprises in these series from the normal expectation of the terms of trade moving against underdeveloped countries are in Asia and Australia. The former is the result of the bad crops of 1960 in jute and rubber; the latter is ascribable to the pattern of price decline in wool which makes the 1953 base a misleading one.

THE FUTURE

But my task, as I understand it, is primarily to suggest what the future holds as terms of trade for developing countries. The analysis worked out in my monograph in 1953–54[11] in emendation and support of Singer/Prebisch seems to have fit the facts of the last decade adequately enough. Will the years ahead provide more of the same?

Unfortunately, in present circumstances, it is virtually impossible to project the terms of trade into the future. If the world institutional framework remained unchanged, it would be relatively safe to follow the forecaster's law that tomorrow is more likely to be like today than anything very different. The Colin Clark forecast which has held true for the Soviet bloc, where simple manufactures are in far greater abundance than foodstuffs and raw materials, relative to demand, seems unlikely to overtake the underdeveloped world for some years ahead. The difficulties which India faces in agriculture, while serious,[12] seem less formidable than those it encounters in steel.

But a change has occurred, and largely in the attitude of economic authorities toward commodity price stabilization or regulation on a world basis. The GATT 1958 Panel of Experts recognized the difficulties of efforts at maintaining prices of primary products, but found in principle for this course of action:

> It is desirable to supplement general stabilization policies with measures for the stabilization of particular commodity markets where such measures are practicable and are innocuous on other grounds.[13]

[11] Kindleberger, *op. cit.* (Note 4).

[12] The GATT report, *International Trade, 1961* (pp. 14–16), suggests on the basis of its view of internal requirements and export possibilities, that agricultural production will have to grow by 120 per cent in Southeast Asia between 1956–60 and 1975, i.e. from $18 billion worth at 1956–60 prices to $41 billion. If the 1950 decade rate of growth obtained in the area, agricultural production would expand over this period only by 60 per cent. If the needed 5 per cent per annum rate of growth is not achieved with the aid of "highly sustained efforts," the report states that foodstuffs prices will have a persistent tendency to rise, in particular for animal products. It is thought that there are limits on the availability of non-commercial surpluses from developed countries. For Asia these are estimated to rise threefold, but only from $500 million at 1956–60 prices to $1.5 billion.

[13] GATT, Panel of Experts, *op. cit.,* (Note 7), para. 35, p. 7.

The conclusion is carefully qualified, but the enunciation of a change in principle tends to escape the restraint of the qualifications. In 1950, the Department of Agriculture was the only agency in the United States supporting international commodity agreements. By 1962 the Department of State had taken leadership in promoting the coffee agreement in the interest of political stability in Latin America. As early as 1955 the United States relaxed its opposition to the Commission on International Commodity Trade of the United Nations. The United States may not join all commodity agreements to which it is invited (*vide* tin), nor does it regulate its activities in the interest of these, as in the case of its rubber sales from stockpile. But commodity agreements, councils, study groups, and local organizations have become respectable as well as ubiquitous. The task of contemplating the future course of prices then becomes one of forecasting how effectively these organizations will perform, and what the political response to their success or failure may be.

The reaction of the GATT secretariat to this breach of the ancient orthodox stand against international price supports is to estimate the probable volume of trade in various classes of commodities from continental groups for 1975, but to calculate the value of trade on the assumption that 1975 prices will be those of 1956–60 on the average. The primary-product prices of 1956–60 are some 13 per cent higher than those of 1961, but are adopted as a working hypothesis. "This . . . subsumes the organization of some form of international action to support prices."[14] It is noted that if 1975 prices are those of 1961 instead of those of 1956–60, the projected trade deficit of the underdeveloped countries ($3.4 billion excluding Middle East petroleum countries and non-commercial imports) would be $2 billion larger.

This sort of partial-equilibrium analysis of output and trade, in which volume is estimated independently of prices[15] may be the best that one can do in making projections, but it is not very satisfactory. It is particularly disconcerting that a projection which assumes that prices are held up by international action emerges with the result that there is likely to be upward pressure on agricultural prices. It is certainly helpful to project what will happen to volume, given certain assumptions about prices, and what will happen to price, given certain assumptions about output; hopefully, the projections will converge to give a useful picture of what the

[14] GATT, 1961, *op. cit.* (Note 7), p. 13, n. 3.

[15] The GATT study (*ibid.*) assumes that income per capita will grow at 3 per cent a year in the underdeveloped areas, and population close to 2 per cent on the average. The volume of trade adopted for 1975 is, on the basis of 1956–60 as 100, 130 in foodstuffs, 125 in agricultural raw materials, and 225 in fuel and metals, or 165 (roughly 3 per cent per year) over-all.

future holds. But it is hardly tolerable to have the volumes that are produced with certain price assumptions yield price conclusions of a contradictory nature.

THE DISEQUILIBRIUM SYSTEM IN COMMODITIES

It is ironic that just at the time the Soviet Union appears to be discovering the price system, the Western World over a wide spectrum of commodities and countries is in process of abandoning it. Since the early 1950's, the machinery for intervention in international trade and price formation has been multiplying rapidly. Commodity problems are discussed in the UN Committee on International Commodity Trade, in the Food and Agriculture Organization's Committee on Commodity Problems, at the regional UN Commissions, the OECD and, since November 1961, GATT itself. On top of the UN, FAO, regional, and specialized groups, GATT adopted "procedures designed to establish the basis for the negotiation of practical measures for the creation of acceptable conditions of access to world markets for agricultural commodities."[16] During 1961 and 1962 discussions were held within GATT, as well as within the OECD, the European Economic Community (EEC), bilaterally between Britain and the supplying countries, and within the FAO Committee on Commodity Problems as to what to do to hold up the London price of butter. Failing international agreement to limit exports, the United Kingdom imposed import quotas. The episode neatly illustrates the extent to which the disequilibrium system has taken over the market mechanism. The occasion for the excitement was the expansion of French production which dropped that country from the ranks of the importers and required a place for it among the exporters with as much as 61,000 tons in total in 1961.

International agreements are found in only a limited number of commodities — wheat, sugar, tin, coffee, and (now lapsed) olive oil. The wheat agreement operates primarily through the efforts of the United States which holds a year's volume of international trade off the world market.[17] In sugar, the international agreement is less significant than the allocation of the United States import quota, an equal or more thorough-

---

[16] GATT, *International Trade, 1962,* p. 31.
[17] The International Wheat Agreement does not meet the entire range of problems faced in that commodity, and in particular not the sale by the United States of surplus grain under Public Law 480, but it was not the only organization in the field. There are in addition the FAO Group on Grains, the GATT Group on Cereals, established in February 1962, and of course the EEC.

going interference with the price system, which has lately turned up an interesting record of high-pressure lobbying in Washington by representatives of foreign countries. The tin agreement ran short of supplies in its buffer stock when production difficulties in the Congo, Indonesia, and Bolivia sent the price up; what would happen to world prices turned on the attitude of the United States stockpiling authorities with respect to whether they held onto their considerable supplies or, as in rubber, sold some off. The newest agreement in coffee is of interest because of the fact that within it there are an agreement of the producers of mild coffees of Central America to export less than their quotas in an effort to stabilize (raise) the prices of these varieties, and an Inter-African Coffee Organization with the leading policy objective of maintaining minimum prices. The Organization of Petroleum Exporting Countries (OPEC), established in 1960, has in its turn the principal objective of restoring the prices for crude petroleum reduced by the oil companies in August 1960.

Whether they are formed into a producers' alliance as in cocoa, bananas, and citrus fruit; an international advisory committee as in cotton; a study committee as in jute and allied fibers and proposed for the hard fibers, in lead and zinc, coconut and coconut products; or merely into a subcommittee of the FAO Committee on Commodity Problems meeting on the "Economic Aspects of Rice," the producing countries, occassionally in company with the importing countries, find themselves proposing to disturb the price and volumes which would clear the market in the absence of special stockpiling measures and production and trade controls. Not in all cases is action taken. In principle, the study group operates on the same basis as French planning — convening producers and consumers so that they may become acquainted with one another's intentions and adjust their own operations to their estimate of the totality of the others. In practice, more studious attention is given to the opportunities to maintain prices through a mutual restriction of output or at least of exports.

There is no basis for the developed countries' taking a patronizing view of these attitudes on the part of the underdeveloped. The United States agricultural program should provide a disturbing object lesson in the difficulties of large-scale intervention in the price system, but fails to move either the public or, along with indigestible surpluses, the Congress. Initiated to support the family farm, it now provides high profits for stockholders in corporate farm enterprises operated by contract managers. With peasant agriculture beginning to disappear in Western Europe, it might be thought that these countries would approach a "special regime for agriculture" with some diffidence, especially after the undistinguished record of the European Coal and Steel Community in coal. Established to "integrate" the market for coal, the ECSC not only failed to interfere with national policies of price controls, investment subsidies, and averaging of costs between high and low-cost producers, departing from the efficient policy of equalizing marginal costs, but also, despite econometric projections, overlooked the threat of competitive sources of energy. When it was hit by oil, the ECSC proved itself incapable of getting a Community-wide competitive solution but let each country adopt its own disequilibrium solution.

The disequilibrium system takes many forms, but its basic variants are two: (1) price too low: shortages, rationing, subsidies to maintain output; (2) price too high: surpluses, encouragement of sales and especially dumping, acquisition of surplus stocks, restriction of production.

The disequilibrium system can perform useful functions when the allocation of resources to production and of output to consumers is taken care of in other ways. It serves to distribute income in appropriate ways — restraining profits in wartime when the price is held down, and maintaining incomes when price is held up. Applied to foreign-exchange systems, the disequilibrium system — multiple exchange rates — can be used in many ways: to collect revenue for the government, improve the terms of trade, redistribute income, and even speed up development by allocating profits to growth industries. Its weakness is that incentives are created to undermine the desired pattern of expenditure and production and to lead to breakdown; to divert exports from the high rate to the low one, and imports the other way, in exchange control systems; to produce too little of the commodity when the price is held down and too much when it is held up. With adequate pressures to hold these economic incentives in check, the disequilibrium system can function effectively in the short run — as in time of war or great structural transition such as reconstruction from war. In peacetime, over long periods of time it inevitably breaks down.

It may be argued that the object of study groups, international agreements, etc., is to find and hold the long-run equilibrium price; that they are concerned with the short-run stabilization plan, not the slippage of the terms of trade against primary product and underdeveloped countries. This may be true in some cases. In the most important ones, however, the task seems to be to maintain the historic price, not the equilibrium one, and if economics knows anything it knows that this is a tough task. In oil, OPEC wants the August 1960 price, not one which will equate the long-run demand and supply. It hopes to hold the supply down and that the long-run demand will catch up with it. But it is faced with the necessity of making room in the market for French and Libyan oil, possibly that to be produced in Africa below the Sahara, the Russian sales to the west, and gas from the Netherlands, the Sahara, the Soviet Union, and perhaps overseas. In wheat and cotton, the United States recognizes that American corporate farmers could make money at prices more than 25 per cent below present support levels. And the same is true in coffee where the problem is recognized as finding the political equilibrium price, not the economic equilibrium.

Another defense of the disequilibrium system runs in terms of *tu quoque*. Manufacturers maintain prices; why should not governments act *in loco manufactorum*? Where competition is sharp, and entry is easy, it is true that there is no difference between manufacturing and primary production. The international agreement in cotton textiles to limit exports is exactly analogous to the international agreement to limit exports of butter, except that the latter could be enforced by import quotas in a single principal importer. Sir Donald MacDougall once forecast that automobiles would be the textiles of tomorrow. This projection has been falsified thus far. Entry into automobile production has been successfully undertaken by a number of developed countries with new models exported by Sweden and the Netherlands in addition to the United States, Britain, Germany, France and Italy, and successful local production in such countries as Australia and Canada. The returns are not yet in on the success of Japan in exporting. But production in developing countries — Argentina, Brazil, India, Israel, South Africa, to name a few — does not yet make the grade. None of these seems able to reduce costs far enough to enable it to compete successfully, in a market-oriented industry, with imports. It is not entirely clear whether the failure to achieve successful entry into automobile production in these countries is due to scale, labor skill, management, material costs, component-supply deficiencies, or some other factor. So long as the developed countries have the production possibilities to provide for themselves what they get from the underdeveloped countries, but the developing countries cannot with equal efficiency produce the manufactures they want and now import, the chances of primary-producing countries maintaining prices in the same way as manufacturers in developed countries must remain slight.

The developing countries may argue that their only need is for the same degree of price stability achieved by developed countries in primary products. Here it is necessary to make a distinction between competitively produced commodities (corn, cotton, meat, tobacco, wheat, wool, etc.) and those minerals (aluminum, coal, copper, iron ore, lead, nickel, petroleum, and zinc) and materials (newsprint and woodpulp) which are produced under oligopolistic conditions. In the first group, government intervention has maintained domestic prices in a number of countries, at great expense to the consumer and the taxpayer, but without devising a system which is capable of extension to the world as a whole. The so-called Baumgartner plan put forward by the French to GATT and calling for world price maintenance in international trade in temperate-zone foodstuffs, with surpluses produced at these prices donated by the producing countries to developing countries, has evoked no favorable response. The prospective diversion of U.S. and Commonwealth exports from the European Economic Community will exacerbate a situation which is proving increasingly difficult to maintain in the United States.

The second group has maintained prices well, except for lead. The prices of only two other commodities, copper and iron ore, are below the 1953 level, and two, nickel and aluminum, have risen substantially in price by 1960–61, to 127 for nickel and to 119 for aluminum. But aluminum producers are not happy. In November 1961 the U.S. industry put forward a proposal for a "voluntary Government-negotiated system of trade among free world nations" for the purpose of "rationalizing international trade in aluminum products." One spokesman noted that 20 per cent of the industry's capacity was idle and that this "has created the stiffest kind of price competition, which has driven profit margins down and down."[18] Similarly the oil industry, which has received government support at the state and national level in the United States, as well as from the British government and the OPEC, and has maintained prices for reporting purposes, has experienced widespread discounting. These oligopolist industries have maintained prices and profits longer than in the competitive industries not supported by government, but in so doing have encouraged entry at home and abroad at a faster rate than even the rapid expansion in demand.

In a world operating under the disequilibrium system there is not one price to be forecast for each commodity, but several. With a "special regime for agriculture," as in the EEC, or trade discrimination against tropical products from elsewhere than the former African colonies, there will be at least two prices. In some commodities, such as sugar, there will

---

[18] *New York Times,* November 20, 1961, p. 47.

be virtually a separate price for each country, and several for the United States. If the world develops in the direction of the price supports along with Public Law 480, one price may be zero and the terms of trade of some developing countries will approach infinity — a positive price for exports and free imports. But it is hardly useful to attempt to forecast the terms of trade of developing countries or of primary products under the disequilibrium system.

This much can be said: The National Planning Association seems to have been optimistic in 1960 in predicting for 1965–70: 7¼-cent bananas, 30-cent Bahia cacao, 33-cent coffee, 28-cent copper, 14.6-cent lead, crude petroleum rising at 1 per cent a year, iron ore up by 35 per cent, 5½-cent sugar (for Cuban premium supplies), and 13-cent zinc.[19]

Further, it is possible to reject the GATT projection for 1975 using 1956–60 prices, since the organization of international action which that presupposes can be predicted to fail if undertaken. It seems probable that the price of primary products will slip over-all, and that in one or two commodities where stabilization efforts have been made and failed, the dumping of redundant stocks on the market will result in very large price declines.

Some small allowance should perhaps be made for the possibility that the terms of trade will shift against manufactures in favor of primary products because of (a) the population expansion; or (b) a belated realization of the Colin Clark 1942 forecast that developing countries shift out of primary production into manufactures at a faster pace than is warranted by the differences in income elasticities of demand. On the first score, I remain skeptical despite the cogent points put forward by Sir Robert Hall.[20] Demand may increase, but price will not until the supply curve shows some tendency to point upward. There may be some price rises in quality foods — dairy products, meat, fish, etc. — but for the grains, oils, and simple proteins the supply curve looks flat over the years ahead to 1975 and even beyond.

Clark's prediction appears to have worked out in the Soviet bloc where foodstuffs and raw materials have been neglected in favor of simple machine tools, defense equipment, and especially steel. Is the underdeveloped world likely to follow this path? I see no prospect that it will. There is some doubt that the terms of trade really favor primary products over manu-

[19] Louis O. Delwart, *The Future of Latin American Exports to the United States: 1965 and 1970* (Washington: National Planning Association, Inter-American Research Committee, 1960), pp. 19, 22, 24, ff.

[20] Sir Robert Hall, "Commodity Prices and the Terms of Trade," *Lloyds Bank Review*, No. 63 (January 1962), pp. 1–15.

factures in the Soviet Union. One would have to have not only marginal social values for Soviet commodities — a difficult task in view of the disequilibrium price system used there — but also some adjustment for what is reputed to be the poor quality of some consumers' goods. But it seems to me unlikely that any country outside the Soviet bloc would today contemplate the reorganization of agriculture which would cripple output in that sector.

Forecasting is too risky in a disequilibrium world. It is safer to discuss policy. The urgency of policy discussion, moreover, is enhanced not only by current price trends but by the decision to hold a world trade conference under the sponsorship of the United Nations in 1964, a decision taken in the absence of a consensus and against the votes of the United Kingdom and the United States. The conference, it appears, will discuss the state of commodity prices, the impact on trade of the European Economic Community, and the proposals for commodity price stabilization. At the present writing, it is hard to see how it can do otherwise than fail.

POLICY

A world trade conference meeting in the spring of 1964 would have little difficulty in agreeing on two propositions of an uncontroversial nature:

1. that developed countries should strive in every possible way to maintain income stable and, indeed, expanding;
2. that developing countries should strive to increase their capacity to reallocate resources as between primary products and manufactures, so as to be able to take advantage of the relative profitability of each.

Proposition 1 encounters difficulties of execution, where there are such constraints as balance-of-payments weakness, or inhibitions such as reluctance to use fiscal policy to expand national expenditure. But the goal has been accepted, and its achievement would help the primary producers.

Proposition 2 meets virtual consensus. If it were put stronger — that developing countries should shift resources out of primary products into secondary manufacturing — it would encounter objection from those who, like Colin Clark in 1942, believe that planned industrialization is likely to be carried too far, and would run the risk of tipping the terms of trade in favor of primary products and against manufactures.[21] But if it is put in terms of increasing capacity to reallocate resources between primary products and manufactures so as to take advantage of relative profit opportunities, there can be no objection.

Beyond these two propositions, however, there will be difficulty. The least controversial conclusion, widely agreed to by international organization and governments but difficult to put into practice, can be stated as:

3. that developed countries should be prepared to accept increasing imports of manufactures from developing countries.

Intellectually reasonable, this proposition runs into the difficulty that imports of, say, textiles from developing countries threaten to wipe out one of the least productive sectors of the developed countries, and one which frequently possesses political power. Lancashire MP's and Southern Congressmen are facts of life. One can debate strategy and tactics in working toward responsive adaptation in developed countries as economic development creates new imports. It is clear that some battles will be lost. The principle, again, should be accepted.

It is also fairly widely agreed to among the experts:

4. that revenue duties on coffee, tea, and tobacco in some European countries have become so high that they act as a major restraint on consumption and import demand and should be reduced.

This implies that the demand is elastic at going prices. If this is so, the duties could be reduced with increases both in the value of imports and in revenue from the additional volume. If demand is relatively inelastic, the effect of tax reduction, in the absence of action by the exporting countries, would be limited to internal finance and income redistribution changes in the importing countries. But there is a possibility that the consumption taxes in Europe would be replaced by export taxes in the producing countries. This makes tax reduction the equivalent of foreign aid. One could as easily collect the tax in the importing country and turn the proceeds over to the exporters, as has been suggested in connection with the policing of valorization schemes. But it is an unsatisfactory form of foreign aid, because it is tied to the volume of exports of primary products. As such it works to retain resources in what may prove to be wrong lines.

---

[21] It is interesting to observe in the *New York Times* for November 21, 1962, that Premier Khrushchev now denounces the "blind" race for more and more steel production.

What can be generally agreed to is the reduction of these consumption duties where it will expand volume without cutting revenue. This will apply only where the demand has an elasticity substantially higher than one and where the tariff is a substantial proportion of the final selling price.

We do not propose to examine schemes for insuring the terms of trade. These are typically concerned with short-run stability, which is ruled out by our terms of reference. Where the insurance proposal has a subsidy element in its payment features, it becomes a matter of foreign aid, discussed below. Our discussion of commodity-price stabilization deals not with means but with ends, in four basic propositions:

5. that all intervention in the formation of primary product prices be completely abandoned in the very near future, and that instead, the rate of foreign aid to developing countries be adjusted to the requirements of their development programs in the new price situation;

6. that the United Nations embark on a program of international commodity-price stabilization as a long-run normal part of the international economic system;

7. that a series of programs of commodity-price stabilization be worked out on an empirical basis, either ignoring the fact they will not work in the long run, or recognizing it, but in the hope that something may come along to change the situation.

8. that a certain amount of temporary commodity-price stabilization be undertaken in a limited number of emergency cases, but that these be recognized as transitional and exceptional in the long-run structure of the international economic system with which the world hopes to emerge.

Proposition 5 will have a strong appeal to many groups in developed countries. It is the analogue of the Friedman proposition that foreign aid ought to be abandoned by the United States and replaced by the removal of tariffs on imports from developing countries;[22] or of Pechman's appealing suggestion that the exceptions to income taxation have become so widespread among all classes of taxpayers that the time has come to clear away all exemptions for the blind, the over-sixty-five, those with excess medical expenses, home-owners, married, parents of children, owners

---

[22] Milton Friedman, "Foreign Economic Aid: Means and Objectives," *Yale Review,* Vol. 50 (June 1961), pp. 533–40. The two propositions can be combined thus eliminating foreign aid: i.e., abandon intervention in international price formation and tariffs on imports.

of municipal bonds, producers of crude oil, etc. — and start a clean slate with a lower rate of tax applied to all incomes.[23] There is a great intellectual attraction in the heroic catharsis which rids the system of the labyrinth of encumbrance and intervention which distorts it. But it is hardly sensible as a political prescription. Before one can adopt a radical solution toward agriculture in the United States, for example, one must not only build urban opinion; one must destroy agricultural political power, reshape the political parties and the congressional committee structure; etc. Proposition 5 is a counsel of perfection or despair. Rigorous logic is not useful for policy purposes. The Congress of the United States is opposed to international commodity agreements, committed to domestic price stabilization in general, and supports commodity agreements in those commodities which the United States exports. Moreover, it is true that the developing countries exaggerate when they describe the situation of commodity prices as "reaching proportions of extreme emergency"[24] or "critical" and about to "impoverish many countries.[25] At the same time, it is impossible to contemplate the political consequences of a further sharp decline of commodity prices which would follow abandonment of existing efforts to hold prices up, and the sale of surplus stocks now held off the market.

Proposition 6, for generalizing commodity agreements world-wide, is the equally unrealistic, or possibly even more unrealistic remedy put forward by the developing countries acting as a bloc in the United Nations. Much of the present difficulty arises from prices being held too high, which encourages new entry. More of the former means more of the latter. Acceptance of the principle of international commodity price stabilization by the U.S. government and various bodies, including the GATT Panel of Experts, has not been accompanied by any increase in skill at making such stabilization function. On the contrary, the reluctant acceptance of the goal without provision of successful means has worsened the position.

The 1964 United Nations trade conference will doubtless see a renewed drive on the principle of commodity price stabilization. It should be resisted, and the previous acceptance in principal withdrawn. General commodity price stabilization might be tolerable if it were accompanied

---

[23] Joseph A. Pechman, "Erosion of the Individual Income Tax," *National Tax Journal*, X, 1 (March 1957), 1–25.

[24] See "Commodity Woes Worrying Latins, Falling Prices for Staples Creating Wide Concern," *New York Times*, June 10, 1962.

[25] See "Neutrals Voice Economic Fears, Worry on Commodity Prices Emerges at Cairo Parley," *New York Times*, June 11, 1962.

by strenuous efforts at long-term reduction in output or, more generally, at such increase in the capacity of resources engaged in primary production to let stabilization be temporary and, when it proved unprofitable, come to an end with the re-establishment of prices as the allocator of resources. In actuality, the stabilization of commodity prices is accompanied in virtually all cases by a relaxation of the pressure to remove sources from the industry, and even by efforts to expand production at the new and remunerative price, either through more intensive methods which beat acreage controls or through producing in new regions not covered by production controls.

The fact is that the world does not know how to stabilize commodity prices in ways which will produce the appropriate distribution of income without messing up the allocation of resources in production. The move from the British agricultural program of income guarantees and freely fluctuating prices to the Common Market special regime for agriculture, with its pegged prices and variable levies, is a backward step. In the United States, the failure to move from price supports to the wrongly maligned Brannan plan of income subsidies has been close to disastrous. The need is to move from price stabilization to income subsidies, with strong price incentives to readapt resources into economically efficient lines, and income subsidies — international aid — to assist where the distributional pressure of equilibrium prices is insupportable. "Adequate, fair, and equitable prices" are a mirage. It is not appropriate perhaps to say, "Aid, not trade"; but, "Aid, not subsidized prices," while not as poetic, makes good sense.

Proposition 7 will appeal to the cynical. In the oil industry, for example, it was long recognized that the world price was too high and that uneconomic entry was being encouraged; meanwhile profits were fine. It does not pay to worry about long-run solutions: the problems press today, and if the immediate is the enemy of the ultimate, the immediate is here and the ultimate still far away. Something may turn up, as World War II did, making a blessing out of the evil of heavy stocks of cotton and wheat owned by the Commodity Credit Corporation. The Princes of Serendip made out very well in ignoring or miscalculating the consequences of their policies. We may do as well. It is better to have monopolized and lost than never to have monopolized at all.

Proposition 7 would command a majority of United Nations votes. "Don't stand there; do something — anything." The developing countries will insist that they are not in position to contemplate ultimate consequences, since they face immediate problems. For the United States to reply to emergency appeals with proposals for long-range study seems either patronizing or evasive. Various groups in this government, like the Department of State on the coffee agreement, will be moved to join the search for stop-gap measures — regardless of consequences and regardless of the qualifications with which the experts surround their approval of commodity agreements. The United States and Britain, having failed to stop plans for the United Nations trade conference, will probably have to support some short-run measures for commodity price stabilization put forward by the majority. It seems probable that they will be no more successful in the long run than the UN Committee on International Commodity Trade, established finally after the United States reluctantly gave up persistent opposition.

This leaves Proposition 8, the use of a few price agreements in emergency situations, while working for their ultimate removal. If the general principle of price stabilization be abandoned, the problem can be reduced in size. The OPEC, for example, can be served notice that the rest of the world is uninterested in supporting their efforts. The aluminum industry — hardly a case for compassionate attention — can be required to work out the competitive solution. Some commodities which look low in price, like wool and rice, can be ignored because of the success of the market in adjusting to equilibrium prices. And other commodities, which look high in a historical sense, like jute, can be seen to involve tough residual problems.

CONCLUSION

In emergency commodities where price stabilization is undertaken, these measures should be coupled with aid to assist in the necessary diversification and expansion of other lines of output. Some of the diversification can take place in other primary products. The capacity of Egypt to switch between cotton and wheat, or of East Pakistan and India to grow either rice or jute, helps to stabilize the prices of both. The one-crop producers must contemplate diversification into other primary products as well as into manufacturing.

To sum up: not much primary-product price stabilization, then, and all of that temporary, and accompanied by foreign aid for the purpose of alleviating dependence on limited specialization.

STATISTICAL APPENDIX

Table 1. Dollar Relatives of Primary Products

(1953 = 100)

Commodity (country of quotation)	1951	1954	1955	1956	1957	1958	1959	1960	1961	1962 (first half)
Aluminum* (U.K.)	79.0	99.4	106.4	121.7	125.4	117.2	114.6	118.5	118.5	116.0
Bacon and ham (Denmark)	97.1	94.2	98.7	106.5	98.1	101.0	96.1	96.8	95.5	98.7
Bananas (U.S.)	102.0	100.0	101.3	102.0	105.9	103.9	102.6	96.7	100.7	n.a.
Beef (Argentina)	79.2	101.1	94.7	75.2	71.9	83.4	94.2	99.1	90.1	90.3
Burlap (India)	245.0	95.9	88.7	81.5	83.0	81.1	80.6	95.5	109.1	116.6
Butter (Denmark)	86.1	100.7	103.5	105.9	85.6	70.8	101.4	87.5	80.2	91.0
Cacao (Ghana)	110.7	166.5	134.2	91.8	82.4	133.1	115.8	92.4	72.0	72.2
Coal (U.S.)	104.4	96.8	102.0	114.5	119.2	115.7	111.8	107.9	s.n.c.	s.n.c.
Coconut oil (Philippines)	102.0	82.8	69.9	66.7	68.5	94.7	116.5	92.1	71.3	68.5
Coffee (Santos, U.S.)	92.9	133.9	97.5	99.9	98.0	83.6	64.8	63.1	62.1	59.5
Copper (U.K.)	87.4	99.3	141.1	128.4	85.6	78.2	94.8	97.1	91.0	92.8
Copra (Philippines)	98.7	84.1	74.1	71.1	77.7	102.4	127.5	98.4	77.0	75.3

Table 1 (*continued*)

Commodity (country of quotation)	1951	1954	1955	1956	1957	1958	1959	1960	1961	1962 (first half)
Corn* (U.S.)	113.3	101.3	89.2	91.8	82.3	79.7	77.2	73.4	71.5	70.0
Cotton (U.S.)	126.4	103.3	102.1	81.8	83.6	84.8	77.8	72.0	76.0	74.9
Fish (U.S.)	100.9	100.4	91.6	90.2	95.6	117.3	125.3	112.9	s.n.c.	s.n.c.
Flax* (U.K.)	150.9	99.4	97.8	87.9	83.9	74.8	74.8	75.8	77.6	77.6
Hemp (Philippines)	161.4	71.2	78.1	95.0	117.1	102.2	151.2	140.4	114.1	100.9
Hides* (U.K.)	118.9	88.1	77.6	84.9	86.5	82.7	117.6	92.4	82.4	80.0
Iron ore* (Germany)	81.4	88.8	94.5	104.1	109.5	104.7	91.4	92.8	93.1	s.n.c.
Jute (Pakistan)	200.0	105.7	104.4	108.2	118.9	110.7	100.6	127.7	177.0	127.0
Lead (U.K.)	176.1	104.8	115.4	126.1	103.0	79.0	76.4	77.5	69.6	62.8
Linseed oil (U.K.)	94.2	63.1	57.8	77.8	66.2	61.8	57.8	61.3	67.1	51.6
Lumber* (U.K.)	114.0	99.9	108.4	110.1	107.8	99.7	91.3	99.9	102.7	98.0
Mutton and lamb (N.Z.)	75.2	115.0	127.4	130.2	137.6	124.2	109.0	114.5	102.8	96.8
Newsprint (Canada)	87.1	100.1	100.4	103.0	104.8	104.4	104.7	105.1	104.6	104.8
Nickel*	90.1	101.0	107.8	109.0	124.2	124.2	124.2	124.2	130.4	133.0

Commodity										
Nitrates* (Chile)	93.9	92.7	90.2	83.1	73.7	76.1	75.5	83.3	81.1	s.n.c.
Olive oil* (Spain/France)	110.0	77.1	87.5	121.9	98.6	82.4	75.3	74.9	71.7	79.0
Crude petroleum (Venezuela)	95.3	104.3	104.0	101.4	110.1	110.5	102.9	101.4	101.4	101.4
Petroleum products (U.S.)	95.4	98.0	99.1	105.2	111.1	106.6	104.8	107.0	107.0	99.7
Pulp (Canada)	102.2	98.9	97.3	97.8	101.6	100.0	100.5	98.9	99.4	91.5
Quebracho (Argentina)	81.6	100.9	100.5	99.1	90.2	79.2	81.8	57.6	48.9	56.2
Rice (Burma)	66.9	74.9	59.6	54.7	53.3	56.2	51.5	48.6	53.6	53.4
Rubber (Malaya)	251.4	100.0	169.5	143.6	131.8	119.1	150.5	160.4	124.1	117.3
Sugar (Dominican Rep.)	161.1	92.4	91.5	96.1	148.2	107.0	93.0	102.8	102.8	s.n.c.
Tea (U.K.)	97.5	139.2	149.2	132.2	133.9	128.6	126.6	130.9	123.1	116.9
Tin (U.S.)	133.1	96.7	99.3	106.1	101.3	99.8	107.1	106.4	118.8	123.8
Tobacco (U.S.)	103.7	102.2	101.6	105.3	106.5	115.2	117.0	114.8	121.3	125.0
Wheat (Canada)	104.3	86.6	84.7	84.2	82.3	80.4	83.3	81.8	82.8	86.7
Wool (Australia)	138.6	91.9	77.6	81.6	90.0	61.5	63.1	63.2	65.0	66.3
Zinc (Canada)	155.8	102.0	114.0	124.2	109.3	91.4	105.2	113.4	102.2	94.7

Source: International Monetary Fund, *International Financial Statistics*, various issues (data since December 1961, converted from 1958 base to 1953), except for items marked with asterisk, which are from United Nations, *Monthly Bulletin of Statistics*, converted to dollar base and 1953 relatives.

s.n.c. — series not continued in sources.

POTENTIALS AND HAZARDS OF DIRECT INTERNATIONAL INVESTMENT IN RAW MATERIALS

CHANDLER MORSE

Barely a century has passed since the emergence of international investment as a major influence on the course of human events. Excluding loans to governments, a very large part of such investment has been in raw materials directly, or in related lines such as transport. If we exclude Western Europe, the United States, and Japan, the preponderance of direct foreign investment in the development of natural resources has been substantial. Much of such investment has been in Canada, Australia, New Zealand, and the Republic of South Africa, where the institutional setting and — with the exception of South Africa — the sociocultural conditions are broadly similar to those in the investor countries. A more controversial fraction has been in countries where the environment differs markedly from that of the investors.

CHANDLER MORSE has been professor of economics at Cornell University since 1950, serving also as chairman of the University's Modernization Analysis Workshop (since 1962); as chairman of the Economic Survey Mission to Basutoland, Betchuanaland Protectorate, and Swaziland (1959); and as director of the Cornell Social Science Research Center (1954–56). From 1947 to 1950 he was with the Department of Economics at Williams College; in 1946–47 was assistant director of research and statistics, Board of Governors, Federal Reserve System; and during World War II served with the Office of Strategic Services. From 1929 to 1941 he was with the Federal Reserve Bank of New York and Board of Governors of the Federal Reserve System. Mr. Morse is co-author (with Harold J. Barnett) of *Scarcity and Growth* (1963), and author of "The Functional Imperatives," in *The Social Theories of Talcott Parsons* (1961). He was born in Brooklyn, N.Y., in 1906; received his B.A. at Amherst College and his M.A. at Harvard University.

Because of their current interest and increasing importance, the potentials and hazards with which I shall deal will be mainly those of investment in countries with cultures, histories, and institutions different from our own. But some potentials and hazards are peculiar to investment in raw materials as such, and so will be found also in countries with Western structures; and some are characteristic of international investment generally, regardless of industry or location. I shall not make much of these distinctions, but it is well to recognize that they exist.

On first consideration, the concepts of potential and hazard as applied to international investment seem straightforward and simple. But when one undertakes to deal with them systematically on the broad scale here attempted, these virtues vanish. Potentials, presumably, are expected or contingent benefits, but they are also opportunities to avoid actual or contingent costs, account being taken of all favorable and unfavorable possibilities, non-economic as well as economic. Hazards are the reverse. Since benefits and costs cannot be defined or evaluated without specifying to whom the advantages or disadvantages are expected to accrue, the adoption of a global perspective entails serious difficulties. One obvious simplification is to abstract from the problems of East-West competition in production and distribution of raw materials, and this I shall do; the problems of cold economic warfare will be ignored. This shrinks the globe, and leaves us to consider four groups of potentially interested parties: the international firms that undertake the investment and operate the enterprises; the host countries, in which the enterprises are located; the investor countries, where the firms are domiciled; and third parties — all those, including any of the three foregoing groups not directly involved, whose interests are at stake but who are passive rather than active participants in the relevant decisions. But space will not permit consideration of all possible combinations of conflicting or mutual interests among these four groups of interested parties, so I shall deal almost exclusively with the relationships between direct foreign private investors and host countries.

There is also the problem of choosing the right level of generality, the right degree of particularity. At one level of analysis it is clear that international investment in natural resource exploration and development confers widely shared benefits by contributing to the growth and development of the host countries, by augmenting the world's raw material supplies, by yielding widely dispersed gains from trade, and so on. But these potentials imply hazards: competition for the means to achieve more rapid rates of growth and development; gluts of raw materials; instability of prices; efforts to employ dependence on supplies of or markets for raw materials as bargaining weapons in the conduct of foreign policy; disturbance of established ways of life. What appear as communities of interest when viewed in broad perspective, resolve, as we approach them more closely, into conflicts of interest concerning the allocation of incremental benefits and costs. Increased production carries the potential of mutual gain; competition for a share of the gain entails the hazard of absolute loss.

To simplify the discussion, it is helpful to recognize that potentials and hazards imply problems — problems of realization and problems of avoidance. Problems, in turn, imply efforts to resolve them by changes of policy, practice, or institutional arrangements. I shall therefore adopt a problem-focused approach. In so doing, I shall assume, for the most part, that the potentials and hazards implicit in the problems are plain and need not be identified explicitly. To some extent also, the implications for policy, practice, and institutional change will be left to speak for themselves, although some broad generalizations will be attempted by way of conclusion. The topics to be considered are:

> basic problems peculiar to international investment in natural resources; initial problems arising out of institutional differences; dynamic problems arising mainly out of company operations, policies, and practices; constructive approaches to the reduction of hazards; potentials and hazards in political perspective.

Basic Problems Peculiar to International Investment in Natural Resources

Several circumstances distinguish development of capacity to produce raw materials overseas from other types of direct international investment. One of these, not universal but very common, is the *location* of mineral deposits and favorable sites for tropical and subtropical plantations. Because it is so familiar one need only note its major consequences. Production of raw materials is largely for export. Mines and, to a lesser degree, large-scale agricultural or forestry operations, tend to be remote from urban centers so that provision of utilities and social services becomes a substantial business venture in its own right. So do the provision of transport and communications between the site and the outside world, and the provision of consumable supplies for the labor force and their families. The scale of the investment required is thus substantially greater than for raw material processing and manufacturing; and the operation of a mining or plantation community involves social and political responsibilities which can only be handled by large organizations capable of exercising many talents other than business acumen.

Unique risks and uncertainties constitute a second set of distinguishing circumstances for international investment in natural resources. The best known of these, and one which has been the subject of much investigation and debate at the United Nations, is instability of raw material export proceeds.[1] Given the conservative bias of large international enterprises, and their tendency to seek a rapid recovery of capital in risky and uncertain situations, instability of sales often leads to an excessive evaluation of the profit margins deemed necessary in good years to make up for bad ones, and so raises the effective supply price of capital above what it would be with less instability, or the same instability but greater predictability. The host countries, looking at results *ex post* and not much inclined in any case to evaluate highly the risks incurred by foreign enterprises, are more impressed with the problems that instability creates for them than with those it creates for the investor. Most prominent among these problems are balance of payments difficulties. Another, alleged to have operated in Cuba and potentially operative elsewhere, is that the secondary effects of export variability on domestic income and expenditure create uncertainties in many fields and deter investment generally.[2]

A risk peculiar to raw materials is that associated with exploration for minerals, especially petroleum.[3] Only financially strong enterprises can afford to gamble on the possibility that there may be long periods in which costs are incurred without return.[4] Since the prospects of eventual payoff are greatly improved if exploration is conducted over an extended period in a number of geographically dispersed locations, it is clear that the international majors and a few large independents have a great advantage over smaller enterprises, or even government monopolies, in searching for oil in regions where its occurrence has not been conclusively established, or sometimes in developing known reserves. The inability of the Argentine government monopoly to finance either exploration or development on an

---

[1] A useful discussion will be found in Henry Wallich, "Stabilization of Proceeds from Raw Material Exports," in Howard S. Ellis (ed.), *Economic Development for Latin America* (London: Macmillan, 1961). Also see section below headed "Constructive Approaches to the Reduction of Hazards."

[2] See "Comments" by Jose A. Guerra, in Ellis, *op. cit.* (Note 1).

[3] See United Nations, Department of Economic and Social Affairs, *Petroleum Exploration — Capital Requirements and Methods of Financing* (Sales No.: 62.II.B.3), New York, 1962.

[4] *Ibid.*, p. 15, where it is noted that companies invested $40 million in Guatamala between 1956 and 1959, with no petroleum being produced, and that other similar examples could be cited.

adequate scale led to adoption of a policy of opening these activities to private investment, with impressive results.

Analogous risks, though on a much smaller scale, occur in plantation agriculture. Gestation periods for some crops, such as coffee and cocoa, are so long that market conditions may change materially between planting and harvesting; crop yields and costs are highly and unpredictably variable; and ignorance of unique local conditions often plagues new ventures, especially in the tropics and semi-tropics. Experience on one continent, and even within a given region, often is a poor guide to results achievable elsewhere within the area. Crop failures are often the first but seldom the last of the risks encountered, for the salvaging of sunk costs will frequently require the initiation of research and experimentation over a considerable period on crop varieties, disease control, rainfall, soil conditions, fertilizer needs, suitability of soil for irrigation, improved livestock breeds, and so on.

Largely because of ignorance of conditions, one of the most uncertain agricultural areas is Africa. The groundnut scheme in Tanganyika is only one — the most notorious — of several projects involving international investment and aid that turned out badly. The study of such experiences, says Kimble, "is illuminating not so much for the evidence of folly and unjustifiable optimism it discloses as for the insight it gives us into the nature of tropical Africa — its environments and peoples, and our still lamentable ignorance of both."[5]

In addition to the problems created by the unique locational aspects and uncertainties of investment in production of raw materials, there are several which reflect the peculiar political importance of natural resources. Locally, there are the disturbing consequences of alienating land from the indigenous inhabitants, or denying them access to lands once regarded as free, by methods that differ from or contravene the traditional procedures for allocating rights of cultivation, grazing, or hunting; of obtaining spe-

---

[5] G. H. T. Kimble, *Tropical Africa* (2 vols.; New York: Twentieth Century Fund, 1960), I, 169, see pp. 163–93 for a general discussion of problems. For a full-length discussion of a success, see Arthur Gaitskell, *Gezira—A Story of Development in the Sudan* (London: Faber and Faber, 1959); and of an instructive failure, K. D. S. Baldwin, *The Niger Agricultural Project* (Oxford: Blackwell, 1957). Also see John Phillips, *Agriculture and Ecology in Africa* (London: Faber and Faber, 1959), Book One; *The Development of Agriculture and Forestry in the Tropics—Patterns, Problems, and Promise* (London: Faber and Faber, 1961); and V. D. Wickizer, *Coffee, Tea, and Cocoa—An Economic and Political Analysis* (Stanford: Stanford University Press, 1951), Part IV. The annual reports of the Colonial Development Corporation, London, are a fruitful source of information concerning a wide variety of hazards and potentialities.

cial rights and privileges with respect to subsurface resources, which, in most parts of the world, are regarded as belonging to the community as a whole; and especially of depleting the mineral resources of the region without apparent replacement by alternative forms of productive wealth, or other enduring provision for the future welfare of the local population.

This latter characteristic, above all others, has been responsible for making the international production of raw materials as much a political as an economic problem. Levin has made a scholarly and illuminating study of the reasons for the long stagnation of most raw material export economies and for their recent "revolt."[6] This revolt of the export economies has given international investment in raw materials a new political dimension, with companies and host countries in the roles of protagonists. It has also added a new dimension to the international politics of raw materials, in which host countries and investor countries oppose each other. The increasing dependence of the industrial nations, particularly the major powers, on overseas sources of supply was not regarded with concern so long as production was in the hands of their own nationals, and host countries were passive.[7] But increasing independence of the latter, and their occasional expropriation of, or insistence on government partnership in, foreign enterprises indicate that old views concerning the political economy of natural resources and national security are due for revision.

INITIAL PROBLEMS ARISING OUT OF INSTITUTIONAL DIFFERENCES

Because so much international investment in raw materials has been in countries affected but little by the Euro-American tradition, the mere existence of sociocultural differences has been, and continues to be, a source of problems. I call these "initial" (or static) problems because they reflect

[6] Jonathan V. Levin, *The Export Economies* (Cambridge: Harvard University Press, 1960), pp. 2–4. A noteworthy and topically important instance of the non- (or anti-) developmental impact of export-oriented raw material production is found in Cuba and other Caribbean islands. Consider, for example, Henry Wallich's observation: "In his classic study, *Azucar y Poblacion en las Antillas*, Ramiro Guerra has shown how under circumstances where labor is plentiful and land is not, the sugar industry tends to drive out small landowners and producers of competing products and to establish *a plantation routine that blocks all development including its own.*" *Monetary Problems of an Export Economy* (Cambridge: Harvard University Press, 1950), p. 11. Italics added.

[7] See, for example, E. H. Davenport and S. R. Cooke, *The Oil Trusts and Anglo-American Relations* (New York: Macmillan, 1924), especially Chapters VII, XX. Herbert Feis, *Seen from E.A. — Three International Episodes* (New York: Knopf, 1947), pp. 164–65, 181–82, 189–90.

given conditions, and so become manifest at the outset of the investment process; and also to distinguish them from a further set of problems which I call "dynamic" because these arise both out of efforts of the parties concerned to solve the initial problems, and out of the continuing impact of the foreign enterprise and its operations on the host society. The distinction between initial and dynamic problems is somewhat arbitrary, like many of the other distinctions made in this essay, but all of them are convenient. I divide the initial problems into two groups: those arising out of political and legal differences, and those arising out of sociocultural differences.

Political and Legal Problems

Political. From the standpoint of international investors and their governments, colonialism and economic imperialism were highly functional: they permitted Western capital and enterprise to operate with a minimum of fear that changes in the local balance of political power, peculiarities of indigenous law, or the application of strange concepts of justice and equity would require the foreign investor to operate under highly unwelcome conditions. Adaptation there was, but mainly on the side of the host society.

There is little current interest in the means that were employed to secure such adaptation. They have lost favor (to the point where we like to forget they were ever fashionable), and no present purpose would be served by dredging up aspects of this unsavory past, but I commend to those interested the series called "Studies in American Imperialism," edited by Harry Elmer Barnes. The first studies in this series dealt with Bolivia, Cuba, and Santo Domingo,[8] a selection which attests both to the acuity of the initiators and the viability of the problems left in the wake of history thoughtlessly made. To attempt a general summary of these problems would divert this paper from its proper course. Also, it would be otiose, since the heritage of bitterness against the often synonymous anath-

---

[8] Margaret A. Marsh, *The Bankers in Bolivia;* Leland H. Jenks, *Our Cuban Colony;* Melvin M. Knight, *The American in Santo Domingo* (all New York: Vanguard Press, 1928). Two later studies which came to my attention are: Charles D. Kepner, Jr. and Jay H. Soothill, *The Banana Empire* (Vanguard, 1935), and C. D. Kepner, Jr., *Social Aspects of the Banana Industry* (New York: Columbia University Press, 1936). For more recent, economically oriented treatments of the Latin-American scene, see J. Fred Rippy, *The Caribbean Danger Zone* (New York: Putnam's Sons, 1940); *Globe and Hemisphere* (Chicago: Regnery, 1958); and *British Investments in Latin America* (Minneapolis: University of Minnesota, 1959).

emas of foreign enterprise, Western capitalism, and (in Asia and Africa) white supremacy, is an omni-problem on which many another rides.

It is of relevance, however, to note how political pressures have caused the old methods of fitting Western enterprise into a strange environment to lose favor. One alleged reason why these pressures developed in the raw-material countries is that foreign investors showed little respect for law or the legitimacy of power. Of Venezuela, for example, Lieuwen remarks that, under Gomez, the petroleum companies had "almost complete freedom of action, dealing only with the dictator, and making a farce out of the law when the occasion demanded."[9] But after the death of Gomez, and especially after World War II, the situation changed, largely because of the altered balance of political power: the companies became "more willing to go beyond minimum obligations."[10] Something of the same kind has happened in many other countries, which have either thrown off colonialism or risen against foreign economic domination. Indeed, as the activities of international companies have come to depend less and less upon the favorable exercise of arbitrary domestic or foreign political pressure, they have come to be governed more and more by the rule of law, as attested by the sudden appearance (in recent years) of studies dealing with the legal problems involved in the conduct of multinational business operations.[11] Such problems often involve conflicts of law, but such conflicts are less strident, as a rule, than those of politics. They are also less familiar, and for that reason I shall dispose of them less cavalierly.

[9] Edwin Lieuwen, *Petroleum in Venezuela—A History* (Berkeley and Los Angeles: University of California Press, 1954), pp. 117–18. For details see especially pp. 34–38, 61–62, 67–71, and Chapter VI.

[10] *Ibid.*

[11] Milton Katz and Kingman Brewster, Jr., *International Transactions and Relations—Cases and Materials* (London: Stevens & Sons, 1960), p. 2. For discussions of legal problems relating more explicitly to international investment, see the following publications of the International Legal Studies Program of Columbia University: Wolfgang Friedmann and Richard C. Pugh (eds.), *Legal Aspects of Foreign Investment* (Boston: Little, Brown, 1959), containing chapters on each of forty countries, and two summary chapters; Wolfgang Friedmann and George Kalmanoff (eds.), *Joint International Business Ventures* (New York: Columbia University Press, 1961); A. A. Fatouros, *Government Guarantees to Foreign Investors* (Columbia, 1962). Also see E. R. Barlow and Ira T. Wender, *Foreign Investment and Taxation* (Englewood Cliffs: Prentice-Hall for Harvard Law School International Program in Taxation, 1955); and Robert A. Wilson (ed.), *Proceedings of the 1960 Institute on Private Investments Abroad* (New York: Matthew Bender, for the Southwestern Legal Foundation of Dallas, Texas, 1960), which contains discussions of both regional law and specialized problems. Also see Northcutt Ely, *Summary of Mining and Petroleum Laws of the World* (Washington: Bureau of Mines Information Circular No. 8017, 1961).

Legal. Katz and Brewster[12] stress the difficulties of projecting an image of the international legal order in systematic terms. These difficulties, they observe, partly reflect differences in basic values. But even where this is no obstacle, there is wide variation in the room left for individual mobility and choice, and in the willingness to make expectations reliable by permitting rights to become vested with legal protection.

Differences in the reliability of expectations based upon (presumptive) rights are a major breeding ground of problems for international investors. But lack of legal protection for presumptive rights is not the only source of difficulty. There are also differences in laws and in the operation of the whole juridical apparatus. The lawyer versed in a federal system, like that of the United States, is familiar with the problems of having to take into account more than one legal system. The problems are mitigated, however, by the presence of an overriding constitutional instrument which sets standards and techniques for reaching a workable approximation of "equal protection," "privileges and immunities," and the unhampered flow of "commerce . . . among the several states."[13] This is lacking in the international sphere.

A first task is to examine actual differences among legal systems and practices, and to determine what sorts of problems they create. Two categories of such problems may be identified. One arises because of the fact of "foreignness": Aliens and their activities are treated differently from nationals. The other is due to the overlapping and conflict of laws, and to the sometimes inept or inconsistent efforts of sovereign states to effect workable accommodations. Indeed, three systems of law are often involved: that of the foreign country, that of the home country, and the applicable corpus of public international law.

Relevant materials frequently contain language or commentary which suggests that nations may exclude aliens as they see fit, and that courts will defer in such matters to the decisions of political authorities. But this points to a doctrine that sovereign decisions affecting aliens are beyond review and redress — that "foreignness would imply absence of legal protection." This is not the case in practice: "The common interest in international mobility, communication and dealing and the reciprocal interest in fair treatment of nationals abroad finds expression in both municipal legal systems and public international law." (P. 8)

---

[12] Katz and Brewster, *op. cit.* (Note 11).
[13] Katz and Brewster, *op. cit.* (Note 11), p. 4. The following is based on their discussion, especially pp. 6–9, 83–85, 122, 171, 258, 277, 495, 549–51, 603, 615, 635, 695, 727, 748, 779–81, 823–33, and 850–56.

The extent to which the "common interest" has found such legal expression varies substantially from region to region. This is significant in the present context because international investment in raw materials is concentrated in countries where, for historical and cultural reasons, official perception of the common interest, and of what represents reciprocal fair treatment, has differed from that of private foreign investors and their governments. As a result, neither side has moved far toward mutual accommodation.

Nowhere is this so true as in the acquisition, retention, and use of property. These activities, carried out in one state by nationals of another, raise questions of which the implications "reach deep into the prevailing concepts, assumptions and habits of thought concerning the nature of a state, the structure of society and the organization of economic effort." In some societies, especially those with feudal or communal social arrangements, "the concept of land ownership and the concept of alienage tend to appear mutually exclusive. By definition, an alien is one outside the society, and therefore outside the fused political-social-land system. The idea of the ownership of land by an alien seems to imply a self-contradiction." (P. 83)[14]

Differences in social organization, then, are one source of the legal difficulties faced by aliens who wish to own and operate productive assets, especially those of a land-extensive extractive character, in countries other than their own. Differences in economic organization are another source of legal problems. An atomistic type of private-enterprise society needs and develops concepts of property and its use different from those appropriate where economic activity is organized along more centralized or oligarchic lines. Because countries seeking rapid growth and development are likely to rely more on the centralized than the atomistic mode of organizing major new economic activities, the desire for rapid economic growth and development means that the legal concepts confronting Western investors in such countries will often seem inappropriate and misguided. The situation is especially acute with respect to large foreign owned or operated corporations, which are often regarded as essential to growth and development. Attitudes inherited from an earlier period of

[14] In the British African protectorate of Basutoland, for example, no person may have recognized rights to the use of land who is not a member of the Basuto Nation. The concept of private ownership does not exist in Basuto law where, as in much of Africa, title to the land is held in trust by the Paramount Chief on behalf of all the people. To be a Basuto is to qualify for allocation of land by which to support one's family.

colonial or quasi-colonial status have made the emerging nations especially sensitive to and dubious of this form of ownership and control. The resulting conflict of aims and emotions has activated dynamic sociopolitical processes which have led to frequent shifts of policies, thus compounding the problems arising from static initial differences.

The attribute of foreignness often means that opportunities to acquire, hold, use, or dispose of property may be assured, limited, or frustrated in a multitude of small ways. Problems of larger scope and import often arise when the government of a state takes the property of, or annuls a contract with, a foreigner, for such problems reflect conflicting principles of economic and social organization and development. The issues involved in both the smaller and the larger problems are too complex, and the state of law too unsettled, to justify detailed discussion here, but certain points may be made. Thus, there is ambiguity in the terms typically used, such as "taking," "expropriation," "confiscation," "nationalization," and "seizure" (all in relation to property); or "annulment," "cancellation," "repudiation," and "arbitrary refusal to perform" (all in relation to contracts). There are such questions as whether regulation or taxation is designed to give effect to a broad economic or social policy, with the injury to the alien a mere by-product; or whether the injury to the alien is one of the purposes, perhaps even a primary purpose, of the measure. Sometimes the distinction between such a measure and expropriation is quite plain; sometimes it shades rather clearly into covert expropriation. In cases of overt expropriation the principle of compensation may be accepted, but the determination of what is "fair" recompense may find the parties poles apart. And many governments, rejecting an unqualified rule, "insist that the requirement of compensation applies only in the case of expropriation which involves discrimination against aliens or against particular aliens. Others lay emphasis upon the freedom of states to expropriate property in the course of a general program of economic or social reform without payment of 'compensation' or at least without payment of 'full' or 'prompt' compensation." (P. 833)

This whole question led to a lively debate in the United Nations as the result of a resolution, introduced in December 1952, which contained the proposition that "the right of peoples freely to use and exploit their natural wealth and resources is inherent in their sovereignty."[15] A number

---

[15] Quoted by Hyde, *American Journal of International Law*, 50 (1956), 854, excerpts from which are reproduced in Katz and Brewster, *op. cit.* (Note 11), pp. 850–56. The discussion of the UN controversy is based on these excerpts.

of issues became entangled in the ensuing debate, which lasted several years.[16] One of these involved the principle of (political) self-determination, and the related question of colonialism. Another involved the principle of economic self-determination — that is, of a state's power, generally recognized as a matter of law, to control and use its natural resources, and therefore to acquire property within its jurisdiction; and the fact that this power does not nullify the power in a state to make so-called concessions (agreements) covering the importation of capital for natural resource development purposes. It should be noted, however, that if a state takes property or terminates a contract in violation of such an agreement, it may be difficult for the injured party to find effective remedy without — or even with — diplomatic intervention, and that such intervention will not now be as readily available as in an earlier day.

The foregoing problems concern the treatment of aliens, and the conflict of principles, in the matter of property and its use, but this by no means exhausts the list. I shall not extend further this discussion of legal hazards and problems, but it may be useful to observe that overlapping and conflicting or inconsistent laws, sometimes reflecting different patterns of thought, sometimes defying solutions of a clearly rational or equitable sort, are found in (1) the realm of regulatory measures, particularly attempts to enforce competition in foreign commerce,[17] to extend labor and welfare requirements to foreign or international activities, and to ration and control the disposition of foreign exchange; and also in (2) the familiar and complex field of taxation.

Sociocultural Problems

For reasons that are not difficult to fathom, difficulties and problems created by sociocultural differences originate from circumstances analogous to those in law. And they are at least equally intransigent. The contrasts between what is indigenous and what is alien, between views of what is desirable, proper, just, or workable, arise out of deepseated dif-

[16] Indeed, the debate still continues. The *New York Times* of December 5, 1962, reported that the United States had criticized a resolution on sovereignty over natural resources passed by the Economic Committee of the General Assembly by a vote of 60 to 5, with 22 abstentions, "after weeks of debate." The criticism was directed at an accepted Soviet amendment which, according to the United States, "implied that there was no restriction whatever on a country's taking over property owned by foreign interests."

[17] See United Nations, *Report on the Ad Hoc Committee on Restrictive Business Practices* (ECOSOC, 16th Sess. Supp. No. 11), cited in Katz and Brewster, *op. cit.* (Note 11), p. 603.

ferences of social organization reflecting adaptations to the natural environment which, for the most part, were functional.

Many cultural differences, to be sure, are largely accidental — historical nonconformities of knowledge, skill, taste, degree of economic rationality — and these often yield rather readily, though not rapidly, to the gentle impact of cultural diffusion. More difficult are the problems that arise out of differences in fundamental assumptions and social structure,[18] which show up as contrasts in goals and values,[19] in ethical and behavioral norms, in opportunities for change of social status. Particular sources of difficulty are low valuation of manual work, low prestige value of success achieved in operating an industrial enterprise, high distrustfulness of others (in Latin America, especially); and such ethical and behavioral norms as dishonesty and corruption in business and government; high absenteeism and high turnover in the work force; tardiness, long lunch hours, and slipshod work among executives; and the tendency, often correlated with the high sense of hierarchical status found in many of the societies where international investment in raw materials is important, to block or hamper the promotion of rival executives. Values and norms like these do not give way readily under mere contact with foreign ways, and are therefore a source of continuing friction.

DYNAMIC PROBLEMS ARISING MAINLY OUT OF COMPANY OPERATIONS, POLICIES, AND PRACTICES

A foreign company faced with a battery of what I have called initial problems will attempt to solve them. These efforts, together with the effects of company operations on the market for labor, the distribution of income, and the balance of payments; on the level and employment of skills, the social structure, and the standards of life; and on political processes, bring other problems and new problem-solving efforts in their train. Sometimes these lead to a steady build-up of tensions, culminating in the explosive dynamics of revolt; sometimes the evolutionary dynamics of cumulative and observable improvement are the result.[20] The focal point

[18] See Allan R. Holmberg, "Methods for the Analysis of Cultural Change," *Anthropological Quarterly*, Vol. 34, No. 2 (April 1961).

[19] See Robert Fleming, in *Activities of Private United States Organizations in Africa*, Hearings, HR Comm. on For. Aff., 87th Cong., 1st Sess. (May 1961), pp. 238–39.

[20] Elizabeth Hoyt has called the collective impact of foreign operations "the upset equilibrium." See "A New Diplomacy for Underdeveloped Areas," *Quarterly Review of Economics and Business*, I, 3 (August 1961).

of criticism in all such cases has been the failure of foreign investment to contribute sufficiently to general economic growth and development in the host countries. This allegation, in its quantitative and qualitative aspects, is the concern of the present section.

The Quantitative Dynamics of Company Operations[21]

A convenient starting point for discussing the quantitative effects of company operations is Singer's familiar thesis that foreign investment, especially in the development of raw materials, has often made little contribution to economic growth and development in the host countries, and sometimes may have had a retardative effect.[22] Singer argues that specialization in export of raw materials, largely as a result of investment by the industrialized countries, has (a) deprived the host countries of most of the secondary and cumulative effects, (b) diverted these countries into types of activity offering little scope for technical progress or internal and external economies, and (c) caused them to suffer further injury because of an adverse trend in the terms of trade of their exports.

The first two points distinguish what I term the quantitative and the qualitative aspects of international investment. The third, covered in Kindleberger's essay, elsewhere in this volume, is not dealt with here. Singer suggested, and I agree, that the quantitative processes, considered in isolation from the qualitative, are relatively unimportant in the case of un-

[21] For a stimulating theoretical and empirical macroeconomic study of the issues with which the following discussion is concerned, see Dudley Seers, "A Model of Comparative Rates of Growth in the World Economy," *Economic Journal,* LXXII, 285 (March 1962). His central conclusion is that, "It is very likely that rates of growth in the world [in industrial and primary producing countries] are once again diverging, and Marx's prophecy of the impoverishment of the poor may be fulfilled on the international plane." (p. 75).

[22] Hans Singer, "The Distribution of Gains between Investing and Borrowing Countries," *Papers and Proceedings of the American Economic Association* (Supplement to *American Economic Review*), May 1956, pp. 473–85. It should be stressed, however, that the superabundance of unskilled labor in underdeveloped countries is an obdurate fact that goes to explain the weak impact of direct investment in raw materials on the host countries. The standard theoretical discussion is the article by W. A. Lewis: "Economic Development with Unlimited Supplies of Labor," *The Manchester School,* May 1954. Another relevant analysis, concerned explicitly with the impact of foreign investment, is that of Hla Myint, "An Interpretation of Backwardness" (*Oxford Economic Papers,* June 1954). Both of these are reprinted in Agarwals and Singh (eds.), *The Economics of Underdevelopment* (Oxford University Press, 1958). For factual background there is a useful series of studies by the International Labor Office, particularly: *African Labour Survey* (Studies and Reports, New Series, No. 48, 1958), *Why Labour Leaves the Land* (Studies, etc., No. 59, 1960); and *Employment Objectives in Economic Development* (Studies, etc., No. 62, 1961).

derdeveloped countries: The most important contribution of an industry is its effect on the general level of education, skill, way of life, inventiveness, habits, store of technology, creation of new demands, etc. But quantitative benefits provide the means and motive force for other changes. They thus merit consideration on their own terms.

Let me begin by considering the findings of an attempt to evaluate the applicability of the Singer thesis to Venezuela in the period 1900 to 1953.[23] To establish a benchmark, Moore defines the conditions under which foreign investment in a raw material export industry would have no quantitative effect whatever on the host country. This would be so if all equipment, supplies, and labor were imported; the entire product exported; and proceeds left wholly abroad (or spent for imports). Nor are these conditions wholly unrealistic. Except for the use of unskilled labor, sometimes needed only in small amounts, it was rather closely approximated in many situations.[24] In any case, the magnitudes of the streams of effect flowing from the foreign enterprise into the host economy relative to those flowing abroad are not difficult to estimate, and Moore therefore concludes that the Singer thesis held for Venezuela in the period 1900 to 1930. The Venezuelan government received in taxes and royalties only about 10 per cent of the value of exports as payment for the depletion of the country's natural wealth, and income accruing to Venezuelan factors of production used in the petroleum industry was negligible. Also, the industry had little effect on the over-all proportion of capital to labor and did little to serve as a growing point. But it could only be said that the industry had a retardative effect on Venezuelan development if it is argued, as seems reasonable in the light of later experience, that in this early period the country was inadequately compensated for her natural resources.[25]

[23] John Robert Moore, *The Impact of Foreign Direct Investment on an Underdeveloped Economy: The Venezuelan Case* (Ph.D. thesis, Cornell University, 1956).

[24] *Cf.* Levin, *op. cit.* (Note 6). He sees the gross proceeds of exports as divided among foreign factors of production — defined as those which remit income abroad — and domestic factors, defined as spending at home. But among the domestic factors, the most important group consisted of "luxury importers." The existence of foreign factors and luxury importers "goes a long way toward explaining the lack of development in many of the export economies." (P. 7.)

[25] Moore, *op. cit.* (Note 23), pp. 84–85. In considering what would be adequate compensation to a country or region which could be impoverished by depletion of mineral resources that were not replaced by alternative productive resources, it is well to remember that U.S. oil companies receive 27½ per cent depletion allowance, allegedly to compensate them for the costs of discovering and developing new oil fields, so that they can stay in business. What does it cost to keep a *country* in business?

As noted earlier, the Venezuelan situation began to change in the 1930's. Direct political pressures were brought to bear on the companies, regulatory legislation was enacted, and governmental policies were framed with a view to assuring the accrual of larger benefits to Venezuela.[26] Largely in consequence of these measures, petroleum began to make a positive contribution to Venezuelan growth and development in the 1940's. By 1953 the percentage accruing to the government was more than three times as high as in 1900–1930; and changes in tax rates increased it further in 1958.[27]

Meier, apparently believing that the criticism of foreign investment in raw material export industries has been overdone, presents a number of counterarguments.[28] While this conclusion that international market forces did not inhibit development is too sweeping — it excludes, for example, any consideration of the consequences of heavy-handed political influence like that exerted by foreign investors in Cuba, and the kinds of disruptive social change that Furnivall describes for Burma[29] — Meier recognizes that "the classical optimism regarding development through trade has not been vindicated for the poor countries." (Note 28, p. 176)

This state of affairs is attributable, in Meier's view, far more to obstacles within the host countries than to the impact of foreign investment and trade. Some raw-material countries, favored by the nature of the export industry and its location, will benefit much, others little. But Meier considers sociopolitical conditions to be the crucial determinant in either case. His conclusion, which is the same as that implicit in Moore's study, is stated explicitly: The crucial need is for domestic policy measures which will produce "sufficient social and political change, as well as economic change, to make the economy more responsive to the stimulus from trade." (Note 28, p. 191)[30]

Moore and Meier thus agree on the importance of policies. But both

[26] Moore, *op. cit.* (Note 23), pp. 136–38; also Lieuwen, *op. cit.* (Note 9), Chapter VI.

[27] For figures showing similar favorable trends in other countries see the essay in this volume by Grunwald.

[28] Gerald M. Meier, *International Trade and Development* (New York: Harper and Row, 1961).

[29] Jenks, *op. cit.* (Note 8); J. S. Furnivall, *Colonial Policy and Practice* (New York: New York University Press, 1956); Myint, citing Furnivall, observes that "the result of the 'free play of market forces' under conditions of fluctuating export prices is the well-known story of rural indebtedness, land alienation, and agrarian unrest." Myint, *op. cit.* (Note 22).

[30] Limiting factors affecting the choice of policy are rigorously explored in H. B. Chenery and M. Bruno, "Development Alternatives in An Open Economy: The Case of Israel," *Economic Journal,* LXXII, 285 (March 1962).

authors disregard an increasingly important determinant — company policies, which play a major role in what I am calling qualitative dynamics.

The Qualitative Dynamics of Company Policies and Practices

Should the developers of natural resources concern themselves only with obtaining an economically efficient flow of extractive output, or should they endeavor also to reduce the backwardness of the people and the society? That is the nub of the conflict that has been slowly emerging between the point of view of foreign investors concerning the potential to be realized through their enterprise, and that of host country governments. That these do, in fact, represent different goals has not always been recognized, as Myint significantly observes.[31] Or, perhaps, it is more correct to say that the goals are different so long as they are not made to converge by the adoption of such appropriate public policies as:

1. those designed to modify the share of net income accruing to the government of the host country;
2. those concerned with putting this windfall effectively to use in promoting economic growth, and development — what the Venezuelans of the thirties called "sowing the petroleum";
3. those designed to force or induce companies to make more positive contributions to growth and development, both (*a*) by increasing the share of income that accrues to domestic factors of production, and (*b*) by adopting more appropriate policies and practices with respect to such matters as: living arrangements and social conditions generally; training, advancement, and treatment of personnel at all levels; working conditions, collective bargaining, and the handling of workers' grievances; local procurement of supplies and services; and the use of political influence and propaganda.

Share of Income. J. C. McClintock, an official of the United Fruit Company, observed that the word "concessions" was "certainly appropriate" to describe the agreements of the past, and then referred to a "new business philosophy, based on participation."[32] Up to the beginning of the fifties, according to McClintock, UFCO paid no taxes of any kind

---

[31] In Myint, *op. cit.* (Note 22).

[32] In Dan H. Fenn, Jr. (ed.), *Management Guide to Overseas Operations* (New York: McGraw-Hill, 1957). For the terms of initial UFCO concessions, of modifications proposed, resisted, and achieved, and of the processes by which changes were brought about, see Kepner and Soothill, *op. cit.* (Note 8).

in many of the countries in which it operated, whereas at the time he was speaking it often paid 34–40 per cent.

This is only one instance among many of a long struggle to win an increasing share of income,[33] a struggle which has steadily become more sophisticated.

In the petroleum industry, to take the leading example, host countries have shown increasing concern for such matters as taxation, expensing, allocation of costs and revenues among the several operations of the vertically integrated companies with which they deal, pricing, and market structure. As a result of these efforts concession agreements have been successively modified, companies have been made to conform to the letter and spirit of their contractual undertakings or of general regulatory legislation, fuller information has been obtained concerning the results of operations, companies have been led voluntarily to make certain changes favorable to the host country, and so on. This is too large a subject to examine in detail here, but a couple of general observations may be made. One, suggested earlier, is that the raw-material exporting countries as a group have benefited substantially from the changes in distribution formulas that have occurred since the war. Another is that there is still ground to doubt that the return on private investment in natural resources has been reduced to the point where it approximates the true, competitive, long-run supply price of foreign capital, even after allowing for the additional (but reducible) risks and uncertainties considered in the section above dealing with international investment. Thirdly, this doubt will remain as long as the light of full publicity on the results of overseas operations remains dimmed, for this inevitably creates suspicion that the companies have something to hide. In the case of Middle East Oil, for example, Mrs. Penrose[34] notes the incentive for oil companies to adopt accounting and other techniques designed to produce a maximum effect on public relations with a minimum of actual concession. Serious study is hampered because important facts are missing. Finally, the oligopolistic market structure in many of the international raw materials, the degree of

---

[33] See for example: Raymond Vernon's forthcoming study of economic development in Mexico, especially Chapter 3; Lieuwen, *op. cit.* (Note 9); Benjamin Shwardran, *The Middle East, Oil and the Great Powers*, 2nd ed., rev. (New York: Council for Middle Eastern Affairs, 1959), Section 2, and S. H. Longrigg, *Oil in the Middle East*, 2nd ed. (London: Oxford University Press for Royal Institute of International Affairs, 1961), pp. 57 ff. and Chapters X, XVI. A more generalized survey of the evolution of Mideastern concession agreements will be found in George Lenczowski, *Oil and State in the Middle East* (Ithaca: Cornell University Press, 1960), Chapters IV and XI.

[34] E. T. Penrose, "Profit Sharing Between Producing Countries and Oil Companies in the Middle East," *Economic Journal*, LXIX, 274 (June 1959).

overlapping ownership, the technical, managerial, or financial incapacity of most host countries to operate modern mineral enterprises, or to gain access to markets if they did, tends to place the weight of the bargaining power on the side of the companies.[35]

Use of Government Share. The will and the skill of governments vary widely when it comes to using their share of income from foreign investment in raw materials to further economic growth and development. The aim should be to make sure that the depletion of natural resources does not reduce but, rather, increases national productive capacity. This is the same as saying that development of natural resources should provide the means to reduce — eventually to eliminate — economic, social, and political backwardness.

But the government share in raw material income is only one of the factors contributory to the attack on backwardness. Even in the exceptional cases where, relative to current national product, the government share is so large that the public development program can be financed entirely from this source, the program may be smaller than it could be because the proceeds of royalties and taxes are diverted into private pockets or spent ineffectively.[36] No matter how large or how small the public

[35] This is not the place to tackle the thorny problem of profits earned in international raw material investment, but two points are worth noting with respect to the controversial world-wide petroleum industry. First, there are serious observers who believe that oil companies have practiced deception in the preparation of their accounts. See Lieuwen, *op. cit.* (Note 9), p. 67; also Robert Engler, *The Politics of Oil* (New York: Macmillan, 1961), who refers to "what Senator Brewster called a 'liberal education in tax evasion'" (p. 222), and who later asserts: "There is ample evidence that all these illustrations of corporate foreign relations and domestic deception took place with the knowledge, consultation, and active intervention of responsible officials in the State and Treasury departments and in the American Embassy in Saudi Arabia." (P. 228.) Second, a recent economic study concludes that "Perhaps the most one can say is that study of the limited data available [which suggests that annual profits in the range of 30–60 per cent of invested capital have not been uncommon in both the Middle East and Venezuela] leaves one with the *impression* of unusually high profits in Middle East Oil. It is, moreover, an impression which, in the writer's experience, is borne out by conversation with oil men who are familiar with the facts." (Wayne A. Leeman, *The Price of Middle East Oil: An Essay in Political Economy* [Ithaca: Cornell University Press, 1962]), p. 79. It is probable that a similar view is also justified concerning the results of major mining operations in Africa, Asia, and Latin America. Also see Penrose, *op. cit.* (Note 34).

[36] Saudi Arabia and Kuwait are the cases that come most readily to mind. For a less dramatic but more typical example, involving Northern Rhodesia, see Taylor Ostrander, Assistant to the Chairman, American Metal Climax, Inc., "The Place of Minerals in Economic Development" (mimeo), a paper presented to the Council of Economics at the 92nd Annual Meeting of the American Institute of Mining, Metallurgical, and Petroleum Engineers, Dallas, Texas, February 27, 1963.

revenues attributable to the development of natural resources by foreign enterprise, or how honestly and efficiently they are employed, the impact of such development will be greater if it is conceived as only one element in a process that is quantitative and automatic only in a limited sense. To an increasing extent this is being realized. Recognizing that foreign enterprises have failed to contribute as much as they reasonably could to the development process, or even have hindered it, host governments have begun to concern themselves with the policies and practices of these enterprises. Since the potentialities of such policies and practices have been relatively neglected in the economic literature I shall consider them in some detail.

Company Policies and Practices. An increasing awareness that backwardness is not an ineradicable feature of the environment in which they operate, and that its elimination brings enduring benefits even if it also entails immediate costs, can be found in the top management circles of some large international companies, and among students of the special management problems that arise in the conduct of overseas operations. This is a significant, if still limited, break with the not so distant past, and is the consequence of the social and political pressures brought to bear on the companies both at home (the criticisms of economic imperialism) and abroad (the protests against foreign domination, arrogance, discrimination, and greed). Conclusive illustrations of the effects of criticism at home are hard to come by, but Lieuwen provides a concise description of how growing protest in Venezuela brought about changes in company behavior patterns.[37] Not only protest, but also the observations of management personnel in the field, of consultants, and of independent investigators have often led companies to adopt changes in policies and practices which, if sometimes introduced mainly for their public relations effect, also represent substantive improvements.

Since the war, in short, there has been a new approach: the voices in the United States calling for change have had a different tone from those of the preceding era, and have come largely from a different source. The prewar scholarly critics of economic imperialism tended to be historians and social scientists, concerned above all with the interests of the foreign

---

[37] Lieuwen, *op. cit.* (Note 9), pp. 80–88. A similar interplay of protest and reform — and also of suppressed or thwarted protest — is found in other areas and reported, less succinctly, in the literature on Middle East Oil; mining in Northern Rhodesia, Peru, Bolivia, and Chile; plantation agriculture in the Caribbean region, Central America, and Southeast Asia.

country and its people, and with what they regarded, when judged by this criterion, as the immorality of corporate behavior toward the export economies. The new generation of analysts does not talk of economic imperialism. It stresses recognition and promotion of mutual interest with the host countries. Taking a long, wide view, which embraces the national interest as well as that of investors, and which recognizes the restructuring of political power that has attended the collapse of colonialism, the analysts of overseas operations seek to find the sources of discontent and to eliminate them. In this they have been supported by research initiated by individual scholars, research organizations, and international bodies, often acting at the behest of the host countries.

One of the early expositions of this new approach was made by the head of public relations for an American oil company in the Middle East.[38] Since then a growing literature has questioned whether "private investment does, in fact, necessarily contribute to the accelerated progress of underdeveloped areas,"[39] and has urged business firms to sponsor research on the disturbing social effects of their operations in foreign lands.[40] In the remainder of this section I shall discuss the major issues that have been reviewed in this rapidly growing literature against the background of socioeconomic and political problems created by foreign investment and, more generally, by the processes of growth and development.

The case for review and revision of company policies and practices arises because of criticisms and pressures in the host countries. These are manifested in the press, in the demands of trade unions, in mass movements of protest, in the growth of xenophobic attitudes in the platforms of political parties, and so on. From the host country point of view, the international companies are seen as removing natural wealth without adequately compensating the nation (witness the Brazilian slogan, "the petroleum is ours"), as exercising undue domination over economic life, as interfering in internal political affairs, as discriminating against nationals of the country economically and socially, as procuring abroad

[38] W. Jack Butler, "Public Relations for Industry in Underdeveloped Countries," *Harvard Business Review*, September–October 1952.

[39] Lincoln Gordon, "Private Enterprise and Economic Development," *Harvard Business Review*, July–August 1960.

[40] For example, Hoyt, *op. cit.* (Note 20); John Fayerweather, *Management of International Operations* (New York: McGraw-Hill, 1960); Fenn, *op. cit.* (Note 32); and *idem, Business Responsibility in Action* (New York: McGraw-Hill, 1960) pp. 89–122.

supplies and services that could be obtained locally and, in general, as failing to contribute sufficiently to realization of the potentials regarded as residing in the natural resources being developed.

Among the consequences of these sometimes distorted perceptions are efforts to force foreign enterprises to behave in a desired manner by levying special taxes or duties on items imported by foreign companies and personnel; utilizing multiple foreign exchange rates to achieve financial or other economic benefits; restricting transfer of earnings, depreciation allowances, and capital funds; requiring reinvestment of a certain proportion of inside funds; limiting foreign ownership to a stated percentage; enacting highly protective labor legislation; threatening expropriation; and in other ingenious ways exerting leverage to achieve aims believed unattainable otherwise.

In addition, and outside the realm of governmental action, the ways in which the people in the host countries perceive foreigners and their activities seem to be at least partly responsible for low worker productivity, reflecting a "conscientious withdrawal of efficiency," to use Veblen's phrase, and other types of intentional or partly intentional non-co-operation. Other factors contributing to the difficulties of productive resource development are bad labor-management relations, whether trade unions are recognized or not; the rise of militant anti-Western and anti-capitalistic labor leaders or political parties; and increase in the degree of social and political instability. The new approach, discussed above, represents an attempt to reduce or remove the causes of these public and private actions by correcting abuses, endeavoring to make a more substantive contribution to growth and development, and in general conforming more to the criteria and motivations of an indigenous than of an expatriate enterprise. The changes in policies and practices that have been recommended and, in some cases, put into effect in recent years will be considered under the following heads: (1) acculturation of expatriate personnel; (2) personnel policies; (3) social services; (4) relations with the government; (5) public relations; (6) political activities; (7) economic contributions to growth and development.[41]

1) ACCULTURATION OF EXPATRIATE PERSONNEL. The term "cultural shock," employed to describe what happens to Americans and Europeans sent abroad under technical assistance and other aid programs,

---

[41] For a discussion concerned mainly with the economic considerations affecting the decisions of American and European companies to undertake direct investment (especially in manufacturing), see C. P. Kindleberger, *International Economics,* 3rd ed. (Chicago: Irwin, 1963), Chapter 20.

has become part of our modern vocabulary. But the term is new, despite the fact that for a century or two, large numbers of Western expatriates have lived and worked as members of colonial or corporate administrations in these same areas. In earlier times the Westerners took their cultures with them, setting up social enclaves isolated from contact with those who could not or would not become Westernized, and enforcing conformity to Western methods, standards, criteria, and forms of organization by those who participated in the activities of (or for) Western enterprises. There was cultural shock, but in reverse, and not observed or reported as such.[42] Reported and observed instead were the irresponsible behavior, low standards, and inferior values of indigenous workers and administrators: absenteeism, lack of discipline and punctuality, backward bending supply curves of effort, low levels of aspiration, low evaluation of manual work, and so on, through an almost endless list of popular clichés.

To call these clichés is not to characterize them as nonsense, for many of them have firm foundations in fact. It is only to suggest that thought should not stop with factual observation, as has so often been the case. Whether one would wish to modify the values and norms reflected in the phrases, or deem it better or wiser to accept them and adapt to them, familiarity with the culture in a large sense, with its historical roots, and above all with its functional attributes, is essential. Not only academicians like Hoyt, and Whyte and Holmberg,[43] but businessmen too are coming round to this view.[44]

[42] This is only partially correct. E. M. Forster's novel of the early twenties, *A Passage to India*, acquired renown because of its insight into the phenomenon of what we can now term inverse cultural shock. And in France, both before the war and in the early postwar years, several scholars showed a keen awareness of what was happening in the colonies. See René Maunier, *The Sociology of Colonies*, edited and translated by E. O. Lorimer (London: Routledge & Keagan Paul, 1949), in two volumes; O. Mannoni, *Psychologie de la Colonisation* (Paris: Editions du Seuil, 1950) translated as *Prospero and Caliban* (London: Methuen, 1956); Henri Labouret, *Colonisation, Colonialisme, Décolonisation* (Paris: Larose, 1952). For a stimulating suggestion and analysis of parallelism between inverse cultural shock and the social cleavage between employers and workers that accompanied industrialization in the West, see Reinhard Bendix, *Work and Authority in Industry — Ideologies of Management in the Course of Industrialization* (New York: Wiley, 1956), Chapter 7, especially pp. 444 ff.
[43] Hoyt, *op. cit.* (Note 20); William F. Whyte and Allan Holmberg, "Human Problems of U.S. Enterprise in Latin America," *Human Organization*, Vol. 15, Special Issue, No. 3 (Fall 1956).
[44] Butler, *op. cit.* (Note 38), for example. Also see Fenn, *op. cit.* (Note 32), and David E. Lilienthal, *The Multinational Corporation* (New York: Development and Resources Corporation, 1960), especially pp. 18–27.

2) PERSONNEL POLICIES. Foreign enterprises have been criticized for (*a*) employing monopsonistic labor practices; (*b*) not providing effective opportunities for the training and promotion of indigenous personnel; (*c*) delegating insufficient responsibility and maintaining excessively close supervision over the work force, in both blue- and white-collar jobs; (*d*) being excessively paternalistic; (*e*) failing to provide effective machinery for collective bargaining or for settling grievances and disputes, for being neglectful of working conditions, and for bungling labor relations generally; and (*f*) failing to select expatriate technical, supervisory, and executive personnel with sufficient care, failing to provide them with specialized training for their overseas assignments, and failing to screen out those who maintain attitudes of superiority towards indigenous personnel and their culture.[45]

Few companies, presumably, are open to serious criticism on all of the foregoing points, yet few are likely to get an altogether clean bill of health from an impartial observer. To summarize the pros and cons on so long a list of charges is manifestly impossible. I shall therefore confine myself to presenting a sample observation on each point.[46]

  a) *Labor Recruitment.* It is almost inevitable that individual firms engaged in the exploitation of exportable raw materials should often be the sole buyers of wage labor. But even when there are several firms in the same market for labor, they often have either a tacit

---

[45] Fayerweather, Fenn, Lieuwen, Whyte and Holmberg, *op. cit.* (Notes 40, 32, 9, 43); Lenczowski, *op. cit.* (Note 33), Chapters XI, XII, XIV; *H. R. H. The Duke of Edinburgh's Study Conference on the Human Problems of Industrial Communities within the Commonwealth and the Empire, 1956* (London: Oxford University Press, 1957), in two volumes, *passim.* Kepner and Soothill, *op. cit.* (Note 8), Chapter XII; Frederick Harbison and Charles A. Myers, *Management in the Industrial World* (New York: McGraw-Hill, 1959), Chapter 19; Walter Galenson (ed.), *Labor and Economic Development* (New York: Wiley, 1959); John C. Shearer, *High Level Manpower in Overseas Subsidiaries: Experience in Brazil and Mexico,* Research Report Series No. 98 (Princeton: Department of Economics and Sociology, Princeton University, 1960); Alexander S. Lipsett, *Chile: Star in Ascent* (Brownsville, Texas: A. S. Lipsett Associates, 1962) pp. 23–48. Also such background studies by the ILO, Geneva, as the Studies and Reports Series (Note 22) and the mimeographed reports of the *Petroleum Committee,* Sixth Session (1960) Vols. I, II, III; *Committee on Work on Plantations,* Fourth Session (1961), Vols. I, II, III. Also National Planning Association, series of studies on United States Business Performance Abroad, especially, *Aluminium Limited in India* (1962), and *United Fruit Co. in Latin America.* Also, *Activities of Private U.S. Organizations in Africa,* Hearings, Subcommittee on Africa of HR Comm. on For. Aff., 87th Cong. 1st Session, 1961, testimony of F. Taylor Ostrander and statement by Mobil International Oil Co. Also, The United Africa Company, Ltd. (Unilever subsidiary), *Statistical and Economic Review,* No. 22, (January 1959).

[46] Authors mentioned are cited in Note 45 unless otherwise identified.

or an explicit agreement concerning wages.[47] In some circumstances there may be ground for legitimate concern lest bidding for labor in an area create much wider wage differentials than have been customary, or lead to inflation with little or no increase in real wages.[48] But ordinarily wage differentials are one of the channels through which economic development is transmitted, and there is little if any social justification for preventing their appearance. In general, an excessive concern for maintaining a stable structure of wages, and a tight hold on the organization of the labor market, as under the recruiting system for mining labor in the Republic of South Africa, is likely to reflect monopsonistic intent.

b), c) Advancement of Indigenous Personnel. Although many companies have instituted training programs for employees at all levels, and some have reduced the numbers of expatriate personnel to remarkably small proportions, even in the top echelons, Shearer reached the conclusion that the great majority of the firms he studied employed far higher proportions of costly Americans (the ratio of the cost of imported to equivalent indigenous manpower was about 8 to 1) than could be justified by any quality advantage over nationals who could be substituted for them. Institutional frictions, especially protection of their jobs by the expatriate Americans, were held to be largely responsible for persistence of this disequilibrium. Whyte and Holmberg found that, by failing to allow those under them to make decisions for themselves, many expatriate managers in Latin America acted so as to reinforce the very habits of behavior they presumably wished to change. Fear of working himself out of a job was often a factor tending to make the North American act in this way.[49]

d) Paternalism. The latter two authors also criticized paternalism (provision of company housing, community services, and so on), remarking that it is costly from the management standpoint and does not appear to build loyalty or create harmonious labor-management relations. Many management people have come to this conclusion, but fear the consequences of abandoning long-established paternalistic arrangements. Where workers are truly dissatisfied, however,

[47] See Margery Perham (ed.), *Mining, Commerce, and Finance in Nigeria* (London: Faber and Faber, 1948), p. 95 ff. Also Myint, *op. cit.* (Note 22).

[48] See remarks by J. Terry Duce in Fenn, *op. cit.* (Note 32) and discussion from the floor. Also see NPA Business Performance study of Firestone in Liberia.

[49] See also Harbison and Myers, *op. cit.* (Note 45), p. 383.

as they were in one of the older camps of the Creole Petroleum Corporation, Whyte and Holmberg believe that a way to effect mutually beneficial change should be discoverable. And, citing the Orinoco Mining Company as an example, they suggest that it may seldom be necessary to provide paternalistic living arrangements at the outset of a new venture, or it may be possible to plan for their early withering. A further point, noted by Butler, is that many paternalistic services are merely thankless tasks which cause management to be blamed for numerous off-the-job grievances. The ILO, partly for this reason, has recommended that governmental authorities, both national and municipal, be brought in to assist with or to take over the job of running the communities in which labor lives. And Ostrander has characterized as "the newest form of benevolent paternalism" the effort of the American Metal Climax–Rhodesian Selection Trust partnership in the African Copperbelt to replace paternalism with individual or group responsibility.

A somewhat different point of view is expressed by Galenson. He regards paternalism as a necessary and inevitable concomitant of modern industrial development. And Myers, in the same volume, observes that in India "paternalism" and "welfare activities" are required of the employer who expects to reduce absenteeism and maintain employee morale.

Whether to be paternalistic or not is a question that is usually answered in terms of what is best from the employer's standpoint. More attention could well be paid to the effect of paternalism on the elimination of backwardness. Which consequence is more important: demonstration effect or the cultivation of self-reliance?

e) Labor relations. The structure and role of labor unions, and the policies of overseas managements toward labor, vary widely. Latin-American unions, for example, generally lack the kind of organization that enables the union to reach its members on their problems; and contract negotiations give the impression of "being influenced, if not completely determined, by people who are not even in the room: government officials."[50]

Partly for this reason, presumably, labor relations in the paternalistic Chilean copper industry (where wages, working conditions, and social status, at least in the three American companies, are far better than those in other sectors of the Chilean economy) recently have fallen back into the pattern of perennial conflict, largely empty

[50] Whyte and Holmberg, *op. cit.* (Note 43).

collective bargaining, and governmental intervention — a "spectacular breakdown in industrial relations."[51] At something like the other extreme stands Indaluco (Indian Aluminum Company, Ltd.), which has been characterized as ranking among India's most progressive employers in every significant field of employee relations — wages, welfare measures, working conditions in the factory, and the general approach of management.[52]

f) Selection and training of personnel for work overseas. Fayerweather's study of administrative attitudes and relationships appropriate to work in a foreign culture is perhaps the most systematic approach to what has only recently become recognized as a problem requiring special attention. With a few notable exceptions, he observes, managements have barely scratched the surface of the problem of training men for foreign work. Stress should be placed on selecting men of higher quality than in the past, and on developing the skills required of U.S. executives in their relations with foreign executives. One aim should be to create a better understanding by Americans of what it means to be an indigenous executive in a U.S. company, viewed with something akin to suspicion both by colleagues in business and compatriots in society.

3) SOCIAL SERVICES. The need for social services — provision of housing, sanitation, public utilities, medical care, recreational opportunities, educational facilities, programs for women, and the like — arises because of the comparative isolation of most large raw material enterprises. The questions at issue are those concerned with the degree of paternalism that is appropriate: the extent to which companies provide all facilities on their own terms and according to their own standards, with or without subsidies, or offer financing and other facilities to individuals and groups who make their own choices and decisions, compared with the extent to which they leave or transfer such responsibilities to indigenous governmental authorities.

We have already observed that American opinion is turning toward the view that paternalism has been overdone, although there are proba-

[51] Lipsett, *op. cit.* (Note 45). He also reports, by way of contrast, that under the contract currently in force in the economically depressed Chilean nitrate industry, labor relations are stable and peaceful: "management relies extensively on union collaboration and participation; constant efforts are made to draw the men close to the industry and give them an insight into its particular problem."

[52] National Planning Association, *op. cit.* (Note 45). Indaluco has not attempted completely to avoid paternalism, for this is deeply ingrained in Indian culture, but it has limited its provision of services to employees (see pp. 47 and 64).

bly cultural differences governing what is appropriate. In general, however, companies engaged in the development of natural resources cannot avoid providing some services themselves, nor accepting a measure of responsibility for those provided through other channels. In either case the problem is mainly one of making sure that the types of houses and services provided are what the workers and their families want. Either through ignorance or false economy, attempts are seldom made to discover these wants. Aramco, which has been co-operating with the government to help employees acquire houses of their own, provides an example of an effort to adapt to local conditions.

4) GOVERNMENT RELATIONS. Partly for the reason just mentioned, Aramco illustrates the extent to which, under certain conditions, it may be necessary to develop facilities for dealing with governmental agencies.[53] In 1958, this company had a specialized government relations staff headed by a vice president, general manager, and assistant general manager. Under them was a policy and planning staff and two operating departments, one of which handled relations with the central government and one those with the local governments in the three main centers of operation. Government relations at the national level are likely to be less multifold but more complex than those at the local level. They may arise because one of the parties wishes to revise the concession agreement,[54] new legislation is proposed, or the government threatens expropriation.

5) PUBLIC RELATIONS. Where governments remain firmly independent but somewhat sensitive to domestic political breezes, there is often a clear private advantage to be derived from efforts to make the climate of public opinion more favorable. Understandable, therefore, but not necessarily approvable, is the emphasis placed by some foreign enterprises on public relations. Butler's article and Lenczowski's discussion (Chapter XII) suggest that the praiseworthy activities of the oil companies in the Middle East have often been initiated for their favorable effect on the public image of the corporation. Nearly all of what Butler recommends is strongly on the track of making a positive contribution to welfare or development, yet one wonders whether policies adopted by managements because they have been persuaded of their public relations value will not tend to emphasize appearance more than substance, to maximize publicity rather than achievement. Such doubts are easily overstressed, but it

---

[53] Lenczowski, *op. cit.* (Note 33), Chapter VI, which also discusses Iraq Petroleum Co. (IPC).

[54] See Lenczowski, *op. cit.* (Note 33), Part Two, pp. 63–199, for a discussion of the issues.

is appropriate to note that Lenczowski devotes approximately eight pages to a discussion of the companies' "refutation by deeds" of the criticisms to which they have been subjected (treated in Chapter XI), and more than thirteen pages to a discussion of public relations in the Madison Avenue sense.

No industry can match petroleum in the scale of its international operations, in its political importance, or in its awareness of and reaction to the latter. One must therefore beware of generalizing from oil to other cases. Yet individual companies, or an extractive sector dominated by two or three foreign firms, are often so important to the countries in which they are located that their local influence is analogous to that of petroleum in the world at large. With due allowance for differences in the intensities of public opinion to which companies are subjected, and for the effect of this on their policies, the behavior patterns of the oil industry may not be unrepresentative.

6) POLITICAL ACTIVITIES. The dividing lines between government relations, public relations, and political activities are often blurred, as Engler's study clearly shows. But the distinction is being made increasingly in favor of the first and second against the third.[55] Butler, for example, says that political activity may pay off initially but not in the long run. He advises neutrality, aloofness from the shifting political tides, perhaps because of the risk of backing the wrong horse. Lilienthal distinguishes between such unsavory activities as secretly subsidizing rebel leaders and keeping cabinets on a payroll and actions that, having inevitable political consequences, should perhaps be discussed with local policy makers. Because of the latter's increasing importance, corporate managers overseas must be thoroughly familiar with local politics, but as students and observers, not as participants.

7) ECONOMIC CONTRIBUTIONS TO GROWTH AND DEVELOPMENT. The contribution of foreign enterprises to growth and development in the countries where they operate is affected by all of the policies discussed so far, public as well as private, but there are some specifically economic potentialities still to be considered: (a) local procurement versus importation of supplies and services; (b) provision of economic services to the community at large (public utilities, transport, electric power, communications); (c) research on problems of concern to the entire economy; (d) provision of technical assistance to indigenous enterprises, pri-

---

[55] A relevant discussion, though concerned solely with political activities in the United States, will be found in Michael D. Reagan, "The Seven Fallacies of Business in Politics," *Harvard Business Review*, Vol. 28, No. 2 (March–April 1960).

vate and public; (*e*) provision of marketing facilities for indigenous products other than those produced by the company; (*f*) financial assistance to indigenous enterprises; and (*g*) facilitation of local participation in ownership.

While each of these activities has its exemplars (as shown below), no companies, presumably, have engaged in all of them, and some may have undertaken none. The total impression is that, though promising great returns to all parties, a broad, imaginative approach has been wholly lacking. At least one industrial spokesman, however, visualizes the as-yet-unrealized possibilities:

> The copper companies [in Northern Rhodesia] might have made it possible for minerals development to spill over on a broader scale into general economic development by a program of deliberately developing indigenous enterprise around the copper industry. Industrial and foreign *investor statesmanship* can see to it that any central enterprise deliberately stimulates the maximum amount of satellite local entrepreneurship by subcontracting wherever possible, by hiving off parts of the central enterprise for transfer to local enterprise, by giving capital subsidies and management training to help get such satellite activities under way, etc. Such a policy would superimpose a *new objective of a longer run nature* on normal management decisions based on efficiency alone. The objective would be the *creation of a healthy economic environment* within which the central enterprise would live. The aim, by the way, would be the development of *native* entrepreneurship, not satellite enterprises under expatriate control. This is one way modern management might see its development task today. It is a *new concept*. It would result in some greater tendency for mineral development to contribute to broader economic development. It could be done by mining companies alone, without encouragement or direction from the state.[56]

The following examples of specific economic contributions to growth and development reveal the difference between what has been attempted so far and what might be done with more imagination and effort.

    a) Aramco has for some time been trying to increase the volume of its local purchases. To this end, it has abolished commissaries for Western personnel, at least in the vicinity of economically developed indigenous communities, thus directing trade to local stores. It has also endeavored to acquire more of its supplies locally, and to utilize local contractors to an increasing extent in construction, maintenance, and transport operations.[57] The Liberian Mining Company,

---

[56] Ostrander paper, *op. cit.* (Note 36), italics added.
[57] Lenczowski, *op. cit.* (Note 33), pp. 230–32.

too — in contrast to Firestone, which takes pride in the elaborate import and distribution system it has built up and maintained — appears to have encouraged the growth of Liberian-owned and -operated businesses to supply its needs and those of its personnel.[58]

b) Oil companies in Venezuela have opened company roads to public use and supplied natural gas to Maracaibo. Many instances could be cited in which railroad services and electric power, developed primarily for company use, have contributed to local growth. This appears to have been much less true of communications facilities, however.

c), *d*), *e*) Firestone's research activities in Liberia, which have developed a breed of disease-resistant cattle and more productive strains of dryland rice, and its research on tropical diseases, illustrate what can be done to increase the stock of generally useful knowledge. This company also provides free rubber trees to Liberian growers, together with technical assistance in the art of rubber growing, a guaranteed market (at a price set by a formula that has been criticized), and facilities for transporting the rubber.

f) The rendering of financial assistance to indigenous enterprises has been a policy of a number of foreign companies (Aramco, for example), but perhaps the most ambitious effort is that of Creole Petroleum, which in 1961 set up a wholly owned subsidiary, the Creole Investment Corporation, for the exclusive purpose of making equity investments, on a minority share basis, in existing or new Venezuelan enterprises in industry or livestock and crop agriculture. As of February 1962 it had approved eight proposals involving a total commitment of $2.5 million. Although the amount involved was small, the initial reaction of business, the public, and the government was reported as favorable.[59] If experience continued to be favorable, Standard thought it might initiate similar ventures in other countries where it operates.

g) Although many countries restrict foreign ownership of enterprises, there is sometimes a problem of obtaining local participation because the citizens of the country are too ill-informed concerning the corporation as an institution or are too poor to acquire shares even if they were available. There are at least two cases in which companies have endeavored to overcome these difficulties.

[58] *Activities of Private U.S. Organizations in Africa* (Note 45), pp. 22 and 178.
[59] Memorandum provided by Standard Oil Company (New Jersey), the American parent of Creole Petroleum.

One, in Tanganyika, is mentioned in Gaitskell's essay in this volume. The second involved the Liberia Mining Company, which executed a scheme for financing the local purchase of shares in a new venture on favorable terms, accompanied by efforts to explain what the offer involved.[60]

These cases, like most of those cited in other connections, had unusual features and are not, therefore, subject to generalization. But they illustrate that a combination of will and ingenuity can make sharp breaks with past behavior patterns, both foreign and indigenous, presumably to the long-run benefit of all concerned. Of these two requisites, the more problematic is "will." There can be little doubt that where foreign investors see the adoption of policies conducive to growth and development as involving their interests, even in a somewhat roundabout manner and over the long run, they are likely to adopt such policies. To some extent this is a matter of knowledge, perception, breadth of vision, length of time horizon. But to a considerable extent it depends on the political power of those excluded from the internal economies and affected by the external diseconomies generated by the private operation — upon their ability to capture private benefits which are not publicly shared, or to convert into private costs the social costs that are ignored in the private calculus. By and large, therefore, the question whether there is conflict or mutuality of interests depends on the political context, broadly defined. This context has changed significantly in the past generation or so, and is certainly destined to change further. In the following section I consider some of the constructive broad-scale steps that have been taken or accelerated in the past decade, largely because of the enhanced political power of the raw-material countries, and in the concluding section I consider some of the political and social issues still to be faced.

Constructive Approaches to the Reduction of Hazards

Preceding sections have endeavored to identify problems. Now I undertake to indicate the major lines along which systematic efforts to work out solutions have been running. To be considered are: (1) proposals for ameliorating or offsetting the effects of instability in primary commodity trade; (2) the trend toward establishment of international joint business ventures; (3) the use of international arbitration procedures;

[60] See *Activities of Private U.S. Organizations in Africa, op. cit.* (Note 45), p. 180, for details.

(4) guarantees for international investors; and (5) possibilities of stand-ardizing legislation relating to mineral and other natural resources.

Combating Instability in Primary Commodity Markets

Efforts to remove the causes or soften the consequences of instability in the markets for primary commodities go back to the interwar period,[61] but the postwar period has witnessed a substantial increase in the amount of research and thought devoted to the problems of commodity trade. This work, undertaken chiefly at the United Nations under pressure from the raw-material exporting countries, is now largely centralized in the UNESCO Commission on International Commodity Trade (CICT).

The CICT began its activities in 1955,[62] concerning itself initially with gathering data,[63] but subsequently with the analytical and statistical ex-amination of measures proposed for dealing with instability. The latter are conveniently summarized in a twelve-page note issued by the UN Secretariat early in 1959, which deals briefly with (a) international com-modity agreements covering particular commodities; (b) international compensatory measures; and (c) national stabilization measures.[64]

[61] See Wallich, in Ellis (ed.), op. cit. (Note 1). Also Edward S. Mason, Con-trolling World Trade (New York: McGraw-Hill, 1946).

[62] For references to earlier work by the UN, and for numerous other references to studies of commodities and commodity problems, see Wallich, op. cit. (Note 1). Not mentioned by Wallich are two UN reports in which most of the stabilization ideas currently under discussion were brought forward for consideration within a broader context: National and International Measures for Full Employment (Sales No.: 1949. II.A.3); and Measures for International Economic Stability (Sales No.: 1951. II.A.2). A recent source of basic information is a document prepared by the UN Secretariat: Measures to Deal with Fluctuations in Primary Commodity Mar-kets — Replies of Governments to Questionnaire Circulated by the Secretary-Gen-eral (E/CN.13/L.69, March 29, 1960).

[63] Among the studies that have emerged are: Fluctuations in Commodity Prices and Volume of Trade–Pilot Study of Non-Ferrous Metals (E/CN.13/L.49, April 24, 1957); Impact of Fluctuations in Economic Activity in Industrial Countries on International Commodity Trade, by A. J. Brown (E/CN.13/L.68, March 8, 1960); Report on the Study of Prospective Production of and Demand for Primary Com-modities — Non-agricultural Commodities Over the Medium Term (E/CN.13/ L.66, March 25, 1960); a twin study, by FAO, on agricultural commodities (E/CN.13/L.70); and Agricultural Commodities — Projections for 1970 (E/CN. 13/48, CCP62/5, published as Special Supplement to FAO Commodity Review 1962).

[64] Examination of Measures Applied or Proposed for the Solution of Problems Connected with Primary Commodity Trade — A Guide to Measures for Dealing with Fluctuations in Primary Commodity Markets (E/CN.13/L.61, Jan. 20, 1959). The alternatives, and the variants within them, are discussed succinctly and evalu-ated critically in Boris C. Swerling, Current Issues in Commodity Policy (Essays in International Finance, No. 38, Department of Economics, Princeton University, June 1962).

Under the heading of agreements covering particular commodities three main types are distinguished:

    multilateral contracts for purchase and sale at stipulated prices;

    quota restrictions on export and/or output; and

    buffer stocks.

In practice, two or even all three types are often combined. It has been suggested also that simultaneous negotiation of agreements on several commodities might sometimes be advantageous. Many countries would then have stakes in the agreement as both exporters and importers, and loss of markets to uncontrolled substitutes could perhaps be minimized by bringing them within the scope of the agreement. One difficulty with specific commodity agreements is their limited coverage, and for this reason it has often been emphasized that more generalized approaches are desirable. Another difficulty with commodity measures is that, while there is wide agreement that interference with market forces should be minimized, the administrative complexities of arrangements that are effective and also meet this criterion become overwhelming, especially if weight be given to consumer as well as producer interests. National stabilization efforts for particular commodities encounter these same problems, but also create the possibility of inconsistency between the domestic and the international features of a country's commodity policies.[65]

Because of these and other difficulties with the commodity-by-commodity approach, there has been an increasing tendency to try to work out more generalized compensatory arrangements of a financial, or even a monetary,[66] character. Measures to provide financial compensation for swings in primary export proceeds (instead of trying to prevent the swings), may focus on sales of particular commodities, on aggregate export proceeds, or on current account receipts in the balance of payments as a whole. The compensation may take the form of loans;[67] of unconditional unilateral transfers (gifts); or of contributory schemes, incorporating a social insurance principle. If initial UN ideas should be adopted the insurance schemes would involve the partial use of loans in

[65] "At a time when we urge institutional reform upon the leaders of underdeveloped societies, the United States demonstrates its conspicuous inability to cast off a discredited agricultural policy." Swerling, *op. cit.* (Note 64), p. 7.

[66] The buffer stock technique, if widely employed, would have clear monetary implications. These, perhaps, are best considered on their own terms, as in the rather Utopian proposals to establish a commodity reserve currency.

[67] A recent decision by the International Monetary Fund has made it easier for member countries, especially exporters of primary products, to draw on the Fund when export proceeds suffer temporary declines. See *International Financial News Summary*, March 8, 1963.

lieu of outright settlement and would provide for a measure of unilateral transfer from the higher income industrial countries to the lower income raw-material countries whenever repayment in full by the latter would entail undue hardship.[68] The differential appeal of the several compensatory alternatives to paying and receiving countries is obvious, and this might make it hard to reach agreement. There are also deep-seated technical difficulties. Some arise out of efforts to limit the possibilities of manipulating export proceeds so as to generate claims to compensation.[69] Others relate to the determination of norms from which compensable deviations are measured, to the effects of such norms on producer behavior, to the optimal (or minimally feasible) scope of the scheme, and so on. Clearly, the more general the scheme becomes the farther the problem is removed from the arena of instability in primary commodity markets as such and the closer it comes to the related problems of (a) stabilizing world income, (b) providing an adequate stock of international liquidity accessible to all comers, and (c) determining the appropriate magnitude and allocation of unilateral transfers of all kinds from the industrial to the developing countries. Nonetheless, it seems clear that each of these problems should be attacked on its own terms, recognizing that each solution will contribute to the effectiveness of the others while avoiding the institutional and administrative involvements of a monolithic approach that attempts to solve all international economic problems at once.

If this is accepted, there is much to be said for an insurance scheme to stabilize export proceeds as a whole. The UN economists concluded that the insurance machinery, so applied, was flexible in its relationship to other policies and more likely to prove complementary to than incompatible with other international commodity stabilization schemes.[70] More importantly, however, an effective insurance scheme might increase the political feasibility of permitting flexibility of relative prices to bring

[68] The insurance idea was systematically developed in a report to the UN: *International Compensation for Fluctuations in Commodity Trade* (Sales No.: 61.II.D.-3). It has since been explored and retrospectively subjected to a statistical test in at least two UN documents: *Consideration of Compensatory Financial Measures to Offset Fluctuations in the Export Income of Primary Producing Countries — Stabilization of Export Proceeds Through a Development Insurance Fund* (E/CN.-13/43, January 18, 1962); and *International Compensatory Financing in Relation to Fluctuations in the Prices of Primary Commodities: Application to Individual Commodities* (E/CN.13/45, CCP/62/11, February 6, 1962).

[69] Insurance schemes for individual commodities are particularly open to such manipulation. See UN study of February 6, 1962 (Note 68).

[70] UN study of January 18, 1962 (Note 68), p. 185.

about efficient resource allocation, as advocated in Kindleberger's essay elsewhere in this volume.

The insurance of export proceeds thus seems like a promising device. The initial examination of its feasibilty indicated that a scheme could be instituted at a cost which should not appear inordinately high to any of the participants, even those industrial countries with relatively stable exports that might expect to be net contributors rather than net beneficiaries.[71] A major question, however, would be whether the major prospective contributors would join, for otherwise the viability of the scheme would be seriously compromised.[72]

Joint International Business Ventures

Considerable light on the advantages, disadvantages, and prospects of business ventures owned jointly in two or more countries has been shed by Columbia University's International Legal Studies Program, and particularly by the volume that appeared two years ago.[73] The present remarks are based, however, on Blough's summary of the program's findings.[74]

The joint international business venture, according to Blough, is a partnership in the practical although seldom in the legal sense, which brings together persons, corporations, or governments from two or more countries. It is regarded in many quarters as one of the possible keys to the problems of foreign investment in underdeveloped countries.

Foreign enterprises that enter into joint arrangements must be willing to face the problems involved in equity participation, perhaps to a controlling degree, by nationals of the host country and/or the host government. Indeed, it is becoming popular in underdeveloped countries to encourage and promote, if not to require, the use of joint ventures. It is thought that they are less likely to involve foreign control of political and economic life, are more likely to pursue suitable training and promotion policies, and will provide greater assurance of satisfactory division of profits.

From the standpoint of the foreign investor there also appears to be a balance of advantages over disadvantages. The joint venture seems to con-

---

[71] *Ibid.*, p. 184.

[72] *Ibid.*, pp. 155–56.

[73] W. G. Friedmann and George Kalmanoff (eds.), *Joint International Business Ventures* (New York: Columbia University Press, 1961).

[74] Roy Blough, "Joint International Business Ventures in Less Developed Countries," in Wilson, Southwestern Legal Foundation, *op. cit.* (Note 11), pp. 513–36.

tribute to good management, to better public relations, and to improved relations with government (although cases in which joint arrangements have hurt public relations have been cited). Although some businessmen are opposed to the international joint venture as a form of organization, others are enthusiastic. To some extent the differences reflect personal experience (or temperament), but also the fact that some industries and countries are better suited to this form than others. Although it has not been widely used so far, the trend in the less developed countries is toward serious consideration of the joint venture as a possible solution to the problems of meeting the legitimate interests of the principal parties concerned. Joint ventures will not solve all problems, for there is a basic conflict over distribution of income and there are other issues which are not readily resolved. Still, Blough considers that the results of the Columbia study are on the whole very favorable to joint ventures.

International Arbitration of Business Disputes[75]

The problems posed by international conflicts of law and related matters were touched upon in the section on "Initial Problems." Arbitration is a way of partially by-passing formal legal procedures and reaching settlements on privately agreed terms. The practice began with domestic and international commercial disputes, but in recent years has begun to spread, though slowly because of the greater issues and obstacles involved, to disputes concerning the rights of international investors. A substantive law of foreign investment has not yet been developed, and Domke believes that determination by fact-finding and decision-making bodies might therefore become the primary source for development of such law.

The oldest commercial arbitration system is that in Great Britain, where a London Court of Arbitration, established in 1892 within the framework of the Chamber of Commerce, has come to be used by businessmen all over the world. World-wide arbitration facilities have also been maintained since 1923 by the International Chamber of Commerce, headquartered in Paris. The American Arbitration Association, organized in 1926, has panels of both national and international arbitrators.[76]

Enforcement is a serious problem in international arbitration. Some-

---

[75] See Martin Domke, "International Arbitration of Commercial Disputes," in Wilson, Southwestern Legal Foundation, *op. cit.* (Note 11), pp. 131–84.
[76] *Ibid.*, pp. 146–49.

times, but by no means always, there are relevant provisions of law which do not conflict, concerning jurisdiction; sometimes, where a government has been directly involved from the outset, as in a concession agreement, enforceable arbitration clauses may have been introduced into the relevant instruments. But the case of investment is especially difficult.

Because of the importance of this problem the UN has taken an active interest in suggesting the establishment of suitable arbitration machinery for the protection of foreign investors.[77] A report of the Secretary General in February 1960, quoted by Domke, emphasized that what was lacking was not so much a definition of investor's rights, as an effective forum in which to enforce them: Neither foreign courts and agencies, nor the support of his own government, seem to provide certain protection against unfamiliar and arbitrary infringements. Domke then observes that the UN document suggests the use of arbitration as an alternative. And he approvingly quotes a member of the Netherlands delegation as having said, during discussion of the report, that:

> . . . from a practical point of view, the certainty that disputes concerning the treatment of investors can be submitted to the judgment of arbitrators is even more important than the establishment of fixed rules for such treatment. Rules are not much use to the private investor if he cannot compel compliance with them, but, if he can bring his case before an impartial body, he knows that substantial justice will be done even if it is not based on any codified set of rules.

It is perhaps natural that, out of such beginnings, there should have emerged a feeling that there is need either for new arbitral bodies or for the adaptation of existing facilities. The Secretary General, in a press conference in March 1960, expressed a preference for the latter course.

A point that needs to be made in conclusion is that arbitration is perhaps seen by investing countries both as more necessary and more impartial than by borrowing countries. Borrowers often perceive the alleged unwillingness of investors to make funds available without protection as evidence of a greedy concern for excessive profits. And, to the extent that they recognize the possibility of disputes arising because of legitimate differences of views concerning facts, the interpretation of contracts and laws, or the jurisdiction of legislative and adjudicative systems, they often distrust the objectivity of arbitration mechanisms and procedures,

[77] See *Ibid.*, pp. 177–79, 183–84 for a brief summary of UN activities and citations of UN and other relevant documents.

especially when these are created by, operative within, and obedient to the legal and economic norms of the investing countries. Until the aims and operative premises of lenders and borrowers correspond more closely than they do now it is doubtful that the requisite basis of trust and understanding, needed for mutual acceptance of institutions to resolve conflicts, will come into being.

Investment Guarantees[78]

Investment guarantees may be given either by capital-exporting or capital-importing countries. The latter are more common, but also less specific, consisting of general statements concerning the treatment of all foreign investors and providing assurances of fair treatment, non-discrimination, and the like. Although specific guarantees also are sometimes provided by the borrowing countries — as in the cases of concession agreements, guarantee contracts, and grants of administrative approval of a proposed investment after application to an appropriate agency — neither the general nor the specific guarantees of capital-importers have sufficed to create an investment climate satisfactory to foreign investors generally. For this reason, some of the capital-exporting countries have endeavored to fill the gap as a matter of foreign economic policy. The United States took the lead after World War II, followed by Japan, West Germany, and to a smaller degree Great Britain. The possibilities of setting up one or more European funds or agencies for the guarantee of overseas investment have also been discussed.[79]

The investment guarantee program of the United States was inaugurated in 1948 to provide protection against non-business risks such as expropriation, non-transferability of earnings, and war. Investments may be guaranteed either by the Export-Import Bank[80] or the newer Development Loan Fund (DLF), which is not discussed by Fatouros. The guarantees available from the DLF, which are broader and more flexible than those of the Export-Import Bank, may be made to "foreign firms . . . in-

[78] The most comprehensive, and also recent, treatment of these matters is another in the Columbia series of international legal studies: A. A. Fatouros, *Government Guarantees to Foreign Investors* (New York: Columbia University Press, 1962), which contains an extensive bibliography. A useful study of the guarantee program of the United States is that by Marina von Newmann Whitman, *The United States Investment Guaranty Program and Private Foreign Investment* (Princeton Studies in International Finance, No. 9, Department of Economics, Princeton University, 1959).

[79] Fatouros, *op. cit.* (Note 78), pp. 121–22, 111–17.

[80] *Ibid.*, pp. 101–11, 117–19.

ternational consortiums . . . anybody who is friendly"; only normal business risks are excluded.[81]

Fears that the assumption of responsibility by the capital-exporting country would encourage capital-importers to behave irresponsibly, and that normal investor risks, assumed by government, would become a burden on taxpayers, have not been realized. Host governments have understood and accepted their responsibilities, and so far no formal claim for payment under the guarantee has been presented. This is in one sense a measure of the program's success, but it also means that the program has not been tested under stress. Perhaps the favorable if limited experience so far is responsible for an improvement in the attitude of business circles toward the program, and for a recent increase in the value of guarantees outstanding and applied for.

Investment guarantee programs should not be confused with the investment provisions that have been included in the bilateral treaties of Friendship, Commerce, and Navigation (FCN treaties) concluded by the United States since the war, or with proposals for a multilateral international investment code which were incorporated in the Havana Charter and have since been debated at the UN, the Council of Europe, and elsewhere.[82] A basic difficulty with these approaches is that they are partly founded upon an assumed identity of interests between the capital-exporting and the capital-importing countries. That such an identity exists is by no means obvious, especially where the capital-importers are the less developed countries (which is one reason why the United States has been able to conclude only half a dozen such treaties with such countries, and why the three treaties which were signed but not ratified were with such countries). In the section dealing with institutional differences it was noted that there were divergent views concerning such matters as the title to subsurface resources and the taking of private property owned by aliens. Under the circumstances it is hardly likely that capital importers generally will come to regard the views of capital exporters as worthy to prevail because of their greater rectitude. Another problem is that a code or treaty can hardly afford substantial protection to foreign investors without limiting the sovereignty of all participating states, which even some of the capital exporters would presumably resist. There is the further fact that capital-importing countries would have no assurance of receiving an adequate

---

[81] Whitman, *op. cit.* (Note 78), p. 45, except the quotation, which is from Representative Judd as reported in *Activities of Private U.S. Organizations in Africa, op. cit.* (Note 19), p. 74.

[82] See Fatouros, *op. cit.* (Note 78), pp. 69–101.

and continuing capital inflow in exchange for their loss of freedom of action. Finally, according to Fatouros, most of the proposed draft codes are one-sided because they protect investors without attempting to safeguard the host state's interests. It is sometimes said that the foreign investor needs protection more. But even if this doubtful contention were true, it does not follow that investors' duties toward the host state should not be included in a comprehensive investment code.

Bilateral treaties are easier to negotiate than a multilateral code would be, partly because they can be tailored to meet the special circumstances of each situation. But despite this flexibility they suffer from most of the same, only partially remediable, disadvantages. In both cases, differences in interests and points of view are too wide to be spirited away by agreement on broad, abstract principles.

Standardized Legislation

The greater the similarity between juridical systems the less the need for specialized adjudicative mechanisms and institutions of the kinds discussed in preceding pages. And while persistent differences in social objectives, institutions, and mores will preclude perfect harmonization of law, some movement in this direction can be expected. The possibilities in a field of present relevance are outlined in a paper by Ely.[83]

Serious and systematic consideration of legislative possibilities have advantages because issues are raised in specific and concrete form, and the experiences of countries with similar objectives but different legislative provisions can be compared. The subject of comparative law, especially when applied across differing cultural systems, is relatively new. Ely has approached his task mainly from the standpoint of countries which, having newly acquired both independence and the hope of finding and exploiting mineral resources, wish to draft a minerals statute *de novo,* but this is not the universal case. Nor is it the sole problem, for tax law and commercial law also bear importantly on the problems of international investment in raw materials. There are thus many opportunities for constructive revision and codification of basic economic statutes, a process that might well begin with appropriately specialized research in comparative law and comparative legal experience like that in the Columbia Uni-

---

[83] Northcutt Ely, "Legislative Choices in the Development of Mineral Resources," paper presented to the UN Conference on the Application of Science and Technology for the Benefit of the Less Developed Areas, Geneva, February 1963 (Washington: U.S. Government Printing Office).

versity program, and be extended to provide concrete guidance for the drafting of legislation, as in Ely's paper.

The focus of this section has been on efforts to reduce hazards, to ameliorate the risks and uncertainties that inhibit the flow of private investment or diminish the net benefits accruing to investors and host countries. Inevitably, in view of the problems considered, the measures and institutions discussed were narrow in scope and technical in nature. Politics, domestic and international, was present but largely ignored. The time has come for its crucial role to be recognized.

POTENTIALS AND HAZARDS IN POLITICAL PERSPECTIVE

The political dimensions of the problems we have been considering have frequently been apparent, sometimes explicit, but never central. In bringing them to the fore, I necessarily enter a realm of greater speculation and controversy.

Private Power and Social Objectives in Less Developed Countries

The social irresponsibility of private enterprise is an old theme. But the theme is not dead, especially when applied to private foreign investment in natural resources in non-industrial countries. Preceding pages contain numerous items to support this contention, and many more could be provided. There is, for example, Lincoln Gordon's assertion of the need for business, especially in underdeveloped countries, to recognize its social obligations.[84] In a similar vein, there is the remark of Monsignor Ligutti that, "To save itself, capitalism must realize its social purpose — service to society — and act accordingly" in its overseas operations.[85]

The implication of such views is that business has failed to carry out its obligations to society, and must be persuaded to mend its ways. But the premise, it seems to me, is wrong, and the remedy misconceived. Private enterprise is socially a-responsible rather than irresponsible, and socially responsible business behavior must be imposed by society through its institutions, not achieved through voluntary action by so-

[84] Gordon, "Private Enterprise and Economic Development," *op. cit.* (Note 39).
[85] In Fenn, *Management Guide to Overseas Operations, op. cit.* (Note 32). Compare also Engler's conclusion that, "The central consideration arising from the analysis of the politics of oil is the incompatibility of a socially irresponsible system of power with the goal of a truly democratic society." *Op. cit.* (Note 35), p. 484.

cially minded executives.[86] While some business leaders clearly have a sense of social responsibility, and some companies do attempt to pursue policies shaped by a conception of the public interest, these are not inherent norms of our form of socioeconomic system. The logic, function, and organization of private enterprise are such that the social consequences of its actions are of no compelling concern to those who make decisions unless institutions or political processes convert such consequences into private benefits or costs. The untrammelled business executive either proceeds, in his capacity as profit-maximizer, along the efficiency path defined by the parameters of his situation, or tries, in his capacity as business strategist, to induce parametric shifts advantageous to the profitability, survival, or growth of the enterprise. It is thus the role of a society's political institutions to control the parameters of private choice functions so that socially beneficial lines of action will coincide with privately advantageous decisions, whether these are economic or strategic in character. Such control has been established (though incompletely) in the industrial countries — partly through the device of establishing and maintaining competitive markets — but it has not operated to the same degree in the underdeveloped countries. That is why Marx's predictions went awry in the Western world, where the force of the contradictions of capitalism has been largely dissipated through the operation of political processes, but turned out remarkably well in other regions where tensions due to conflict of private and social interest have frequently cumulated to explosive levels.

Admittedly, the people and governments of the host countries often exaggerate the severity and durability of the conflict between public power and foreign private power; and these distortions of the degree of conflict militate against its resolution. Yet the existence of exaggeration is no ground for refusing to acknowledge the underlying realities. The transition of the major raw-material countries from colonial or quasi-colonial status to political independence has meant the end of a long period of relative — and sometimes nearly complete — laissez faire for direct foreign investment. Inevitably, the change has been accompanied by strains and problems. Companies have lost or been threatened with losing valuable special privileges in the host countries. Host governments, mindful of long lists of actual or alleged grievances, and eager to explore the meaning of sovereignty, have imposed or threatened to impose ham-

---

[86] Support (though not responsibility) for this view will be found in Francis X. Sutton, Seymour E. Harris, Carl Kaysen, and James Tobin, *The American Business Creed* (Cambridge: Harvard University Press, 1956) pp. 354–60.

pering constraints and unworkable demands on company operations. The notion that private enterprise is an exploitive, even a conspiratorial, form of control over the means of production dies hard in areas where experience often lends credence to the belief.

Perhaps more important, however, is the new governments' lack of understanding of hard economic facts, and especially of the limitations they impose both on the companies and on the governments that wish to maximize the contribution of company operations to local welfare and growth. The consequence is often governmental inaction accompanied by mutual suspicion, hostility, and frustration; or action that, in an effort to derive greater social benefits, discourages initiation or expansion of private productive activities. That the new business climate in the raw-material countries should thus be different from the old, and less satisfactory to investors, is the inevitable consequence of political change. That it should also differ from and be less satisfactory than the business climate in the investor's home countries is also a consequence of change; but this need not be taken as inevitable — not, at least, in countries that want foreign capital.

The Problem

Given these equivocalities, it is not strange that the raw-material countries are currently wavering between two choices. One is to foreswear private enterprise and go wholly over to socialism in whatever form or version they find attractive. The other is to create the sort of sociopolitical context that simultaneously will (*a*) permit private enterprise to function efficiently as a device for realizing the mutually beneficial potentials of co-operative endeavor, and (*b*) so resolve the conflicts of distributive interest that the economic surplus produced by the private sector is allocated in a manner promotive of economic growth and development. If the second of these choices is to be made it is important for both the private foreign investors and the host countries to recognize and accept that it is contrary to the nature of private enterprise to be socially responsible, and that therefore the success of the system from the social point of view depends on the institutional context within which it operates. Deny the crucial relevance of that context and one inevitably passes through the looking glass into a Marxist vision of capitalism, with all its implications for a forceful reorganization of economic activity along socialist (read "socially responsible") lines.

Thus, I question reliance upon exhortation, upon urging business operating overseas to act in a socially responsible manner, for I believe that, normatively speaking, it has only those social responsibilities that political action has made coincident with its private responsibilities. Sometimes, to be sure, private enterprise abroad acts in a socially responsible way without being compelled to do so. Sometimes, too, far-sighted international corporations, perceiving a convergence of private and public interest, adopt continuing policies of a socially beneficial character which are more progressive even than those of the host government itself. But behind such actions, I suggest, there will usually be found a perception of political writing on the wall and an estimate of net advantage in the long term. The major problem, therefore, would seem to be that of formulating the political writing. For it is society, particularly its political sector, that is ultimately responsible for the fulfillment of social goals, even where immediate responsibility is left with individuals and private organizations. No good can come from failure to face this fact squarely. What is needed, consequently, are systematic efforts to help the raw-material countries equip themselves with the sociopolitical goals, values, institutions, and processes that are prerequisite to the efficient and socially beneficial operation of private enterprise, whether domestic or foreign.

So to define the problem is a far cry from solving it. To transport a modern corporate enterprise, complete in all its operative essentials, to a premodern environment is remarkably easy; but it is impossible to transport a sociopolitical system, as the records of colonialism and satel-litism show. Some method for strengthening indigenous developmental processes in such systems must therefore be sought.

One difficulty is that, failing to acknowledge the need, we fail to tackle the problem. Taking an a-political view, we profess to believe that capital, technology, and rising per capita incomes are effective weapons against revolution when the fact more often is that a restructuring of society is a prerequisite to putting capital and technology to effective use. But such restructuring is seldom if ever a goal of business strategy.[87]

The contrary, indeed, is often true, and this creates a second difficulty. Foreign companies, accustomed to operate in a highly privileged and un-

---

[87] An analogous point concerning foreign aid is made by Lucian W. Pye, in "Soviet and American Styles in Foreign Aid," *Orbis,* Summer 1960. The nub of his analysis is the observation that, in principle, technical specialists must take orders from "the 'broker' in values, the politician;" but in American practice, this is not the case. No matter whether the technical specialists are the managers and engineers of private enterprises or experts provided under foreign aid programs, the point is the same: politics is either ignored or wrongly practiced by technicians who should be receiving rather than providing political guidance.

trammelled manner, are likely to resist change, even though change is often favorable to business prospects rather than otherwise.[88] Fear of uncertainty, stimulated by reformist polemics, has frequently led foreign companies to make common political cause with powerful indigenous elements favorable to the status quo.[89] Though less frequently (or less openly) than before, the political power of foreign private enterprise is thus employed to prevent the imposition of social responsibilities hitherto ignored. For private enterprise does possess and exercise political power.

Such doctrine is today regarded as strange and unacceptable: the dominant Western ideology of fundamental harmony between public and private interests hinders our perception of disharmonies abroad, and hampers our efforts to deal with them. When Herbert Hoover, Jr., at a conference session on "American Business Abroad and the National Interest," said: ". . . while American business is faced with challenging opportunities abroad, it must also be prepared to shoulder corresponding responsibilities" — something which he referred to as the "hallmark of industry at home"[90] — he was ignoring the political differences that make business more responsible at home than abroad. By the same token, he was overlooking the need — in the national interest of the United States — to eliminate the differences.

Investment, in short, should be brought to recognize, as some of the leading international companies already do, that the loss of old privileges is inevitable and irreversible, and that there is no inherent reason why

[88] For example: "The United Africa Company, both because of its size and ubiquity . . . was the target most often selected as the local representative of Britain's economic imperialism . . . . But this animosity was modified once political power was transferred to the African; today business for such firms is better than ever." Edward and Mildred Marcus, *Investment and Development Possibilities in Africa* (New York: Bookman Associates, 1960), p. 191. In general, the stronger and more socially conscious the political regime in the host country, the more satisfactory for both investor and host will be the policies and practices of the foreign enterprise. Consider, for example, the case of Indaluco, mentioned in the section dealing with dynamic problems arising out of company operations. See also the testimony of Chad C. Calhoun, of Kaiser Industries, concerning their relations with Ghana on the Volta River Project, in *Activities of Private U.S. Organizations in Africa, op. cit.* (Note 45), pp. 65 ff. But this may not always be true of companies established under a once pliant regime that has given way to a progressive one.

[89] The difficulties of carrying out the reforms called for under the Alliance for Progress at least partly reflect the power of such elements.

[90] Fenn, *op. cit.* (Note 32). When asked how business operating abroad could figure out what their national responsibilities were, Hoover replied that they were: "Good common sense, business honesty, and the mutuality that must be a part of any sound business deal." One can be confident that when Terry Duce said: "Whatever Aramco does abroad is done with an awareness of its national responsibility," he had rather more in mind than Hoover's vacuities. (*Ibid.*)

private enterprise should be more favored abroad than at home. A correlative problem is to bring Westerners generally to recognize the need for a change in the balance of public and private power in the raw-material countries, and to accept actions by their governments predicated on that view.

Changes are also required on the capital receiving end. Host countries need to be brought to a wider appreciation of the relationship that should obtain between private enterprise as the chief economic agent of society, and government as the chief political agent. The developing countries need not approve a private enterprise, and may eschew it. But if they accept it, they must do so on terms. There is nothing absolute about these terms, which are subject to initial negotiation and later change, but at any given moment the "opportunity terms" existing elsewhere in the private enterprise world set a limit to what a given "independent" government can successfully achieve.

Western Interests and the Raw Material Producers

The question is whether anything can be done to make the views of the several parties more realistic — that is, to bring them closer together. The national interests of the United States, of the Western world generally, and of the underdeveloped countries will be better served by recognizing that the achievement of effective working relationships between foreign enterprises, on the one hand, and the peoples and governments of host countries on the other, is a major problem worthy of special study and attention. Such relationships would be privately profitable but, to an increasing extent, they would also be socially beneficial. However, their achievement requires that we do something more than exhort private enterprise to shoulder social obligations which are not defined with clarity and which, in the absence of appropriate institutional arrangements, are not private responsibilities in any case. It also requires that we do something more than castigate host countries for actions and activities brought on by our own past mistakes. What is this "something more" that is required?

There is little that the governments of the investor countries can or should do directly to bring host countries to realization of the proper scope of private enterprise, or to help them achieve a proper balance between public and private power. But Western governments can facilitate these changes indirectly, by acknowledging their desirability and by taking a broader view of the national interest than has been their custom. International companies, as we have noted, are often urged to act in the national interest as if it and the private interest were closely similar. But why is it assumed that an impersonal corporate personality should be the agent of the national interest of the investor country and not of the host country? The answer, surely, lies not in the investor country's higher moral claim to the company's loyalty, but in its stronger political claim.

There is no permanent basis for this stronger political claim. It reflects a historical asymmetry in private-public power relationships which lies at the root of many current problems, particularly in the sphere of private international investment in natural resources. The Western nations would serve their own interests well by recognizing this asymmetry and lending their support to its elimination. This they can do most effectively by pressing strongly for solutions to the problems discussed in earlier sections of this essay (and also in Gaitskell's essay, in this volume, which has a range of application far wider than its specifically African context) — problems which, as we have seen, are already on the agenda.

Note: Revision of the original draft of the section on political perspective was greatly aided by discussion at the RFF Forum. I am also indebted to my colleague A. E. Kahn for a number of helpful comments.

INTERNATIONAL TRANSFERS OF KNOWLEDGE AND CAPITAL

EGBERT DE VRIES

This essay will concentrate upon the development of existing and potential resources, both human and material, in the developing countries. To be sure, the interchange of knowledge and capital between high-income, industrialized countries has many institutional and organizational aspects; but these are not our special concern. In the case of Eastern European countries, the flow of knowledge to and from the industrialized countries of the "West" at times has aspects of spying; capital investment between them is almost nil. But both the "West" and the "East" must carefully consider the organization of transfer of knowledge and capital to the developing countries.

Until the Great Depression it seemed that market mechanisms were

---

EGBERT DE VRIES is Rector of the Institute of Social Studies, The Hague; director of the Netherlands Universities Foundation for International Cooperation; vice chairman of the National Organization for International Aid, and vice chairman of the Board of the African Study Center at Leyden. From 1950 to 1956 he served with the International Bank for Reconstruction and Development, first as chief of the Economic Resources Division of the Economics Department, then as chief of the Economic Division of the Technical Operations Department, and later as chief of the Agricultural Division. From 1947 to 1950 he was professor of tropical agricultural economics at the University of Wageningen, and adviser to the Netherlands Ministry of Overseas Affairs. From 1924 to 1941 Mr. de Vries served the government of the Netherlands East Indies, for the latter four years as head of the Division for General Economic Affairs. From 1941 to 1946 he was professor of agricultural economics and dean of the Agricultural Faculty at the University of Batavia (Djakarta). Mr. de Vries was born in the Netherlands in 1901 and educated at the University of Wageningen.

adequate to cope with these problems. A large part of Asia and Africa had bilateral flows of knowledge, entrepreneurship and capital from their respective metropolitan countries. Dominions and independent countries had access to loans in the main financial centers; generally their doors were open to private investment from a variety of sources.

In a few cases — for instance in the oil industry (mineral and to some extent vegetable oil) and for some of the nonfuel minerals (gold, diamond, copper) — a concentration or cartellization had gradually taken shape.

Government and business circles in the developing countries had to adjust to the ebbs and tides of the world market for capital and the desire to invest overseas. Interestingly, at least in Great Britain, this flow was anticyclical. In times of industrial overproduction (steel, shipbuilding) and unemployment in England, British capital sought more intensively for employment abroad.

All this changed dramatically after World War II. The reasons are complicated, but the main strands can be recognized.

a) The United States came out of the war as the only large nation capable of assisting other nations in their attempts to reconstruct their economies. This involved three important flows of governmental funds (UNRRA, British loan, Marshall Aid).

b) Already during the war, financial circles agreed that there would be a need for global monetary and banking institutions (Bretton Woods).

c) At the end of the war, the United Nations from its inception carried the notion of organized flows of knowledge and capital.

d) Even during the execution of the Marshall Plan, the United States strengthened greatly its governmental channels for both types of transfer (Export-Import Bank, Point 4).

e) Great Britain followed, in a more modest way and on a different pattern in 1950, with the Colombo Plan for Asian Commonwealth countries. All this was put into motion during the first five years following the war. The next decade gave rise not only to continuation and expansion of these efforts (with the exception of Marshall Aid) but also to the development of a variety of other channels:

f) The metropolitan countries in Europe — Great Britain, France, Belgium, and even Portugal and the Netherlands — expanded greatly governmental or semi-governmental grants and loans to their overseas territories or to friendly nations after independence.

g) The European Economic Community started off with a socio-economic development fund for its associated members, primarily in Africa.

h) The Sino-Soviet countries likewise initiated their programs for the transfer of knowledge and capital.

i) The United Nations and the International Bank diversified and expanded their instrumentalities (Economic Development Institute, International Finance Corporation, International Development Association, Special Fund, *et al.*).

j) Several other countries started bilateral programs for foreign aid and co-operation (West Germany, Japan, *et al.*).

k) Non-governmental agencies (religious institutions, foundations) undertook to enlarge the flow of knowledge and development assistance.

In the private sphere, borrowing facilities on the capital markets which had dwindled were not revived. But the desirability of continued or even expanded direct private investment overseas was emphasized.

This list is not exhaustive. It is meant to illustrate the rapid growth in numbers and intensity of channels of transferring knowledge and capital.

It is possible to classify the forms of transfer and the nature of the services transferred in a variety of ways. A classification has often been coupled with a scale of preference or rejection. The rapid development of the instrumentalities is one reason why several of these judgments became obsolete within a few years. For instance, the fight between proponents of multilateral or bilateral intergovernmental aid seems to be fought without a general preference evolving.

It seems preferable to begin discussing the characteristics of various organizational and institutional aspects without political connotations. Political considerations, of course, greatly influence the modalities of the flow of both knowledge and capital, and their impact will vary from case to case, but it should be possible to analyze the process without political judgments.

Resource development requires an application of knowledge and capital, human and material resources, which have to be concentrated upon specific programs, projects, and enterprises. Transfers into an integrated whole will be necessary under all circumstances, but will play a vital role where both knowledge and capital are inadequate. Conceptually, in resource development all elements (human and material) must be seen as components of an integral process, where knowledge, skill, experience, muscle power, entrepreneurship and imagination of human beings are matched to equipment and machinery in a socioeconomic-political framework.

If the word "process" is used here, more is meant than the observed sequence of events or phenomena in a certain spatial (geographical) environment. These changes in the relationships between man and nature become a process by the magic wand of human purpose and design. Without this finality — the hoped for reward for endeavor, sweat, and risk — no development of "natural" resources can be considered. People can happen to find treasures or they can exploit existing resources, but this is not resource development and may not even lead to resource development. And, incidentally, in changes of economic, social, or political structures (relationships between men), man's objectives similarly make the series of social phenomena a process.

Without exaggeration, one may state that the transfer of resources cannot fruitfully be studied without taking into account the objectives, the goals of the action taken. And in our times there must be identifiable objectives at both ends for there are no more empty lands. The process of transfers undoubtedly can and should be judged on the basis of efficiency — the relation between accepted purpose and means applied.

Must the process be integral? This indeed is a modern idea. There have been times when in practice (and in theory) priority in the process was given to one specific factor in resource development.

In the early decades of rationalism and liberalism (1780–1850) this specific element was considered to be a liberation of individual entrepreneurship from social and political shackles. It was taken for granted that experienced, even if unskilled, labor and profit-seeking capital would always be available in an expanding market, under a system of internal law and order and international free trade.

At a later stage, when the nation-state became more profoundly established and enterprise became institutionalized, including the international markets for capital, it was considered that capital was the moving force. Well-directed investments would, if necessary, be supported by national governments (even overseas). Management and well-trained labor to be engaged and scientific research to be organized and applied were assumed to be available when adequately paid for.

At a later stage again in certain societies, first of all those adhering to total planning, it was considered that the political will had to be the moving force, mobilizing the state with all its human and capital resources.

In our times, in resource development involving international transfer of knowledge and capital, the need for a combination of at least all these elements is recognized. It would be impossible to develop mineral, forestry, or energy resources without the active co-operation of the government or governments involved, wthout organized research, capital resources, entrepreneurship, highly capable management, and experienced labor. The art of combining the manifold elements in a successful enterprise calls for an integral approach. In this collection of essays our attention is focused here upon the elements knowledge and capital — both most important in the process, but not all-inclusive.

TRANSFER OF KNOWLEDGE

Knowledge is a cumulative asset of mankind. Given the right institutions and organization, it would be freely communicable — with some temporary legal restrictions on its application and a time- (therefore resource-) absorbing process through study, teaching, training, and learning. In principle international transfer would be hardly more complicated than intranational and generation-to-generation transfers. But in practice it is a great deal more complicated, and not only because of cultural and language barriers.

There are good reasons to review what complications are actually interfering with effective international transfers.

First, historically the accumulation of knowledge has been spread unevenly among continents and nations. During the period of colonial administration it did not matter so very much that Asian and African natural resources were studied in the European capitals and universities. These were also the places of decision-making. But at the moment of independence in many new countries the basic data, even statistics, were found lacking for ongoing programs because the plans were ready-made in Paris or London. Two things happened during and after World War II. First, the institutional arrangements for this accumulation became clogged. In recent history many channels of developing knowledge through expeditions, surveys, field and laboratory research have lost in efficiency. This would especially be the case during the process of acquiring independence and in the early years of newly won national independence. At the same time there is need for new accumulation of information and knowledge at points where present decisions are being made. This is part of the process of "decolonization" of the world.

Secondly, science and technology are developing at a speed which makes it difficult, if not impossible, to become and remain "up to date." This is the world-wide "technological explosion" of our age. It is well known that the Soviet Russian Academy of Sciences has organized a grandiose instrumentality to collect, classify, and screen information from all around the world in the field of science and technology. No other nation seems to be adequately equipped to do the same. Although in the aggregate various institutions in the United States jointly have accumulated more knowledge about foreign countries and societies, nowhere is the material easily accessible or "in stock" for a smooth transfer.

I submit that as a result of these tendencies the *collection and transfer of basic data is dangerously interrupted and inadequate* for rapid resource development in the developing countries. For many projects and programs in Asia and Africa data may be hidden in European files, but these are hard to find and by no means up to date.

The *new* instrumentalities — technical assistance activities, university contracts included — are in principle of a temporary nature. Personalities in these programs change even more rapidly than the activities themselves. There are fewer lifetime careers in research on non-Western resources than during the "colonial period." Furthermore, there is little chance that the new findings are:

a) properly evaluated against earlier observations (the "expert" cannot find the data or is not being given the time to process them scientifically);

b) properly communicated to scientists in the country or area where the expert worked (limitation of time of contract and shortage of adequate counterparts or local team members);

c) effectively added to the stock of knowledge on a global scale (often the reports are confidential or are being filed by governmental or intergovernmental agencies and almost inaccessible);

d) adequately brought together in specific scientific institutions or documentation centers and thus made available for general use.

Some attempts are being made to overcome these formidable obstacles through research grants to scholars and scientific institutions, but some gaps will be very difficult to bridge. An enormous amount of basic information on countries that have suffered from wars and civil wars may be irretrievably lost. Some of it might still be recovered if a systematic search were conducted, but with the death of prominent scientific workers and former civil servants in developing countries the chances of re-

trieving older data on the societies in transition, useful for future resource development, become very slim indeed.

As an instance where most of the data collection started afresh one
may mention the Mekong Valley program. (I leave aside the possibility
that more use might have been made of data hidden in French institutions.) And as a happy example of sustained effort, hydrological and
engineering data on the Nile River collected over several generations
have made it possible to draft the High Aswan Dam project.

Under the present rules of the international game it is very difficult or
well-nigh impossible for intergovernmental organizations to act as a
reservoir of basic information on natural resources. Even for the Special
Fund of the United Nations this task would be too heavy, and the desire
of governments for quick advice and fast project development tends to
work against spending money for this purpose.[1] The major foundations
in the United States (and increasingly in Europe) and the larger universities or specialized institutions all around the world would be more
free to perform this role. But, with notable exceptions, their resources
are generally inadequate to perform systematic data collection and distribution.

The main measures for improvement of resource development fall
within four categories:

1. First of all, there is an urgent need to *develop scientific institutions
in the developing areas* (for the smaller countries preferably on a regional basis), with adequate documentation, personnel, buildings, and
funds. The sequence is given in the order of priority of need. In reality,
very often the reverse happens. Somebody makes funds available, buildings are set up, personnel from abroad brought into empty buildings.
This temporary staff then tries to find or train local scientific staff and
collect a documentation.

2. Secondly, as a backstop it is necessary to *maintain and develop
partner-institutions,* mainly in Europe and North America. These should
no longer be called mother-institutions. Difficult as this may seem, it is
necessary within overseas university programs to stimulate independent
partner-institutions in the countries of special interest and operation.
But it is likewise necessary to keep a full supply of basic knowledge in
the traditional great scientific centers. Transfer of knowledge both ways

---

[1] At the recent UN Conference on The Application of Science and Technology
for the Benefit of the Less Developed Areas, at Geneva, a proposal was made to
initiate a major UN effort for resource development.

may well largely take the form of microfilms. Technically, the means of transferring and retrieving data is much more advanced than is often believed. We should make full use of the new methods.

3. Thirdly, it is indispensable to *train basic research workers* on a much larger scale. Of course, these people should also have a reasonable opportunity to add to the flow and exchange of knowledge through research assignments after training. Institutionally, this process is still very inadequately organized. Many young scientific workers from the developing countries find no research facilities in their own countries.

4. *Exchange* of teaching staff, of research workers and postgraduate students adds greatly to the potential of a transfer of knowledge. But these assignments and fellowships should not be ephemeral; they should be geared towards a two-way traffic in transfer of knowledge. In other words, they should fit in a pattern of institution building as indicated under categories 1 and 2 above.

Not all knowledge is free after it has been developed, and transfers are often difficult or have to be contracted for.

Private industry, especially in mining and forestry, is accumulating a great deal of highly important information on resources. Obviously, this knowledge is part of the assets of a particular concern.

Consulting agencies undertake, on the basis of a contract, to investigate and make available to their principals basic data and possible applications. Because of the fee involved, this information is generally restricted to a limited group.

Last but not least, there is a great amount of basic scientific knowledge which is considered of national interest and therefore essentially non-available for an international transfer. The delineation of this area of secrecy is very difficult; it is well known that no screens are impermeable, but their existence does impede the legal transfer of knowledge.

Implicitly, and even explicitly, there has been a plea for enlarged channels of transfer of knowledge about resource development all around the world. The main argument is not that anything communicable should be freely transferred. It is rather the character of knowledge as a cumulative asset which asks for transferability. Transfer of knowledge adds to the common stock. Those who give freely are likely to profit most. It is in their own self-interest for the advanced institutions (and parts of the world) actively to promote and subsidize this transfer, for they are likely to benefit most.

The promotion of research and the transfer of its results must be considered an investment of great importance. It is therefore necessary to develop systematically those instrumentalities which promote greatest efficiency. It is clear that much remains to be done.

TRANSFER OF CAPITAL

Capital resources when used and applied are capable of returning not only their own investment but also profit, and in the long run they tend to flow in the direction of maximum surplus. Profit maximization, if not the only or primary motive for all investors, is the rule on the capital market. Capital resources are unevenly distributed among continents and countries and it is unlikely that an equilibrium would exist at any moment and a flow of capital be considered a "natural" phenomenon. But as a process, the international transfer of capital is nowadays institutionalized in a great number of organizations. This is in a sense the sign that the "free flow" meets with obstacles. The international markets for capital are not readily accessible to customers from the developing continents.

Under present rules of the international game, investment capital is generally free to move into an area or country, into or within a specific branch of industry. At this stage, it is eagerly sought after and perhaps therefore cagey. Once it has been invested, the capital often is no longer free to move out, or sometimes it is difficult or impossible to transfer interest and amortization. Such experiences make potential investors or lenders reluctant to venture their capital resources. As a result, an increasing percentage of capital transfer uses governmental or intergovernmental channels. But at the same time there is a general recognition of the value, even necessity, of capital transfers in the private sector. Thus an ambivalent attitude is being created and maintained. Most governments in developing countries declare solemnly that they would welcome private investments. At the same time, conditions congenial to private (new) investment are hardly present. Foreign enterprise, if not forthcoming, is being invited; foreign enterprise, if traditionally present, is being resented. Would it be possible, if desirable, to shift completely to public investments? Would it be possible, if desirable, to revitalize private investment for productive investment and have recourse once more to the private capital market for the infrastructure?

I do not believe that declarations of good will, or even the establishment of an international ethical code of investment, will solve the dilemma. The investments of today are protected by the hope of a continuous flow of investments. Even this promise does not always afford adequate protection. The investments of yesterday are in an even more precarious position. If one looks at the considerations of potential investors, governmental and private, one finds that the "natural" flow of capital into areas of scarcity (hence high surplus value) is hampered mainly by the inordinate risks felt to exist by potential investors.

A demonstration of the effect of political risk upon investment is the constant, sometimes surreptitious flow of private capital to "safe" countries with a low interest rate. For the investment (or hoarding) of capital from Asian and Latin-American countries, Switzerland, Belgium, and the United States give highly desirable opportunities. Because of frequent evasion of tax or currency regulations, the magnitude of this transfer of capital is hard to assess; it is however very considerable. A large part is hidden in export — and import — transactions. It has been estimated that some $25 billion to $30 billion of Latin-American assets have been transferred into the United States and Europe during and since World War II. Much of this transfer is based upon safety rather than high profitability.

Of course, if the assessment of risks reverses the "natural" flow of capital from low interest areas into a flow from countries with great scarcity of capital, it seems clear that measures to ensure more transfer towards the developing countries must tackle the general conditions of operation rather than merely the overt organization of capital transfer.

But here one encounters a formidable obstacle in the fact that the majority of the developing countries *are* a bad risk. Investment risks have not only been made high by specific governmental measures; in many of the developing countries foreign exchange income varies widely, even wildly, in the short and long run as a result of heavy dependence upon one or two primary commodities. The free transfer of profits and depreciation allowances cannot be guaranteed under all circumstances, let alone the free repatriation of investment, even if governments had all the will in the world to do so. Investments outside the primary sector are even more vulnerable than those in mining and plantations. Public utilities offer services which are near-monopolistic and therefore are the first target of "price stabilization" in an inflationary situation. In effect, this practice has amounted to gradual confiscation of the property in many instances. Investment in manufacturing industries, even with temporary high protective duties, has to overcome the many hurdles of lack of local managers, skilled labor, and the supporting framework of scores of other industries as a supplier or market. Even with low wage levels for local labor, industry in the developing countries starts off as a high-cost industry.

Perhaps even more importantly, there is diverse opinion on the role of capital goods and capital as an economic factor. The importation of capital goods is valued highly, but the connotation "with interest to be paid for their use" is looked upon somewhat differently. It is commonplace, if not perfectly logical, that developing countries expect the producer and exporter of capital goods to sell on long-term producer credit. Thus the burden of capital formation — temporarily sacrificing consumption — is carried not only during the period of production but also during installation and the early years of effective use. Although contractors generally find full compensation in price levels, none of the parties concerned can estimate the chances of repayment. Thus inadequacies in channeling capital goods are a heavy cost and risk to both parties.

The purely economic answer would be the promotion of labor-intensive against capital-intensive industries in the developing countries. Capital goods, if of a less complicated nature, could more easily be produced in these areas, almost on the spot, as industry grows. This would reduce the need for transfer of heavy equipment.

Interesting calculations have been made, for example by the Netherlands Economic Institute (Tinbergen), on the best combination of labor and capital under conditions of mass underemployment and scarcity of capital. Even on paper, however, it is not very easy to arrive at a maximization of social returns with much labor and little capital. In practice, it is even more difficult: unorthodox types of management would be necessary.

In essence, attempts to substitute labor for capital in industry is an attempt to simulate European and North American conditions of the early nineteenth century in present-day early stages of industrialization. The idea itself may run counter to the ambitions of governments of the newly independent countries; but this would be a political consideration and we want to abstain from such. A more important question is: to what extent is such a "factor-mix" admissible under present-day technological circumstances?

Unfortunately, the answer must be: only to a very limited extent and in selective cases can a nation save on capital by the use of labor.

First, with all due respect to infant industry and the commensurate protective measures permissible under the General Agreement on Tariff and Trade, one does not promote uneconomic inefficient production if there are other possibilities. Some processes, such as spinning and oil-seed crushing, and the steel and petrochemical industries, are only feasible in rather large-scale units that are capital intensive and labor extensive. Wages would have to be below zero to substitute for capital in a foundry, as the Chinese communes learned with their "backyard iron production." Because of technology (transferable knowledge) it is impossible to introduce early nineteenth century processes into a new industrial program.

Secondly, the comparison with early industry in England, Germany, Belgium, or Switzerland fails because although there is a surplus of agricultural labor (even with skill), there generally is a shortage of skilled manufacturing labor as much as of capital in most of the developing countries. And skilled or even experienced manual labor cannot be transferred internationally. It may be redirected from hand looms to mechanical looms, from blacksmithery to small-scale metal industry; it may be trained and retrained; but it cannot be transferred. It is in fact easier and more commonly done to transfer managerial skill than experienced labor. Developing countries generally have a shortage of skilled labor as much as of capital goods. Large-size labor-intensive industry (manufacturing) requires many skilled workers.

Inevitably, therefore, one cannot conceive of rapid resource development without very sizable capital transfers. (Incidentally, there is an almost full complementarity between the factors of production. It is inefficient, for instance, to build a dam and irrigate a valley if the practice of using irrigation water is not well established.) The need for capital goods, often of a complicated nature, cannot be reasoned away even on economic grounds of substitutability of capital and labor. A balance or (shifting) equilibrium based upon the idea of complementarity of both main factors of production will have to be established. It will be necessary to study more carefully the implications of the transfer to and the use of capital goods in a culturally and politically foreign environment.

The costs of the use of capital goods fall within five categories: (*a*) labor for operation, (*b*) materials used in the process, such as fuel and oil, (*c*) maintenance and repair, (*d*) depreciation, (*e*) interest on the use of capital resources. In the consideration of attracting and making available capital resources, people generally concentrate on the last items: the cost of borrowing and the possibility of transferring interest and amortization (depreciation).

I submit that a comparative quantitative study of all costs involved in the transfer of capital goods is needed. Especially, the problems of maintenance and repair are highly important. They are linked with protection against weather (dust, rust), with spare parts and their storage, with the careful treatment of the machinery by the operators, with periodic checks and maintenance facilities. The International Bank would have access to cases where success and failure of a project depended primarily, if not solely, on the effective utilization and maintenance of capital equipment.

Many factors are involved. Some are of a technical character. Nature (climate and soil) is often very unfriendly. Machinery, if it is equipped against all contingencies, becomes too expensive; if tailor-made for specific circumstances, it likewise becomes too expensive because of the small numbers produced; if too well protected, it becomes complicated and vulnerable to neglect; if spare parts are lacking at a crucial moment, great damage may be done. But this last danger is now commonly known and manufacturers do not complain if their principals order spare parts for the next ten years, thus enlarging the order. The Public Administration Division of the United Nations (stores management) would have revealing data at its disposition.

Even more important is the "ethos of machine use." The man who would take care of his horse, cow or buffalo before eating, bathing or sleeping is inclined to leave the machine unattended and uncared for at the blow of the whistle. Machines are dead. Of course, there is a great difference between owning an animal and operating somebody else's machine, especially if somebody else is in the corporation, the government, or the *sovkosz*.

The "ethos of responsibility" for a specific piece of machinery has to be extended to a small group with effective checks and balances. Thus it becomes part of business management and to a very large extent is only transmissible through personal contact and contagious care for the equipment. This again means a transfer of knowledge (stretched into care and responsibility) through demonstration and training. Also, adequate rewards for carefulness and alertness must be introduced.

For a piece of heavy machinery with a useful life of twenty-five years, maintenance and depreciation taken together is more expensive than the interest on a loan. But for a tractor with 10,000 hours of effective work, maintenance alone may be as important as depreciation and several times the burden of interest on a loan for the amount of the purchase.

In passing I want to stress that a general low level of income in a country does not mean that the cost of labor for operating the machinery is proportionally less. Where seven Norwegians can handle a trawler, there is need for twelve to fourteen Japanese and for twenty to twenty-five Indians on the coast of Travancore. Also, fuel and other ingredients to keep the machinery going generally are more expensive in the developing countries.

There are some examples of very efficient use of heavy equipment, including earth-moving equipment, in the developing countries. The conditions for their success and the comparative costs of operations should be studied and publicized to the advantage of all concerned. But case studies are rare and the knowledge available is not widely communicated.

If the risk of transferring capital is considered high, capital must be expensive. Private capital will have a greater preference for short-term supplier investment than for long-term basic resource development.

Some of the managerial and perhaps even political risk can be reduced through the joint venture approach, which has shown remarkable success in some cases but has been hard to realize in others. It would be essential in a joint venture that both capital and management (again material and human resources!) can gradually and progressively pass into the hands of nationals in the country of operation. It is highly desirable, therefore, to study objectively the performance of public national and intergovernmental agencies in this field. Theoretically, there is great scope for tripartite joint ventures — national funds, foreign enterprise, and international public capital (International Finance Corporation).

A second method of reducing the costs of risks — in this particular case political and monetary risks — is the introduction of a multilateral guarantee. A scheme, originally proposed by E. H. van Eeghen, Amsterdam, has been studied by International Bank staff. Its implementation would require an international treaty between both capital-exporting and capital-importing countries.[2]

A third way — not yet given shape — might be a "co-operative organization of borrowing governments" in order to raise money in the capital markets of the world. This suggestion might specifically cover such general investments as escape the eye of the potential investor, who increasingly looks for identifiable single projects for investment — which, by the way, is disturbing the balance from a general point of view.

There is a close relation between risk and cost of capital transfer, but differences between the two should be recognized. Many investments would be highly profitable if risks were reduced, and the increasing flow of supply would tend to reduce interest rates and at the same time would be conducive to the development of instrumentalities of transfer.

[2] International Bank staff report, March 1962.

In the private field, there is an internal equilibrium through the policies of various concerns and firms. Decisions are periodically being made on the feasibility of expansion and branching out in location and type of foreign investment.

In the public field, there is an almost perfect state of persistent disequilibrium. For some types of projects, but only in countries which in themselves are "credit worthy," the International Bank plays an increasingly important role on commercial terms. The International Development Association makes capital available at very long term and at minimum interest. The Development Fund of the European Economic Community in the first five years made grants available and will now have both grants and loans, the latter applying equally to the various bilateral programs. Lucky is the country which finds its needs covered from such a variety of sources in the right proportion and magnitude.

If there is any equilibrium in the total investment program of a given country it is because of the interchangeability of local resources (tax money), with funds derived from international loans and investments. The skill of managing a government budget and over-all development program has indeed become an art. Most governments show ability in handling flexible programs, but of course there are tremendous losses in works undertaken but unfinished or stagnating over years of low-ebb financing.

One might conclude that it is important to increase the total flow of capital transfers, but it is equally important to streamline the present body of capital transfers.

The Points of View of the Developing Countries

We will now depart from our original terms of reference, which excluded political consideration, and try to look at the whole picture from the viewpoint of the government and businessman of a developing country.

Usually, after the first days of hopeful expectations — "they" must help us, "they" are committed, it is "their" promise and responsibility, "we" are so important (for one reason or another) — there follows a period of sobering thoughts and even frustration. Assistance is not forthcoming in the measure expected.

Technical assistance is a bureaucratic process which puts a strain on local human resources as well. Investors and lending agencies ask more questions than anybody can honestly answer. Thus, there comes a time of disappointment generally resulting in the statement that any assistance from anywhere is welcome. But not all assistance can be handled easily. Sometimes there is a multitude of helpful sources of knowledge and capital; so many that all kinds of jokes develop around this theme. It is said that two years ago the Government of Burma counted sixty-nine public and private agencies ready to help Burma — too many, of course, to be effective. When the Government of Burma then declared that it would accept help only from governmental or intergovernmental agencies, even The Ford Foundation had to leave Burma. Was this necessary in order to take a deep breath before another take-off of world-wide transfer of knowledge and capital into Burma? Or was it a withdrawal into the more limited field of the domestic resources of Burma and one or more neighboring countries?

A number of governments welcome loans and grants from both "East" and "West." Partly they do so in order to be able to maintain that they are not committed politically. This has resulted in the complaint, frequently expressed, that they are playing both ends against the middle. "Blackmail?" If a government — such as the United Arab Republic — maintains substantial contacts with both "East" and "West," it becomes vulnerable to a cool reaction from both sides. It can easily be "blackmailed" back, and this has happened in several cases.

Most governments of developing countries welcome private enterprise. But the majority are unable to back up their declaration because of external and internal economic and political vicissitudes. They then are accused of "lip service." This may be true, but what can a poor government of a low-income country with a lopsided, vulnerable economy do? "Muddling through" is indeed an art of survival in difficult days.

With regard to planning for development, most countries have now been persuaded that they need a development program. The United Nations, the International Bank, and U.S. missions have played an important role in this process. Paradoxically, the Soviet countries, with their emphasis on total planning at home, have elected to make deals with developing countries on an ad hoc basis rather than as part of a comprehensive plan. (Soviet Russian aid to Mainland China in 1948–53 and to Cuba in 1960–62 may be exceptions.) The reason may well be that there is less commitment on either side if ad hoc arrangements prevail.

Many governments have only been able to establish a systematic program for resource development with outside technical assistance, but this advice is not always welcome if the recommendations involve changes in internal financial or economic policy. Of course, governments have the right to reject recommendations, but the frequent discrepancies between advice, the acceptance of a plan, and its execution point to serious deficiencies in the channels of communication between various agencies and the nations concerned.

With regard to technical assistance, including the social, medical, and educational fields, the main troubles for a developing country are the manifold discontinuities, the lags and inadequate co-ordination between the numerous agencies. Nevertheless, even if it is a wasteful process which may lead to omissions and delays, rarely do receiving governments lack a variety of valuable analyses and recommendations. Their main problem is to translate these into policies and programs of action. To the objective outsider, groups of countries, especially the smaller ones in more or less similar conditions, might profit a great deal from joint programs of technical assistance. Comparative studies, for example among Central American or West African countries, would give perspective to the various governments (and their officials). It would certainly bring about a better use of the scarce top-level experts in development. There is some hope that the Mekong Co-ordinating Committee will become a focal point in joint planning and resource development, with the river and its tributaries the unifying element.

But the desire among governments to make a co-operative endeavor does not go deep. The Western European governments performed rather well during the Marshall Aid years and through the European Payments Union. The Alliance for Progress has a harder time to achieve a "take-off" in the direction of joint planning for reforms and development. This is understandable, but it is not a very happy phenomenon.

In spite of these limitations, development programs in most cases are not merely shopping lists for most urgent needs. More and more countries have lived through a succession of planning efforts and are applying the experiences gained in the process.

THE POINTS OF VIEW OF THE DEVELOPED COUNTRIES

If I use the term "developed" against "developing," it is only shorthand to indicate countries that are net-exporters of capital and knowledge. Governments of such countries have to be careful in many directions.

First of all, they cannot avoid establishing a policy in this process —

a national policy first of all, the promotion of world peace and international co-operation included. The intricacies of the problems make the implementation difficult, even if the national policy is well established. But secondly, problems become more complicated if governments have to convince a parliament year after year that sizable amounts of taxpayers' money are well spent. Publicity may work both beneficially and adversely to the success of the programs. And thirdly, each of the exporting or potentially exporting countries faces a continuous pressure of demands on scarce supplies of experts and funds.

If there were a unified world resource to be allocated over more than a hundred countries and territories, one would need excellent data and a highly developed computer. In the absence of these instruments allocation becomes a political expedient, even if this had not been the intention at the outset.

The exporting countries, and the United Nations and its agencies, as well as other intergovernmental bodies, try to solve these problems by dividing them. For the United Nations, this is mainly done through its specialized agencies — with the frequent overlaps. For the U.S. government, it is mainly done by regionalization and even country allotments. For the Bretton Woods agencies and their offspring, it is done by a selection of types of projects on the basis of recognizable returns to the various investments. In the EEC social development fund, there is frequent consultation on the basis of an allotment by country (or small groups of countries in the second five-year period). In the Colombo plan organization, it is done on the basis of a "market" of give and take at meetings of cabinet ministers. The Alliance for Progress uses a number of these devices.

As the joint efforts towards world development proceed, the complexities and sheer magnitude of the task become more apparent. The Special Fund of the United Nations is specifically designed to promote, support, and carry out "pre-investment research." Fortunately, the managing director and the governing council of the Fund keep their terms of reference flexible and wide. Out of a total sum of about $250 million earmarked for its various programs,[3] the subdivision is roughly:

surveys — $90 million;
research — $50 million;
training — $100 million;
planning — $10 million.

[3] Supplement No. 11 to the Official Records of the 30th Session of the Economic and Social Council.

The requests for assistance from the Fund over the first four years of its existence have run into over $500 million. At the last meeting of the governing council, in January 1963, the managing director felt it essential that $100 million in resources for the 1964 programs be forthcoming.

On an annual level of about a $10 billion[4] investment in resource development, one must envisage some $500 to $600 million for pre-investment research. Thus it is clear that the present level of the Special Fund is inadequate. One may state so even if large parts of the Expanded Technical Assistance Programs are added. Even if governments were to take upon themselves 75 per cent of total activities — a very optimistic assumption — the Special Fund would need some $100 to $150 million annually for surveys and research as a preparation for investment programs in the developing continents.

Reviewing the results of all these genuine efforts to reach a high degree of consistency, some serious gaps remain. This has led to the "consortium" idea, where a group of important donors discuss with the recipient country what its basic and most urgent needs are, and where an effort is made to cover these from the total potential investment or aid.

In the circles of exporting countries there also has arisen the need to consult each other concerning the total need on a global scale and the ways this is covered or left uncovered. The Organization for Economic Cooperation and Development finds here a most important field of activity. It leads to a comparison of effort, an attempt to measure each country's share and capacity to carry part of the burden. Unfortunately at present it is leading to a tendency to pass the buck onto "stronger shoulders." It might presumably also lead to improved or new channels of information on a comparative basis and increased flows of capital funds.

A Few General Considerations

If "unity of purpose and unity of action" comprise the acme of any cooperative effort, much is left to be desired. It is difficult to achieve unity within one given governmental structure; it is well-nigh impossible among twenty-odd intergovernmental organizations, even within the United Nations family. For many actors in the game a direct special purpose fol-

---

[4] Some $5 billion in agriculture (soil and water), the remainder in other resources.

lowed by action, unhampered by other agents of development, is a desirable goal. But this can rarely be achieved, not even within an "authoritarian" government. Therefore, efforts at systematization of the channels of communication, both for knowledge and capital, would be useful.

I do not believe that one need wait for a world government in order to work for reduction of waste, friction, and loss of time (all resources) in international transfers.

To sum up, I shall pinpoint the problems related to the development of *natural* resources of the developing countries.

1. The systematic collection of information on potential and existing world resources requires full international co-operation.[5] The international geophysical year was a striking example of great scientific and practical interest. The international soil survey is another example. But we need to know much more about the weather, soils, minerals, forests, aquatic resources, ocean currents, etc.

2. The Special Fund of the United Nations needs a substantial strengthening of its activities. These needs have already been discussed above. One also would want the Special Fund to ensure the preservation of all important new basic data at various scientific centers for future use.

3. There is a tremendous amount of information buried in archives and out-of-the-way publications. It would be highly advisable to organize the collation of existing data. Universities, national academies of science, with the support of private foundations and governments, would here find a fruitful field of action of great scope.[6]

4. It would be necessary to have first-hand or parallel information in the developing countries either on a national or, for the smaller countries, co-operative (regional) basis.

5. Systematic training for the development of relevant information on existing and potential resources should be initiated. I would prefer an action on the basis of "problems related to resources" rather than of specialized fields of knowledge. As we all know, resource development at present is an interdisciplinary field of considerable complexity.

[5] Clearly substantiated by the UN Conference on The Application of Science and Technology for the Benefit of the Less Developed Areas, Geneva, February 1963.

[6] Modern techniques offer new opportunities. *Cf.* Bertram M. Gross, "Operation Basic: The Retrieval of Wasted Knowledge," In *Journal of Communication*, XII (June 1962).

6. Last but not least, it is necessary to strengthen and co-ordinate more efficiently the numerous governmental, intergovernmental and non-governmental efforts to channel persons, information, and funds toward the general goal of international development and co-operation.

CONCLUSION

The international flow of knowledge and capital is big business. If private channels are included, some $8 to $10 billion annually are involved in research, education, and investment. But in view of the needs of a rapidly growing world population, resources are really scarce. Waste is against all principles of resource development and management. There is ample scope for improvement. Therefore, a concerted effort for improvement of the total process is overdue.

INDEX

NATURAL RESOURCES AND
                    INTERNATIONAL DEVELOPMENT

EDITED BY MARION CLAWSON

        designer: Edward D. King
      typesetter: Connecticut Printers, Inc.
       typefaces: Text: Times Roman. Display: Granjon
         printer: Universal Lithographers, Inc.
           paper: Perkins & Squire GM
          binder: Moore and Company
  cover material: Columbia Riverside Linen